TERMINATOR

THE AUTHORISED JULIAN DICKS STORY

KIRK BLOWS

POLAR
PUBLISHING

First published in Great Britain by
Polar Print Group Ltd
2, Uxbridge Road, Leicester LE4 7ST
England

Text © Copyright 1996 Kirk Blows
Design © Copyright 1996 Polar Print
Group Ltd

ISBN 1 899538 07 0

Edited by Julian Baskcomb

Designed and Printed by
Polar Print Group Ltd
2, Uxbridge Road, Leicester LE4 7ST
Tel: 0116 261 0800

*Photographs and illustrations are
courtesy of:*
Steve Bacon, Richard Austin,
Sporting Pictures (UK) Ltd, Allsport,
Associated Sports Photography,
Empics Ltd, Popperfoto, Colorsport,
John Cocks, Roy Beardsworth.
Remaining photographs are from the
private collection of the author or
from albums and scrapbooks owned
by various West Ham supporters or
members of Julian's family. We have
been unable to trace the sources of
all these pictures, but any
photographer involved is cordially
invited to contact the Publishers in
writing providing proof of copyright.

Front cover photograph: Richard Austin
Back cover photograph: Sporting
Pictures (UK) Ltd

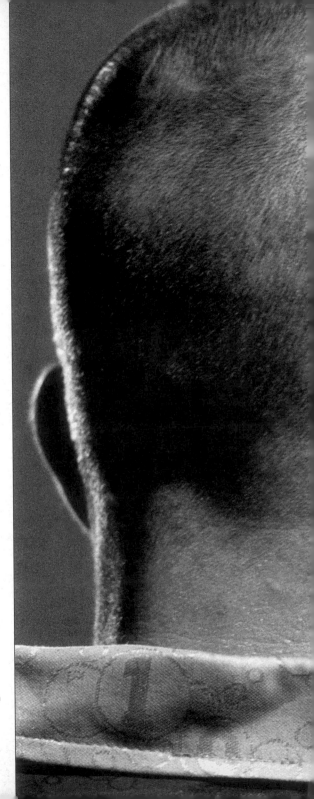

ACKNOWLEDGMENTS

Many football journalists have no doubt pondered the possibility of writing a book about the life and times of Julian Dicks, probably in order to capitalise on the player's public profile and exploit his notorious reputation and image. Hang the story on his numerous sending-offs and sensationalise the many controversial moments of his career and Bob's your uncle - you've got a cut-and-paste biography that meets minimal expectations.

But that wouldn't be telling the whole Julian Dicks story. So, intrigued by the challenge of discovering what really makes the man tick, I set about making contact with as many people associated with his life as possible, not just to talk about his career as a player but to find out who the **REAL** Julian Dicks is.

The objective was not to attempt to repackage or represent him as a player or person, or apologise for any areas of his past, simply to probe Julian's background and reveal more about his true character and personality. The assistance of others was therefore essential, so it's special thanks to…

Julian Dicks (for his co-operation and for telling it like it was), **Kay Dicks** (for her candid conversation and the tea), **Kattie** and **Jessica Dicks** (for finding mummy and daddy's long lost wedding photos!), **Carol, Ron** and **Grantley Dicks** (for hours of invaluable interview time and the use of their personal photographs and press cuttings), plus, in alphabetical order: **Martin Allen, Ian Bishop, Billy Bonds, Tony Cottee, Roy Evans, John Green, Don Hutchison, Martin Kuhl, Frank Lampard Snr, John Lyall, Lou Macari, Alvin Martin, John Moncur, Jimmy Quinn, Harry Redknapp, Janet Rodgers, Ron Saunders, David Seaman, Graeme Souness, Peter Storrie, Ron Veal, Steve Whitton** and **Danny Williamson** (for being willing to contribute their memories and thoughts of Julian towards this project).

Also thanks to **David Mellor's** producer for taking my call on his 606 radio show. No thanks to a certain ex-England boss and a current TV pundit for ignoring my faxes and phone messages. Cheers, guys.

On a more personal note, the author would like to extend his deepest gratitude to: **Rachel Anderson** (for letting me tell it the way it was), **Julian Baskcomb** at Polar Print Group (for not pestering me over deadlines – can I have the rest of my advance now?), *Hammers News Magazine* publisher **Tony McDonald** (for encouragement and not wondering where his editor had occasionally disappeared to), **Steve Blowers** (for the loan of the odd scrapbook or ten), **Cathy Howes** and **Jo Davies** (for support while listening to endless lager-fuelled waffle) and, finally, to fellow West Ham season-ticket holders **Gerry Levy** and **John Raven** (for promising to buy the book when it comes out!).

May you enjoy…

ABOUT THE AUTHOR…

Kirk Blows has been a West Ham United supporter for the majority of his 33 years and therefore has almost as little hair as Julian (unfortunately not by choice). Prone himself to the occasional rant and rave from his position in the Boleyn Ground's East Stand, he inevitably felt an instant rapport with the defender who quickly became a cult hero after joining the Hammers in March 1988.

Presently the editor of Hammers News Magazine, West Ham's official monthly publication, Kirk spends a large percentage of his life annoying his neighbours in London's Maida Vale with his collection of horrible heavy metal albums (acquired during his past secret life as a rock journalist). Not surprisingly then, he lives alone but, as is typical of a West Ham fan, he's the eternal optimist!

He exists on a diet of double sausage, egg, beans and chips and the occasional Hammers victory over Tottenham Hotspur or Manchester United.

CHAPTER 1

HEADLINE MAKER

AS days at the office go, Monday, September 11, 1995, was not a good one for Julian Dicks. With just under 35 minutes of West Ham's televised home game against rivals Chelsea played it was hardly looking like one of the best anyway, with the East Londoners going 2-0 down thanks to goals from Dennis Wise and John Spencer. But within just a few minutes of the latter's strike, an incident took place which would influence the course of events for the Hammers' No 3 for some considerable time to come.

Few could have imagined the consequences of the next few seconds as Julian hassled Spencer for the ball just a yard or so outside the penalty box in the bottom left-hand corner of the Upton Park pitch. But as the Chelsea striker went down under the challenge, Dicksy leapfrogged his opponent only to bring his right boot down on the floored player's head.

"That's a little bit of retribution," stated pundit Trevor Francis on the live Sky Sports commentary, making judgement following an earlier incident that had seen Spencer booked for swinging his boot wildly at the West Ham left-back. "Dicks made a note of it, waited for his moment, and made an equally rash challenge with no attempt to play the ball."

As the TV cameras showed Julian turning back onto the pitch after retrieving the ball, an expression of disbelief crossed his face and a four-lettered expletive fell from his mouth. For referee Robbie Hart had moved to caution him for his involvement in the clash which left blood pouring from a wound that required Spencer to have eight stitches in the side of his head. To this day Julian has denied the strong suggestion that the contact between boot and head was a result of a deliberate stamp on his part – as implied by the likes of Sky's soccer analyst Andy Gray, who turned the spotlight squarely on the Hammers man as numerous replays of the moment were aired to the watching millions.

"We went shoulder to shoulder and Spencer fell over," says Dicks, as he attempts to explain the incident. "I tried to jump over him and didn't even know I'd landed on him until I saw the blood running down his head. The referee booked me for shirt-pulling but never saw any stamping and neither did managers Harry Redknapp or

THE SUN, Tuesday, September 19, 1995

Rash...Dicks goes flying in | Clash...boot clobbers Spencer | Gash...wounded Spencer in agony | Bloodied...victim John Spencer

DICKS TO SUE MELLOR OVER 'ANIMAL' BLAST

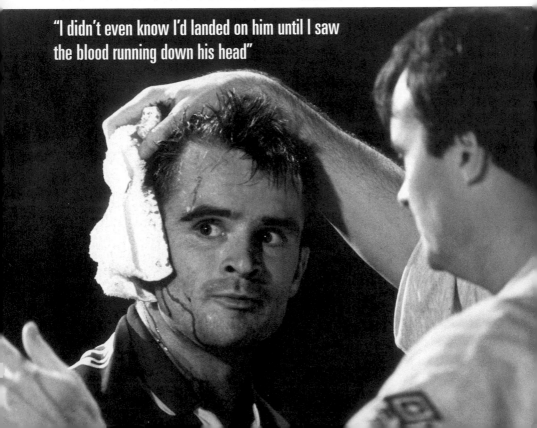

"I didn't even know I'd landed on him until I saw the blood running down his head"

Glenn Hoddle. At half-time Spencer asked me if I'd meant it and I said, 'No, I tried to clear you.' He asked me if I was sure and I told him I was positive. I said, 'If I'd meant to have caught you, I'd tell you.'"

> "Harry came out and asked, 'Did you mean it?' I told him I hadn't and he said, 'You f***ing liar!'"

The 19,228 crowd – the large majority, of course, being Hammers fans – left the game reflecting on Chelsea's 3-1 victory (with a bloodied and bandaged Spencer scoring again to make his 25th birthday a memorable one – if his sore head allowed him), with few aware of the controversy that would explode over the next few days. Not only did Sky focus much of their post-match analysis on the clash but it had pride of place as the lead story in the following day's edition of *The Sun*, with a sequence of pictures showing Dicks making contact with Spencer. "I had a feeling the press would make the most of it, simply because of my past disciplinary record," he says. "It had been quite good in the two years up to then, but as soon as something like that happens everybody's back on the bandwagon again, trying to get me up in front of the FA. If it had been anybody else involved, it wouldn't have been blown up so much – especially by Andy Gray. He showed the incident so many times with his stupid video cameras. If you do that you get other people believing it.

"Everybody believes what Andy Gray says but, at the end of the day, only I know if I meant it or not. And people won't take my word for it. If Gary Lineker had done it he'd be believed straight away, but because it's me and the reputation that I've got, I obviously meant it. Even John Spencer said after the game that I didn't mean it and people should take into account his point of view as well."

It was the big talking point over the rest of the week: did Dicks mean it? So much so, that even Hammers boss Harry Redknapp – obviously unhappy at what he'd seen – saw fit to toss the question the player's way a couple of days after the game. "I was out kicking a ball against a wall in training and Harry came out and asked, 'Did you mean it?' I told him I hadn't and he said, 'You f***ing liar!' I said, 'Harry, I swear on my kids' lives, I didn't mean it.' It was only when I did that that he believed me," reveals Julian.

But if Dicks was the enemy as far as much of the public were concerned, it was Andy Gray who was the antagonist in Julian's eyes. "I thought Gray was bang out of order when he

"I thought Andy Gray was bang out of order"

said I should have been sent off – that was disgraceful! It's not nice when you're branded as a nutter and a headcase," he says. And the war of words between the two men continued in the future.

But as the dust of the Spencer clash began to settle towards the latter part of the week following the Chelsea game, it at first appeared that there would be no further inquiry, with referee Hart making no special mention of it in his report – apart from having booked Dicks for tugging at his opponent's shirt. With Spencer and his club not pursuing the matter, some newspaper stories indicated that Julian would not be charged over the affair. What the defender was not immediately aware of, however, was that – as a result of the publicity and what had been aired on television – the FA had sent a video tape to the referee, asking him to take another look and allowing him the opportunity to re-evaluate the situation. Whether Hart felt under pressure to revise his opinion is open to question, but certainly the FA wanted to be seen to be taking action.

Spencer, for his part, seemed quite content to accept Julian's explanation and apology, despite experiencing some pain. "It was a shoulder charge and as I went down he put his foot down and I got my head in the way. But during the game he apologised," said the Scottish international, who sportingly showed no malice towards Dicks and mocked, "What a way to celebrate a birthday – by having eight stitches inserted in my head. It was the first time I've needed them and I cried like a baby!"

As West Ham went to Highbury on Saturday, September 16, what was needed was for Julian to go about his work in a quiet and efficient manner, keeping a low profile. What took place, however, was more the complete opposite, proving that Dicks is not somebody who will allow past events to compromise his game. First he was booked for a foul on Glenn Helder – which prompted a fiery reaction from Julian, who strongly suggested to the Dutch winger that he was guilty of diving. Then, in the 43rd minute, a somewhat desperate challenge on Ian Wright on the byeline resulted in him conceding a penalty. While many thought another yellow card (and a subsequent red one) could have appeared, referee Alan Wilkie gave Julian the benefit of the doubt and, on closer study, the attempt to make contact with the ball was a lot closer than it originally appeared – ill-advised that the challenge was in such a precarious position.

Fortunately for Dicks and the rest of the Hammers, Wright wasted the opportunity to put the Gunners ahead, sending his shot wide of the top corner. But despite a half-time warning from

> "I felt he deserved to go. In fact, I thought he could have gone earlier"
> — HARRY REDKNAPP

Harry Redknapp to exercise caution, Julian committed himself to a tackle on that man Wright again, 10 minutes after the re-start. Again, it looked worse than it actually was, with Wrighty's histrionics disguising the fact that Dicksy just may have got a touch on the ball (although video evidence is inconclusive). But with the Arsenal striker spectacularly hitting the deck right in front of Alan Wilkie, it was little surprise when the red card finally appeared.

"I thought I was harshly done by at Arsenal," complains Julian. "I thought that Glenn Helder dived when I got the first card. It wasn't a nasty tackle but the referee booked me straight away, without giving me the benefit of the doubt. I guess he could have booked me for the penalty I gave away but I think I did touch the ball. It was slight, though, and I'd have been surprised if the ref had noticed it.

"Harry did warn me at half-time, telling me to go steady otherwise I'd get myself sent off. I told him I would but that's just the way I play. If I think I can win the ball I'll try to do so. Harry came in after the game and said, 'You've let us down.' And I said, 'Yeah, I know I have.' Maybe the last one on Ian Wright looked bad, but I got a touch on that too. As soon as I saw the referee coming towards me I just started walking.

> "As soon as I saw the referee coming towards me I just started walking"

Coincidentally, Alan Wilkie had been the last referee to show Dicks a red card, with him also handling the match at Derby County in January 1993 (which saw Julian go off for the third time in four months). Not that this was recognised at the time of the Highbury dismissal. "I wasn't aware that it was the same ref who had sent me off nearly three years earlier," admits Julian, who places little significance on the fact.

It was a miserable day all round for Hammers fans, who saw Arsenal win through another, more successful, Wright penalty (after Dennis Bergkamp hit the

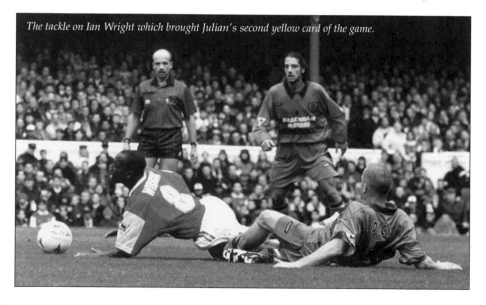

The tackle on Ian Wright which brought Julian's second yellow card of the game.

turf following a Steve Potts challenge) and their team finish the game with only eight legitimate outfield players, with substitute 'keeper Les Sealey coming on and playing in a striking role after midfielder John Moncur had to leave the field suffering with double vision.

Not surprisingly, Harry Redknapp was not amused with Dicks' red card. "I was very disappointed. He knew he was on thin ice. I told him at half-time we couldn't afford to go down to 10 men and that it was important to be professional and not go diving in," says the Hammers boss. "I felt he deserved to go. In fact, I thought he could have gone earlier. The referee gave a penalty when he pulled down Wrighty as he was cutting in on goal, so surely that's a booking as well. It was a bad day all round and I was disappointed with both incidents involving Julian that week."

As Dicks tried to come to terms with another knock-out blow, he found few friends in his corner. Yet he found an ally in his former Birmingham team-mate David Seaman, with the Arsenal 'keeper sympathetic towards his plight. "It's just the kind of player Julian is," says the England man. "He's a hard tackler and if it's not timed properly it can look spectacular. But he's as honest as anything. He's not a dirty player and he doesn't cynically go over the top. He's hard but fair.

"He's had a lot of criticism, which I think has been a little bit unjust, but he's stuck to his job and the things he's really good at. He always had an amazing left foot and he's got a great shot. He's been a great player," he adds in tribute.

Not that many of these qualities were acknowledged as the media went to town over the whole affair, with the sending off coming at the worst possible time following the Spencer debacle. The press coverage was predictably explosive ('*Clown Jules sent off for the NINTH time,*' screamed *The People* (incorrectly – see end of book), while the *Daily Express* aired the view that '*Julian Dicks displayed suicidal tendencies*'), yet the biggest criticism of Dicks came not in the papers the next day but on MP David Mellor's 6.06 phone-in show on *Radio Five Live* just an hour or so after the game.

Said Mellor on his show: "This animal has been sent off today and should have been sent off in the week," referring to the game involving Chelsea – who the former Cabinet Minister happens to support. Julian did not hear the comments himself, but was informed by his agent the next day. "We got a taped copy of the show and I heard it then," says Julian. "He said I was an animal and didn't deserve to be a footballer. He got people to ring in and say things like I should be kicked out the game and he agreed with them.

"I wanted to sue Mellor's bollocks off"

"At the end of the day, I'm not an animal. If David Mellor wants to call me things then he should meet me somewhere and we can discuss it there and then. But to say things on the radio when I've no right of reply is out of order. He wasn't at the Arsenal game so he can't have seen the tackles that got me sent off. He just jumped to the same old conclusions. I wanted to sue Mellor's bollocks off."

Dicks did indeed consider taking legal action against the Tory MP and the story that he was investigating the possibility broke in the tabloids on Tuesday, September 19 – the same day that the FA confirmed that they were charging the player with bringing the game into disrepute following the injury to Spencer (as a result of hearing referee Robbie Hart's new interpretation of what had taken place after watching video evidence).

The conflict with David Mellor may have given the press another opportunity to run the sequence of photographs showing Julian catching Spencer with his right boot but, incredibly, this wasn't the only story to put his name in the papers that day. For Dicks had captured the front page headlines as well!

'Soccer star's girl, 6, hurt in revenge attack,' wrote *The Sun*.

'Soccer star's twins attacked,' said the *Daily Star*.

For all the headlines Dicks had helped create during his controversial career, this was the first time that his name had appeared on the front pages of the newspapers. And it came about as an indirect consequence of the Mellor comments. "We don't know anyone else who can get away with what he does," says Julian's wife Kay. "I'm surprised he's not taken off air because I'm sure some of what he says must be libellous. He's got no right to say such things – you don't live in a greenhouse and throw stones. We were so annoyed afterwards."

> "There are wars going on and kids dying, and they put ME on the front page"

So annoyed, in fact, that the couple approached solicitor Rory Mulvihill. "The Mellor programme got out of hand with people going over the top about Julian. It developed into a have-a-go-at-Julian-Dicks session," said the lawyer at the time, indicating that he was sending a letter of protest to the BBC.

Mulvihill did indeed put his complaints down in writing, issuing a statement pleading for the media to lay off Julian, as the constant bad publicity was now affecting his children – daughters Kattie and Jessica – who'd been subjected to some abuse at school.

"I spoke to my solicitor about the incident and he put out a press release," confirms Julian. "We stated exactly what happened – that one of my kids had been tripped up at school – and that was it. But the papers blew it up so much it was ridiculous. The point of the statement was to tell the press that the stick I was getting was affecting my children, so they should cut it out and leave me alone. But they thought 'sod that' and whacked me on the front pages. My solicitor didn't realise how much effect it would have – he couldn't apologise enough.

"It surprised me as well. There are wars going on and kids dying, and they put *me* on the front page. It just didn't make sense. The last thing people want to know about is my family when you've got battles going on in Bosnia. I'm used to appearing on the back pages but being on the front is a bit different."

Julian became aware that he'd made cover headlines when he received a call from his mum, Carol. "She asked if I'd seen the papers and I said, 'No.' So I went out to get them and the press were still outside the house. It was crazy."

SOCCER STAR'S GIRL, 6 HURT IN REVENGE ATTACK

The newspaper vultures had already descended the previous evening (getting directions for the house from the local chinese takeaway!), once they'd got wind that something involving Julian's daughters had occurred at their school. "It was about 10 o'clock in the evening and we were getting people knocking on the door, asking if they could see the children because they understood that they'd been beaten up at school," remembers Kay. "We just said it was a load of rubbish but they wouldn't leave us alone. In the end they had to leave because they're obviously not entitled to be on your property.

"The next morning, at about half-past six, there were a load of press outside again. The story was in the papers and it was a weekday, so obviously the kids had to go to school. The press followed them down the road, trying to get them to speak, but they just ignored them."

Like Julian, Kay was somewhat dismayed at all the publicity. "When things start affecting the girls, or if it's got no significance with football, then I don't like it," she says. "Julian is big enough to look after himself, and so am I, but when our children get involved it's not fair on them. I don't want my daughters in the papers. Our personal life has got nothing to do with anybody.

"I felt gutted because the stories were a load of crap"

"The media attention was pathetic. The papers would send women round to ask, 'Are the children all right, have you got any comment?'"

The stories that appeared on September 19 were rather exaggerated. Said *The Sun*: *'The daughter of soccer star Julian Dicks was attacked at school – in revenge for one of his clashes on the pitch. Terrified Jessica Dicks, six, was shoved and kicked by a playground yob, aged only ten. The tiny lout, who also harassed Jessica's twin sister Kattie, yelled as he struck: "Your dad's a bully!"'*

"I felt gutted because the stories were a load of crap," says Julian. "Jessica was tripped up and told, 'Your dad's a cheat' – and that's it. She was okay but I was annoyed because it was an older kid. We went to see the headmaster and it was all sorted out."

Kay was happy with the way the school handled the affair. "They dealt with it straight away," she confirms. "I went down there to see the headmaster, Mr Bewick, and he kept the boys behind in assembly until they owned up. That was as soon as it happened, just after the Chelsea match, and then came all the headlines.

"It was blown up out of all proportion – you'd think Jessica had been beaten up or something. Primary school boys are so into football that they're going to say things to the girls. That's okay as long as they're not nasty, as long as it's just a laugh and a joke."

The press stories understandably spread concern throughout the Dicks family, with Julian's mum Carol confirming that "friends were willing to take the girls on holiday to the Isle of Wight" to allow them to escape the alleged hostilities at school and their position under the media microscope (although that wasn't deemed necessary).

John Spencer himself was alarmed at the stories suggesting retribution from Chelsea fans, detaching himself completely from such people. "It's disgusting and I can't condone it," he said. "For people to do this supposedly on my behalf sickens me to the bone. I said on the night of the game it was an accident and I spoke to Julian and he confirmed that. I accept that and so should everyone else."

But people didn't accept it and Julian predictably received his fair share of 'hate mail', although this was dismissed in light-hearted fashion. "He had a lot of bad mail come to the club after the Spencer and Arsenal incidents," confirms West Ham team-mate Danny Williamson, "but he'd just come into the changing room, stick it on the table and have a laugh and a joke about it. He'd say, 'Have a look at what some idiot has sent me,' and share it with the lads. I think that was his way of not allowing it to get to him."

> "If anything, those incidents probably helped him as a person"
> — TONY COTTEE

The way Dicksy coped during this period of adversity impressed several of his playing colleagues. "He handled it brilliantly," says John Moncur. "It means a lot to him to do well and it must hurt him when he's criticised like he was during that time – he wouldn't be human otherwise. But you've just got to sling it out of the window and I think he succeeded in doing that. He just says 'bollocks' to it all and that's it."

Striker Tony Cottee also admired Julian's resolution. "He coped very well with it," he says. "You had photographers at the training ground and people camped outside his house. It must be very difficult to deal with it all but he did. If anything, those incidents probably helped him as a person and he seemed to respond to the situation. He went through quite a traumatic period but from that time onwards he started to play his best football and didn't have any more disciplinary problems at all."

Incredibly, Julian soon embarked on a 26-game run without picking up a single booking and it's a transformation that was acknowledged by David Mellor on his 6.06 show when he was contacted by the author of this book on Saturday, October 12, 1996. "I think things are definitely much improved for Julian," he said. "He went through a bad patch, culminating in that incident with John Spencer, but I think that what Julian has done in recent times is to be applauded." Mellor (who had also attacked Dicks following a tackle on Manchester United's Andy Cole in January 1996 – "Mellor was out of order," stormed Hammers MD Peter Storrie at that time, who said he was considering sending a letter of complaint to the BBC) then went on to acknowledge Julian's efforts towards charity concerns, before asking John Ley of *The Telegraph* (sitting alongside him) for his view on the player's progress. "Some players find a maturity when they're 21, some when they're 31, and Julian's finding it now. I wonder if he's knocking on the England door," said the reporter.

"Now that would be a turn-up for the books and give you another chapter to write about," concluded Mellor, not realising that Julian's involvement at international level had already been addressed! (See chapter 24.)

The Spencer episode was not immediately over, however. For Dicks still had to face the FA's disciplinary commission and answer the disrepute charge, with people still debating the intent behind the contact with the Chelsea player's head. Allowing agent Rachel Anderson to oversee his defence, the mission was simple – to prove his innocence. "Knowing him as I do, and talking to everybody in the aftermath, I knew he hadn't meant it," says Rachel. "Julian knew he hadn't done it on purpose and so did Spencer, because you know if someone's being aggressive towards you during a game – and that wasn't happening.

"So it was up to us to prove it."

Referee Alan Wilkie puts Dicks in the book at Highbury.

CHAPTER 2

IN THE DOCK

I N the wake of the furore over the clash with John Spencer, Julian discovered that he was to be charged by the FA of bringing the game into disrepute not by letter or phone call – as you would expect – but by teletext!

The date of the hearing, October 19, was officially confirmed in writing to his agent Rachel a few days later, with the venue named as the Royal Lancaster Hotel, just a few minutes from the FA headquarters in West London.

As Julian, Rachel, West Ham manager Harry Redknapp and MD Peter Storrie arrived for the inquiry, complete with the team of men who would hopefully convince the FA of the accused's innocence ("we employed top lawyers, a physical education expert – Peter Harrison – and a chap who was an expert in body language and movement," says Rachel), Dicks met up with the official in charge on the night in question, Robbie Hart – who'd had a change of heart having looked at video evidence of the clash.

"Before we went in the referee shook my hand and said that he hoped I got off with it," reveals Julian. "Yet when the FA sent him the video asking him if he wanted to change his mind about the incident, he said, 'Yeah, I would've sent him off.' And he came up there on the day and told me he hoped I got off! I felt like smacking him there and then but I don't think that would have done any good somehow."

During the three-and-a-half hour hearing, the three-man commission (comprising Barry Bright, Ted Powell and Alan Turvey) heard Dicks' lawyers point to his improved disciplinary record prior to the Chelsea game (with him not having been sent off for nearly three years) and the fact that referee Hart was only five yards away and had deemed the skirmish only worthy of a yellow card for shirt pulling. They also had a letter from Spencer, indicating he considered the clash to have been accidental, but the Chelsea man was not present at the hearing to speak in Julian's defence. Dicks had spoken to him by phone and the Scot had appeared to have been willing, but it's thought that then-Blues boss Glenn Hoddle intervened and put the blocks on his player assisting Dicksy's case.

The key defence, ultimately, had to come from the expert in body language. "He proved categorically that there was absolutely no way that Julian could have avoided making contact – in fact, he did everything he could to avoid hurting him," says Rachel.

The witness indeed offered a convincing argument on Julian's behalf. "He was superb," adds the player. "He replayed the incident on the video monitor and he testified that it was impossible for me to miss him. The FA must have had an inkling that he was right because they only gave me a three-game ban and fined me the cost of the hearings (believed to be around £3,000)."

With the inquiry finding Dicks guilty, he was then asked to leave the room while they arrived at the three-match penalty. When they called him back in and announced the punishment, it came as something of a relief to Julian: "Once they found me guilty I thought I was going to get hammered and get a 15-20 game ban. I was relieved but annoyed because the ban suggests they weren't sure and in that case I should've been found not guilty."

"Referee Robbie Hart came up there on the day and told me he hoped I got off! I felt like smacking him there and then"

Whether the FA had already made up their minds to bring a guilty verdict is open to debate, but Julian was of the view that the powers of the game had wanted to be seen to be taking action. "I think they found me guilty because they wanted to make an example of me," he says. "You've got other players breaking faces and getting away with it, but John Spencer needed eight stitches and I got charged," he complains, clearly feeling that his reputation had gone before him. Certainly, his agent feels it was a contributory factor: "It's unfortunate that, historically, he's got a bad reputation – some of it justified but a lot of it not – and the FA don't always look at the facts in front of them in isolation. The referee changing his mind was the main thing."

The FA were clearly in a difficult position, though. They'd brought the charge on the basis of TV pictures, the media hysteria and the referee changing his view of the incident. They therefore felt compelled to take action, despite the strong case from Julian's defence and the fact that, at the end of the day, only one person really knew what intent there'd been in Julian's mind – and that was Julian himself. The commission couldn't *prove* Dicks had meant to make contact with Spencer, they could only *assume* it, and consequently they fell someway short of the maximum punishment they could impose.

The press reaction was a mixture of hysteria, anti-Dicks propaganda (take a bow, Simon Barnes of *The Times* – 'Dicks has taken great pains to look like a psychopathic convict,' he remarked) and some intelligent comment from some of the better-informed writers, such as Rob Hughes (also of *The Times*) who expressed concern about the precedent set in a case that was concluded with the burden of proof

Peter Storrie: Confused about outcome.

seemingly overlooked. *'I doubt that it can be proved, other than by confession, that Dicks landed his boot on the head of John Spencer with malice aforethought,'* he wrote, pointing out that the case against Wimbledon's John Fashanu had been dropped after it being recognised that 'intent' couldn't be substantiated. *'This is treading on dangerous ground,'* he added, clearly worried about the implications of the FA finding Dicks guilty on the basis of them *thinking* it had been a deliberate act.

The verdict left all those in Julian's camp, including Peter Storrie, somewhat uncertain in their reactions. "Harry and I were very forcefully behind Julian," says the West Ham MD. "We helped to defend him, he had the club's full support and we were disappointed that the verdict went against him – and then surprised that he was given such a small sentence, which gives one the impression that no-one was really sure. The panel themselves must have felt there was an element of doubt, otherwise he'd certainly have got a lengthier sentence. In the end, we didn't know how to feel about it – disappointed that he'd been found guilty or pleased that he'd got off lightly."

Former chat-show host Michael Parkinson, writing in one of the broadsheets, certainly felt that Dicks had 'got off lightly', claiming that the Hammers player *'couldn't have had a better result for stamping on a player's head than three weeks off work.'* *'Yet another miscreant becomes a martyr,'* he complained, pointing out that while Spencer's loyalty to a fellow pro was praiseworthy, it was somewhat misguided given that *'his face was in the turf when assaulted so he was hardly in the best position to judge exactly what was intended.'*

> **"The panel themselves must have felt there was an element of doubt, otherwise he'd certainly have got a lengthier sentence"** – PETER STORRIE

It could also be suggested the standard ban – which is what Dicks would have got had Robbie Hart shown him a red card on the night – was also designed to dissuade him from appealing against the verdict, smacking him on the wrist rather than kicking him up the backside while leaving plenty of room for the punishment to be increased should the FA be forced to ratify their decision.

Harry Redknapp was not surprised by the outcome, but could see the irony of the situation. "Football has had cases where players have admitted things as being intentional but they have not been punished, yet Julian had a letter from Spencer saying that he considered it to be accidental and he is found guilty. It's unique!"

After the case, Julian unleashed his frustration by attacking Andy Gray for his comments on the night of the Chelsea game. "As far as I am concerned he instigated all this," he fumed. "He's the man who put me in front of the FA. John Spencer tried to help me and I'll be ringing him to thank him for that. But I've no intention of speaking to Andy Gray and I will certainly never shake his hand. I accept he's got a job to do and know that football is a game of opinions. But he should keep opinions like that to himself. As a player he was hardly whiter than white himself – yet he does a thing like this to me. But my conscience is clear."

> "I've no intention of speaking to Andy Gray and I will certainly never shake his hand"

Gray, naturally, defended his ground. "I was asked a question and gave an honest opinion," he responded. "But I am deeply saddened by his words. If you ask 90 per cent of the population watching, I am sure they would agree with me. For 20 years I had similar problems with the FA and I understand what it means to a player. I would not put a player through it if I didn't believe what I felt."

Later in the season, feeling somewhat victimised following similar treatment from Gray over the tackle on United's Andy Cole, Dicks felt obliged to pursue the Sky man for some sort of showdown. "I got my agent, Rachel Anderson, to ring him up and arrange a meeting at an hotel or bar somewhere so that I could chat with him, without the press around, to find out what he had against me."

Gray declined the proposal (also ignoring calls to speak to this author), countering it with an offer for Julian to appear on his talk show. "He wanted me to go on his show and chat about it there. But he wouldn't meet me one-to-one," says Dicks, who was naturally reluctant, feeling as if he would be at a major disadvantage. "I wouldn't go on the show because Andy Gray is experienced at talking on television and I'm not. And if I met him in private I could tell him that he's a liar if I wanted to."

Given their contrasting philosophies, it's probably just as well that the two men have not been locked in the same room together. But, oh, to be a fly on the wall...

18

CHAPTER 3

ACCIDENTS WILL HAPPEN

JULIAN DICKS – all 7lb 10 ounces of him – was delivered into the waiting arms of his mother Carol at Keynsham Hospital in Bristol on August 8, 1968. "I was an accident," suggests Julian, and it's a view that neither of his parents really argues against. With their first son Grantley having been born less than two years earlier, there were no immediate plans to further expand the family, despite Carol initially intending to have four children with husband Ron. But along came Julian unexpectedly, actually arriving "late" for his first challenge. "The doctors said the noise I made when I was having him was something else!" says Carol.

With the addition of Grantley and Julian – so named because their mum wanted them to be "different" – it meant that, within a few years, three quarters of the Dicks family living at 4 Kenmare Road in Bristol's Knowle West district would be gripped by the fever of football.

Dad Ron, a fork-lift truck driver at Courage Brewery, was on his way to integrating himself into the local soccer scene, playing right-back for Eagle House before then establishing his name as a tough tackler for Keynsham Town in the Western League. Ron would also play for Welton Rovers, Frome Town, Somerset FA, Shepton Mallet (who he went on to manage) and Redwood Lodge by the time he would hang up his boots. And football was always his main passion. "I would have loved to have been a pro, but I was never really good enough," admits Ron on reflection, despite training as a youngster with Bristol City.

"It was football, football, football," remembers Carol of those early years. "Ron was never around. He was either training, playing or out with the lads, while I was at home. He was always like that and he never changed. But the children never lost out on anything, I made sure of that."

One thing they did lose out on, strangely, was watching their father in action. "He wouldn't let me watch him play in case he broke his leg or got badly injured," says Julian, while Ron himself recalls rather different reasons for keeping his sons away from games: "I was the sort who never swore in front of my kids and when you're playing semi-pro park football you've got all the language and it's not very nice. So I

> ## "The people who he played football with used to say he was a horrible bastard"
> — JULIAN ON HIS FATHER AS A PLAYER

didn't want them to go when they were young, although Grantley and I later played together in the same team (Redwood Lodge).

Yet despite Julian only witnessing his father play competitive football on just one occasion – a friendly game, as people recall – there's no doubt that he would very much develop in Ron's mould, inheriting several key aspects of his personality and some which can safely be considered as family characteristics – on the pitch, at least. "He's got my aggressiveness," says Ron, "and Grantley's the same. As a player I was always aggressive. I always hated losing – I'd cheat rather than lose. And I was pretty vocal." Julian's main image of his father on the pitch, meanwhile, was of him being "a very hard footballer", claiming, "The people who he played football with used to say he was a horrible bastard." While Ron's disciplinary record was not good, however, it would hardly make for as grim a read as his son's in future years.

Ron and Carol Dicks may have both been born in Knowle, in the southern part of Bristol, but they were actually living in the Lawrence Weston district of the city (in council property) after getting married prior to Grantley's birth. They moved to their three-bedroomed, semi-detached, terraced house in Kenmare Road as a result of an accident involving their first son while Carol was pregnant with Julian. "I was doing the washing at the communal laundry one day," she recalls, "and Grantley, who was

The Dicks brothers...
Julian and Grantley

just a toddler, was playing with some other kids when his thumb went into a box of live wires. There was a big stink about it because the wires had just been left exposed in the wall, with no cover on them. I'd already requested a move with the council, but for some unknown reason we got a three-bedroomed house, when we had just one child still. That was unheard of in those days."

And it was at this house, complete with front and back gardens and a drive alongside, that Julian would spend his childhood years – right up until the age of 14, in fact. Although Ron Dicks remembers Knowle as being "not too bad" in the early seventies, the area was in obvious decline. "I wouldn't live there now if you gave me a *free* house," he says today from his nearby home in Bridlington. "But it was all right then. We didn't want to live anywhere else and never really considered moving away."

The really bad districts may have been Hartcliffe and Withewood, but as the area deteriorated it's understandable that Julian's strongest memory of Knowle West is how it was in his later years there. "It was a bad area, a rough place to live, with drugs and everything there," he says. When he was younger, though, he could at least play football outside in relative safety. "I used to go out on the streets to play football until eight or nine o'clock at night and we just learned to look after ourselves as we grew up."

That growing up process revolved around two main activities: football and fighting. As soon as Julian – or Juju, as his mother called him (and occasionally still does!) – was old enough to do either, from around the age of five, he'd be in one of the gardens with Grantley chasing if not a ball then a brawl. "We were like normal kids, we played football in the street and things like that," recalls Grantley. "I suppose we were quite close. But we did fight a lot, I must admit." As their father remembers only too well: "You'd look outside to see them playing football and they'd be fighting. To be honest, the fact that Julian and Grantley were both like that was probably because of me. And you had to be a little bit aggressive living in Knowle West."

Much of the scrapping between the two brothers would either be playful or over the smallest of issues. "Every day we used to fight between ourselves," admits Julian, "but if there was a fight out on the streets we'd always stick up for each other. It was just brothers for you. We used to have our own rooms and if there was something in his bedroom I wanted I'd go in there and nick it. And if he caught me he'd lump me one. It was over silly things really."

Mum Carol supports the view that their behaviour was typical of young boys, although the aggression was very much part of the desire to come out on top rather than to hurt anybody. "Neither of them used to really win because I used to split them up

> "If there was a fight on the streets we'd always stick up for each other. It was just brothers for you"

eventually," she says. "But the aggressiveness to win – that's always been there. That has never changed from when Julian was tiny."

These childhood years would shape Julian's footballing character significantly. When he started playing, it wasn't about winning games, it was about winning the ball. And then games would be won. To that end, the two brothers developed their own sport when they were alone together – murderball. "We used to stick the ball in the middle, stand 10 yards apart, say 'Go!' and run at each other. We used to do that in the back garden for hours and hours," recalls Grantley. Julian remembers the clashes well: "We'd come in and smash each other. And that's where it's all probably come from," he says, referring to his tenacious trademarks. "If you stuck one of us in goal it got boring just taking shots, so we'd stick the ball in the middle and run in and clatter each other."

"If you stuck one of us in goal it got boring just taking shots, so we'd stick the ball in the middle and run in and clatter each other"

Back indoors too, football was the prevailing theme and main influence throughout the boys' formative years. "It was all because of their dad," says Carol, who remembers the regular sessions in front of the TV. "Whether it be *Match Of The Day* or *The Big Match*, Ron would get his beer in, the kids would have their lemonade and we'd all be sat in front of the telly, with Ron one side of the boys and me on the other. Grantley was a Liverpool fan, Julian supported Man Utd. And when they drew 3-3 one year – oh it was bedlam in that house!"

Despite the city of Bristol offering two football league teams – City and Rovers – there was no serious allegiance to either, with Ron, Carol and the kids only bothering to visit City's Ashton Gate ground (the closest of the two, in Bedminster) if the likes of Manchester United were coming to town. Dad was mostly playing himself at the same time anyway, so trips to games were few and far between, although Julian does remember the likes of Chris Garland and Norman Hunter in City's colours. It was the red of Man Utd rather than that of Bristol, however, that held the biggest attraction, thanks to the legend of one man – George Best – who Julian still describes as "my idol".

Inspired by George and spending so much time kicking a ball around his garden and immediate streets, while surviving several bouts of murderball, Julian started taking the game more seriously around the age of seven, imagining what it would be like to be a top soccer star. "I can remember asking my mum how to write my autograph and then copying it," he says, "and from that point on nothing else interested me." Ron Dicks remembers his son's declaration of intent from around that age and had no reason not to take him seriously, admitting, "That's what I wanted him to be."

Julian was now attending Novers Lane Primary School (where mum had become a dinner lady), which at least offered him opportunities to indulge in his football interests, if not any academic ones. "I just used to pray for the breaks," says Julian, confessing that lunch would be sacrificed for the sake of a game, generally with older kids who were friends of Grantley. "I just wanted to get in with them and play football. School work didn't interest me."

Such was her young son's reluctance to entertain regular school work, Carol would understandably feel quite frustrated at Julian's laziness. "He was a little sod," she says. "He had a brain but he'd never use it, because all he thought about was football. All he wanted to do was kick a ball, go up to the park and do things like that." This still didn't stop her offering him plenty of encouragement as far as football went, particularly with Grantley having a two-year headstart in the game. "People always used to say, 'Grantley's gonna make it, Grantley's gonna be the one.' But I used to pick out Julian because he was little and say, 'No, our Ju will do it.'" she says.

Young 'Juju'

In those years at Novers Lane, Julian was indeed small for his age. But he was mischievous with it and, as Carol says, "He had a little cockiness about him that the other kids used to like." Grantley also remembers how Julian's cheekiness would endear his brother's class-mates to him during his time at school: "Kids would hang around him because he used to muck about. He wouldn't get into major bother but he used to like winding the teachers up – which he did most of the time. Kids liked him because they thought he was funny."

Back at home, Julian was far too preoccupied with all things football to exercise any discipline or take pride in looking after his own room. "The two children always had their own rooms and if you went into Julian's it was always like a bomb had hit it," says Carol. "Yet I'd go into Grantley's room and it would be tidy. Sometimes I'd suddenly hear, 'Mum, our Ju's been in my room again, it's a

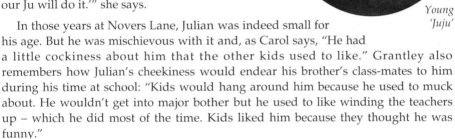

"He was a little sod. He had a brain but he'd never use it, because all he thought about was football" — MUM CAROL

mess!' And I'd go up there and everything would be pulled out. I used to have a go at him about his room but it was pointless. He'd also have his stick insects up there in a four foot tank. I remember the time the poor little buggers died and it stunk!"

Then there was the occasion when, at the age of eight or nine, Julian fell down the stairs and hit his head on the radiator at the bottom, needing six stitches in his head.

This wouldn't have been quite so embarrassing had Julian not deliberately jumped in the first place!

But for all his cheek and bravado, there was another, more sensitive side of Julian's character which often revealed itself when given the opportunity. He'd always be willing to help out elderly neighbours by putting their bins out for them, while a retarded girl by the name of Maria Mancini, who lived a couple of doors away, came in for special attention. With other kids making fun of her disabilities, Julian would do his best to offer his protection.

"He used to look after her and was the only person she would get on with," remembers Ron Dicks. "If anybody else came near her she'd pinch them and scratch them. I've seen her chase kids away who were taking the mickey out of her, but he used to look out for her and that's what he was generally like as a kid." Although only a kid himself at the time, his relationship with Maria also reflected Julian's affection for children in general. Indeed, when slightly older, both he and Grantley wanted Carol to have a baby girl – and they weren't bothered where it came from! "They wanted me to have another baby, adopt, foster – anything – as long as it was a little girl," Carol recalls.

> "He said, 'Come and see what I've got!' So I put my hand in the bag and felt this furry thing. He'd brought a baby seagull home!"

It was for animals, however, that Julian showed a special attachment. During his time at home he kept hamsters, gerbils, rabbits, fish, insects...you name it, he did his best to keep it confined in his bedroom. "I came home one day and there were 22 babies in the rabbit cage!" he exclaims. "One of them was born with damaged back legs and I can still remember my old man putting it into a bag to suffocate it – because it was too expensive to get a vet to put it down. But it wouldn't die so he shoved it into the oven and gassed it. I cried my eyes out for days."

Then there was the story of Horace the seagull. Julian had gone on a school trip to Brownsea Island, near Poole in Dorset, and returned to meet his mum with a bulging football bag and a big grin on his face. "He came to me and said, 'Come and see what I've got!' while opening his bag and telling me to stick my hand in," says Carol. "So I put my hand in the bag and felt this furry thing. He'd brought a baby seagull home! I said, 'What are you doing with that?' and he told me that a man said he could have it because it had lost its mum and would die if it was left on its own.

"I just didn't know what we were going to do with it. Eventually we got a box with some chicken wire on the top and it had to live in the kitchen. It was just a ball of fluff with two little legs sticking out the bottom, but we brought it up to be a fully fledged seagull."

The bird was swiftly named Horace by Julian and the two boys would fish for eels and buy whiting and sprats from the fresh fish shop to feed him. "The eels

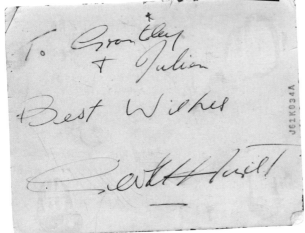

An early West Ham connection!... A picture of Ron Dicks with Geoff Hurst and Glenn Hoddle in the Canaries is signed on the back 'To Grantley & Julian. Best Wishes. Geoff Hurst'

would be a foot long – they used to hold them up and let the seagull gobble them," recalls Carol. "And when it was learning to fly, they'd take it out into the garden. It would flap its wings and go a bit further and higher every day."

The main family pet, meanwhile, was a cocker spaniel known as Frome, named after one of Ron's football teams. Carol had not wanted the dog initially – "because I knew who was going to end up with it!" – but Ron's scheme of taking her over to the owners of the dog who'd just given birth to pups worked a treat and she inevitably fell in love with it and brought it home.

"Julian used to stick Frome in goal!" she laughs. "The boys would put Frome at one end of the garden and kick the ball at her. She'd be diving for the ball and saving shots. Mind you, they used to stick me in goal and fire a ball at me as well. They broke my glasses and gave me headaches on more than one occasion."

Something else that gave Carol headaches was Julian's appetite for food – invariably the wrong kind. "Ooh, he was a sod," she says. "My mum used to give in to him and he used to have choc ice and chips for Saturday dinner. He's always loved junk food. Grantley, on the other hand, would eat anything. He'd have liver and kidneys and Julian would say, 'Oh no, I'm not going near that.' He wouldn't eat proper food and in the end I used to give up and let him eat what he wanted. He'd say I used to stuff him with vegetables, but to a degree I was soft with him."

When a telling off was required, for either of the boys, a smack across the legs would generally suffice. "My dad's never hit me or my brother, but if we'd done something wrong we'd know about it," says Julian. Punishment would often result in them being sent to their rooms, although Carol laughs at that idea now: "Why we sent them upstairs I'll never know because they used to have a snooker table and just about everything else up there! They never wanted for anything. I can remember buying them skates, bikes, go-karts…"

When it came to football kits, however, Julian and Grantley said they could make it up themselves and they found themselves white T-shirts, white shorts and long white football socks which became an impromptu Leeds United kit. "We bought them their boots – Julian always wore Puma and Grantley wore Adidas – and I can remember taking a photo of them outside the house, with all this white gear on and a ball under their feet," smiles Carol.

Back at Novers Lane, things were taking place – not in the classroom ("My mind would just wander," explains Julian), but out on the playing fields. Julian had started playing for the school football team and was not only enjoying it but excelling at it. Despite his diminutive size, he was proving a mighty handful up front, banging in a plentiful supply of goals with his left foot. "I thought I was Pelé," he admits.

A memory that wasn't fun, however, was of the game that Julian finished playing, only to walk off the park to discover that his grandad Edward had just died. Ron's father (known to his family as Poppy Dicks) had been a useful player too, by all accounts, and his enthusiasm for the game was certainly strong enough for it to continue down the Dicks family line.

The Novers Lane team often attracted proud parents to watch their kids in action, but one day a different figure appeared on the touchline. He wasn't cheering

anybody on or shouting anybody's name out, unlike the rest of the support. He was merely watching and observing. And caught in his gaze was 10-year-old Julian Dicks.

Ron Dicks (far left with beard) with Frome Town.

26

CHAPTER 4

ENTER THE TWO RONNIES

RON VEAL was a Bristol based scout, working on behalf of Aston Villa boss Ron Saunders. Their relationship had gone back many years, to the time when Veal's goalkeeping son Robert played under the manager at non-league Yeovil.

First asked by Saunders to scour the Bristol region for talent to send down to Yeovil, Veal continued to look for young players for him as the manager moved up the league ladder – first to Oxford United, then Norwich City. It was for the East Anglian club that the scout enjoyed most success (with 22 of the 30 youths he sent there being signed as apprentices or professionals) and he worked briefly for John Bond ("we didn't get on at all," offers Veal) at Carrow Road while Ron Saunders had a short spell at Manchester City. The two Rons soon linked up again, though, at Aston Villa. And it was during this period of their relationship that Ron Veal began to run his eye over Julian Dicks.

"I knew the schools because my son had played for Bristol Boys and the county," explains Ron as to why he was spending time watching 10-year-olds. He was also running a pub in High Ridge, so leaving his wife to look after the business, he'd be off on scouting missions – all for good will too. "I wasn't getting any money out of it," declares Veal. "I was doing it purely for Mr Saunders because he was so good with my boy. If he'd have asked me to go to Scotland I'd have gone and all I would have claimed is my petrol money."

Julian was still at junior school when the Villa scout spoke to his parents for the first time, following a game at Novers Lane. "He'd gone in to get changed and we were sitting in the car park," says Carol, "when a teacher brought Ron over and introduced us, saying he was a scout for one of the Birmingham clubs and that he'd like a few words with us. That was when Julian was about 10, but he always stood out a little bit. If Julian scored too many goals they used to put him in goal to give the other side a chance. He always wanted to win and was very competitive, but there was no big-headedness in him at all."

Much of Julian's footballing development at this stage stemmed from the elimination of virtually everything that might usually distract kids of his age. He had no pop music idols, didn't spend all night in front of the telly, there were no computer games then to be gripped by and, despite making the move from Novers Lane to Merrywood Boys Secondary School at the age of 11, was no more inclined to think about homework than he had been previously.

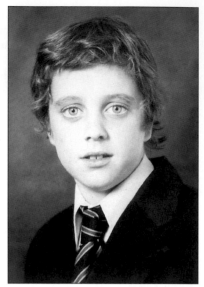

Julian, aged ten

Indeed, the amount of effort that Julian put into his schooling was, according to his mum, "whatever he could get away with". And with Carol spending more time at home with the children than Ron, it was inevitably her who had the burden of trying to push them into making more of an effort. "It was always me who used to help them with their homework – when it was obvious they had some," she says, although Grantley was a little less reluctant in his studies than Julian. Ron, meanwhile, had some slight concern at the poor grades (mostly Ds and Es, apart from the A he would get for PE) Julian's reports would show – when he bothered to bring them home or not hide them, which wasn't often – but felt there was little he could really do to alter his son's chosen course. "Whatever I said to him would go in one ear and out the other. All he wanted to do was kick a ball," he says. One thing Ron and Carol were adamant about, however, was that Julian at least attended classes. "I never bunked off school," confirms Julian, "that's something my mum and dad were very strict about."

What he used to get up to at school though was anybody's guess, especially given his scruffy appearance which suggested he'd spent most of his time rolling around the playground. "He used to come home looking like a bag of rags, flicking his tie as he walked along the pavement," says Carol. "You could have a crowd of boys but you could always tell my two – shirts hanging out, blazers all over the place, ties being flicked, dirt on their faces…"

Reflecting the local area, Merrywood Boys was a little on the rough side. Julian had his mates – Jeff Hazel, Gary Bourne, Lee Gardener, some of whom were friends of Grantley's and hence older – but as his brother says, "If you couldn't look after yourself, you got picked on." Julian was never a victim as such, but still had his fair share of fights. "I got beaten up loads of times but I could hold my own," he insists. But again, if either brother got involved in anything when the other was around, they'd leap to each other's defence. "That happened on the football field as well," adds their mother. "They would always look after each other – people would say, 'Watch it, the Dicksies are about.'"

Inevitably small gangs would form, but Julian's mob were not the type to go round bashing little kids or anything like that. More often they'd have fights with rival schools, such as Hartcliffe, which was even rougher. About three or four miles apart, they'd meet halfway for their battles. "But as we got older it got out of hand, with chains and things like that turning up, so I never got involved in that stuff," says Julian.

Other 'bad boy' behaviour included nicking sweets from newsagents, breaking windows with footballs and, when slightly older, experimenting with cigarettes. "I used to nick money from my mum and dad, maybe a quid or so, and go and buy a packet of Embassy No 6," Julian confesses. "They did catch me a couple of times – my mum would find the money in my rolled up clothes and put it back on the shelf without saying anything."

By far the most serious 'crime', however, took place following a visit to the local Bristol Corporation golf course with Grantley. With a putter and pitching wedge in his hands, Julian swiftly succumbed to temptation. "I said to my brother, 'I'm gonna nick these.' So we played two holes and went round the back of the forest where another hole was and shoved the two sticks down my trousers, which left me rather stiff-legged as I walked out!

"It was about six weeks later when a copper stopped me in Melvin Square and asked me where I'd got the clubs from. And, of course, they had BC – Bristol Corporation – stamped on them. I said I'd found them and, as I was only 30 seconds from my house, said, 'If you don't believe me, I only live there. You can ask my parents.' But the police put me in their car, took me to the station, shoved me in a cell, took my belt off and pulled the laces out of my shoes – basically removing anything I could hang myself with!'

> "The police put me in their car, took me to the station, shoved me in a cell, took my belt off and pulled the laces out of my shoes – basically removing anything I could hang myself with!"

With Julian's parents out, he had to wait for Grantley to break the news to them when they returned home. To say Ron and Carol were annoyed is an understatement – not with their son, but the police! "We went up to the station and I went absolutely potty," says Carol. "They'd taken his belt and laces off, not fed him and kept him there for hours. I said to the copper, 'You want to do something better with your time, you've really got to be joking!'"

Fortunately for Julian, however, he managed to manoeuvre his way out of trouble, even though he was threatened with a court appearance. "Fortunately it never went that far," confirms Julian, "because my parents said, 'Look, he's being watched by Aston Villa and we obviously don't want this to ruin his chances of a career.' So it got dropped, although I think I got a clout round the head from dad!"

Ron Veal had continued to keep tabs on Julian's footballing progress, watching him on a regular basis. "I followed up on him about four times a year until he was 14," he reveals. "I used to watch him and make notes of the dates in my book." And Julian was indeed making progress, not to mention a name for himself, following his initial Novers Lane exploits. Playing for Boco Juniors and Raleigh Sports (the latter along with Grantley) at under-12 level, he made an instant impact with his tenacity and eye for goal.

A Raleigh Sports news-sheet acknowledged Julian's ability and contribution following his two goals in the 3-2 victory over Warmley in the 1978-79 GYFA U-12 Cup semi-final with the following lines: *'It was Julian Dicks, showing enormous skill allied to a willingness to run and fight, who opened the scoring with a super lob after 15 minutes. The brilliant little forward struck again with a great long range drive to give Raleigh a 2-0 half-time lead.'*

The very same sheet opened out to reveal a double-page profile of the Dicks brothers, detailing various information including their likes. It reveals that Julian's nickname was 'Eyes', he was a fan of *Starsky & Hutch*, his favourite meal was steak and chips with a shandy(!) and that his hobby was collecting football cards. Strangely, though, it lists his favourite player and team as Tony Woodcock and Nottingham Forest (who admittedly were faring slightly better than the team he actually supported, Manchester United).

Carol would watch her two boys and play 'coffee lady', producing a hot flask at regular intervals during the winters when it got too cold. But Julian was proving a hot property himself, picking up rave notices in the local press that featured the results and performances of teams in the junior leagues. *'Julian Dicks, son of Frome Town and Somerset County skipper Ron Dicks, hammered six goals for Boco Juniors in a 17-1 thrashing of Wick in the Hanham Minor League,'* said one report, while another strangely opted to put the emphasis on one of his team-mates, despite getting a hatful of goals: *'Mark Cooper, son of Bristol Rovers player-coach Terry Cooper, was among the goals as Boco Juniors beat Stoke Lane 10-2 in the Hanham Minor League this week. Six of Boco's goals came from Julian Dicks.'*

And so it continued...: *'Five-Goal Julian Raleigh Star'* was the headline over a story which confirmed Raleigh Sports' triumph in the Avon and Bristol Federation of Boys' Clubs U-13 five-a-side soccer area finals, with Julian's five goals substantially helping them on their way to a 7-0 thrashing of Sea Mills.

Julian's success meant that he was swiftly representing Bristol Boys, assembled from the best local youths, often finding himself playing with boys two years his senior. *'Grantley and Julian Dicks are in the Bristol Boys U-13 soccer squad for this season's programme of representative matches,'* said one newspaper clip which illustrated such an occasion. Back at school, however, Carol Dicks was less than happy with the way her son was being treated.

"The rows I used to have with the school because of how they used to use Julian!"

*Julian with the
1980 Isle of Wight
trophy (Under 12s).*

she complains. "He was two years younger than Grantley but they used to play in the same team, yet when an older boy came in they used to drop Julian. They'd say he was too young. I used to blow my top!"

On May 4, 1980 Julian played his first game at a league venue – Bristol Rovers' Eastville Stadium – when his Boco Juniors side (in their second season) met Bridge Farm United in the Hanham Minor League Cup Final. The team-sheet notes said everything about the quality of the young forward: *'The player behind our success. Plays for Bristol Schools at U-13. Prolific goalscorer with over 80 goals.'*

By this time Julian was playing on Sundays for West Town Harriers, the youth side managed by his father Ron that was meant to feed prospects through to Bristol City. Their big rivals were Parkway, the equivalent side for Bristol Rovers, and both these teams would battle it out for supremacy, particularly when they came up against each other. "It was always niggly when we played against them," remembers Julian. "You'd have all the parents fighting each other! My mum's terrible – she really shouts her head off."

As well as Ron Veal, City scout Jock Rae had his eye on Julian, recommending him to the club's manager, Alan Dicks (no relation!). But, according to Carol, when told Julian was just 11, Dicks apparently replied, "Oh, he's got 10 years yet before I want to have a look at him." ("That's what he was like," she says.)

It was with West Town Harriers that Julian found himself attracting the attention of a scout working for *another* league club in the summer of 1980. Little could he know then how he would ultimately figure in that club's future, for it was West Ham United. A representative of theirs, Mike Dove, had shown interest after Julian won the player of the tournament award after a competition on the Isle of Wight.

"They took him up to London and he played in a couple of trial games," recalls Ron Dicks. "I think it was Bill Nicholson, who was doing some scouting for West Ham, who finally said, 'He can pass but he's got no pace.'"

"Mike Dove was really disappointed that Julian never made it. To think that West Ham could have had him for nothing!" – CAROL DICKS

Carol was also present on the day West Ham turned Julian down. "They had Ron and I in an office, with Julian outside, and they explained to us that they didn't think he was good enough. They said he's not quick enough and was much smaller than the rest of the boys. So Ron said, 'Well, how old do you think he is?' They said that they assumed he was the same age as the rest of the boys – 13 years old. When Ron said that he was only 11 it was like, 'Oh!'

"Mike Dove used to pick us up at Victoria Coach Station and take us to Chadwell Heath for those trials. He was really disappointed that Julian never made it. To think that West Ham could have had him for nothing!"

Undeterred by the East London club's rejection, Julian carried on playing as much

Julian with Bristol City manager Alan Dicks (no relation) behind. "Oh he's got 10 years yet before I want to have a look at him".

football as he could force into his time. What didn't please him was that the Merrywood school tried to get everybody to play rugby as well, and it's no surprise that both Dicks boys participated reluctantly, Julian generally giving the ball away as fast as possible to indicate his disinterest. Not that he was worried by the physical aspects of sport, despite his size. "You'd get stuck in on the football pitch and you had kids that started crying or those that just got on with it. I just got on with it," he says.

One match, in particular though, may have been significant in the development of Julian's temperament on the field of play. "I suppose he was about 12," recalls his father. "He hadn't been that aggressive before then, but somebody stepped on his hand during the game and left a cut on it, like an egg, and he started crying. He started to walk off the pitch and I said, 'You don't come off the pitch crying, son, you get back on there and like it.' He stopped crying and went back on. And since then he's been more aggressive. Whether that had anything to do with how he is now I really don't know."

Inevitably, fights occasionally broke out on the pitch and Julian would show a new resolve. "If you booted somebody and they lumped you one you'd end up fighting," admits Julian. And if Grantley was around then he'd be in there as well, of course.

Meanwhile, Ron Veal, still working for Ron Saunders at Villa, was ready to make his move, undeterred by what some people had started to say about Julian. "He wasn't getting into trouble but some teachers said his temperament would let him down," he remembers. "But I said that I didn't think so – if you treated the kid right he'd be alright. That's what I found and I had no trouble with him.

"At one point I spoke again to his mother and father who were watching him and I said, 'I'd like to take him to Villa.' And they said that he was down for Bristol City. I said, 'That's okay, but I can tell you that I used to be a big shareholder there and I know what's wrong there that you don't.' Even though his father was running the

BRISTOL SCHOOLS' FOOTBALL ASSOCIATION

THIS

CERTIFICATE

IS AWARDED TO

Julian Dicks

Who has played in the

BRISTOL BOYS UNDER *14* **XI**

SEASON 19 *81/82*

P. W. Sale

TEAM MANAGER

P. Robson.

CHAIRMAN B.S.F.A.

junior Bristol team, West Town Harriers. Anyway, he said, 'Yeah, I should think so.' So I took Julian up for a trial, along with his brother Grantley. The chief scout up at Villa was initially more interested in Grantley. But I said, 'Julian's the one!' And so it proved. The thing is, he *wanted* the ball. The ball was *his*. Even though it belonged to the club, it was *his* ball. And that's what I like about a player. If he lost the ball he'd try and get it back."

With Julian still only 13 years of age, though, he was still too young to sign on the dotted line, although he was well aware of their wish to take him. "They said, 'When you're 14, we want you to sign,'" he confirms.

Julian could easily have been playing in the claret and blue of Aston Villa, if only Ron Saunders had not found himself in an untenable position at Villa Park shortly after the above verbal agreement was made. "I was sacked by Villa, but still had three years to go on my contract, so it was me that finally walked out," Saunders explains. Soon afterwards, he was back in management, a short way across town at Birmingham City. And just as Ron Veal followed him to the Blues, so did Julian. Indeed, when Saunders first saw Julian, he asked Ron Veal, "Where did you find this kid?" before exclaiming, "What a boy!"

Not that the manager should have been too surprised, knowing full well that "when Ron Veal said a kid was good, he was good. In my opinion he was one of the best youth scouts in the country.

"He had a lot of ability," says Saunders of the young Dicks. "He was a very well-balanced player for a kid and knew what it was all about – he had a good head. He always wanted the ball and a blind man could have told you he could play."

34

It therefore became a formality that Julian would be offered schoolboy forms for Birmingham City as soon as he turned 14. And when he was invited up for a meeting at St Andrews, he was faced with what would be the biggest decision of his life. "There was myself, Ron Saunders, Ron Veal and my parents in the manager's office," Julian remembers. "They said that they wanted me to finish my schooling in Birmingham, live in digs up there and train with the club three or four times a week. They gave me time to make a decision and I decided to sign. Mum and dad got stick from people for letting me go, but they allowed me to make my own mind up – they said it was entirely up to me."

The club offered to find Julian an appropriate school, pay him a nominal wage and arrange to accommodate him at a hostel with other young Birmingham players. But while some parents may have made a decision on their son's behalf, Carol and Ron were content to leave the decision in the hands of Julian himself. "I said to Julian that if he wanted to do it then it was entirely up to him," claims Carol, "because if we didn't let him do it, all we would have got from him at a later stage was, 'If you'd have let me do that I would have been all right by now.' I thought we'd just take the consequences if he didn't make it."

"I was getting into more and more trouble – fighting and nicking stuff. God knows what I would have done if I hadn't have got away – maybe I'd have ended up in prison"

Ron Dicks, of course, could have opposed the move because of his position with West Town Harriers, but he appears to have been content to let his son join the Midlands club. "We had a chat about it with him but I thought it was an ideal opportunity for him," he says, admitting that his own feelings were influenced by the changing environment in Bristol. "At that point, Knowle West was starting to get a bit naughty. He was at that age where the kids he was mixing with were a bit dodgy. He could have gone the other way."

Scout Ron Veal indeed had the same view that a move away from Knowle West would be doing Julian a favour. "They lived in a part of Bristol which was a little bit wild," he says. "You had to be a man to stand it around there and I thought the best thing for Julian was for him to get away. But that didn't often happen for people and he was very lucky."

Julian did not necessarily want to leave home, but the opportunity to join Birmingham was too good to miss and, yes, he probably knew it was his chance to avoid Knowle's looming pitfalls. "I was getting into more and more trouble – fighting and nicking stuff," he concedes. "God knows what I would have done if I hadn't have got away – maybe I'd have ended up in prison. But playing football was something I'd always wanted to do – there was certainly nothing else I could have done – and here was my chance, so I took it."

Back in Bristol, however, the reaction to the news that a 14-year-old boy was leaving home to join a football club halfway up the country was not favourable. Ironically, especially given Julian's loathing of school work, one major voice of dissent was from Merrywood Boys. "They didn't say anything to me but in the local paper, Pete Bell, his sports master, said that it was a not a good idea to let a lad of 14 go away from home," remembers Ron Dicks, who, according to Ron Veal, also had to suffer the indignity of eventually losing his position at West Town as a result of his son's defection. "Once they found out that Julian had signed for Birmingham, Ron was given the sack," the scout states. "Terry Cooper was the manager at the time and he told him to go. Ron didn't mind because Julian was doing so well and if he'd have signed for Bristol they'd have only had him for a couple of years before selling him anyway, because that's what they do with all their boys. That's why they've got no team."

As Julian's departure became more publicised, so did the reaction against it, causing even more media attention. "We took a lot of flak, we really did," says Carol. "The newspapers used to phone up, the teachers used to say things and other parents said, 'Do you think you've done the right thing? Fancy letting him go away at 14!'"

The *Bristol Evening Post* ran one large story about the news on August 25, 1982, quoting Julian as saying, *"It doesn't bother me having to go away from home because it is the best thing for my future in football."* It was a view not shared by Bristol Schools FA chairman, Peter Bale: *"Personally I feel that the boy is too young to be taken away from home to live in a hostel,"* he said. *"I happen to know him particularly well as he is a pupil at Merrywood, where I teach, and is in my house at school. Julian has a lot of ability and will be a loss to Bristol Boys' under-15 squad this season. But having dealt with a lot of young players, I would not consider his potential greater than quite a few other lads."*

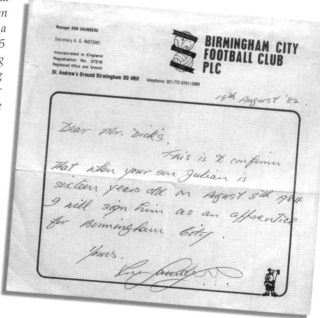

With that final, stinging comment ringing in his ears, Julian headed off to Birmingham – with boots in bag and signed confirmation from Ron Saunders that he'd be taken on as an apprentice on his 16th birthday in hand – to prove the few cynics wrong.

CHAPTER 5

BLUES BROTHERS TO BRUISE BROTHERS

I N September 1982 Julian moved to his new home, Park View Guest House, a residence for young Birmingham City players run by Janet (a sort of Blues *mother*, if you will) and Brian Rodgers at 42 Tennyson Road in the Small Heath district. The couple had started looking after apprentices in their previous home and after taking on Pat Van Den Hauwe – who had been staying with Brian's mother (along with former West Ham player Alan Curbishley) – they'd formed an agreement with Birmingham to look after the club's new recruits to the Midlands (at a cost of £30 a week per head) in a larger, seven-bedroomed property.

Park View was a lovely house, complete with swimming pool and park opposite (hence the house name), but despite its welcoming appearance there was an initial possibility that Julian (or rather the club on his behalf) would be house-hunting elsewhere.

"I didn't want him!" admits Janet Rodgers. "I was quite adamant I wasn't going to take him because I'd got some pros and apprentices and they were all about 17 or 18 years old. Julian was only 14 and would have to go to school. I just thought that he wasn't going to fit in at all with the older boys. Ron Saunders came to see me about it, wanting me to meet his parents, and I said, 'No way, I just haven't the time to look after a schoolboy.' But Ron told me he was sure I'd really like Julian if I met him.

"I was still quite adamant that I didn't want him but Julian came up one afternoon with his parents and everything I'd said just went out the door. I found myself saying, 'Yes, alright.' I took to him straight away and all my fears came to nothing in the end."

The date of Julian moving to Park View coincided with a midweek Birmingham City fixture against a Liverpool side featuring Graeme Souness at St. Andrews. After tea at Janet and Brian's, Julian and his parents watched the game together in one of the club's executive boxes before saying their goodbyes. "Afterwards, my parents went one way and I went another and my mum started crying and then so did I. And then I thought I'd made the wrong decision," admits Julian on reflection.

Carol Dicks then received a call from her son the following day. "He said, 'You were crying, weren't you?' and I said, 'No, I was not!' And he said, 'Oh yes you were!'"

Many kids of 14 might not have been able to deal with the potential trauma of leaving home to join a big city club in another part of the country but Julian's integration into his new environment was made easier by the fact that – in addition to the support given by Brian and Janet ("they were as good as gold and treated me like their kid") – two vital people took him under their wing: fellow resident at Park View, Martin Kuhl, and club manager Ron Saunders.

"The only player I was really friendly with was Martin," says Julian. "He was on the fringe of the first-team when I moved in and I used to look up to him and he looked after me."

Martin Kuhl (who originated from Sandhurst and joined Brum after being released by Chelsea) remembers Julian's arrival at the house: "He was a scrawny little kid with big eyes – a real ugly little duckling. When we first saw him we wondered what all the fuss was about, but when he got playing he had a special left foot – he was made out of rock and he'd go through a brick wall for you."

Martin admits that he's tried to dismiss the theory that he took Julian 'under his wing' – because of his own 'hard man' reputation (having been sent off six times over the years) – but acknowledges the welcome that both he and, indeed, Janet and Brian gave the youngster: "The Rodgers were great. Janet took to Julian like he was her own kid. There were people there she didn't really like and had trouble with, but the ones she took to were probably Pat Van Den Hauwe, myself, David Coles (whose place in Martin's room went to Julian when he left) and Dicksy. The four us were like her children."

Julian indeed settled in well. "For a young lad to come up from Bristol and be away from his parents like that and be happy was fantastic," says Janet. "His whole life was football and he really enjoyed it. Some of the lads, like when I first had David Coles, were on the phone to home every five minutes."

> "He was a scrawny little kid with big eyes – a real ugly little duckling" – MARTIN KUHL

Martin Kuhl took to his new co-tenant so much that, after a while, he'd even invite Julian on dates with his girlfriend Sharon. "Julian was like a younger brother," he says. "We took him everywhere – zoos, fun-fairs, the pictures – he was always welcome to come along. Living away from home can be lonely, so we were like a big family. Sharon liked him and he was as good as gold."

And Julian was more than happy to spend time with the couple who would eventually get married and remain together. "You don't think about being a gooseberry when you're 14!" he admits, reflecting on those (mostly day) trips out.

At the club a further protective arm was being thrown around Julian by Ron

Early days at Brum... Julian (centre) with Ron Saunders.

Saunders, to the extent that, after a while, many players started calling him "son of Ron" as a result of him getting preferential treatment. "Youth team manager Keith Bradley tried to give me a second-hand pair of trainers," Julian recalls, "so I went to tell Ron Saunders and he told him to give me a new pair. From that day Keith and I never really saw eye to eye."

Another example of Ron's sympathetic handling of Julian came some two years later when, aged 16 and playing as an apprentice against West Bromwich Albion's youth side, he was sent off for the very first time after making a tackle. "Nobby Stiles was manager of the West Brom kids and he came up to me and said, 'Don't worry about it, just carry on the way you are and you'll be all right,'" recollects Julian. "It was nice of him to pull me to one side and say that, but Keith Bradley wanted to fine me. But Ron Saunders stopped the fine."

Carol Dicks remembers the fatherly hand the club manager extended to her son, talking of how Ron used to sometimes pick Julian up from the bus stop after school and give him lifts home: "He loved him. There was no reason for Ron Saunders to go past the bus stop but he'd pick him up in his Mercedes. Julian would sit there playing with the ashtrays and electric windows, pressing all the buttons and having a great time.

"There was a period when every time he turned up he seemed to be with Ron Saunders. I can remember waiting outside Highbury with the Birmingham team coach pulling up, and Julian getting off and going to the boot to get the kit out. There were lots of things like that."

But Ron purely saw it all as being part of his responsibilities as a manager. "We looked after *all* the kids," he says. "That was one of the pleasures of being a manager – it was your job to look after players and discipline them accordingly, for their own benefits."

For all Ron's efforts to help Julian, however, Janet Rodgers did not take to certain aspects of the manager's character. "I didn't like him," she says. "When we first got involved in looking after footballers for Birmingham, Jim Smith was in charge. He was just a down-to-earth, really nice man, but Ron always seemed very superior in his attitude. He would acknowledge me and if I had any problems I could phone him, but I didn't like him. Yes, he was protective of Julian, and that was probably why some of the other lads did resent him a little bit, because he was a favourite of Ron's."

These "other lads" were predominantly the group of apprentices in the Rodgers household who Janet referred to as "the Londoners". At the club itself – like at Park View – Julian was being embraced by an older group of players. "Even at 14, when the other kids weren't in, he was like a semi-apprentice, doing jobs that apprentices would be doing," remembers Martin Kuhl. "When the schoolkids turned up he eventually trained with them, but when they went home Julian would stay with the rest of the apprentices. So he had an early education as to what would be coming."

As for education in the more traditional sense, Julian was attending classes at Washwood Heath, where he'd been allocated to various O-level standard classes. Not surprisingly, given his continuing lack of interest in school work and single-mindedness towards football, he was clearly out of his depth and soon he was demoted to elementary classes – not that his grades improved much.

There was little doubt that he was happy in his new environment, though, and – as his parents could detect when he returned to Bristol at weekends – he was showing obvious signs of maturing too. "I thought he grew up quickly," states Ron Dicks. "He went away as a boy and came back a man. As the months went on you could see him growing up."

And he needed to grow up too, at least in the physical sense. "He was very, very small," declares Ron Veal. "When I first took him up there, it looked as if you needed to put a pump in his mouth and pump him up. I said to the governor (Ron Saunders) that he'd have to get some steaks down him." Indeed, it's reckoned by Julian that he probably weighed just six-and-a-half stone when signing as a schoolboy.

There was plenty of football being played in those early days – much to Julian's delight, of course. In addition to playing for Washwood Heath and later the Birmingham youth side, plus the training sessions he was enjoying with the club outside of school hours, Julian's trips south saw him turn out for Raleigh, Boco and then Fairfurlong and Hanham. Some people involved in the local soccer leagues in the west country, however, tried to oppose his presence. "A lot of them thought that because Julian was getting extra coaching elsewhere, they'd suggest that he shouldn't be allowed to play for any team in Bristol. 'He's not a Bristol lad,' they used to say, because he didn't live in Bristol any more. But it was no different to him going to boarding school and coming home at weekends – they wouldn't stop a boy then," argues Carol.

> "I thought he grew up quickly. He went away as a boy and came back a man" – Ron Dicks

Eventually Boco chief Bob Boyd successfully fought against such unjustified prejudice with the league authorities and Julian continued to play. Not that Julian was too eager to go home once he'd become absorbed into his new life in Birmingham anyway – at least as far as Janet Rodgers was concerned. "He never wanted to go home," she says. "I shouldn't say that but he didn't. He was really quite happy up in Birmingham."

It had always been suggested by his parents that nobody would have any problems with Julian as long as he had things to keep him occupied in the rare times he wasn't playing football. And it would seem he certainly had plenty to do, both at home and – as Julian would come to call his football responsibilities – work.

While still a schoolboy he received £8 pocket money from his club, which went straight to Janet. This money was earned back by mowing the lawn in the back garden and taking his landlady's boxer, Ali, for walks in the park. "Julian absolutely adored that dog," says Janet. "He used to do all sorts of errands, such as going down to the shops for me and taking the dog for walks. That helped me no end because even finding time to take Ali out in those years was quite an effort."

Julian was also more than happy to take on such responsibilities as doing his own ironing during these times, which all helped to develop his own sense of duty. No longer were things just left to others (although Janet would still clean his room and "find a few dirty books under his bed!"), not if he wanted to make it as a footballer.

It was with this main mission in mind that Julian realised that all the duties put his way at Birmingham's Elmdon training ground would have to be accepted, no matter how unpleasant. These included ensuring that the changing rooms and shower areas were clean, particularly when he was later made Chief AP (during his apprenticeship), which meant telling the other boys what to do to keep Keith Bradley happy. "If he saw just one speck of dirt he'd make you do the entire wall again. And it was the same with all the floors," remembers Julian, who sometimes wouldn't get home until 9.30pm. Later, after his school days were over, he'd be at Elmdon at nine in the morning, getting things cleaned and prepared for the pros

NOTICE OF AMENDMENT TO THE AGREEMENT OF AN APPRENTICE PLAYER

It is hereby agreed by ...Andrew Richard Waterhouse........................,

the Secretary of the ....BIRMINGHAM CITY FOOTBALL CLUB PLC.................,

of ......ST. ANDREW'S GROUND, BIRMINGHAM B9 4NH..........................

on behalf of the Club, and ......Julian Andrew Dicks.....................

of ......42 Tennyson Road, Small Heath, Birmingham.....................

Apprentice Player, that the Agreement entered into on the

..........9th July................. 19..84.... by the said Club and Player be

amended to read as follows:

CLAUSE 10. Wages

£ ...26.25........ per week from ..2nd September 1984.. to ..8th August 1986...

£ .... per week from .... to ....

(Fill in Any Other Provisions Required)

Clause a)
Clause b) Remain same

Signed by the said ...Andrew Richard.....

......Waterhouse........................

and ......Julian Andrew....................

........Dicks........................

In the presence of the Parent or
Guardian of the Player

.....Julian A. Dicks.
(Player)

........Awaterhouse..
(Secretary)

..........4. 9. 84......
(Date)

Signature ....

Occupation ....

Address ....

....

42

who'd arrive at 10am. "And if things weren't spotless you'd get whacked – and I mean whacked!" he emphasises.

Often he'd clean the showers out only to see mud chucked in there again. "And he'd clean it all up again without saying a word because he knew it was his job," insists Carol Dicks. "I think it was in his mind that if he didn't do it, then he wouldn't make it as a player. They'd make him clean the toilets and everything and he'd just buckle down and do it."

> "Ron Saunders was an iron man but he loved Dicksy because he was his sort of player"
> — MARTIN KUHL

At the end of each season, the dressing rooms would need to be cleaned down and once again Julian would know about it if he failed to do the job adequately. "If they weren't done properly he'd get soaked," remembers Martin Kuhl. "Like Ron Saunders, Keith Bradley was a very strict man and if things weren't done right the whole building would have to be done again. If Dicksy let the lads down he'd get his come-uppance."

Bradley's methods may not have endeared Julian towards him but Saunders was untroubled by his coach's ways. "Keith was possibly a little rigid, but he was very genuine and did a tremendous job for me. He was a lovely fellow," he says.

Bradley also left an impression on Martin Kuhl. "The lads used to take the mickey out of him but compared to a lot of people around nowadays he wasn't a bad coach," he says. "But they were all strict there. Ron Saunders was an iron man but he loved Dicksy because he was his sort of player. If you gave a hundred per cent and had something special in your feet, the gaffer would love you."

Back at Washwood Heath, as Julian neared the time to leave school in his final year, the careers officer invited him for a discussion on his future. "He asked me what I wanted to do when I left school and I told him I was going to be a footballer," says Julian. "He said that not many people actually made it in football, maybe one in a hundred, and I just said, 'Well, that one will be me then.'" Later, the headmaster had a word in the careers officer's ear and Julian never saw him again.

Julian eventually left school after taking exams in maths, English and science, among others, but it was all irrelevant. He didn't even bother to get his results, for his apprenticeship at Birmingham had long been guaranteed – for the last two years, in fact.

Julian's apprenticeship was confirmed on August 22, 1984, just after his 16th birthday, and it was around that time that two significant things happened (apart from his earnings rising to £26.25 per week). The first was his breakthrough into reserve team football; the second was his shift into a left-midfield role.

Throughout his time in youth and reserve team football, Janet Rodgers watched every game. "I'm not an expert on football, although I got more interested because of the lads, but there was something about Julian that just stood out," she confides. "He was so above a lot of the other kids, you could tell he was a natural. He'd always go

TODAYS LINE UP

KETTERING TOWN	V	BIRMINGHAM CITY
ALL YELLOW		ALL BLUE

		From:
	1	LEE WILLIAMS
ANDY MEADOWS		KEVIN ASHLEY
MICK PAYNE	2	JOHN FRAIN
BEN WILLIAMS	3	MARTIN WEIR
ANDY SMITH	4	PETER SHEARER
ADIE RINGROSE	5	IAN GORE
TONY KIRKLAND	6	TOM DEVESEY
MARK McKAY	7	STUART STORER
PAUL BIRCH	8	JULIAN DICKS
COLIN MARSHALL	9	GUY RUSSELL
JOHN SELLERS	10	ROBIN JUDD
JON INWOOD	11	MICK CLARKE
GORDON ANDERSON	12	

Referee:	J. Ashworth (South Luffenham)
Linesmen:	P.M. Keach (Bedford)
	J. Cutts (Wyton, Hunts.)

Other Matches at Rockingham Road

Sat. Dec. 8th Res. V. Corby Hazeltree K.O. 2.15 p.m.
Tues. Dec. 11th V V.S. Rugby (Midland Floodlight Cup) K.O. 7.30 p.m.
Sat. Dec. 22nd V. Barrow K.O. 3.00 p.m.

Forthcoming Home Youth Matches:

Jan. 15th V. Milton Keynes City K.O. 7.30 p.m.
Jan. 23rd V. Wolverton Town K.O. 7.30 p.m.
Feb. 5th V. Enderby Rangers K.O. 7.30 p.m.

Printed by Stamford Swiftprint Ltd., 10 St. Mary's Hill, Stamford, Lincs. Tel: (0780) 51551

Left: The programme from an early FA Youth Cup appearance.

Above: Julian captained the Birmingham side which beat Aston Villa 4-1 to win the Sunblest Midland Youth Cup.

in for a tackle. I would never have called him dirty, though, like some people have since labelled him."

Carol and Ron Dicks also showed their son support, although the costs of journeys from Bristol to Birmingham prohibited them attending too many of his games. One match that stands out for both Julian and his parents is an FA Youth Cup quarter-final tie against Newcastle when he was 16. A crowd of 5,000 or so watched a team featuring Paul Gascoigne, Ian Bogie and Joe Allon secure a 2-1 home win for the Geordies, before they completed the job with a 3-0 trouncing at Birmingham.

Strangely, Julian has no recollection of his one trophy (apart from his Young Eagle of the Month awards) collected during his days as a youth team player – the 1985 Sunblest Midlands Youth Cup – which he lifted as captain!

One of the earliest reserve games that Julian remembers playing at St. Andrews was against Shrewsbury. "I used to look after Jim Blyth and Wayne Clarke's boots and on that day we won 3-1, so I got a £6 bonus," he recalls.

On the pitch, Julian was already showing himself to be an "aggressive" character – collecting his first red card for Birmingham's second-string (ironically against West Brom again) for 'foul and abusive language'. He may have just have been dividing his energies between the youth and reserve teams at this time, but it's worth acknowledging the influence of the likes of Pat Van Den Hauwe, Mick Harford, Mark Dennis, Noel Blake, Robert Hopkins and Martin Kuhl, who gave the Birmingham first-team a distinctly physical presence during the mid-eighties.

"As a young lad, even as a schoolboy, these players took him under their wing," says Kuhl. "I think they realised he was a good player. The lads loved him and big Mick Harford thought the world of him."

These players welcomed the young Dicks into their training sessions when the other kids weren't around and were happy to share their knowledge and experience. "He was brought up with the fact that you won the ball at all costs and you were taught even the dirty tricks of the game," says Kuhl. "He was brought up with it from the age of 14. He'd hear us talking and ask us things and train with us. He knew what it was all about and I don't think it's done him any harm.

"As a team, we trained how we played. That was the way we were coached. We'd have stitches needed after accidental clashes of heads. Ron Saunders would play in the five-a-sides – I caught him once and he wellied me off the park! But we made 50/50 tackles and we got up and got on with it. We'd never show we were hurt. But one thing that people didn't realise was the amount of skill and class in the team – it was unbelievable. Big Mick Harford is still playing now; Tony Coton could play outfield as well; Pat Van Den Hauwe did well in his career.

"We used to look after each other, on and off the pitch. If you got done in a tackle, somebody else would take care of him. Teams like Wimbledon think they were the first to do it. We could do it but we had more about us than they did. People like Mark Dennis and Mick Harford had class, but perhaps it was their reputation as nutters – especially Dennis – that cost them an England place."

Julian had enough obvious talent of his own though, to impress the senior players at St. Andrews. "He had a sweet left foot and was good for his size in the air. He was only skinny but he used to wear baggy shorts," laughs Kuhl. "You could tell he could play. That's why most of the lads took to him. After training we used to stick around and ping balls to each other and he'd join in – he was one of the lads, even though he was younger than the rest of us."

Rather than his parents worrying about the people around Julian in his early days at Birmingham, they felt comfortable with the support he was getting. "A lot of people say he turned out the way he did because of who he was with at Birmingham," Carol says. "But they protected him, they really did. They wouldn't let him get into any trouble. He'd go to nightclubs with some of them and they'd always look after him. I wasn't worried about him at all."

One of the clubs Julian occasionally visited was Faces, managed by Janet's husband Brian. Having gone along with his landlord, Julian invariably – and inevitably – had to hang around until late, although no real drinking took place on his part. For the older players, though, the nightspot was considered a place where a drink could be had without the threat of trouble.

Trouble did take place, however, when people broke Janet Rodgers' 10.30pm house curfew. "I had a few coming in a bit late and drunk," she admits. "It was a nightmare sometimes but I knew that if I'd have informed the club then they'd have got the sack and been on their way."

> "A lot of people say he turned out the way he did because of who he was with at Birmingham, but they protected him, they really did"
> — CAROL DICKS

There was still one incident, though, which had people at Birmingham City asking questions about the wisdom of letting their players reside with the manager of a top city nightclub. "I remember two Scottish lads who said they were going to the pictures one Friday night, before a youth game the next day," says Janet. "They went out but what I didn't know was that they'd gone to the club. They had to knock me up to get in and, of course, they were virtually paralytic. I went absolutely berserk! They went up to their room and then Martin came down, asking for a bucket because they'd been sick. Brian gave them a real telling off.

"We didn't report them, we thought we'd let it go, but I think it was Pat Van Den Hauwe who had an important match for the first team that afternoon and he must have let it out. My husband and I were summoned down to the club and given a real dressing down over it. In fact, Ron Saunders at one stage was thinking of taking the lads out of the house, because he didn't think it was the right kind of environment for them. But Brian argued that he didn't encourage the lads to go there, which he didn't."

> 'Bristolian Julian Dicks, 16, could make his debut for Birmingham today, when they take on Charlton in the Midlands'

Apart from the curfew, another rule was that no players could bring girlfriends back to Park View. "They'd all be at it otherwise," protests Janet. "It would have ended up like a brothel. Although Pat Van Den Hauwe was a bit of a problem in that respect, being older than the others."

Despite his aggressive nature on the pitch, Julian was considered as being relatively placid in his social habits off it, preferring to remain focused on his footballing priorities as he turned 16 and allow the older players to pursue girls in the clubs.

By that stage his sights were set firmly on the first-team, where the large majority of his Birmingham mates were, of course. And some time after his sixteenth birthday, Julian thought his chance had come. "It was a home game," he recalls, "and Ron Saunders said to me outside the first-team dressing room, 'Come in here,

INJURY-HIT Birmingham include a 16-year-old in their squad to travel to Manchester City today, writes Dave Horridge.

Julian Dicks is one of three apprentices manager Ron Saunders has lined up for a match that could see him without all three first-choice forwards.

Mick Harford and Wayne Clarke are still doubtful with the injuries that kept them out of Wednesday's Milk Cup replay at West Bromwich and they have been joined by Robert Hopkins with a damaged knee. Full-back Brian Roberts, hurt in that game, is a definite

Ron turns to the City kids

non-starter along with Gerry Daly and Mark Jones.

Said Saunders: "It was difficult enough to name a squad—I'm dreading having to pick a side."

Peter Shearer and Ian Brown, both 17-year-old apprentices, played at the Hawthorns and it seems certain that at least one of them will be on duty at Maine Road.

one of my midfielders has gone down injured – you're playing!' I s**t myself! So I went in, got my gear on and saw that everybody was looking at me. Then Ron said, 'You're not playing really.' And I felt so small. Some of the players had a go at him about it but it was only meant in good humour, although I didn't find it funny!"

Manufacturing such a scenario, however, was Ron's way of giving players on the fringe a taste of what it's like to get the big call-up to first-team duty. "Because a lot of them think it's a doddle and then on the day they're washed out with nerves before they go onto the pitch," he argues. "So that kind of thing was an exercise to get them mentally ready."

There were a couple of occasions at the tail-end part of that 1984-85 campaign (Birmingham's promotion year from the old Second Division, when they finished second in their first attempt at returning to the top flight) when it was speculated that Julian – still in midfield at that point – might make his first-team debut.

'Midfield player Julian Dicks, 16-year-old son of former Shepton Mallet manager Ron Dicks, is named in Birmingham City's squad for tomorrow's Second Division match away to Manchester City,' reported one Bristol paper, while a Midlands story – headed *'Boys Brigade: Ron Turns To City Kids'* – ran: *'Injury-hit Birmingham include a 16-year-old in their squad to travel to Manchester City today. Julian Dicks is one of three apprentices the manager has lined up for a match that could see him without all three first-choice forwards.'* "I'm dreading having to name a side," said Saunders before that game.

The injury crisis continued, offering hope to Julian as he gained another place in the first-team squad. *'Bristolian Julian Dicks, 16, could make his debut for Birmingham today, when they take on Charlton in the Midlands,'* suggested one paper back in his home town.

It wasn't to be on either occasion. But as Julian looked towards his 17th birthday, things were about to radically move on in his life. The 1985-86 season would prove to be a significant year for him – in more respects than one.

CHAPTER 6

FIGHTING FOR THE FIRST TEAM

AUGUST 6, 1985 was a momentous date in the Julian Dicks diary. Not only had he broken into the Blues first-team for the pre-season games by then, but he returned to his home city as a goalscoring hero, netting an equaliser just two minutes from time in a friendly match against Bristol Rovers.

'Sixteen-year-old Julian Dicks came home to Bristol to spare the blushes of First Division Birmingham at Eastville. His 88th minute equaliser, poached from an ill-judged Phil Bater back-pass, robbed Rovers of a victory they deserved. And the goal made it a perfect night for a player seemingly on the threshold of an exciting league career,' said the Bristol Evening Post. "The boy is making tremendous progress and is going to be a very good player," added Ron Saunders of Julian, who'd only been on the pitch for 10 minutes, having replaced David Geddis as a substitute.

Less than three weeks later, the serious business began, with Julian named on the bench for Birmingham's third league fixture back in the First Division. The Blues had won their opening game at St. Andrews – 1-0 against West Ham – and were attempting to bounce back from a 3-0 defeat at Watford with another trip down to London, this time to Chelsea. "We travelled down Saturday morning and had lunch at an hotel on the Thames," recalls Julian. "Ron Saunders got us into a big room and named his squad. He told me I was going to be sub but I thought, 'He's told me that before, he's winding me up again!' He'd have this big marker pen and use it to show what he expected from you. I didn't really take much notice but when he named his subs I was one of them.

"Once the whistle went for the start of the game I started to get a bit nervous on the bench, but as soon as I got on the nerves went and I just enjoyed it."

Julian replaced striker David Geddis again, being told by his manager to score him a goal. Despite one close effort, however, it wasn't to be their day, with Brum going down 2-0. Saunders offered a "well done" after the game – "even though I was knackered," Julian adds. "I thought that that would be it – the injured players would come back and I'd be bombed out, but I was sub again a game or so afterwards."

After being named as a substitute again (although not playing) in the match at

Everton on August 31, Julian only had to wait a week before being awarded the injured Des Bremner's No 7 shirt for his first league start. And what a fixture for him to get his big break, with the Blues playing arch rivals Aston Villa at St. Andrews in front of nearly 25,000 people.

Julian was told he'd be playing on the Friday before the game and naturally got little sleep that night. In fact, it was one of the few occasions he was genuinely nervous about starting a match and he certainly made his mark come the big derby debut itself. "I went to clear the ball and I caught Paul Birch, cutting his eye open," Julian remembers. "After that I just went on and on. I had a header cleared off the line and had a 25-yard volley which was going into the top corner. I thought, 'I've scored here!' but Nigel Spink, the Villa 'keeper, palmed it away."

Dad Ron was present at the game, which finished with a 0-0 scoreline, and witnessed the clash with Birch. "I remember some guy putting his head down low

September 1985: Julian with Paul Birch – debutant Dicks cut the Villa's player's eye open.

and Julian kicking him," he says. "But he didn't get booked for it. The referee gave him a warning and said, 'Seeing as it's your debut...' But he played quite well, considering that he was just 17."

'Julian Dicks' introduction to league football was in a game so fast and furious that three passes in a row would have merited a lap of honour,' reported one national paper rather disgruntled with the quality of the football on show. The local headlines, though, were dominated by Dicks' close efforts: *'Teenager Julian Dicks came close to marking his full First Division debut with a glorious winner in the Second City battle of St. Andrews,'* said one, while the *Sunday Mirror* wrote: *'A brilliant flying save by 'keeper Nigel Spink saved Villa's bacon. His acrobatic skill prevented 17-year-old debut boy Julian Dicks from notching a marvellous match winner in this dour Midlands derby. Dicks did everything right as he raced after a waist-high ball to hammer in a vicious left-foot volley. The ball was flying into the top of the net until Spink took off to tip it over.'*

One paper even went so far as to say that *'the 17-year-old was the one good thing to come out of the dreadful 0-0 derby'*, while Birmingham skipper Billy Wright hit back at the criticism, claiming that his side dominated a game against "the worst Villa

> **"I went to clear the ball and I caught Paul Birch, cutting his eye open"**

side that I have played against in a long time" and commending Julian on his performance. "We had a young lad making his debut in midfield and I was worried as to whether or not he could handle such a game mentally or indeed physically. But after a quiet start, after he got rid of his nerves and settled down, Julian had an impressive match and could have won the game for us in the last 10 minutes."

Julian was modest about his start, though. "I never expected a chance like that so soon," he admitted after the game. "I read the manager's comments about my debut being two or three years ahead of schedule and that's got to be right, grateful that I am for the chance."

Ron Saunders insists that, despite the injury situation, Julian had gained his place on merit, remembering certain qualities in his game: "As a youngster he showed great enthusiasm and put tremendous effort into his game. Of course, there's a thin line sometimes between giving a hundred per cent and going a little bit over the top," he says, before elaborating on the young Julian's on-field character. "I never really thought he had any problems with his temperament. Only that, as a competitor, if anyone

---

TEENAGER Julian Dicks, came close to marking his full First Division debut with a glorious winner in the Second City battle of St Andrew's.

The stocky Bristol born midfield player, who will not be 18 until next month, forced goalkeeper Nigel Spink into making a blinding save ten minutes from time.

Spink dived to his right to push the ball out for a corner and with two minutes remaining, again had to make a brilliant stop to prevent Robert Hopkins from giving Blues victory.

In the end, the contest between the two old enemies ended with Blues maintaining their unbeaten home record.

beat him he'd get after them very quickly. And he did everything he could to stop them doing whatever they wanted to with the ball.

"He had a way, and no doubt still does, of playing his games very simply. There was nothing extravagant or prima donna-ish about the way he played. So, whatever games you put him in, you knew before you started exactly what you were going to get."

Following the good write-ups, Julian kept his place in the team for the following week's 1-0 victory at Ipswich Town. With Des Bremner returning from his rib injury, though, he had to be patient in the next few months, making occasional midfield starts or being named on the bench depending on the team's injury situation and form. There was no danger, though, of Julian getting too big for his boots, despite his early call to first-team duty. "If you did start getting big-headed one of the pros would always lump you one to bring you back down to earth," Julian says. "I was still cleaning boots at that time and if they weren't done properly I'd get a slap. But that was all part of growing up."

Coincidentally for Julian, the Blues played against Bristol Rovers again in the second round of the Milk Cup, and although he did not figure in the 3-2 first-leg win at Eastville, he was in the starting 11 for the second leg which the Blues won 2-1 after going behind. *'At least one Bristol footballer was happy after Rovers' cup dreams were shattered last night,'* stated one paper wryly the following morning.

> "If you did start getting big-headed one of the pros would always lump you one to bring you back down to earth"

After a reasonable start to the campaign (Brum winning their first three home games before the Villa match), things started to take a turn for the worse in October. But rather than Ron Saunders changing things around and bringing the likes of Dicks into the side, the poor run of form only encouraged the manager to restrict Julian's chances even further. "I've no doubt that if the team was struggling, he would have been left out or rested – for his own good," concedes Ron. "It's hard enough for a youngster coming into a winning side but it's a damned sight harder coming into a struggling side."

Despite the club gaining promotion the previous season, the writing had long been on the wall. "We actually came back up with seven free transfers in the regular team," Ron admits. By this time the likes of Pat Van Den Hauwe, Mick Harford, Tony Coton, Mark Dennis and Noel Blake had all been offloaded – some for big money – and even Saunders was questioning City's chances of survival in the top flight without investment in the squad. Billy Wright vowed to prove the knockers wrong: "Even the manager, who has been angered by not being able to buy new players, has backed up his argument by saying we could go down by Christmas unless we buck up our ideas. But that's not the attitude among the players," said the captain in the Midlands' *Sports Argus*.

"My job at the Blues was to sell a player almost once a month to keep the club afloat," declares Ron, reflecting on the club's '80s decline. "The problems were financial and the job I went there to do was to balance the books. We brought Mick Harford in and got an astronomical amount of money from Luton for him. We sold goalkeeper Tony Coton to Watford for £300,000 and paid a lot less (£100,000 to Peterborough) for David Seaman. It was a case of wheeling and dealing all the time.

"My main strength was in coaching and knowing what we wanted. But I got just as much pleasure from signing younger players – that no-one else rated, quite often – and getting them at the right price and developing their game. But during that season things were as bad as at any time I'd been there. And you knew that if you weren't able to strengthen you had problems. End of story."

Martin Kuhl remained throughout most of the changes, but was frustrated at having seen a good squad dismantled, particularly in the time just prior to Julian's introduction to the side. "Virtually every one of that squad got sold – even Dicksy in the end. But I think if the players had been kept together it could have been a hell of a team. And when we did well the fans were magnificent," he says.

> "My job at Blues was to sell a player almost once a month to keep the club afloat" – RON SAUNDERS

But gates were down (starting the season off around the 11,000 mark but ending with a miserable 6,256 against Arsenal) and Brum had both feet planted firmly on the downward 'poor investment=poor team=poor results=poor attendances=poor gate receipts=poor investment etc' spiral while trying to cope with a growing overdraft. Eventually, it was the small things that intimated how bad things were to the players, such as the withdrawal of sandwiches at the training ground and people being reminded to turn light switches off in changing rooms to avoid waste.

The decline of the club was also reflected in the circumstances of the Rodgers. From having 22 players at one time at Park View, numbers had dwindled to the point that, with only three or four lads (Julian included) in such a big house, Janet and Brian opted to move to a smaller property at 185 Richmond Road, Olton – a much nicer area about eight miles from Small Heath. "Birmingham were having a bad time and we could see the writing on the wall that things were going to fold up," says Janet. Martin Kuhl, by that time, had found his own place and Julian was sharing with Lee Williams, a young goalkeeper.

The team that Julian was introduced to league football with included 22-year-old David Seaman in goal and midfield battlers Kuhl and Robert Hopkins, but it had obvious deficiencies up front in Wayne Clarke, Andrew Kennedy and David Geddis. The latter hit five goals in six games in September, but the attack disintegrated after that, with November seeing the Blues go goalless for six games. That was during a run that saw the team pick up just two points in 14 games, the last three of which had seen Julian deployed as a left-back because of injury to Brian (Harry) Roberts.

The next game was a home FA Cup third round tie on January 14 with Altrincham. It was a day of disaster.

"I can remember when Altrincham beat them in the FA Cup," says Ron Dicks of the non-leaguers' sensational 2-1 victory. "Birmingham were having a bad time and you could see it happening. Julian was gutted."

It was a feeling that grew as the consequences of the catastrophic result (which Julian describes as his biggest embarrassment in football) began to sink in. "Ron Saunders came in on the Monday and got us all round and said, 'I'm resigning.' And that was it," says Julian. "I felt gutted because he really had looked after me. If it hadn't have been for him and Ron Veal I wouldn't have got the start that I did."

Martin Kuhl was also disappointed to see the manager depart, recognising his qualities. "I think the reason Ron did it was to take the pressure off the players," he says. "He was a real players' manager. He had that iron rod of fear about him but he'd do anything for the players. He came in and said, 'You're going to get stick as well, I think it's fairest if I just resign.'"

"He just said, 'You, f*** off over there with the kids!'"

Saunders himself, however, implies it was more the constraints he had to work under than the Altrincham debacle that brought about his resignation: "It was nothing to do with the result. I can't say why I resigned without having a go at one or two people – which I'm not prepared to do," he says. "But the cup game was a bad experience for the club and the players struggled to put it together. You get days like that when the wheels come off."

The fact that assistant manager Keith Leonard's subsequent caretakership of the team was short and sweet was pleasing to Julian. "He just binned me," he declares, "telling me to work with the youth team and reserves. He tried to change everything but it didn't work."

Enter new manager John Bond, who was moving into Ron Saunders' vacated chair for the second time (having previously done so at Norwich City). "I remember his first day," says Julian. "We had a game on the training pitch and I was playing up front with Wayne Clarke. He was telling me to 'spin and go away', so I was spinning and going one way. He wasn't explaining it very well, just getting angrier and angrier that I wasn't doing what he wanted, and he just said, 'You, f*** off over there with the kids!' So I got off to a great start."

Getting starts at all under John Bond at first was difficult, with Brian Roberts returning to the left-back berth and Julian having to be content with a couple of substitute appearances (in the 5-1 thrashing at Sheffield Wednesday and the 2-1 home defeat by Tottenham). But another injury to Roberts gave Dicks his chance in the home match against Luton Town, six games from the end of the season. "The manager said, 'Who wants to play left-back?' and I stuck my hand up. And he said, 'All right, you're in!'" he recalls.

Julian comes up against Viv Anderson at Highbury in November 1985.

Inevitably for Brum, who were staring relegation squarely in the face, former Blues striker Mick Harford grabbed both goals in the 2-0 win for the Hatters. "I shall be very sad to see them relegated. I've still got a lot of old mates here," said Harford after the match. *'The most significant compensation for John Bond was the outstanding performance at left-back by 17-year-old Julian Dicks,'* offered one press report the next day.

"I had a really good game, getting up and down and crossing balls," remembers Julian, "and the day after that the manager gave me my pro forms and I was in the side."

The standard wage for a professional then at St. Andrews was £80, but such was Julian's self-belief he audaciously asked for more. "John Bond asked me what I wanted before seeing the chairman and I said, '£140 a week plus £50 an appearance.' He told me that I wouldn't get that and I said, 'Well, you just asked me, that's what I want.' So he went to see the chairman and he said, 'Yeah, give it to him.'"

> **"We had a competition who could get booked the most"** – MARTIN KUHL

Assistant manager Fred Davies said, "We felt he did very well against Luton last Sunday and this is the least we could do for him," of the two-year deal awarded.

Dicks won't have great memories of those final six games of the 1985-86 season – they lost every single one of them (including a 4-1 crash at Newcastle and a 5-0 spanking at Liverpool), to finish in 21st place – but the team's awful performances had little effect on his desire to play and show what he could do. "Once you get into the first-team, it doesn't matter if you're at the top or bottom – you want to stay there, even if the team's getting relegated," he insists.

Birmingham, of course, went down. Back at his mum's, there was much grief over the team's sad plight. "I was sitting in front of the telly crying when I heard that they'd gone down," admits Carol. "I can remember ringing him up about it shortly afterwards and he just said nothing about it. I said, 'Aren't you upset about it?' and he said, 'Well, what can I do about it?' He's the same now – 'I've done my bit, what else can you do?'"

The Birmingham sales continued, though, with David Seaman being sold to Queens Park Rangers for £225,000 in the summer of 1986 (Cambridge's Roger Hansbury replacing him between the sticks), and when manager John Bond wrote in his first programme notes of the following Second Division campaign that *'the playing strength is basically the same as that which finished in a relegated spot last season'* it's difficult to tell whether he was speaking positively or pessimistically.

Prior to the big kick-off, the Birmingham squad had ventured down to the West Country for some so-called 'friendly' games, allowing an unscheduled mini-tournament to take place. "Robert Hopkins, Julian and myself had a competition to see who could get booked the most!" reveals Martin Kuhl. "I'd been booked three times, so had Robert, and Julian had been booked twice so far in pre-season. We played Yeovil and me and Hopsy were singing '3-2, 3-2...' to Dicksy, and he said, 'Watch this!' and went and got booked. And he started singing 'three each, three each...' I think the three of us were suspended by September." (He was one month out in Julian's case – he missed three games in October!)

With former Villa star Dennis Mortimer, Vince Overson and Steve Whitton recruited (the latter from West Ham in a £60,000 deal, following a period on loan the previous campaign), the team got a decent start to the new season, winning their first two games. They quickly slid into a mid-table position, though, and although Bond was highly critical of his team's defence (leaking 29 goals in one 13-match spell early season) he was pleased to confirm in November that Julian – who played in the first 11 games (but then had his first suspension) – was going nowhere, despite speculation that he could be on the move. "Julian Dicks is staying at St. Andrews and hopefully he will be part of the first team for some considerable time, despite a lot of 'big' name clubs showing interest," he said, no doubt showing his support for his left-back, in case the board were thinking of cashing-in on another of the club's best players.

Interestingly, two of the clubs interested in Julian, according to press reports, were Liverpool (who he would later join, of course) and Glasgow Rangers, managed by Graeme Souness – the man who would eventually buy him for the Merseyside club. It was also reported that Luton Town (home of ex-colleague Mick Harford) had had a bid of £100,000 for Julian rejected, with John Bond saying, "He is the most promising player I have seen in years. It's always difficult to guarantee that a boy of his age will mature into a great player but I have no doubts whatsoever. He was invited for a trial with the England youth team recently and I feel that was an insult to his talent. Mitchell Thomas (who, ironically, would wear the No 3 shirt for West Ham in later years as a short-term replacement for the injured Julian) is the current understudy to Kenny Sansom in the England squad but Dicks is already a better player."

> "He was invited for a trial with the England youth team and I felt that was an insult to his talent" – JOHN BOND

With the team struggling to find any real momentum and Bond being forced to use his resources economically, it was time for Julian's big ally, Martin Kuhl, to move on, joining Sheffield United in January 1987. Kuhl departed with some great memories of his time at St. Andrews and the managers he played under, disagreeing with the view that the Blues team of the mid-eighties that Julian learnt so much from was a dirty side. "We were a dirty team in the fact that we'd win the ball at all costs and we made it hard to be beaten, but I don't think we were dirty in the respect that we'd go out to break someone's leg or deliberately punch somebody on the nose or anything like that. We'd probably have more fights between ourselves than anything else!" he declares.

1986/87

"We lived together on and off the pitch and I think Ron Saunders loved that. Dicksy realised what it meant to have your team-mates and, at the end of the day, I don't think we were hooligans – we just looked after ourselves and each other."

Kuhl's reputation, fuelled by his years at Birmingham and the players he associated with, continued to plague him throughout the rest of his career, including his spell at Watford. "The lads were out for a beer," recalls Martin, "and (coach) Steve Harrison called me a hooligan. 'You were a hooligan for Birmingham and your team-mates were hooligans,' he told me. That's why I left the club in the end."

John Bond's style of management – in terms of how his teams played and the way he dealt with players – was very different to that of Ron Saunders, but Julian appreciated the approaches of both. While admitting that Ron's teams were "very physical", with a tendency for some players to play the 'long ball', Julian felt the manager tried to bring out the best in him. "He still encouraged us to play – if he thought you could do it. But it's true he was a disciplinarian. The players wouldn't mess around with Ron Saunders. They wouldn't try it on, because he had the respect of all the players."

Julian clearly related to the more flamboyant approach of John Bond just as well, though. "I thought he was absolutely superb," he says. "He was a funny bloke. He had his time to be serious, but the majority of the time he was taking the p*** out of players. I got on very well with him, he was a very likeable bloke, but if he didn't like you he'd let you know about it."

"He liked to play football and even if you were in your own penalty area, he wouldn't want you to lump it, he wanted you to play your way out of trouble. I used to overlap and get down the sides and get crosses in and he loved it."

Bond was so adamant, in fact, that Julian should be preached the correct footballing principles that he threatened to ban Julian from joining the England youth training sessions he'd been invited to following reports that the kids were being coached 'long-ball' techniques that were totally alien to the way he was playing at club level. "Julian tells me he's been asked by England coaches to smash the long ball forwards. I won't allow Dicks to go again to be taught like that," he ranted. "If this goes on it will just confuse Dicks and destroy everything I'm trying to teach him. I don't think it's right that England coaches should try and change a lad's way of playing. If we just keep smashing the ball up front it is going to destroy our game. I'm desperately against it. If this goes on it is going to undermine his development."

John Bond

Julian's impressive performances in a mediocre Blues side were still gaining him rave notices, though. In a series titled 'The Boys Of '87' in the *Daily Express*, the Birmingham left-

> "I have never known a young player more certain to reach the top in football than Dicks" – JOHN BOND

back was featured in an article headed: '*Clever Dicks plays it like an England cert.*' Declaring that Brum could sell him for £250,000, the paper reported John Bond as predicting that 18-year-old Julian could play for England within four years and be worth a fortune. "I have never known a young player more certain to reach the top in football than Dicks," he said. "He has all the attributes. Dicks has a magnificent left foot, he is a good tackler, he passes the ball well, he's as hard as nails and he is receptive to what he is taught. The way I like teams to play means a lot of concentration and a lot of thinking from players. Dicks is good like that and has learned a lot in the last six months. He's one of the jewels of the game."

Yet Julian was starting to gain himself a reputation as a result of a string of yellow cards. "I was starting to get booked nearly every game," says Julian, admitting that the more experienced pros such as Des Bremner, Dennis Mortimer and Steve Whitton would try and help him, although they appreciated the competitive aspects of his game.

"He was nasty on the pitch, which is what you need. His aggression and lack of respect for anybody on the opposition showed itself at a very early age" – Steve Whitton

"Julian was always liable to be booked and get into trouble but he was great to have in your side," says Whitton. "He was nasty on the pitch, which is what you need. And for someone that young to be able to do that and not be intimidated by the older lads, it was so obvious that he was going to go on. His aggression and lack of respect for anybody on the opposition showed itself at a very early age. He knew what he wanted and, rather than sit back and hope it happened, he was going to go and get it and that was obviously a good thing for a youngster to have. It made him stick out a mile. He had a great left foot – he'd be facing the other way yet still be able to knock it 50-60 yards down the line.

"But everybody tried to talk to him about his disciplinary problems. I tried to calm him down but it was very difficult and he had to learn for himself really."

'Young Julian Dicks has had more bookings this season than A-Ha (Norwegian popsters enjoying five minutes of fame around 1986-87),' quipped one newspaper, while manager Bond aired his growing concerns in a newspaper article, while admitting, "It's because he's young and immature. He will improve as he develops."

"I'm still learning the trade," said Julian in his defence in a January '87 edition of Blues News, the club programme, before conceding, "Admittedly I've been reckless in certain aspects of my play but I'm working on it daily and in future I will be more professional in the way I go into things out on the park. The boss and my coaches have said their piece and now it's up to me to do my stuff as a Birmingham City footballer."

In fact, Bond even began to use Julian's disciplinary problems as leverage to try and keep him at the club. "I feel that Dicks requires at least another two seasons with the club," he said. "He needs to iron out a few problems, which would not be possible if he moved on."

It's worth remembering that Julian was still just months into his professional career at this point, so any tempestuous signs could indeed be interpreted as naive, youthful excitement on his part. And he had certainly started to eradicate any initial fears about his size. "He was getting bigger and stronger," says Julian's dad, who saw games whenever he could make it up to St. Andrews. "When he was little he'd hit some guys and just bounce off them but when you're bigger and stronger you hit them and *they* start going over."

Julian's fully committed approach to his game and the Blues cause was certainly appreciated by the fans. One particular element of the hardcore support named themselves the Zulu Warriors and they'd chant "Zulu, Zulu" for prolonged periods at games.

"The trouble was, when he was diving into tackles, the Birmingham fans loved him because of that. And the more aggressive he got the more they cheered him," says Steve Whitton. "He had to learn to relax a little bit and not play to the crowd so much – although I'm sure he still does sometimes because it's always going to be part of his game."

Julian was also popular in the Blues Bar, the supporters' social club situated under the main stand of St. Andrews. Also known as the D Club, most of the Birmingham players would put in an appearance after matches and mingle with fans. This was run by Janet Rodgers in the latter part of Julian's Blues career and he occasionally offered to help out on the beer and skittles evenings and at other functions they'd have down there. "He used to come down and help me with the buffets. He was ever so helpful," recalls Janet.

Carol Dicks has many memories of Saturday evenings in the bar after matches: "We saw quite a few games in the last two years at Birmingham. We were friends with everybody in the Blues Bar, especially Janet and Brian. They were a really nice couple. Our Ju would go into the bar and get mobbed. All the blokes liked him. After a while things were changed and the players stopped coming in, but Julian used to because we were in there.

"I remember once, I came out of the toilets and Julian was in fits. There was this kid there and Ju said, 'Go on, my mum'll laugh, show her.' So this kid pulled down his pants and he had got 'S*** on the Villa' tattooed on his bum!"

Villa were certainly going down the pan themselves in 1987, heading for relegation from the top flight, but Brum were also in danger of slipping through the hole at the bottom of the Second Division thanks to a run of poor results that included a 3-0 defeat at Ipswich, a 4-0 lesson at Leeds United and a dreadful 6-0 collapse at Crystal Palace (the last of which fortunately saw Julian just sitting on the bench).

The season climaxed – if that's the correct term – with a final game, at home to Shrewsbury, with Birmingham needing a result to avoid the drop via the newly introduced play-offs

> "Ju said, 'Go on, my mum'll laugh, show her.' So this kid pulled down his pants and he had got 'S*** on the Villa' tattooed on his bum!" – Carol Dicks

(which in those days took teams down as well as up). "We lost the match and had to wait on the game involving Sunderland, which had a late kick-off, to see if we went down or not. We stayed up but the feeling was horrendous," admits Julian of that Saturday which saw Brum finish the campaign in 19th position.

Chase hotting up for Julian

Not surprisingly, John Bond's programme notes for that game had an air of defeat about them: *"We have reached our lowest ebb in 1986-87. I hope now that we don't drop any lower. We have the facilities to climb back and somebody – hopefully it's me – will grab hold of this club and show the public and media that the Blues are a First Division side."*

By the time the following season kicked off, Bond had been kicked out. "We were training down at the ground," recalls Julian, "and John was up with the chairman, Ken Wheldon, when he came out, jumped in his car and sped off. Some press were there and they said that he'd been sacked. I was sorry to see him go because he was a good bloke."

Garry Pendrey was appointed as manager at the beginning of the 1987-88 season, with the former Blues player leaving Wolves and inheriting the same problems that had made the job so impossible for Ron Saunders and John Bond. "I got on well with him, because I was one of the better players, as such," says Julian of his relationship with Pendrey. "There was myself and Vince Overson, and he was building the team around us. There was all this speculation building about me going to Man Utd and West Ham and he told me that he wasn't letting me go."

With Julian now the Blues' prize player, it seemed inevitable that he would follow in the footsteps of virtually all his big-name colleagues who'd been sold off to keep the club afloat, despite Garry Pendrey's protestations to the contrary. "We are determined to keep our best players and Julian is certainly one of those. He's a terrific lad, with the best possible attitude, is strong and has a very cultured left foot," he said. "Everybody has a price, of course, but it would need to be a very good deal for the club to tempt us to part with him. We need players of Julian's calibre to get back in the First Division."

Steve Whitton took such words with a pinch of salt, however. "I think Garry Pendrey said that for the benefit of the fans. A club like Birmingham, who were struggling for money at the time, just couldn't keep a player like Julian. I always felt that they'd accept any decent offer that came along for him."

Whitton, incidentally, attributed a large proportion of the club's problems of the time to the group of 'big-name' players in the early-to-mid-eighties who failed to deliver. "That's what ruined the club as far as I was concerned," he says. "You had all these top players, earning large amounts of money, but they didn't really perform. People like Noel Blake and Mark Dennis – all they did was pick up their money."

The season started to mirror the one before, with crowds rapidly diminishing (to the six or seven thousand mark) and results erratic (a great 2-0 win at Villa, who would win promotion at their first attempt, followed just a fortnight later by another 6-0 walloping by Palace, this time at St. Andrews). Pendrey's management style, meanwhile, would also have its drawbacks. "He wanted to be one of the lads and people took advantage of him. I didn't think that worked," says Julian.

All the while, there was even greater interest in Julian from other clubs. He'd been linked with Brian Clough's Nottingham Forest, both Glasgow clubs, Manchester United, West Ham, Coventry City and both Merseyside clubs, among others, and Brum's crippling financial situation was becoming more and more apparent.

"All the players had a big meeting in the changing room about what was happening with the club getting further into debt again," remembers Julian, "and Roger Hansbury, our goalkeeper, said, 'There's only one solution and that's to sell Julian.' But Garry Pendrey kept saying, 'I'm not selling, I'm not selling...' But Birmingham weren't going anywhere. They were always going to be a bottom of the table side." (They'd even taken back striker Peter Withe on loan at the age of 36!)

With Pendrey's repeated insistence that his best player would not be sacrificed to help balance the books, Julian decided that if he wasn't going to be allowed to join a club who would be able to pay him more, he would request a new, improved contract with Birmingham. After his first deal being raised to £160 a week, plus £100 appearance money, Julian had earlier in the season signed a contract paying £300 a week, plus £125 appearance money. The club's response to their left-back's request was to offer an extra £50 per week, without the need to sign another contract, but for Julian it wasn't good enough. "That's no good to me," said Julian to his employers, adding that he was looking to buy property. "They said they didn't have the money," he recalls, "so I said, 'Let me go then!'"

About a month later, on the stroke of transfer deadline day in March, 1988, Julian received a phone call from Garry Pendrey requesting that he came down to St. Andrews. After much deliberation on their part, Birmingham City had decided to cash in on their number one asset...

> "All the players had a big meeting in the changing room and Roger Hansbury, our goalkeeper, said, 'There's only one solution and that's to sell Julian.'"

Julian aged 18

CHAPTER 7

LOVE AT FIRST SIGHT?

BY the time that Julian was indicating his willingness to move away from Birmingham City, at the age of 19, he'd rather more considerations in mind than just himself. His main reason for wanting to improve his financial position was that he was hoping to purchase a new property to share with girlfriend Kay Blythe, whom he'd been living with in a maisonette at Marston Green.

Julian had first met Kay at the age of 17, following his move with the Rodgers to Olton, yet the irony is that they got to know each other by regularly speaking at a local chip shop (Julian claiming that Kay "had a load of chains around her neck and I asked her for one"), with both of them unaware that the other was also employed by Birmingham City.

Sixteen-year-old Kay worked for the promotions department at St. Andrews, on the club lottery, while Julian was still an apprentice, on the verge of breaking into the first team and training at Elmdon half an hour away. "The only time I used to go to the ground at that time was on the Friday, to clean the dressing rooms and the players' match boots, and on the Saturday afternoon for the home games," Julian explains, while Kay was based in a different area of the ground from the main stand where the players would enter.

So, oblivious to what each other did for a living, they first met at the chippy, which Julian would occasionally pass while walking Janet's dog. On the first occasion they spoke, Julian was playing the fruit machine with his mate Lee Williams when Kay arrived with some friends. "We got talking to them and they both said they were plumbers and were staying at the Flemings Hotel," recalls Kay, who subsequently stopped for chats whenever they crossed paths in there. "Then I said I'd meet him down there one night and I didn't turn up. It wasn't that I didn't like him, I just couldn't be bothered to get involved. I used to like just going out with my friends and I didn't really want a relationship or anything like that.

"He was really skinny and, because he came from Bristol, I just used to take the mickey out of him. I was horrible. I failed to meet him a few times – I think it's awful now, but at the time I used to think it was funny."

"Her sister Sue used to think I was a poof because my name was Julian and I spoke with a Bristol accent"

Kay actually stood Julian up on four or five occasions but he decided to give it one last go and, to his surprise, she finally turned up. "It wasn't love at first sight but I got on well with her," Julian recalls of their early dates. "I used to ring her up and her sister Sue used to answer. She used to think I was a poof (calling him "the queer kid") because my name was Julian and I spoke with a Bristol accent."

With Julian still on apprenticeship money, elaborate dates were out of the question so initial nights out together were in their mutual local pub, with Kay's parents' place backing onto his digs in Richmond Road. "I only used to earn just over £20 a week so I'd take her down the pub and half my money would be gone!" says Julian.

And for the first month or so, Kay was still under the impression that Julian spent his days playing with pipes and sinks instead of a football. "I said I was a plumber because if people ask you what you do and you say you're a footballer, they think you're a big-head," Julian explains, as to why he kept his true occupation under wraps. But Kay's theory was that he kept the ruse going, even though he'd soon discovered her position at the club, simply because there was nothing he liked more than a joke at somebody else's expense. "He's just a wind-up merchant, basically. He's still the same now – he just thinks things like that are funny," says Kay.

"But there was always going to be a time when I found out. I never used to go to the matches because we were working on the lottery and sorting the money out, but then I got moved across to the main office, working on reception while still doing promotional work. I was at work one day and he suddenly walked into my office. I was gobsmacked! But Julian just laughed."

Kay's ignorance was perhaps a blessing in disguise, though, with the club frowning on employees getting involved with the playing staff. "You weren't meant to have relationships with players," she admits. "A couple of people had already got the sack, but I was luckier – I got on well with the chairman."

Dicksy's relationship with Kay was completely unexpected as far as team-mate Martin Kuhl was concerned, who considered Julian far too introverted to break any ice with a good looking female such as Kay. "It took us by surprise that Dicksy had got a girlfriend," he says. "He was so shy that I couldn't believe that he'd started speaking to Kay. And then one day he started dating her. But she's a lovely girl and he thinks the world of her. She's an absolute diamond."

While living with Janet and Brian, Julian had to adhere to the 10.30pm curfew (which Kay remembers them being quite strict about), but he met Kay on week nights for the odd trip to the pub and, later, the occasional night at Faces. Initially, though, Kay certainly had no long term thoughts about the relationship. "It wasn't that I didn't think it would last, but at that point I certainly couldn't see myself moving away from home or anything," Kay says. "At that point we didn't definitely know if he was going to be kept on at Birmingham.

"He's a hard person to get to know," she continues. "I was a bit off with him at first, but once I'd decided that I wanted to get to know him I suppose it was a bit of a challenge for me. And then the more I got to know him I realised he was really nice. He just makes me laugh. Sometimes he drives me mad – he's always winding me up – and I don't think he'll ever be any different. But he was ever so kind and I enjoyed his company."

Because of Julian's limited funds, however, 'nights out' were more often than not 'nights in'. "We didn't used to go out that much," admits Kay. "He'd usually come round to my mum and dad's house. We were quite happy just to be at home."

Unknown to Kay, her father Peter took an early opportunity to check out his daughter's boyfriend's playing credentials. "He'd not heard of Julian so he went down to one of the games just to have a look," she remembers. "I can remember him coming back and saying, 'He's not bad, he's quite a good player.' But it didn't make any difference to me – he could have been doing anything as far as I was concerned."

On matchdays, Kay would occasionally work until kick-off time and then take the opportunity to watch some of the action involving Julian, but as things between them developed (with Julian spending more and more time at her parents'), she considered that the right thing to do was sacrifice her post at Birmingham, going to work with her dad in the nearby market. "I think Janet Rodgers had mentioned to John Bond that he was sleeping on the settee round at my dad's," assumes Kay. "Of course, the manager had a word with me, although Julian wasn't on the sofa – he had a bedroom. But I just thought in the end that it wasn't fair for me to carry on working there when everybody else had got the bullet."

Puppy love?

Janet, being a friend of Kay's mum's, was well aware of where Julian was spending his time, but she seemed to have no objections to what was going on. "I thought Kay was a lovely girl – and the right one for him, too," she states.

Julian's departure from the Rodgers household, after four years, coincided with them deciding to end their involvement with Birmingham ("I think we'd only got Julian by that time and he was virtually living at Kay's anyway") and move into the countryside, as a result of Brian having rheumatoid arthritis and looking to relinquish his managership of Faces after his 15-year run. "Birmingham was getting a bit naughty, with fights and so on at the club," Janet adds.

As Julian moved in round the corner at Kay's parents, the Rodgers found a place for their retirement in Wootton Wawen, near Stratford-upon-Avon, in January 1987. Brian would later succumb to cancer, passing away on January 2 (Janet's birthday), 1993, with Julian attending his funeral.

A short while after the couple had started living together, Julian and Kay found their own home in Marston Green. "My dad had kept nagging," says Kay. "He just told Julian that we should get our own place, so in the end we bought a maisonette from a lady I used to work with. We were really lucky. We'd not got a lot of money, but the deal allowed us to buy all her furniture, so we had what you'd call a result."

Carol Dicks occasionally visited the Marston Green maisonette and still remembers an incident that reflected Julian's protectiveness towards his family members. "They used to have a shared drive and we pulled up in it one Saturday," she recalls. "The cantankerous old git next door came out and started going at us hammer and tongs, because we were parked on the drive. I just said to him, 'You know who I am, Julian's mother,' and he screamed, 'I don't give a f*** who you are...' The next minute Ju was out the front saying, 'Don't you swear at my mother, I'll have you. You'll be on the floor. That's my mother you're talking to!' He won't have anything said about his family."

The couple would remain in the maisonette for a year, during which time there'd be much speculation about Julian's playing future. Marriage, meanwhile, had been mentioned between the two of them, but the short term priority had been to invest in the home. "We never really made any decisions about it," says Kay. "We were both ever so young and things had happened so quickly. And I think it's better if you live with someone first because you don't really know them until you've done that."

Twelve months later, in March 1988, Julian decided it was time for a move – either to a new house in the Birmingham area as a result of an improved contract, or to a new club and a new part of the country completely. And after some initial discussions with manager Garry Pendrey, he eventually got the summons to St. Andrews to discuss a possible transfer. The Blues had agreed a deal with First Division West Ham United – now the ball was in Julian's court.

CHAPTER 8

ONCE A HAMMER...

WEST HAM fans may have had mixed views on Steve Whitton following his variable performances for the club in the early mid-eighties, but their opinion of him would certainly improve if they were aware of the role the attacking midfielder played in Julian Dicks arriving at Upton Park.

As already detailed, Whitton had joined Birmingham City in August 1986, following a loan spell at St. Andrews, but his allegiance to the Hammers – having always supported them after being born in East Ham – became a vital factor when he became aware that Dicks was likely to be moving on.

"I knew he was going to go somewhere, that was inevitable," says Whitton. "Because I was still living in London I was continuing to train with West Ham and I knew they were looking for a left-back. I spoke to John Lyall about him and more or less said, 'If you don't take him you'll be mad!' I think he had him watched, then he'd asked me about him again: 'Can he do this, can he do that?' He'd ask me virtually every Monday how Julian had played at the weekend."

With speculation growing and Whitton feeling it was only a matter of time before Julian was on his way, he did his best to see that his Birmingham team-mate joined his favourite club. "Steve thought he was a very good young player," acknowledges the ex-Hammers chief, "so while we were aware of Julian, that made us look even more closely at him. He kept on to me about it and was very insistent, saying we *had* to take him."

The left-back position had become something of a problem for the Hammers. Lyall realised it had never been adequately settled following the demise of Frank Lampard's contribution to the side as far back as 1984 and, despite the efforts of Paul Brush, Steve Walford, George Parris and Tommy McQueen, was aware of the kind of character needed to wear the No 3 shirt. "Frank was such a stalwart and good club man that you needed someone very imposing to take over the helm," says John. "He typified exactly what West Ham was about – great commitment, great loyalty and great intelligence – so we couldn't have just *any old* left-back."

Lyall's first efforts to take Dicks to Upton Park were thwarted, however. "I spoke to the Birmingham chairman, Ken Wheldon, and he wasn't keen to sell him. We got close to a deal at one time but then he had second thoughts and said he wanted to delay it for a little while, so he gave me first refusal. Then, a matter of three or four months later, I spoke to him again and he said he was in a position where he felt he could now let him go."

> "There was a great touch there. I wouldn't have bought just a physical player" – John Lyall

With a fee of £300,000 agreed between the two clubs with the minimum of fuss, the deal hinged on Julian agreeing personal terms with the Londoners. Having had the call from Garry Pendrey to come down to St Andrews, Dicks met up with John Lyall, chief scout Eddie Baily and Hammers secretary Tom Finn. Pendrey had a quick word with his player before the negotiations began, though, telling him to "see what they're offering and then come back and see me." The West Ham men made their offer – £650 a week, plus £200 appearance money and a signing on fee – and with Pendrey telling Julian that he thought it was a good deal, a three-year contract was quickly signed.

"I can remember Julian and Kay looking so young as they sat there," says John Lyall. "When they're like that you're hoping you're doing the right thing for them, but Julian seemed very keen."

It was only later that John would realise Julian had played in a trial game for West Ham when much younger, admitting that he'd have probably seen the game, although he has no recollections of it as such. There were no reservations about paying over a quarter of a million pounds for a player he could potentially have had for nothing, though. "It wasn't a difficult choice to sign him, just for his left foot alone. But it wasn't just his power, there was a great touch there. He can pass little three or four-yard balls just as well as he can thump a ball 30 or 40 yards. It was what I call an educated left foot," says John. "I wouldn't have bought just a physical player.

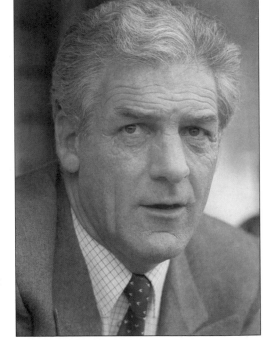

John Lyall

"We saw him play in his early days, not at full-back but the left side of midfield, and I've got reports not talking about him physically but technically – playing one-twos to beat people, getting in early crosses, getting in on the far post and shooting from 25-30 yards.

"People such as Brooking and Bonds were so different but you needed both qualities because one without the other couldn't have survived. And Julian had that mixture."

The deal took West Ham's spending to nearly £600,000 in just over a week, with striker Leroy Rosenior having been recruited from Fulham to help the Hammers guarantee their First Division status. As Julian was putting pen to paper, the hope on the club's part was that he would make his debut less than 48 hours later in a fixture with the left-back's heroes, Manchester United. But there was just one thing he'd neglected to mention to his new bosses – he was suspended!

Lyall was typically understanding, though, recognising that Julian may have feared he was jeopardising the deal if he mentioned it. "You don't buy a player for one game," John says, insisting it would not have made the slightest difference.

Kay Dicks, knowing that Julian was going to be sold at some stage and that a move of house away from Birmingham was pretty much inevitable, had no particular preference where they went. "I was thinking of all these different clubs that were being mentioned and wondering, 'How many miles is that?' But at the end of the day, if you meet nice people it doesn't matter where you are," she says.

Whether she'd have fancied heading north to Glasgow will probably never be known, but there was a possibility that Julian could have been signed by Rangers, with Graeme Souness taking a definite interest in the young Dicks. "I liked the look of him and I was desperate for a left-back," confirms the Scot, "but with his disciplinary record I thought that maybe Scottish football wasn't the best place for him at that particular time. It was a shame because he was obviously going to be some player."

Julian himself would later hear a story that Souness had had a bid of £350,000 rejected by Birmingham just a month before the club agreed their deal with West Ham for £50,000 less, but to this day he's never bothered to substantiate it.

> "With his disciplinary record I thought that maybe Scottish football wasn't the best place for him at that particular time" – GRAEME SOUNESS

While Birmingham were investing a third of their Dicks money on Manchester City midfielder Kevin Langley, Julian's immediate priority was to help steer the Hammers to safety, with them sitting 15th in a division of 21 teams. "When I signed I didn't even look at the league table," he claims. "It was just West Ham, a step up, great!" – a feeling shared by his family.

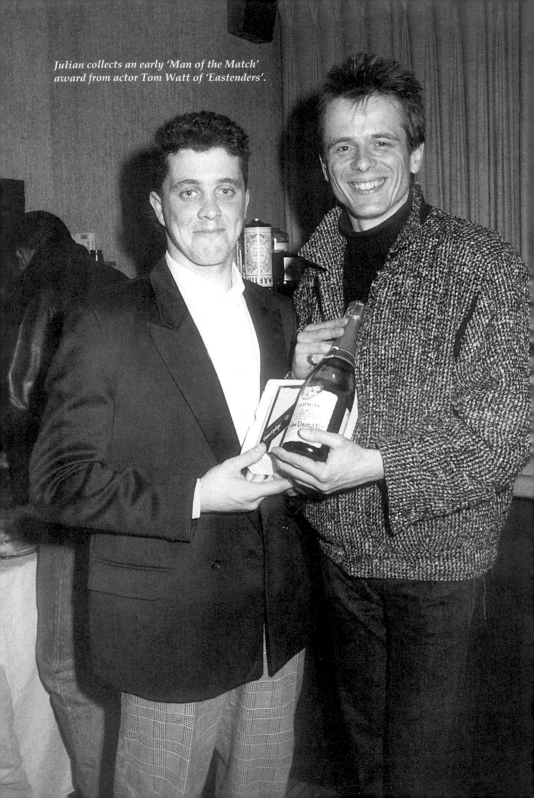

Julian collects an early 'Man of the Match' award from actor Tom Watt of 'Eastenders'.

For most of the Hammers players, Julian was an unknown commodity when he signed for the club. "I wasn't aware of him and hadn't heard of his name," admits Tony Cottee, "purely because he was a young player just making his way in the game. So I suppose I raised an eyebrow when he was signed. I didn't really get to know him that well because I was so caught up in my own events towards the end of my last season at the club at the time. And we were under extreme pressure fighting relegation."

With the United game out of the way (which was lost 3-1), Julian finally made his debut in West Ham's colours in the following week's game at Hillsborough. Despite his efforts apparently winning him a man-of-the-match award from the Sheffield Wednesday officials, the Hammers fell to another defeat, 2-1 this time. Fortunately a point was gained in Dicks' home debut – a 0-0 with Everton – which also saw Julian making an impact in more ways than one. While one paper commented: *'Dicks looks good value for the £300,000 he cost from Birmingham'*, Julian himself remembered the match mainly for a clash with one of the opposition. "I can recall elbowing Trevor Steven in the face by the dug-out. The crowd loved it and it made me feel part of the club," he confesses.

It was an incident that showed typical fire from Dicks and it was this fight and spirit – along with his cultured left foot – that helped immediately endear the Hammers fans to their new left-back. "The fans saw the commitment of the lad. He played and wanted to win for his club. The fans would also readily admire his technique. He had that balance," says John Lyall, who felt he quickly proved to the Upton Park faithful that he was very much in the Frank Lampard mould. "Frank would play for you with a broken leg and Julian had that same attitude – and the fans could see that."

> "I can recall elbowing Trevor Steven in the face by the dug-out. The crowd loved it and it made me feel part of the club"

John had been aware of Julian's growing disciplinary problems up at Birmingham and his habit of inviting yellow cards through his tenacious play. But Lyall also had the intelligence and knowledge of the game to realise there were reasons why Dicks had started to fall foul of referees. "Sometimes things can happen through a lack of ability, a lack of knowledge or it can be carelessness. But you have to try and understand it," he insists. "Some footballers are powerful men. I'm not making excuses for Julian, but he's not the sort of player who, when he's committed himself for a tackle, can readily pull out. He has that angular build – Billy Bonds was another one, a very powerful man. Whether we like it or not, people who do compete will sometimes make bad judgements, in the same way that people whose job is to score miss open goals.

"A tackler must make errors, the same as a passer makes errors. But we tend to say that a tackler mustn't do that and the physical people mustn't make mistakes, because they get yellow and red cards."

Such was Julian's "square build" – somewhat stockier than the lightweight kid of old – that Lyall was tempted to compare him with West German international Hans-Peter Briegel, who gained 72 caps for his country and also delighted with "a hell of a left foot".

There was nothing too delightful about Dicks' error in his second home game for West Ham, however, which cost his club the points in the derby against Arsenal. "I remember giving the goal away," says Julian. "I got the man-of-the-match award and thought, 'Why?' Tony Cottee came in after the game and said, 'You gave a stupid f***ing goal away!' Which intimidated me a bit because I'd only just joined the club. I was ready to have a row with him but he went and got in the bath so that was it."

> "Tony Cottee came in after the game and said, 'You gave a stupid f***ing goal away!'"

The little Hammers hitman detailed the incident in his Claret & Blues autobiography in 1995: *'Months of pent-up frustration exploded on the night of April 12, when our 1-0 home defeat by Arsenal left us just a point above the play-off zone near the bottom of the First Division. We had conceded another sloppy goal and just as John Lyall had started to go over what had gone wrong, I let fly with an outburst. It went something along the lines of "All we ever do is let in rubbish goals" and it was the most upset I'd ever been after a game.'*

But Cottee's outburst had not been a direct attack on his team-mates, regardless of how it seemed to Julian at the time. "I had a go at John Lyall and Mick McGiven, it wasn't at the other players," insists Tony. "It was out of pure frustration at what was going on in my own career more than anything. I made the point in my book that we were conceding bad goals, but I've never been the type of person who would turn round and point the finger at somebody – certainly not a 19-year-old. Maybe I should have been a bit more tactful but it never entered my head that I'd made a comment that might upset one of the players, because I wouldn't do that sort of thing."

Worse was to come, with the club sinking into the play-off position following draws against Forest and Coventry and defeat at Southampton. But an explosive 4-1 win over fellow strugglers Chelsea (thanks to two-goal Rosenior, who also got sent off) secured the points that ultimately ensured safety. "We needed to win to save ourselves," recalls Julian. "I remember hitting a volley, which was going into the top corner, but I think Tony Dorigo cleared it off the line. It helped get the crowd going and we did well in the end."

Which was just as well really, as Julian got on the scoresheet in the final game at Newcastle – putting through his own net with a misplaced backpass past 'keeper Tom McAlister for the Geordies' second and decisive goal in a match the Hammers had to lose by seven goals to have been dragged into the fourth-from-bottom play-off place. It wasn't quite what Dicks had in mind when he told John Lyall he liked to have a pop at goal every now and then!

CHAPTER 9

RELEGATION (CLARET &) BLUES

Julian's first full season with the Hammers didn't exactly get off to the greatest of starts. The team's league form was bad enough – a win and a draw in the first eight games – but the campaign had been preceded with a less than 'friendly' match against Spurs at Upton Park for Alvin Martin's testimonial.

West Ham won 2-0 but the ensuing headlines were dominated by a fracas between Dicks and Tottenham's former Hammer Paul Allen, which saw both men being taken off by their respective managers following instructions from the referee. "We were down on the right-hand side of the pitch, by the tunnel, and Paul got the ball and threw it at me. And it just went off," says Julian of what took place.

John Lyall, concerned about the possibility of losing players for vital league games if dismissed in pre-season friendlies, had tried to avoid such a situation by talking to the match officials first. "We would go to the referees and say, 'If you've got a problem with a player, give us the nod and we'll take him off.' The referee, Danny Vickers, a local lad, came over and told us that the two players were getting a bit upset, so Terry Venables and I just took them straight off."

Lyall applauded the official for his "common-sense attitude" after the game, with Vickers confirming that he'd asked the managers to substitute the players to avoid the inevitable red cards and subsequent two-match bans. One newspaper carried a story with a heading of *'Don't Be A Dope, Dicks'*, with team-mate Alvin Martin pleading: *"Calm down or you'll ruin your career. Julian is a fine defender and a great buy for West Ham. I think he'll become England's next left-back – but only if he cools down."* It hadn't taken Alvin long to assess Julian's strengths upon him joining the club. "When he came to West Ham he was a really quiet, shy lad, but as soon as I saw him I thought, 'Yeah, good player.' He had a very good left foot and was aggressive," he says.

Whereas most players tailor their approach to the game according to the importance of the match, this incident indicated to West Ham fans Julian's total commitment, whatever the situation. "It doesn't matter if it's a league game, testimonial or five-a-side game, I'm always committed and want to win," he says.

"I've always been taught that you play as you train and train as you play. I've always been like that."

Julian's determined efforts were frequently in vain, though, during the 1988-89 season. West Ham had struggled the previous year (having been in decline since their best ever finish in 1986), with striker Frank McAvennie going to Celtic in September '87 and Tony Cottee only getting a proper strike partner in Leroy Rosenior as late as March '88. And when Cottee himself departed, in a £2.2million move to Everton during the close season, the Hammers were always going to be up against it, despite the recruitment of David Kelly from Walsall for £600,000.

Kelly may have had the likes of Tottenham and even Bayern Munich among the clutch of clubs looking to secure his services, but in retrospect it's easy to doubt the survival chances of a team relying on two strikers who'd been plying their trade in the old Third Division the previous season.

"That's the way West Ham had to do it," insists John Lyall. "With players like Mark Ward and Frank McAvennie, you bought them cheap and they became more valuable. David Kelly had a lot of clubs after him and we felt we did well to get him. But he and Leroy were replacing two international footballers."

Cheer up Julian! You are a lot more popular than Allen McKnight and David Kelly – two players who came in for a lot of stick from Hammers fans.

How West Ham came to be a 'selling club' in the late eighties, after setting a world record fee for a goalkeeper when they bought Phil Parkes in 1979, splashing a club record £800,000 on striker Paul Goddard in 1980 and finishing third in the First Division in 1986, is open to conjecture. But the fact was that Dicks came into a side woefully short of genuine firepower, seemingly always suffering injuries in defence to the likes of Alvin Martin and Tony Gale, and having major problems adequately replacing Parkes in goal, with Tom McAlister proving erratic and Irishman Allen McKnight experiencing a baptism of fire after joining in a £250,000 deal from Celtic at the beginning of the 1988-89 season.

"He came in for a lot of stick," remembers Julian of the 'keeper who inspired such headlines that season as *'McKnightmare!'*, *'McNit!'* and *'McTwit!'* following costly and embarrassing blunders. "He made some errors and, obviously, when you're a 'keeper your mistakes are going to be a lot more damaging. For us to be bottom of the table we were obviously all making mistakes but he got singled out and took a lot of blame for the position we were in. It would perhaps have been better if John Lyall had changed things sooner rather than later but he gave him more games and he got worse and worse.

"David Kelly was another one who got a hell of a lot of stick – the crowd hammered him. Everybody says he was always on his backside, but he wasn't the only one who was struggling."

> "It wouldn't have helped him that most of the players were probably trying to help themselves first" – JOHN LYALL

The tough battle for points was of course not a new experience for Julian, given his struggles with Birmingham, but John Lyall considered such difficult situations as being educational for such a youngster. "In many ways, if a player is going to be successful, it can help him because he does have to think," he says. "Lads like Tony Cottee, who came through the system, had had to work out how to score goals because they weren't going to have them laid on a plate every week. Paul Ince had to learn how to be a good midfield player. It was the same for Trevor Brooking, Alan Devonshire and Frank Lampard – they all had to think about the game because the points weren't guaranteed every week. And that's the situation that Julian was in. He came into a team that was working hard for survival, so he had to think. And it wouldn't have helped him that most of the players were probably trying to help themselves first, which is understandable when you're struggling."

Despite the poor results (which included a 4-0 opening day defeat at Southampton, a 4-1 home beating by Arsenal and a thrashing at Luton by the same scoreline), Julian's attitude to the game remained undiminished. He invariably came in for training at Chadwell Heath at 9.30am and spent the best part of an hour in the gym with the ball before the other players arrived. "It concerned me a little bit because he'd be full of sweat, he'd stop for half an hour while the other lads were getting changed, and off we'd go again," says Lyall. "He was that sort of boy, he wanted to improve his game, so he worked a lot individually. And sometimes I felt he was maybe taking too much out of himself, but he loved going into the gym to whack balls against the wall and perfect his touch.

"He was self-taught in a lot of his skills. We certainly tried to help him on the coaching side but a lot of it was self-induced skill and he deserved a lot of credit. You can see why his career has been so good because he developed a knowledge of the game and depth of skill that would make him successful."

Julian's battling instincts were also appreciated by his manager. "Julian is a fighter and he won't give in. From the start I would have looked at him as a West Ham type of lad. He was loyal, wanted to do well, would talk to the senior players and the nice thing about it was that he'd listen to people but make his own decisions – and I think that's very important with a footballer. Some players nowadays would much rather be told, 'Just do this, just do that.' But Julian had his own imagination, his own ideas on football and would try and offer those to you."

"Julian is a fighter and he won't give in" – JOHN LYALL

Julian's character in the dressing room had yet to really develop and flourish though. "He was like Paul Ince," says Lyall. "They were young lads and hadn't reached a maturity where they would talk in the dressing room like a Billy Bonds or Trevor Brooking did. They were the next generation coming through so they were more listeners than talkers."

Back on the pitch, Hammers' league form was desperate, the team winning a paltry five out of 31 games to leave relegation almost a certainty. In the two cup competitions, however, their fortunes improved dramatically, beating Arsenal at Highbury in the third round with a goal from Rosenior and making it through to the sixth round before eventually falling 3-1 to Norwich in a replay at Carrow Road.

It was the Littlewoods Cup run that saw the goals really flourish, with Second Division Sunderland beaten 5-1 on aggregate, First Division Derby thrashed 5-0 and, best of all, league champions Liverpool being humiliated 4-1 in a fourth round tie at Upton Park. It was an astonishing result, given the contrasting forms in the league, with Liverpool fourth in the table and West Ham just one place off the bottom. It was also the Anfield club's heaviest cup defeat for 50 years.

One newspaper report paid special tribute to the West Ham traditions and philosophies which, although ineffective in many of the campaign's league games, suddenly burst to the fore in this tie: *'Their quality is rarely reflected in their results. But almost at full strength and in the mood for a stern challenge, they have the ability to be irresistible. For half an hour even Liverpool could not withstand their force. They were as powerful as a tropical whirlwind, sweeping all before them and going ahead through two spectacular goals from Paul Ince.'*

Julian played his part too, winning the free-kick which led to the Hammers' fourth goal. "I remember getting kicked in the head by Nigel Spackman and having

> "I remember getting kicked in the head by Nigel Spackman and having physio Rob Jenkins tell me that I should go off"

physio Rob Jenkins tell me that I should go off," he recalls. But staying on to mop the blood from his brow, he watched as Tony Gale superbly curled the resulting free-kick into the top corner of the net, before later having stitches in the wound.

It was 21-year-old Paul Ince who grabbed all the headlines, with his two goals capping a superb individual performance and giving notice to the rest of the country that the midfielder had well and truly arrived, following just over a full season's worth of first-team football. Julian got on well with Ince, who displayed no shortage of confidence in his own abilities. "A lot of people say he was arrogant and big-headed, but I like that in people. It shows that they've got something about them," he says. "I like that kind of thing in Chris Eubank and Prince Naseem. I think they're superb, but other people loathe them because of the way they are. And a lot of people didn't really like the way Paul was – it pissed a lot of people off. He was very arrogant and confident about his football ability."

Ince's attitude was reflected in a training ground incident. "Something happened in a five-a-side game, I think it was," says Julian. "There was a bit of a row and Incey turned round to Liam Brady (who'd returned from Italy to join the Hammers in the November of that season) and said, 'I'm the guv'nor here now, you've had your day.' I was standing right by Incey as he said it. But Liam just started laughing at him."

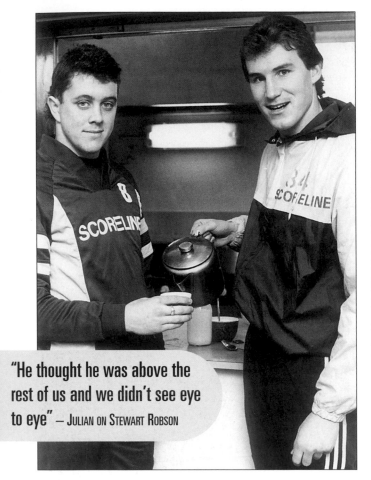

"He thought he was above the rest of us and we didn't see eye to eye" – JULIAN ON STEWART ROBSON

Brady was older and wiser, of course, having seen and done it all in a fabulous career with Arsenal, Juventus, Sampdoria, Inter Milan and Ascoli. Brady commanded respect from all – apart from Ince, it would seem – and the Irish midfielder often sat Julian down to try to talk to him about his habit of picking up bookings and how to gain greater control of his temperament. But Dicks had rather less regard for another ex-Arsenal player then wearing the claret and blue (injury permitting) – Stewart Robson. "I didn't get on with him," confesses Julian. "He came from Arsenal to West Ham and thought he was going to be the dog's bollocks. But it didn't work out for him. It was just the way he was – he thought he was above the rest of us – and we didn't see eye to eye. Quite a few players didn't get on with him."

It was against Arsenal that Julian scored his very first Hammers goal, at Highbury on February 4, 1989, although it was no more than a consolation with the championship-chasing Gunners already two up. It was a great goal, with Julian chesting down a throw from David Kelly, beating defenders Lee Dixon and Steve Bould and firing into the roof of the net with just six minutes left. "I just hit it as hard as possible," remembers Julian.

Yellow cards were rather more frequent than goals for Dicks in those days, though, and six bookings had ruled him out of games against Sheffield Wednesday, Spurs and Norwich just before the New Year. "I think I learned a lot from watching those three games from the side," said Julian after making his return. "It brought home to me certain things that I was doing wrong. When you sit back and watch people like Liam Brady and Tony Gale you realise just how effective the easy ball can become. So I have resolved to play it more simply and play it quick. I am also trying to avoid stupid challenges. I can't say I think about it as I go in for a tackle but I do have to be careful."

John Lyall had few concerns over Julian's behaviour, recognising that his playing style was partly responsible for him being perceived in a particular way. "There may have been the odd occasion where you'd say something was not on, but I honestly can't remember him having a real problem," he says. "Occasionally I felt that he committed himself a little bit early, but you have to look at the type of tackling that those kind of people do. He is what I call a slide tackler. He doesn't tackle standing up, he goes to ground. Dave Mackay used to do the same. But when you miss it looks bad. We always used to say, 'When you go to ground, make sure you get the ball because if you don't, you've either got the ball going into the back of your net or you've got serious problems with the referee.'

"But it's a style of tackling that's traditional in English football. The game is about the physical aspect as well. You can't make it all technical because it then loses its passion. We've got to have people who tackle."

Julian is poised to score his first Hammers goal, at Highbury.

Just eight days after scoring at Arsenal, Julian conceded a penalty as the Hammers crashed 3-0 to Luton Town in a farcical Littlewoods Cup semi-final first leg at Upton Park. The damage had already been done thanks to two Allen McKnight errors, the first of which allowed Julian's old Birmingham colleague Mick Harford (who'd rejected a move to West Ham before the start of the season, citing their lack of ambition – which still doesn't explain why he was playing for Luton) to put the Hatters ahead. But with the vision of Wembley fading, Dicks manhandled Roy Wegerle to the ground to allow Danny Wilson to grab a third from the spot. "I think I grabbed the bloke around the neck," he recalls of an incident which most would have worked hard to erase from the memory banks. *The irresponsible challenge by Dicks on Wegerle might have been born of the frustration of seeing the dreams of the twin towers disappear,'* said one paper almost forgivingly, before adding more bitingly, *'Luton will probably now head to Wembley and West Ham towards the Second Division.'*

Luton did indeed go to Wembley, wrapping up the job on the Hammers with a 2-0 win at Kenilworth Road in the second leg. And once Norwich had dumped West Ham out of the FA Cup, there was then only one priority left – saving their top flight status. And they had to do it in front of a crowd that had long since lost its patience with some of the players, particularly John Lyall's newer recruits. "This crowd has destroyed David Kelly and now they are trying to do the same to me," complained Allen McKnight. And the manager did not escape the fire either.

"John was under a lot of pressure because the fans expected more from the team that we had then," says Julian. "He'd been there a long time and the fans were chanting 'Lyall out!' and stuff."

But the manager worked hard to keep an upbeat atmosphere present at the training ground, trying to take the pressure off the players. "I was just trying to do my job and as you take the winning, you have to take the losing," says Lyall. "Obviously there's pressure when you're bottom of the league but you smile as much as you can. One of many things I learned from Ron Greenwood was that you have to try and give the players the belief that they're good enough."

> "I think I grabbed the bloke around the neck"

And with a final roll of the dice Lyall made two changes to try and turn things around, finally putting 'keeper McKnight out of his misery by recalling 38-year-old Phil Parkes and, at the other end, bringing striker Frank McAvennie back to Upton Park in a bold £1.2m gamble before transfer deadline day.

It basically meant that Lyall had finally spent the money received from the sale of Tony Cottee the previous summer, with the Kelly, McKnight and McAvennie deals wiping out the whole £2 million. Despite his popularity with both fans and players, Frank was unable to rediscover his scoring touch, failing to hit the back of the net in any of his nine appearances that season.

Home defeats by Norwich, Middlesbrough and Southampton – the last of which

There's a ball around here somewhere!

Julian missed through a one-game suspension following a booking (his ninth of the campaign) in the 3-0 loss at Tottenham – looked to have sealed the Hammers' fate, although it's an indication of how much injuries unsettled the team that Dicks still played more games than any other player, despite being banned for four matches that campaign.

The results did suddenly pick up in the final month, starting with a convincing 3-0 win over Millwall on April 22 which saw Julian score his first goal for the Hammers at Upton Park. "I came up for a corner, somebody headed it out and I volleyed it in from about 20 yards. It wasn't a particularly good volley but it went in through the 'keeper's legs!" he explains.

With the team still 10 points adrift of safety with just six games remaining and the headlines being dominated by troublesome 'fans', some of whom had marred the minute's silence for the 95 Hillsborough victims a week earlier, the goals against Millwall were hardly big news. Yet the result seemed to spark some belated self-belief, with the Hammers next going to St. James' Park and securing a 2-1 win to send Newcastle down (as a result of the Geordies having played more games). A 1-0 victory against Luton Town in the last home game kept faint hopes of survival alive and when the team made it four wins on the trot at Sheffield Wednesday – in the first match to take place at Hillsborough after the disaster – a few clubs above them undoubtedly started to get a bit nervy. (The 2-0 win over Wednesday also saw Dicks move into a centre-half position after Tony Gale had gone off with concussion – "It was definitely a position he could play," reflects John Lyall. "He's not tall but he's got great natural spring and is a very good header of the ball. So together with his left foot and aggression, he could certainly play at centre-back.")

Runner-up to Paul Ince in the 1989 'Hammer of the Year' poll.

With three more away games to be played – two up on Merseyside – the odds were still stacked heavily against the Hammers, although as Julian insisted, "Until it's mathematically impossible to stay up, we've got to keep fighting."

> **"You can be philosophical and say it was meant to be, but relegation is such a disappointment because it affects so many people's lives"** – JOHN LYALL

Defeat at Everton should have signalled the end, but a 2-1 win at third-placed Nottingham Forest left the team with a chance of survival that nobody would have granted them four weeks earlier. All they needed to do in their last game was go to Anfield and beat Liverpool, who needed victory themselves to set up a three-point lead over Arsenal (before their head-to-head meeting) in the race for the title.

Despite becoming only the second team to score at Anfield in 1989, thanks to Rosenior's equalising goal after Aldridge had put Liverpool ahead, it wasn't to be. Once former Hammer Ray Houghton had fired past McKnight (back in for the injured Parkes) on the hour, West Ham had to chase the game and their need for maximum points resulted in throwing men forward in the final 10 minutes. "I made a mistake, which set them up for their third goal," recalls Julian, having been robbed by Peter Beardsley in the 82nd minute, and two further goals simply rubbed salt into the wounds. "We all pushed forward to try and get the result but we left ourselves open at the back," he confirms.

Having experienced relegation once before, with Birmingham, it wasn't a feeling Julian wanted to repeat, but he was philosophical about the situation. "It's not nice for the players, supporters or the manager, there are no two ways about it," he says. "When you go down you're gutted. But these things happen in football."

Dicksy's efforts that season were rewarded with a runners-up position in the Hammer-of-the-Year poll (behind Paul Ince), with the fans appreciating the left-back's endeavour. That industry, however, put Julian top of the Hammers' bookings chart with 11 (totalling 41 disciplinary points), with Ince just two cards behind him. Between them, they received 20 of the 43 cautions handed out to West Ham players during that year of struggle.

"The disappointment was that we found the good form too late," reflects John Lyall. "If we'd found a little bit of form two or three games earlier then we wouldn't have had so much of a problem. But it looked so difficult at that point that the pressure was off and we began to play reasonably well. The biggest disappointment was the last game at Liverpool. You fight so hard to try and succeed and when you fail it's a great disappointment. You can be philosophical and say it was meant to be, but relegation is such a disappointment because it affects so many people's lives."

Indeed, it was John Lyall who paid the highest price for the Hammers' relegation (in a season in which they set club records for most home defeats, least home wins, least home goals scored and least total goals scored), with the West Ham board announcing on June 5, 1989 that the manager's contract would not be renewed. "I only found out through the papers," reveals Julian, who received a letter of thanks from the man who'd brought him to Upton Park 15 months earlier. "I thought that was very nice because it wasn't something he had to do. But he'd always been somebody you could talk to. He'd always have time to listen. He was a very nice man but, in saying that, he could also be nasty as well if he needed to. I spoke to him a few times on the phone and he said that if I ever needed advice I could always ring him."

But that was typical of the nature of John Lyall. "You get close to players," explains the former boss. "Those lads keep you in work and it's just nice to thank them for what they did because I was grateful. Years later, I remember seeing Julian in the treatment room at Anfield when I went to Liverpool with Ipswich Town and I spent some time chatting with him. I remember thinking that he was still the same – a nice pleasant boy – and it's on those personal levels that I like to assess the people I work with.

"I can remember him coming into the training ground with his children in the afternoons and he doted over those two. And it was nice to see. He was a real family man. His wife would sit talking to us and he would be pushing these kids around in a twin pram. You could see the fatherly affection. He liked being a dad and there was a closeness with his children."

Certainly, Lyall considered Julian as one of his best ever buys and was probably aware that, despite his left-back's tendencies to occasionally over-commit to the wrong tackle, his team may have stood a better chance of retaining their First Division status had a few more of his type been in the side.

As the media stated upon hearing the news of John's departure from West Ham, after 34 years in various capacities at the club, it marked the end of an era. The next issue, of course, was of who would carry the responsibility of taking the club into a new one…

Father and daughter relax at the training ground with Gary Strodder.

CHAPTER 10
FAMILY BUSINESS

JULIAN and Kay were married at Solihull Registry Office on July 22, 1988, following the news that Kay had fallen pregnant. "I was over the moon," says Julian. "It was just telling her dad – that was the thing! I got on well with him but I didn't know how he'd react. We told her mum and she was happy, and so was her sister. My family were happy as well."

Fortunately, Kay's father Peter was "over the moon" at the news of her pregnancy, with Julian following up with a formal request to do the honourable thing. Permission was duly granted, but with this all happening around the time of Julian's move down to West Ham, there had initially been some doubt about tying the knot. "We didn't know what to do," admits Kay. "We weren't going to get married, but I think people expected us to. We probably got married as much for other people's sakes as ours. I think we just decided that because we were moving away and I was expecting, it would be better if we got married in Birmingham before I moved down, than to leave it until I had the girls. At that point I didn't know it was twins."

Julian was so excited at the news of Kay's pregnancy, especially with always having loved children anyway, that he rushed out the very next day to get 'kitted out'. "I went and got everything – pram, cot, the lot. But then Kay had a scan which revealed she was having twins, so I had to take the whole lot back and change it all!"

Julian's eagerness brought a smile to Kay's face, however. "The shop must have thought he was stupid!" she laughs. "The twins weren't due until December, but you name it and Julian had bought it. I can remember him being with me when I had the scan in the summer. When we were told it would be twins his mouth dropped three feet. He couldn't believe it."

Julian's suggestion of marriage was done in a manner that many would say was typical of him, choosing to surprise Kay with a ring. "We'd gone out one night to a wine bar and it was heaving," Kay recalls. "Julian said to me, 'Close your eyes and give me your hand.' Well, I wouldn't, because knowing him he'd put something disgusting in my hand. He went on for a while and I was telling him to give me whatever it was. But in the end I did as he asked and that's how we got engaged."

*Julian and Kay
share a kiss on their
wedding day.*

The big day – for deliberate reasons – was kept a relatively low-key affair. Julian had never liked being the centre of attention, while Kay was certainly keen to keep things moderate. "I hate big fusses, I can't stand it," she says. "I'd have been quite happy for us to have just gone and got married on our own. I didn't even tell my best friend – she was horrified!"

But Kay's 'best friend' wasn't the only person unaware of what was taking place on that day, with Julian's father Ron and brother Grantley also not being invited. Ron and Carol had split up just a couple of years earlier and, with Carol and her boyfriend Martin present at the wedding, it was considered safest to avoid possible confrontations. "I just thought it would be too much hassle," admits Julian, who also reveals that it was a period of time in which his brother and mother were not getting on too well. "You don't want people having a go at each other on your wedding day. Things were a bit up in the air at that point," he adds.

89

The groom and his mum Carol.

Kay also supported the decision to not send invitations to Ron and Grantley. "They might hate me for it now but you do what you think is right and that's what we did," she says.

As far as Julian was concerned his father did at least know about the wedding, if not necessarily being invited, but Ron denies having that knowledge. "I didn't even know they were getting married," he stresses. "He probably thought I'd try and talk him out of it. Maybe that's why he didn't tell me."

Ron would indeed have probably advised his son to have bided his time, aware of Julian still being a teenager, but he was disappointed to miss the occasion all the same. Dicks' former landlady Janet Rodgers was also downhearted to miss the wedding. "I was quite sad about that," she confides. "When there's a lot of things happening in your life it's easy to lose contact with people, but I'd have liked to have gone to the wedding."

It was Ron Veal, the scout who'd discovered Dicks, who was invited to be his best man. But being good friends with Ron and Carol, he was a little uncomfortable that they weren't both there. "Julian invited my wife Mabel and I up to the ceremony when his father didn't even know he was getting married. That was a bit wrong to me. I tried to keep the boys and their families together. But we're all right about it now and I'm still good friends with his mother and father to this day."

Kay enjoyed her big day, even though she grimaces when looking back upon certain aspects of it. "I looked awful!" she exclaims. "I can't believe what I wore when I look back now. In fact I've hidden our wedding photos – they're terrible. We just looked so young. And because of the move and everything, it was all such a rush. But it was a nice day, it was very quiet and we just went back to my sister's afterwards."

Just in the way that Julian would later tear his football shirts at the collar to avoid the feeling of restriction, he couldn't wait to get out of his smart clothes after the ceremony, changing into his tracksuit at the earliest opportunity. "The only thing Julian didn't like was that somebody put confetti down his shirt," remembers his mum. "He didn't like ties so as soon as the ceremony was finished that was off, then once the confetti went down his neck off came his coat and shirt. I've got photos of him in just his bare chest."

> "Julian invited my wife Mabel and I up to the ceremony when his father didn't even know he was getting married. That was a bit wrong to me" – RON VEAL

With so much taking place, including the wedding, the move down south and Kay's pregnancy, the couple had more than enough on their plate during the summer of 1988 to bother with honeymoons or anything – and that was without

taking into account Julian's pre-season preparations for his first full campaign with his new club.

The Marston Green property had been sold (for £31,000) within 24 hours of it going on the market and Kay remained in the Midlands with her family until Julian – assisted by Hammers kit man Eddie Gillam and residing for the first few months of his West Ham career in an hotel – found their new home. "It took us a while to get the place in Billericay because everybody was getting gazumped," says Kay. "Eddie Gillam

Julian's best man was Ron Veal, the scout who discovered him.

was brilliant. He'd take Julian wherever he wanted to go. We lost one place in Billericay because they put the price up and we didn't want to go any higher. I can remember Julian ringing and telling me that I was going to have to come down the next day to find a house, so I jumped in the car and and we went and had a look at the place we eventually bought.

"I knew I wanted to live in Billericay because I'd driven down the high street and it reminded me of somewhere I knew in Birmingham, so I thought, 'Right, we'll live here!'"

In retrospect for Kay, the middle of 1988 – the summer of change, as it could be called – was a difficult period. "Obviously I knew I was pregnant, but it was July by the time I had my appointment with the hospital in Birmingham. So I had the scan and within two days I moved down to Billericay. So I'd just found out I was expecting twins and then had to move away. It was horrifying. When I look back now I don't know how we did it. There was such a lot going on at once that I don't think we had time to really take it all in. It wasn't until I actually moved down that it really all hit me."

The relocation south in itself was a matter of concern for Kay, with her family roots and ties in Solihull being so strong. "I'd always lived in the same house, apart from when Julian and I got our first place together. So I was dreading the move away, to be honest."

Finally settled into their new Billericay home, and Julian successfully establishing himself in the West Ham team in the early part of the 1988-89 season, the final piece of the new family jigsaw fell into place when Kay gave birth to two daughters – Kattie and Jessica – on December 23, 1988. "It didn't really affect me," Julian says, denying that the disrupted nights and having to attend to the demands of two babies had any impact on his performances at that time. "I was getting up at three or four o'clock in the morning to feed them and things like that and it was a case of carrying on as normal on the pitch – I was still getting booked."

What it did do was change Julian's perspective of things, however. No longer was football the main thing in his life. Now his family were the priority and everything else – soccer included – was secondary. "Before we had kids football always came first, so it did change me in that respect," he acknowledges. "But it didn't change me as a footballer. People say that when you have kids it calms you down and you won't get booked or sent off. But it didn't work out like that."

LIFE UNDER LOU

JULIAN certainly has no problems remembering Lou Macari's first day in charge as the new West Ham manager. "He called me a fat bastard," he reveals.

Needless to say, it wasn't the best way to kick off a new relationship between incoming boss and key player, and the ill-feeling between them remained during their time together at Upton Park. "We used to go into the gym and have five-a-sides and he'd always be on the opposite side. I used to kick shit out of him, really hammer him. But he always used to come back for more," Julian admits.

Lou took over at West Ham in July 1989 after a successful spell at Swindon Town, during which he'd guided the Wiltshire club from the Fourth to Second Divisions. Coach Ronnie Boyce, along with Mick McGiven, had looked after things following the sacking of John Lyall but had not been interested in seeking the manager's job on a full-time basis. "Ronnie told us that he didn't want it," says Julian. "He just didn't need the hassle."

The West Ham manager's chair was certainly not a "hassle" free zone in the summer of '89. Not only did the new man have to win friends quickly, he had to try to get the Hammers back on the winning road while dealing with a number of deeply dissatisfied players – in particular Paul Ince, who was one of the first to express his desire to quit the club following the departure of Lyall. *'It is impossible to envy the man who takes over,'* wrote James Lawton in the *Daily Express*. *'He has a tradition to protect while at the same time satisfying the legitimate demands for success of the West Ham fans who are weary of providing football's artistic interlude. One thing is for certain – he will not get 15 years* (the amount of time Lyall had in the job) *to do it.'*

After Harry Redknapp, Peter Shreeves, Gerry Francis and Ray Harford had been linked with the post, Lou Macari accepted West Ham's offer and immediately told the group of players making noises about leaving (which included Mark Ward and Alvin Martin) that they should honour the contracts they had signed. Ince, however, had other ideas and, under the guidance of agent Ambrose Mendy, saw fit to be photographed in a Manchester United shirt while still a West Ham player in order to seemingly create an untenable situation and force a move through. Despite embarrassed United boss Alex Ferguson feeling obliged to apologise to former Old

Trafford player Macari for the confusion surrounding his interest in the Hammers midfielder, Ince finally got his wish and moved north after playing just one more game for West Ham. "I can't understand what he thought he was doing," says Julian of the shirt incident. "I can only think he thought the deal had gone through, but he was obviously badly advised and it was a terrible thing to do."

Macari was clearly unhappy with much of what he saw when he joined West Ham and his willingness to speak his mind and enforce what he felt were necessary changes did not wash well with players who'd become used to a comfortable environment. "The way some players are reacting you'd think West Ham had got promoted, not relegated," he blasted in one newspaper, while in another he said: "West Ham's style of play did not do them much good last season, otherwise I wouldn't be sitting here today. Maybe the skill emphasis tended to overshadow the need for a fighting spirit. What I want is a fighting team on the pitch."

Frank McAvennie maybe took Lou too literally, however, having a verbal battle with Macari after being asked to take shooting practise before a friendly with Bordeaux, despite only being a substitute, and then lashing out at reserve left-back Tommy McQueen after an exchange of words during a training session. It was Julian who played peacemaker, diving between the two Scots to prevent a fight breaking out.

"I can't understand what he thought he was doing. He was obviously badly advised and it was a terrible thing to do"
— ON PAUL INCE PREMATURELY POSING IN A MAN UTD SHIRT

Dicks had his moments of controversy, too, particularly in a pre-season friendly against part-timers Kiruna in Sweden, when, after scoring Hammers' goal, he was booked for a flare-up with an opponent and then substituted. "We had a fight on the pitch and then their team came to the hotel to have dinner with us," recalls Julian. "I can't remember his name but the guy who I'd had the flare-up with came up to me afterwards and apologised, which I thought was really nice because he certainly didn't have to."

And Dicksy's disciplinary record the previous season caught up with him before the new campaign began, with him ordered before an FA commission to explain the 41 points he had amassed during the year. "They get you in front of three old fogeys and tell you what you've done wrong," he says. "But it's very hard trying to explain to people who've never played the game professionally why you've got booked for a tackle."

> "We had a fight on the pitch and then their team came to the hotel to have dinner with us"

After being fined £500 and banned for one game, Julian pledged to avoid a repeat situation: "People will look at the number of bookings I got last season and get the wrong impression," he said. "I feel I was very unlucky in several games to pick up cautions. I don't like the idea of getting a bad reputation and I'm determined to make sure I don't get booked so many times again."

Before a ball was kicked in the league, press stories started to emerge linking Julian with Spurs. The suggestion that he was 'unsettled' was dismissed as "absolute rubbish", but Tottenham definitely expressed an interest, and looked prepared to pay around £1 million for the left-back. "They didn't make an offer but they asked if he was available," confirms Lou Macari, who was hoping to spend on QPR midfielder Martin Allen at the time. "I think I'd only been there about a month when they made an enquiry, but I wasn't interested. Julian could have been the biggest rogue under the sun but I wouldn't have considered getting rid of him."

Julian's account of the situation is based on contact he had with agent Eric Hall, who was a friend of Spurs boss Terry Venables: "Eric found out about Tottenham's interest and tried to sign me up as one of his players," says Julian. 'I wouldn't sign with him but he offered to do the deal for me. He said he'd arrange for a meeting between Venables and Macari but Lou never turned up. And after that happened a few times Terry obviously thought 'sod this' and left it. And that was that."

The beginning of the 1989-90 season was a strange time for West Ham. While people from afar could speculate about the influence of an 'outsider' going into Upton Park, those inside the camp were not too happy with some of the things Lou wanted to change. One thing the new manager was particular about was diet – and Julian's habit of drinking coke before games was one thing Macari wanted to stamp out.

"I always used to argue with him about it," confirms Dicks. "I'd been drinking coke before games for years and he tried to stop me. We used to go away on Friday nights and he wouldn't let us have chips or dessert. It's okay saying that to a 16-year-old who's starting out but you're talking about 25 and 26-year-old blokes! But if you wanted to have a bet that was okay – like if you wanted to go and stick some money on something before a game, it'd be, 'Yeah, that's alright,' because he's a betting man himself. I remember some of the lads going down to the players' lounge at half-past two on a Saturday afternoon betting on horses and it wouldn't bother him. But if I wanted a can of coke he'd go ape, he'd go mental! I couldn't understand him."

Lou's philosophy was simply that guzzling cola shortly before a competitive match was not a good idea. "It was a habit he got into. And if you don't think it's a good one, or you think it might be advantageous for somebody to stop it, then you talk to them about it. But that would be a minor detail," Macari adds, down-playing the issue. "As a matter of fact, during the week I'd encourage him to drink coke, rather than the alternative – which was alcohol."

Striker Jimmy Quinn, who was brought to West Ham in December 1989 and had previously played under Lou at Swindon Town, could see the impact of his manager's attempts to change things at Upton Park, even though he hadn't been present under the previous regime. "A lot of the players didn't really get on with Lou. The training ground used to do food such as sausage sandwiches but Lou cut all that out and put salads in and that upset a lot of people straight away. And Julian didn't really get on with him. Having played for Lou before I knew what to expect, so it didn't bother me too much. But it was a big thing to change at West Ham at the time because it had been going on for ages."

"The training ground used to do food such as sausage sandwiches but Lou cut all that out and put salads in and that upset a lot of people" – Jimmy Quinn

Macari admits that he called Julian "fat" and felt his weight was a contributory factor to the left-back "under-achieving" – a key word in the manager's vocabulary when reflecting on Dicks' career. Such comment (the sort of thing Julian no doubt saw regularly on his school reports as a child) is clearly not meant as a snipe on Lou's part, more an indication that he was well aware of what the player's capabilities were and of his desire to see him fulfil his potential. "He was a bit overweight," says Lou. "I think it was something of a standing joke. It was a suggestion I'd get from the rest of the staff as well."

Macari raised the point with Julian but felt that he got minimal response. "I think the truth of the matter is that the penny didn't drop sometimes with him," he says. "But, to be fair to him, I think the penny would have dropped had he been surrounded more often by the likes of Billy Bonds and Trevor Brooking. It would have had to have dropped, because those were the habits of those people. But if you're in an environment where everyone's a little bit sloppy or everyone has an opinion similar to the player himself, it's hard to ever get out of it. If it's all 'let's drink and be merry' you've got a job getting any individual to sit up and take notice."

Just six games into the season Dicks was involved in a flare-up during a home game against Swindon Town, as detailed in a press report: *'Trouble erupted midway through the second half when Hammers' George Parris was caught by a reckless tackle from Tony Galvin – and Julian Dicks responded with an avenging foul. The furious Parris then launched himself at Galvin, who was sent flying over the touchline. Referee Alan Seville booked Galvin and Dicks – but surprisingly took no action against Parris.'*

By the time Julian stepped back onto the Upton Park pitch 14 days later (Sep 23), Lou had invested more responsibility in his left-back, not only giving him penalty duties ("There was never any doubt about that. When he put the ball on that spot, it would take a brave goalkeeper to get in the way of one of his penalty kicks," says Macari) but taking the bold step in some people's eyes of making him captain – the second youngest, behind Bobby Moore, in Hammers' history.

> **"The idea was to try to calm me down and keep referees off my back"** – ON BEING MADE CAPTAIN

"I would have tried anything to get him to realise he was an under-achiever," says Lou. "He had more ability and more going for him than he had achieved. Talk of him playing for England probably wasn't even in his mind, yet he should have been – and *should* be – an England player season after season. I didn't really think that before I went to West Ham because, as happens, people's reputations go before them and you make wrong judgements about them. He had a reputation of being bad news, a bad lad, of being misguided – everything you wouldn't want in a footballer."

Having not captained any team since his Birmingham youth days, it was ironic that the West Ham skipper's armband should be handed to him for the very first time against his old side at St. Andrews, for a Littlewoods Cup tie on September 19. "Lou said to me, 'I'm making you captain today.' I thought it was because I was playing against my old side, but it wasn't. And he said, 'I'm making you penalty taker as well.' So it all came at once."

Following in the footsteps of so many respected Hammers skippers, including the most recent – Alvin Martin – Dicks acknowledged the honour of leading the Hammers out, although he was a little surprised. "I thought Lou was joking because Alvin was still playing. But I think the two of them had had a chat about it and the manager decided to give it to me. The idea was to try to calm me down and keep referees off my back," he admits.

To say that Dicksy's first game at Upton Park as captain, against Watford, was an eventful one is something of an understatement. With the team having crashed 3-0 to Brighton seven days earlier (their first league defeat under Macari), the points were badly needed and they were duly secured thanks to a 17th-minute penalty – Julian's first spot-kick for the club. Typically, the game was shrouded in controversy, with Watford manager Steve Harrison not only complaining about the penalty award but accusing Dicks of stamping on winger Rod Thomas.

"Players must be given protection and that just wasn't right," the Hornets' boss blasted after the game. "It was purely unintentional," responded Dicks. "The kid came sliding in and I jumped in the air and landed on him. It was just one of those things. The linesman was right there and saw everything but didn't even raise his flag."

The Watford game had seen the debut of central defender Colin Foster, a £750,000 buy from Nottingham Forest – the second of the new manager's recruits following the acquisition of £600,000 Martin Allen. And Lou made it clear there would be more arrivals – a refreshing change from the stagnancy at West Ham that had developed in the later years under John Lyall.

> "The kid came sliding in and I jumped in the air and landed on him. It was just one of those things"

Early results that season had given optimism to fans hoping for an instant return to the First Division (despite the loss of Frank McAvennie who broke his leg in a clash with Stoke City's Chris Kamara in the opening game, with soon-to-be-sold David Kelly and Stuart Slater taking the No 8 shirt for the first half of the campaign) and notable games included a 5-0 win over Sunderland, a 3-2 victory against Oxford and a 2-0 defeat of Middlesbrough – with Dicks scoring in the last two of those games.

The Oxford win had Julian claiming all the headlines: *'Julian Bravo!'* screamed one paper. *'Blood-and-thunder skipper Julian Dicks hit a stinging winner for West Ham to decide a match of unrelenting thrills.'* Dicks blasted in from 35 yards following a free-kick touched into his path by midfielder Kevin Keen and it was the kind of goal that would become a trademark of his in future times (as was the penalty against Boro).

The Hammers – and particularly Julian – were also having a great time in the Littlewoods Cup. *'You clever Dicks'* was one headline as he scored against former club Birmingham in the second leg of their second round tie. *'The 21-year-old Hammers skipper blasted the nail into brave Brum's coffin with a stunning 53rd minute goal. Dicks latched onto a Kevin Keen pass before unleashing a blistering left-footer into the roof of the net.'* The 1-1 home draw was enough to take West Ham through to a meeting with the other Birmingham club, Aston Villa, in the third round, and after a 0-0 draw with the First Division side at Villa Park, it was Julian who again seized the glory in the replay with another sensational strike from a short free-kick. "It was a bit sad putting out Birmingham but it was great to beat the Villa! Goals will always feel better when they win games like that," bubbled a happy Dicks after the game,

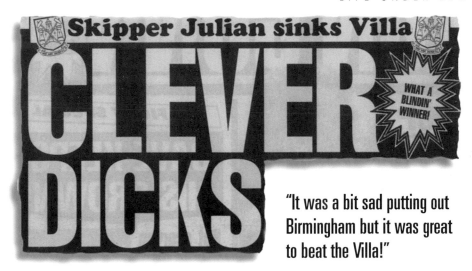

Skipper Julian sinks Villa

CLEVER DICKS

WHAT A BLINDIN' WINNER!

"It was a bit sad putting out Birmingham but it was great to beat the Villa!"

although it was the majestic Liam Brady who won the plaudits following a typically classy performance. "It was one of the best games I have ever seen Liam Brady play," enthused Lou Macari, who was delighted to have seen his team's dominant display against a side who'd thrashed Everton 6-2 in the league just three days earlier.

"Liam's a legend," remarks Julian. "The funny thing about him was that he never used to sprint, he just used to jog everywhere. He'd have five, 10 yards of space around him and he wouldn't sprint. I'd go on the overlap and he'd give me the ball all the time. I'd be sprinting my balls off and he'd just be jogging, but that was just the way he was."

> "The funny thing about Liam was that he never used to sprint. I'd be sprinting my balls off and he'd just be jogging"

Some 21-year-olds may well have found it intimidating to be captaining a side with such a respected, elder-statesman in it, yet Julian shrugged off the extra burden. "As far as I'm concerned, you've got 11 captains on the pitch," he says. "The captain just goes up, flips a coin and says which way you want to kick. You can't just have one person out there shouting their head off, you need a whole team doing it."

Contrary to what some may expect, though, Dicksy's approach in trying to get the best out of his comrades was not to rant and rave at people. "I'm not the kind of person who, if somebody makes a mistake, says, 'You're shit, you shouldn't have done that.' Because that can blow some people's confidence. I'm more of a geeing up person. If you make a mistake, I say, 'Don't worry about it, carry on and do it right next time.'"

Dicksy's captaincy would be questioned, however, after the rumpus that took place during another Littlewoods Cup match, the fourth round tie against

Wimbledon at Upton Park on November 22. It was the night that saw Julian sent off for the first time in his Hammers career and it prompted such an extreme media response that the mud would stick to his boots for many moons to come.

'Dicks sent off as Upton sparks!'

'It's a riot!'

'Dicks sent off but Dons bow out in a new brawl game!'

Those were just some of the headlines in the aftermath of a match that saw Julian dismissed following a late tackle on Dons' midfield terrier, Dennis Wise – just 10 minutes after picking up a first caution for dissent – plus an earlier 17-man brawl, after Wise had fouled Dicks.

'Julian Dicks was sent off as 10-man West Ham won this X-certificate Littlewoods Cup tie that was a disgrace to football,' wrote *The Sun's* Brian Woolnough. *'Martin Allen's brilliant 81st-minute volleyed goal was sadly out of context in a game that had more to do with the profession of violence,'* said *Today's* Rob Shepherd, while the *Daily Mirror* acknowledged: *'The first and worst incident occurred in the 43rd minute, sparked by a reckless two-footed tackle by Dennis Wise on Dicks. The Hammers' full-back reacted wildly*

Julian troops off as Dennis Wise gets treatment.

and within seconds fists were flying. Surprisingly, Wise was the only culprit punished with a yellow card. But it didn't end there, as referee Alf Buksh – who needed a police escort off the pitch – lost control. The final count was six bookings, including Wimbledon physio Steve Allen, and Dicks' dismissal.'

And so it continued: *'This bitter London derby was nothing but a disgraceful exhibition…'*; *'West Ham and Wimbledon heaped more shame on soccer last night…'*; while the *Mirror's* Harry Harris predictably trundled out his usual *'Soccer is in the gutter'* declaration.

Both Dicks and Macari argued against the hysteria as the Hammers and Dons were charged by the FA with bringing the game into disrepute. "I would not call what happened a brawl," said Lou afterwards. "There was some pushing and shoving but it was not that bad. It's all been blown up. I also didn't think Julian Dicks deserved to be sent off. I didn't think he made contact with Wise. But in a way it inspired us and we showed our fighting qualities."

Julian, meanwhile, insisted: "I have played in tougher matches than that. It was a physical game but nothing more than we expected, especially against Wimbledon. There was pushing and shoving but nothing worse. But it certainly wasn't a riot or a brawl. I don't know if I was sent off for two bookable offences or for the tackle on Wise. My first booking came when I pushed a Wimbledon player after two of them turned on Martin Allen. I don't think I should have been booked for that either. I will not change the way I play or my attitude. I will be doing exactly the same in the next game."

Despite his efforts to play it down at the time, the game indeed made a big impact on Julian. "I remember the big brawl. Alvin Martin and Eric Young had a go at each other and then everyone else joined in. There were punches flying everywhere and even the Chicken Run got involved," he says, referring to the surge of fans on the East Stand terracing. "I saw Wise in the players' bar afterwards and I went over and spoke to him. There were no grudges or anything."

> **"There were punches flying everywhere and even the Chicken Run got involved"**

Macari today describes the big flare-up as "a 17-man handbag job" and admits that the most important thing was the win – which had taken Hammers through to the last eight but been totally overlooked as a result of the controversy. "When you win on a night at Upton Park like that, I don't think you're too worried about the press reports the following day," he sniggers.

Press reports that worried Julian, however, were those quoting Macari on his left-back's growing disciplinary problems. He'd already amassed 20 points, prior to the Wimbledon game, and had been sent off for the England under-21 side against Mexico during the summer of that year, prompting Lou to say, "Change your image or forget an England place. Julian just doesn't realise the harm he is doing to himself.

He is one of the most talented young defenders in the country but unless things change he could do himself out of an England career."

Such public comments did not warm Julian to his manager, contravening his ideas of how things should be done. "I think it's all wrong," he argues. "I think Lou should have called me into his office and said, 'Look, you either do this or your England career is going to go out of the window.' Instead, he spoke to the press and I picked up the paper and thought, 'F---ing hell, what's he done here?' You'd think people would have enough bottle to say, 'Come into the office...'"

Lou, however, would not have seen such action as being necessary. "I don't really see what big deal it is," he says of the debate. "I think a footballer is well aware of what he's doing wrong or where he's going wrong. I don't think you need to sit down with him behind closed doors to spell it out to him, unless there's something wrong with his brains.

"Maybe he's a bit misguided when he thinks that some manager calling him in and telling him something face to face is going to make all the difference. If that's so, I'm quite sure there'd have been lots of managers who would have done that."

There was no doubt that Macari was worried about the potential loss of one of his main men through suspension and, although there may not be have been many (if any) one-on-one sessions behind closed doors, the subject of Julian's poor record was still talked about – often in vain as far as Lou was concerned. "I wanted him on that pitch every week," he says. "It's no good him sitting in the stand when he's one of your most valuable players. And I think there have been other people – before and after me – who've tried to help him. A problem that he's had is that he never seems to have realised the importance of not getting into trouble. I don't want to bring up his record since I left West Ham but he's been in trouble season after season."

Having said that, Macari also felt that other factors came into play in respect of Julian getting into bother. "I always felt his reputation got him a few bookings," he admits. "His hairstyle got him some more bookings. And the supporters would be a contributory factor as well. You'd go to an away ground where people had made their minds up about him and they'd continually have a go at the referee over every tackle he'd make. It takes a strong referee not to react eventually to that kind of thing. I felt a lot of referees over-reacted with him. But then, of course, maybe at a later date, he'd give any referee justification in thinking they did the right thing with him by then going and doing something stupid."

Back to the football itself, Julian continued to help out in the goalscoring stakes, netting a penalty in the 5-4 defeat at Blackburn (where Hammers had actually been four goals down!), firing in a rasping 25-yard drive against Plymouth in the little-wanted Zenith Cup (in front of 5,409 people, Upton Park's lowest crowd since 1955) to contribute to the 5-2 win, and another penalty in a 4-2 victory over Barnsley on New Year's Day of 1990.

A month earlier Dicks had had a spot-kick at Upton Park saved by Stoke City

A rare penalty miss from our hero as Stoke fight out a dour draw at Upton Park.

goalkeeper Peter Fox, in a dour 0-0 stalemate that prompted criticism from some sections of the media. *'That's not entertainment, Lou!'* said one paper, describing the team as *'goalless and clueless'*. Given that Hammers had just lost in that nine-goal thriller at Ewood Park just a week beforehand, such words were a shade harsh, although some people had started to air their doubts as to whether the club would be able to maintain their traditions for playing with flair and style under a manager brought in from outside the 'academy'.

The *Daily Mirror's* Harry Harris had asked certain questions in the wake of the Wimbledon fiasco, saying, *'Under manager Lou Macari West Ham are working hard, tackling hard – a force to be reckoned with. Many people may regret that even they are falling into line with professional football's more unsavoury aspects.'*

"I told Lou that all I wanted to do was play football, that I didn't want to get the ball and lump it"

Even Bobby Moore, writing a column for the *Sunday Sport*, commented on the Hammers' harder approach, although he took a more positive view: *'West Ham have certainly changed their style since I used to lead the Hammers! But the Irons' get-tough policy looks like paying dividends in the battle to get out of soccer's hardest league. The player who typifies the new Hammers spirit is captain Julian Dicks. Dicksy has a reputation of being a Rambo on the pitch and he doesn't mince around off it!'*

But it was the actual style of play that some people were raising their eyebrows about, and Julian himself was less than happy with what he was being asked to do under the guidance of Macari. "Everybody spoke about the West Ham academy of football, that we like to play football, but Lou came in and tried to change it," he confirms. "It would be: get the ball, whack it up front. And you can't do that if a team and its players are geared to play football. When you've got people like Liam Brady in the side you can't just lump it. I wasn't the only person to oppose it but I was the only one to say so. I told Lou that all I wanted to do was play football, that I didn't want to get the ball and lump it. It was too predictable and if I don't agree with something, then I won't do it."

> "Wardy went over to the dessert table, grabbed a great big piece of gateaux and sat down eating it. Lou had no control over anybody"

The suggestion that Dicks was asked to compromise his instinct for playing football is strongly refuted by Lou, though: "I don't know what Julian says but he was never asked to play in any different way. He was asked to do what Julian Dicks can do – rampage forward and get back. The only thing I did try and change was for him to not get so many bookings."

Whatever the style of Hammers' play, the concern going into 1990 was the team's position in the Second Division table. Despite the ongoing success in the Littlewoods Cup, the league form had started to wane – alarmingly, in fact. After the 2-0 win over Middlesbrough, West Ham only picked up one point out of the next 18 – and that was in the afore-mentioned Stoke game. "It's nice doing well in the cups but, as any professional will say, it's much better to be top of the league and get knocked out the cups in the first round. The league form was disheartening," says Julian. Four consecutive defeats to Bradford, Oldham, Ipswich and Leicester in December set the alarm bells ringing and Macari responded by ringing the changes. Out went the disenchanted Mark Ward, in an exchange deal that saw Manchester City's Ian Bishop and Trevor Morley head south to Upton Park, and in came Bradford striker Jimmy Quinn (who opened his account in his second game, in the 1-1 draw at Plymouth – a game that saw the final appearance of Alan Devonshire) and, finally, Czechoslovakian goalkeeper Ludek Miklosko, from Banik Ostrava. All this activity was only too welcome for West Ham fans, frustrated with the club's lethargy in the transfer market in past years, but the disappointment of the team's mid-table position offset much of the joy of seeing new players arrive.

Much of the disappointing form could be attributed to the unrest behind the scenes, with some players' poor attitudes being reflected in their behaviour. "We were away one Friday before a game, when Mark Ward was still with us," recalls Julian, "and we were having our food when Wardy asked, 'What's for dessert?' Lou turned round and said, 'You're not having any.' Wardy thought 'bollocks!' and went over to the dessert table, grabbed a great big piece of gateaux and sat down

Celebrating with Jimmy Quinn (right).

eating it. Lou had no control over anybody. He didn't try and play the hard man as such but he tried to lay down his laws. And while he may have had the respect of a few of the lads, the majority of them had no respect for him."

Julian certainly fell into the latter category, and – as already mentioned – he enjoyed giving Lou a tough time in training if the opportunity came its way. "One day, in the gym, I thought I'd broken his leg. It was a 50/50 challenge – I didn't go over the top or anything – but I just went straight through him and he was left on the floor. And he couldn't finish training."

The sight of Julian v Lou in training took some getting used to for a few of the other players, including Ian Bishop. "It was a bit of a shock when I first arrived – it seemed a bit strange to see somebody booting their manager up in the air," says Bish. "To be fair, Lou kept going on the opposite side and coming back for more. But their relationship looked stormy. Julian may have been made captain by Lou but it seemed like a love/hate relationship to me."

Martin Allen also realised the conflict in their relationship. "Julian didn't really like Lou that much," he says. "I think Lou kind of liked him in some ways and in others he wasn't so keen. They didn't have the greatest of relationships."

As far as Lou was concerned, such 'battles' in the gym were all good-natured stuff. "We used to kick one another now and again," he laughs. "And if I didn't come off worse I took a great deal of satisfaction out of that, because most other people did. Actually, I've sent messages back to him since that I'm waiting for a re-match! But, seriously, I didn't have too many problems with him and those I did have I tried to deal with, in his best interests. But I'd be surprised if he indicated that he was arguing with me every day

> "It seemed a bit strange to see somebody booting their manager up in the air" — IAN BISHOP

or anything like that. I used to try, in the best way possible, to take the piss out of him to get a response."

"I used to try, in the best way possible, to take the piss out of him to get a response" – LOU MACARI

Alvin Martin, the senior player at the club, could see that certain players were not responding to the manager's rallying cry and took it upon himself to have words with some of them to try to encourage them to pull together. How much effect this had is questionable, certainly not preventing the team from falling to what was their greatest embarrassment to date that season (although more would later follow!).

An FA Cup third round tie at Torquay – sitting 87th in the league – on January 6 should not have posed too many problems, yet the Hammers were humiliated as they crashed out 1-0. "Their right-winger, Paul Smith, cut in past me and the chap (Paul Hirons) knocked it in," Julian confesses.

News had just broken that Macari was being charged by the FA for unauthorised betting during his tenure as manager of Swindon, but Julian refused to use the scandal as an excuse for the defeat. "We've only got ourselves to blame," he admitted as the Hammers left Plainmoor with their tails firmly between their legs.

"That was when Lou went missing," Dicks recalls. "We were in the hotel on the Friday evening and he wouldn't answer the door to his room, because all the press were there. We went up again the next morning and he wasn't there. God knows where he went."

Macari emerged – looking a worried man – for the game itself and continued to guide the Hammers for the next month or so, even taking them past Derby County (after three games) and into the semi-finals of the Littlewoods Cup. And once again, it was Julian whose contribution proved crucial, scoring a spectacular 30-yarder past England 'keeper Peter Shilton in the first of those fifth round games. "Liam just knocked the ball to me and I hit it and watched it swerve away and hit the post to go in. But Tony Gale made a mistake and Dean Saunders scored to take it to a replay."

Julian then missed the home league defeat by third-from-bottom Hull City (which saw the Hammers slump to 13th in the table) due to suspension, and was also out – along with Martin Allen – for the cup replay at the Baseball Ground. Despite the

MACARI ACCUSED

club missing 15 first-team men (thanks to suspension, injuries and cup-tied players), West Ham escaped with a 0-0 draw. It was an evening that Julian still enjoyed, despite not playing. "Martin Allen and I were in the stands behind the goal with the West Ham fans and we had a great night. They were singing, 'Martin, give us a song,' and then he'd stand up and give them one. Then it would be my turn. We had a great night!"

With Dicks back in the side, the Hammers duly exploited the benefits of home advantage in the third meeting with Derby, enjoying a 2-1 win and prompting Macari to declare his team's performance as "magnificent!"

With the manager about to face an FA inquiry, though, things were about to take a turn for the worse. In the league, Brighton were beaten 3-1 – thanks in part to another thunderbolt strike from 35 yards by Julian – with the players insisting the off-field controversy was not affecting them. "The hearing has nothing to do with us," said Julian, "All we have to think about is the game but obviously we are keeping our fingers crossed for Lou."

Not that Macari had spoken about the issue to the players. "All I could do was read the papers, but if the allegations were true I think it's disgraceful," says Julian. "Betting against your own side is a disgraceful thing to do. It's so hard to believe."

Also hard to believe was the scoreline in the first leg of the Littlewoods Cup semi-final against Oldham at Boundary Park. The Hammers were thrashed 6-0, leaving themselves with virtually no chance of getting to the final. While not using it as an excuse, Dicks felt that it wasn't the fairest thing in the world to expect visiting teams to play on an artificial surface

> "Betting against your own side is a disgraceful thing to do. It's so hard to believe"

when the home side were completely familiar with it. "6-0 was a bit extreme, though," he adds in a moment of understatement.

Just four days later, on February 18, 1990, the Hammers' coach pulled into Swindon's County Ground – with no manager on board. It was an unusual weekend, to say the least. "We got onto the bus before the game but Lou wasn't there," recalls Julian. "I think we were told that he was going by car. But we got to the ground and there was no sign of him. Then it got to the kick-off – and still no sign. So we just thought, 'Well, he's not coming, let's just get on with our game.'"

Assistant Ronnie Boyce assumed the reins of control for the match, which finished in a 2-2 draw. The papers were full of the 'missing manager' stories the next day and, predictably, all eyes were on the Chadwell Heath training ground come Monday morning. "Lots of press were down there, asking where Lou Macari was. Obviously, we didn't have a clue. I don't think we saw him again and it must have been Boycey who in the end announced that Lou had resigned," Julian says.

"Most people were pleased to see him go. I think they were relieved. He tried to lay down laws and he played it all the wrong way. When you've got a situation like that, the players think, 'Sod that, I'm not playing for you today.' I thought he brought a lot of the problems on himself."

Julian spoke out about the departure of Macari in the press a few days afterwards and aired a more sympathetic view: "Nothing was going for him and it was something we all thought would happen. The pressure was so intense it would have got even the strongest man down. We weren't shocked. I think what has happened has affected the whole club."

Lou, speaking in 1996 as manager of Stoke City, says that, whatever minor problems they may have had, he'd love to have Julian in any side of his today. "My main view is that people don't know the real Julian Dicks," he declares. "Deep down he's a nice lad, not a slob or a thug. And he's not just a run-of-the-mill footballer either – he's a very, very good footballer.

"I think that unless you support West Ham or have worked for them and you see him every week, you don't realise how good a player he is. I think people just think of Julian Dicks as somebody with this short, cropped hair who kicks a few people and gets into trouble. And if Julian does kick a few it's because of his enthusiasm for the game.

"Perhaps he's been a little bit misguided in that respect, because he doesn't need to do that. There would be many instances where he gave you an indication he was misguided, but I don't think I'd want to say any more about that because he's been a great player for West Ham. He's got wonderful feet – as a matter of fact, he's the best striker of the ball I think I've ever seen.

"I just want him to know that I'm waiting for another chance – even though I'm 46 – to get back in the gym with him so that I can kick him!"

CHAPTER 12
UPHILL WITH BILL

BILLY BONDS was appointed as manager of West Ham – moving up from his post as youth team boss – on February 22, 1990, and even though Julian had only actually played alongside the Hammers legend on four occasions and the pair of them had little contact outside the training sessions at Chadwell Heath, he was more than pleased to see him move into the hot seat.

"Everybody wanted Billy put in charge – because he WAS West Ham," Julian emphasises. "Everybody respected him for what he'd done as a player and when there's respect for the manager, certain players think, 'I'll do my best for him today.'"

Under Bonds the Hammers showed an immediate improvement, reflecting not necessarily a great change in the way he did things (although, as Julian confirms, Billy did encourage the team to play football) but definitely an increased spirit of unity in the camp. Five of the next seven games were won, including the second leg of the Littlewoods Cup semi-final against Oldham – the team pulling back three of the six goals they'd conceded in the first tie and Julian scoring a penalty. "We went out and gave it our best shot," says Dicks, even though the final outcome was little more than a formality.

The first victory with Bonds at the helm came at Middlesbrough, in a game of mixed fortunes for Julian. First he was booked, then he set up Martin Allen's late winner. *'West Ham's captain, Dicks, did in the end what Bonds used to do – power his way about and inspire by example,'* said one report the following day. *'Brady played immaculately but he didn't win the match – Dicks did. Square-shouldered, high-elbowed, every 50-50 ball was his. Five minutes from the end, realising a little more spirit could snatch victory, he appeared behind the strikers and unleashed a 25-yard shot. It was driven hard but Pears seemed to make a meal of it, knocking it out for Allen to tap in.'*

The booking, which left Dicks facing his third ban of the season after accumulating 32 points, had him seething. "I didn't think I deserved to be booked. I went for the ball and he (Paul Kerr) fell over. Sometimes I feel my reputation goes before me," he complained after the game.

Just a few weeks earlier Julian had spoken about his disciplinary record, in a story

"We give everything for our teams and that's what the fans want to see" — JULIAN ON COMPARISONS WITH STUART PEARCE

comparing him with another left-back who'd played in the semi-finals of the Littlewoods Cup –

Nottingham Forest's Stuart Pearce. *'Dicks is a dead ringer for the current England full-back in approach,'* it stated. *'Pearce's challenge on Coventry City winger Kevin Gallacher, which earned him a booking, was uncannily similar to the offence that brought Dicks a sending off in the same competition against Wimbledon. Also, Pearce's winning goal against Coventry was no better than Dicks' scorching 30-yarder against Derby. Until losing to Oldham, there had been prospects of them lining up against each other at Wembley. The fact the West Ham defender has Pearce's England spot as a long-range target would have added bite to the occasion.'*

"He's a good player and, I suppose, is like me in approach. He goes in hard and always gives one hundred per cent," commented Julian in the same story. "You can't change players like us. It's no good saying we must cut out some challenges. We give everything for our teams and that's what the fans want to see. But I'm learning to control my aggression. I'm still picking up bookings, of course – I'm on 25 or 26 points so far this season. But that's better than usual at this point in a campaign."

The booking at Ayresome Park meant that Julian would miss two games – against

Julian intervenes to help team mate David Kelly at Hull.

Leeds United at Elland Road and the Upton Park clash with Sheffield United – while a thigh injury, sustained in training, ruled him out of making a return at Sunderland. The fact that Hammers lost two of those three games suggested the importance of having their left-back in the side and those dropped points would prove costly come the season's climax.

Julian eventually made his comeback in the home game with Port Vale on March 31, which ended in a 2-2 draw after the Hammers had two penalties saved by 'keeper Mark Grew – one from Dicks and the other from Jimmy Quinn (the last occasion that Julian passed a spot-kick over to another player). "Nowadays I'd take both of them, even if I'd not scored the first, but I thought that if I missed another one it could cost us the game. So Quinny went up and missed as well! After the game it made me feel better that I wasn't the only one who missed," admits Julian, who'd seen his last two penalties saved (having done the same in a recent game against Watford). Afterwards, he revealed that he'd tried placing his recent kicks and pledged to "blast them in future".

Jimmy Quinn had good reason for remembering the Vale game. "We definitely needed to win it, there's no doubt about that," he acknowledges. "When the second penalty was given I looked over to Julian and he said, 'Go on then!' and I was confident enough to take it."

Quinn – or Jimmy 'The Tree', as fans came to know him – had every reason to be full of confidence, having banged in 11 goals in the 11 league games played since his arrival. "Quinny was superb", declares Julian. "He wasn't the most mobile of players but he'd score goals for fun and I was surprised when they got rid of him – especially for just forty grand."

During his 18 months at West Ham, the Northern Ireland hitman developed a good relationship with Julian, with Jimmy and wife Jackie renting a place close by in Billericay. "Our wives became very close – they've been on holiday together and they're still very friendly now," says Jimmy, who occasionally went out with Dicks "for a few pints and a curry" (not to mention a trip to Romford nightclub Hollywoods) from time to time. "Julian can be a difficult person to get to know, but once you do he's not as nasty as people make him out to be. He's got this image that he's built up for himself – and he's got to live up to that. But deep down he's a nice guy, with a lovely wife and a fabulous couple of kids. He's very easy to get on with, although that's not to say he can't be a bit of a rogue at times."

> "Quinny scored goals for fun and I was surprised when they got rid of him – especially for just forty grand"

Dicks was back on target from the penalty spot three games later, completing a hat-trick of wins with a 4-1 mauling of Harry Redknapp's Bournemouth (who gave 17-year-old son Jamie a debut outing) that took the Hammers to within a point of the play-offs. It was a controversial spot-kick against them, however, in the game at

Oldham on April 21 that severely undermined their belated promotion push. "It wasn't a penalty – the player just fell and it was sickening," blasted Julian to the press afterwards. "The penalty changed the course of the game and possibly our season." One paper reported that justice was done, however, after *'referee Keiron Barratt missed a blatant handball by defender Julian Dicks in front of goal.'*

The Hammers' fate was virtually sealed in the next game, at Newcastle, when another Julian penalty (which sparked a pitch invasion by the Geordie fans!) proved not enough to prevent the men in black and white taking all three points thanks to their own mighty Quinn (Mickey) and his winner.

Despite the disappointment of knowing they faced another year of Second Division football, the Hammers ended the season in memorable style, thrashing Wolves 4-0 in a game that saw Liam Brady score a wonder goal on his last appearance after coming on as a second-half substitute. "What a way to finish your career – with a 30-yard screamer! Some of the crowd ran onto the pitch and it was a great way for Liam to bow out," reflects Julian, who picked up the Hammer-of-the-Year trophy for the first time prior to the game. "It's nice because it's from the fans," he says of the award. "They're the ones who watch you week-in, week-out, and they're the ones who pay your wages, so it was a great honour."

The penalty at Newcastle which sparked a pitch invasion by the home fans.

'*Julian Dicks was the star of the show,*' insisted Bobby Moore in his Sunday paper column. '*He was cheered loudly by the all-ticket crowd before the game as he collected his award – and he soon showed why he won the trophy. For the left-back proved one of the Hammers' most dangerous attackers.*'

Dicksy's 14 goals during the season testified to that, making him top scorer (one ahead of Kevin Keen and Jimmy Quinn). Seven of those were penalties and had he not missed three from the spot his tally would have been even more impressive. Add in his capture of the captaincy and his naming in the PFA

Hammer of the Year in May 1990 with runners-up Stuart Slater and Trevor Morley.

Second Division team of the year (for which he received a medallion) and it was without doubt a great campaign for Julian personally – despite topping the end-of-season bookings chart.

In addition to piling up the points, though, Julian was piling on the pounds, according to *The Sun's* Lee Clayton: *'The West Ham skipper has put on nearly half a stone recently because he just can't resist scoffing chocolates, sweets and crisps.'* Dicks' love of a good nosh was obviously having its affect. "I just like junk food," he admits. "My wife does cook proper food but I'd rather have a kebab, a Kentucky fried chicken or a McDonald's."

This was something that Lou Macari had attempted to address earlier in the season, even trying to lure Julian to a health farm! "He went to Henlow Grange and tried to take me with him," says Dicks. "He took about six or seven of the players – including Kevin Keen! He said that Keeny was overweight! He wanted to take me there but I said, 'Bollocks!' and didn't turn up for the coach. As far as I'm concerned you should eat what you feel good on."

And Julian felt good going into the 1990-91 season, continuing as captain and hoping to keep assisting his attack as the Hammers looked to launch a promotion bid. By October 3 he'd scored five times – including a penalty in a 1-0 win over Watford, another in a Littlewoods Cup defeat of Stoke City, a deflected shot to earn a draw at Sheffield Wednesday and a brace (one a pen) in the 7-1 demolition of poor Hull City at Upton Park. Up until that game, though, the Hammers had not always been so convincing in their performances – despite remaining unbeaten in their first 12 league and cup matches – and the early games prompted mumblings of discontent among the supporters. "The fans were frustrated and annoyed and they had every right to be," said Julian in their defence after the Watford fixture. "It was another bad performance and although confidence is okay we've still got problems with match fitness. The lads said afterwards they didn't fancy me for the penalty – and I have to admit I mis-hit it!"

> "If you're getting a couple of grand a week and they're paying your wages, the fans are entitled to have a pop at you"

Billy Bonds complained that the team "didn't play well again" after the beating of Stoke, while the draw with Sheffield Wednesday had Dicks admitting: "The boss had a real go at us and we deserved it."

Dicksy's response gave a good indication of his general view towards the fans. "They pay good money to watch you play and if you don't perform well they've got a right to slag you off," he insists. "I've always thought that. If you're getting a couple of grand a week and they're paying your wages, the fans are entitled to have a pop at you."

The fact the Hammers remained unbeaten during this spell inspired its own

In trouble again... Julian picks up another booking, against Middlesbrough.

confidence, though, and the hammering of Hull had one paper claiming Dicks had *'produced one of the most compelling solo displays of his career. He sets all the standards, tackling like a demon, charging into attack and shooting on sight.'*

It was his second goal of the game that made the biggest impression on Julian. "I played the ball to Georgie Parris, who ran about 40 yards. Because he's quite slow I overtook him and he knocked it back to me for me to round the 'keeper and put the ball in the net. A good game that!"

One goal Dicks would prefer not be reminded about was the own-goal he conceded in the team's 2-1 win in the second leg of the Rumbelows Cup second round tie versus Stoke. *'Skipper Dicks committed defensive suicide to gift Third Division Stoke a shock lead,'* wrote one tabloid the next day to redden his cheeks a little.

And once again, the habit of picking up yellow cards increased his embarrassment. The booking received at Middlesbrough back on August 25 meant he was the first player to be booked in the league in the new season – and three more bookings followed by the time he left the pitch at Bristol City on October 13.

"I know I've got a problem with my temper but I just can't change," he admitted. "West Ham hoped that making me captain would sort out the problem, but it doesn't seem to have happened, does it? I've tried to change but it affects my game. I've spoken to Billy Bonds about it and he understands because he was a similar type of player. But I've always maintained that I will learn from experience because I am still very young."

As West Ham's fans headed back to London after their team's 1-1 draw at Ashton Gate, however, little did they know that the Bristol City game would have far greater consequences on Julian's career than producing just another booking...

CHAPTER 13

CROCKED!

THE 13th day of October, 1990 could not have proved unluckier for Julian. His yellow card and the two points dropped against Bristol City were insignificant compared to the injury incident in the second half of the match.

"I remember it clearly," says Jimmy Quinn, who was nearby. "He was in his own half and the ball was running out of play when he went to clear it up the line and he just continued over the touchline and went over the big bank."

Certainly, Julian will never forget the moment. "There was a two or three-inch dip where the pitch ends and my left foot went off the edge. I never felt any pain but my knee didn't feel right – it felt all limp and loose. There were only about five or 10 minutes to go so I stayed on but afterwards it started to swell up."

The fact that he stayed on says so much about the kind of player Julian is. "That was typical of Dicksy," claims Ian Bishop. "His knee had popped out but he came back and tried to carry on, which you could never imagine anybody else doing. But when he went down you knew something was wrong – that's just the type of fellow he is."

By the time Julian met up with his family – he was back in his home town, remember – the problem had become even more apparent. "We walked into town with him and by that time he could hardly walk," says his father Ron, while mum Carol (who was now living in London) recalls her son complaining of the pain. "We'd taken two cars of fans down to Bristol and said we'd give them a tour of the town and take them to a few pubs while we were down there. We watched the game, went back up to my mum and dad's, walked in and said that our Ju would be up later. As soon as he got through the door he said, 'Mum, me knee hurts!' There were all these grown blokes in the living room looking at Julian complaining to his mum that his knee hurt!"

Yet, despite the knee being examined, Julian played in the next game at Swindon, needing to come off after just 38 minutes. "I went in for a tackle and my knee just locked on me," he recalls.

The first the public knew that there was a risk of Dicks missing games for the club came when stories appeared in newspapers following the Swindon game, suggesting a cartilage operation could well be required. "Julian has been told to crash on and if the knee goes it goes," Billy Bonds was quoted as saying. "Chances of that are 50-50 but it seems more likely than not that he will have to have an op, which means we'll be without him for at least a month."

> "The boy needed an operation there and then. It was obvious to myself but I wasn't in a position to say anything. But for people to have ignored it was not professional enough" – JOHN GREEN

West Ham's current physio-therapist, John Green, was just about to replace Rob Jenkins, the team physio at the time, and while spending some time at the club prior to his official starting date he observed a discussion about Julian's troublesome knee. "Billy Bonds, Rob, Julian and a few other medical people were in the room and I was just standing and watching at the back. I was horrified, to be honest, because the boy needed an operation there and then. It was obvious to myself but I wasn't in a position to say anything.

"It was my opinion that he'd ruptured his ligaments and torn his cartilage at the Bristol game. I could tell just by the way they were moving Julian's knee around, without really knowing what they were doing – the knee was so lax when it was moved about and he had a lot of swelling on it. And for people to have ignored it was not professional enough.

"I'm not really convinced he'd actually seen the club doctor at that point in time. The first thing I heard at the training ground was Rob Jenkins telling Bill and assistant Ronnie Boyce that everything was going to be okay and that he just needed to rest it – which was obviously not the case."

Pushing it to the limit... Julian slides in on Swindon's Tom Jones in the game after he'd injured his knee. He lasted just 38 minutes.

Sickener for Dicks

By LEE CLAYTON

WEST HAM skipper Julian Dicks could face **A YEAR** out of football after badly tearing a knee ligament.

The 22-year-old Hammers ace will have an operation after Christmas to repair the ligament — and will not play again this season.

It is a massive blow to the Second Division leaders who have also lost Ian Bishop and Alvin Martin through injury for their hectic Christmas programme.

And manager Billy Bonds confessed: "It's a terrible jolt. I feel sorry for the lad. You just cannot replace a player of his quality."

Dicks saw a specialist on Monday after breaking down during his comeback for the reserves against Reading last Thursday.

And he said: "When I was told I wouldn't play again all season I was sick. The specialist also said I might not make the start of next season and I know it could be as long as a year."

But Dicks vowed: "I'll be back." Now boss Bonds is now hoping to sign on-loan Tottenham full-back Chris Hughton permanently.

Nowadays, most clubs employ chartered physios such as Green, who are diagnostic practitioners in their own right and who can accurately assess problems and refer injured parties direct to the surgeon. Before the nineties, however, it was felt that some were still operating in the dark ages in terms of their medical set-up – as indicated by the Dicks scenario.

"One of the problems was that Rob Jenkins had no qualifications at all," admits Green. "He was not a chartered physiotherapist and hadn't done any courses. Someone like Rob, without those qualifications, wouldn't make that diagnosis – they would probably see a swollen knee and think he's just sprained the ligaments. But there are specific tests, which if you are qualified you would automatically do, and if they are positive they give you the answer that, with all due respect, was pretty obvious – there was a torn ligament.

"Afterwards I could have kicked myself because I thought that perhaps I should have had a quiet word with someone and said that, in my opinion, he shouldn't play. I told Julian that afterwards and he admitted that he didn't feel he should have played. But that's what Julian is like – he's very stoic and if the manager turns round and says the physio thinks he can play and he needs him to, he's going to try."

And try he did, in the home match against Blackburn Rovers on October 24. "I had a fitness test before the game and I was doing block tackles with Billy on the pitch and I felt okay," recalls Julian. "So I played, but around 10 minutes from the end of the game I went up for a header and as I came down the knee buckled again. Then I knew there was a problem."

Limping off in the 78th minute of West Ham's 1-0 win (their thirteenth undefeated game in the league), Dicks faced up to the likelihood of an operation. "It looks almost certain the cartilage will have to come out," said Bonds after the match. "It's a big blow because Julian is a wholehearted performer, who would play on crutches if you asked him."

Dicks then went to see Brian Roper, West Ham's club doctor, to have the nature of the required surgery diagnosed. "They put a microscope in my knee and told me I needed a cartilage operation," says Julian. "I thought, 'I'll be playing again in six

119

weeks – no problem.' So I went in for the operation and afterwards, as I was coming round from the anaesthetic, Roper was standing over me. He said, 'I've done your cartilage – your meniscus – but your lateral ligament has snapped and your posterior is torn.' He said he'd left them because it was an old injury. So I thought, 'He's the surgeon, he knows what he's on about' – so that was that."

Julian's operation took place on October 31, as the Hammers were heading to Oxford for a dismal 2-1 Rumbelows Cup defeat. It was John Green's second day in his new capacity and he absorbed the surgery that took place on the player's left knee. "Brian Roper did what's called an arthrotomy, which is a very old-fashioned technique of doing a cartilage operation. Nowadays players have key-hole surgery, which means they're back in next to no time, but Brian didn't believe in the modern techniques because he hadn't been brought up with them.

"But Roper was in charge of Julian and the way the club looked at it was that the consultant made all the decisions and the physio just did what he was told. I was told to ignore the ligament injury, just to rehabilitate him as well as we could, get his quads and his hamstrings as strong as possible and he'd be okay."

Green felt that the chances of any player recovering from cruciate ligament injury without surgery, by relying purely on the strengthening of the muscles, was remote, to say the least. "I'd never heard of a player get away with it," he says. Green's confidence in Roper was also diminished when the surgeon diagnosed that Julian's anterior cruciate was damaged (rather than the posterior cruciate, as Julian's memory suggests). "In my assessment, it was his posterior cruciate that was damaged," confirms the physio.

After missing just six Second Division games for the Hammers (in which they'd accumulated 16 points, with Tottenham's Chris Hughton coming in at left-back on loan – and who would eventually join on a free transfer), however, Julian announced that things were going well – having installed a punchbag in his garage on which to take out his frustration – and that he was preparing to make a comeback in the reserve game against Reading on December 6. After initially being ruled out until Christmas time, it surprised many to see Julian start the game against the Royals. But his knee lasted less than 15 minutes.

"We took him off and Bill basically agreed that it was obvious to everyone that what I'd been saying was right," says John Green. "Julian was absolutely livid because he knew he'd wasted the last two months. He could have had the right operation done and been well into his rehab."

Julian was indeed annoyed and declared his refusal to have anything more to do with Brian Roper. "I told the club that I wasn't prepared to see Roper again and that I wanted to see somebody else. They said I couldn't do that. I said, 'I'll pay for it myself, I don't care – it's my career. If I want to go and see somebody else I will, regardless of what you say.'"

Green had set about trying to get Julian to another surgeon, but started to encounter political problems. "It was difficult because no other surgeon would see him without Brian Roper's permission," he says. "And, in the end, I went to the club and said, 'Look, I'm having problems.' And they admitted that it had gone on long enough, said I could take him to who I wanted to and that they would deal with Brian Roper."

Hence Julian and his physio found themselves going to see consultant John King at the London Independent Hospital in Mile End on New Year's Eve. "John King just looked at his knee and said, 'Basically, you've ruptured your posterior cruciate ligament, you've had a cartilage operation which has been done in a very bad way, in that the whole of the cartilage has been taken out rather than just the damaged piece being trimmed up, and as a result of that your knee is now very lax and you need it repaired," explains Green.

Julian's account of the meeting is a rather more blunt: "He was straight as a die and said that my knee was f***ed!" He said, 'You're going to be out for well over a year.' I can remember him saying it. It rocked me back and made me feel sick – literally. He said it was 50/50 whether I would ever play again."

John Green instantly recognised the impact such news had on Julian. "I'll always remember his face when John King swore at him and said, 'We're not f***ing messing around here, Julian. This is a nasty injury.' He obviously didn't expect the consultant to swear at him. That made Julian sit up and take notice and he gained a lot of respect for the surgeon then."

> "I'll always remember his face when John King swore at him and said, 'We're not f***ing messing around here, Julian. This is a nasty injury.'" – JOHN GREEN

The surgery required was also complicated by the fact that Julian had continued playing on the injury after the Bristol City match and then attempted a comeback after the removal of the cartilage. "There was a lot of damage to the other structures in the knee that are there just as secondary support and when they opened him up blood just poured out of his knee," reveals Green, who was present at the operation which took place on January 22, following the initial arthroscopy (the wash-out of the knee) a few weeks earlier.

Wife Kay and team-mates Jimmy Quinn and Trevor Morley paid Julian a visit during his week at the Independent – but it wasn't a pretty sight that faced them. "It was my birthday," recalls Kay. "Jackie Quinn had the girls for me because they were still only little and Jimmy drove me up to see Julian at the hospital. It was terrible. He was in agony. His knee was such a mess. The surgeon came in and said, 'You're not in too much pain then. You haven't bled to death!' His leg was in a contraption that kept moving it so that he didn't get fluid on it – it was terrible."

Jimmy Quinn was also disturbed at what he saw. "I could have cried for him because he was in absolute agony," he says. "It was frightening. It takes a brave man to come through all that to play again and achieve what he has."

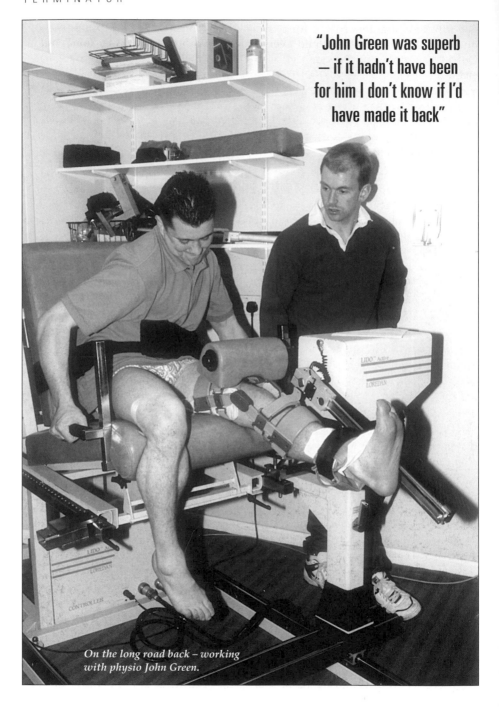

"John Green was superb
– if it hadn't have been
for him I don't know if I'd
have made it back"

*On the long road back – working
with physio John Green.*

As Julian commenced the long and arduous recovery programme, the big question was whether he would ever set foot on a pitch as a professional again. Despite his public insistence that – like Arnold Schwarzenegger's *Terminator* character – "I'll be back!", Dicks had genuine fears that his career could well be over, with the surgeon's words reverberating around in a mind becoming clouded with depression after the trauma of the operation. "I was just thinking, 'Will I ever play again?'" he admits. "I was only 22 and my career could have been over. What would I do? I was really worried. I was wondering what else I could put my mind to and when I thought about it, I realised there was nothing!"

The initial months out of the game were consequently very difficult for Dicks. "For the first 12 weeks he was pretty awful," says Green. "He was very miserable because it just seemed like forever to him. The lads were doing well (going 21 games unbeaten on their way to promotion and also reaching the FA Cup semi-finals before referee Keith Hackett helped Forest on their way to a 4-0 win by sending off West Ham's Tony Gale) and he was struggling."

Julian's father, understanding fully the implications of the injury and subsequent surgery, shared his son's concern but remained diplomatic when talking to him. "I remember him telling me he probably wouldn't be able to play for a year. He was gutted," says Ron. "When he told me it was cruciate ligaments I thought he could be struggling to play again. He never actually said that to me but I thought it might be the case. I never told him, but if it had been 10 years earlier he certainly wouldn't have played again."

Once the cast on the knee was removed, after a short period, Julian had to adapt to life wearing a brace, which was gradually adjusted over a period of 10 weeks to allow greater movement of the joint. During this time, in which he also started his first work with weights to strengthen the movement in the knee, Dicks managed to put his fears to the back of his mind and focus himself on the mission in front of him. "It was hard but I had a lot of help," he says. "John Green was superb – if it hadn't have been for him I don't know if I'd have made it back. I'd do my work with the weights and think, 'F--- it!' It was weights after weights after weights and I'd think to myself,

The brace is on...

'I'm not doing it any more.' But John would come in and say, 'Look, you've got to do it or you won't make it.'"

As far as Green was concerned, however, Julian's rehab – which also allowed for him to start playing golf after three months, helping to shape a routine for his week – was relatively straight forward. "For someone like Julian, once he got his head round things, it wasn't a problem. People may think that he's a bit awkward and, sure, in pre-season sometimes he can be a bit lazy with his running. But he wasn't lazy during his rehab – he knew what he had to do.

"The biggest problem I thought he had was that people just seemed to forget about him. He turned up at Chadwell Heath one day and they'd cancelled training and nobody had even told him. I was in but I wasn't expecting to see him, because I think the lads had gone on a golf day. He wasn't being informed and had gone from being club captain to being basically a leper. That was the attitude in the club towards the injury.

> "He had gone from being club captain to being basically a leper. That was the attitude in the club towards the injury" – JOHN GREEN

"I don't think chairman Martin Cearns really showed him a lot of attention. Or Billy Bonds. I think Bill felt that you just got on with it when you're injured and if you weren't in the squad you weren't important. I know Bill cared about him a lot but I don't think he felt that injuries were something that you worried about. Whereas I think you'd see a different attitude now. The management is a lot better now."

Never has Julian's relationship with West Ham been more strained than during the first nine months of 1990. It was an experience that still leaves Dicks slightly resentful of those individuals who turned their backs on him when he needed their support most. "The chairman and the directors just blanked me," accuses Julian. "I'd be walking up the aisle to the Ron Greenwood Lounge and they'd look at me and look away. They just totally f***ing blanked me. When you're thinking that you might not play again it just makes you feel like you're not wanted."

Such attitudes only served to harden Dicks' resolve and determination to play again, But there were other problems to encounter, though. One particular bone of contention some way into the recovery period was the discussion about Julian being allowed an automatic car, so that he could drive himself into the training ground and up to London for his frequent visits to the Devonshire Hospital (just off Harley Street) for sessions on the Isokinetic machine.

"I obviously couldn't drive my own manual car, so I asked the club if they could get me an automatic," he reveals. "They said, 'We can't do that.' I thought, 'I've put my career on the line for you lot and you won't help me.' That was a big blow. I said, 'Well, what happens when I've got to go up to the hospital?' They said that they'd get a taxi and pay for that because they've got an account. So I'd get a cab, which

On yer bike! Julian was presented with a bike to aid recovery – but was refused an automatic car!

would pick me up from Billericay, take me all the way up to London, wait for me outside the hospital and bring me all the way home. It was like a hundred quid a time! I thought, 'Well, they did tell me to get a taxi.'

"There was one occasion when I was up there for quite a while and the taxi fare was £150. The next day Billy had the bill and said, 'What's this?' I said, 'Well, you told me to get a taxi.' He said, 'Can't you jump on the tube?' I said, 'I've got my knee in a f***ing brace and you want me to jump on the tube?' I told him that I wasn't doing that. He said, 'Well, you can't keep doing this.' So I told him he'd have to sort something out. So Charlie, the security man at the training ground, used to take me up there – and he's the worst driver you've ever seen!"

John Green was also disappointed that the club had not arranged a car to give Julian some mobility. "At that time that would have been a big boost to Julian," he says. "Now, in the regime we've got with Peter Storrie, Harry Redknapp and Frank Lampard, that wouldn't have been a problem. It's just a different attitude altogether."

Julian and Kay had also noticed a 'different attitude' from some so-called friends. "Once you're not playing and getting them free tickets they disappear," says Julian of certain 'acquaintances' who Kay had always been cynical about. "It used to drive me mad because you get a lot of people who want to know you because of what you do," she adds. "If Julian was a bin man or window cleaner they wouldn't have wanted to know. I could probably see that more than he could and it used to really annoy me."

More startling, however, was the discovery that a 'mystery' fellow Hammer was spreading the word that Dicks was finished, with no hope of ever making a return. "It's only through what you'd hear people say, like they'd tell me that a player had said I'd never play again. And people believed it because it came from another player. I used to go out, although I still had the brace on and just had to wear baggy trousers over it. Somebody said, 'I'm sorry about the news.' And I said, 'What?' And they said, 'About you never playing again.' I thought, 'You what?!' You expect supporters to *think* you might not play again, but not for a fellow pro to confirm it."

Ian Bishop well appreciated what kind of impact such gossip would have on Julian, having seen former team-mates endure the emotional suffering of career-threatening injury. "I could understand his feelings," he says. "When you do your cruciate ligaments it's a battle for anybody to try and get back. I've had friends who've damaged ligaments – Paul Lake at Manchester City, for example – people who've made three or four comebacks and still not been right. So there was enough pressure on Dicksy as there was. I don't think he needed other people to imply he wasn't going to play again. But if anybody was going to come back it was going to be him. He was down for a while but he's got such character."

Perhaps the 'mystery' pro had every reason to doubt Julian's return – after all, injury had ruined plenty of other players' careers. "Sometimes people always assume the worst in football," concedes John Green. "And perhaps that's not a bad thing to assume, bearing in mind the type of physio and medical back-up at West Ham in the past – a lot of people had been finished with injuries that perhaps shouldn't have been. People like Stewart Robson were drastically messed up, by Arsenal's doctors and by ours. A lot of players had been badly mis-handled – Alvin Martin (who missed 16 months of football with an Achilles injury from December 1990 to April 1992 and then another 10 months from January 1993), for example. When we took him to a foot specialist instead of Brian Roper, what had taken 10 months with one foot under Roper only took eight weeks with the other under the specialist."

Roper had been involved with West Ham for some 20 years and didn't take too kindly to a young physio walking into the club for the first time and suggesting he wasn't good enough. "He summoned me to Harley Street after John King got involved and basically told me he'd have me struck off," recalls Green. "He was very heavy-handed with me, but I just said, 'Sorry, the club have given me their backing and if you've got a grievance you should take it up with them.'"

With the club about to ask Roper to resign as the 1990-91 season progressed (during which time they searched for a replacement), the doctor passed away. John King was lecturing all over the world and, although he would be available for surgery, he could not offer the necessary commitment to the club. Upon the recommendation of many – King included – Tom McAuliffe was appointed as the new club consultant, with Dr Ges Steinbergs later being recruited as club GP, as West Ham absorbed the lessons of the past.

The negative rumours circulating at this time only made Dicks doubly determined to succeed, and prove the doubters wrong. This meant working even harder and even during the summer months, when the rest of the West Ham players were on holiday, Julian still went into Chadwell Heath every day. To help alleviate the boredom, he bought a personal stereo so that he could listen to the likes of Guns

N' Roses while working with the weights. And, of course, he still played lots of golf. "The children used to think Julian was a golfer," laughs Kay. "They were only two and I don't think they knew what their dad did. If anybody had asked them they'd have probably just said, 'Play golf!'"

With early potential pitfalls such as infections successfully avoided, John Green was more than satisfied with the progress Julian was making. "I was saying to him, quietly between the two of us, 'There's no way you're not coming back from this. Everything's gone well, the operation has been superb, the swelling has gone down quickly, the knee's looking good and every time we go back to see John King we're getting a positive response. Now you can do this, now we can step up and move on.' And Julian could see as well, from going on the Isokinetic machine, how things were improving."

Despite his determination to succeed, the rehab was a long, drawn-out process and any improvement had to be worked hard for. Inevitably, Julian had his down days, which obviously had an affect on Kay at home. "It was horrible. He used to get really grumpy and be not very pleasant to live with, but at the end of the day it was understandable," she says. "If he was having a bad day you felt like you had to keep the girls occupied. You'd be falling over yourself to make him happy but it wouldn't make any difference. I used to go up to Birmingham for the weekend sometimes because we were driving each other up the wall. The girls were busy in the week with playschool and everything, so I'd just go up on Friday and come back Sunday. There was nothing you could do for him anyway.

> "It was horrible. He used to get really grumpy" – Kay Dicks

"Everybody used to feel so sorry for him, but he's not really the kind of person you can sit down and talk to. I tried to talk to him sometimes but, no matter what you said, it didn't make any difference. If he was in a bad mood that was it, you may as well have forgotten it and hope he'd wake up in a better one the next day. He was very stubborn."

As understanding as Kay tried to be with her husband, she could never have fully comprehended what was taking place in his head. She accompanied him to home games, sensing his frustration at not being able to play ("to lose a year in such a short career is like losing 10 years in any other job," she offers) and witnessing first-hand Julian's growing feelings of alienation. "Once you're injured, it's just frightening," she says. "I used to get so annoyed. It's all right when you're doing well but when you're down and out nobody wants to know. I never had one phone call from the club. The only person who ever phoned me was John Green, who was absolutely brilliant, but that was it. Julian went through a phase where he was going out drinking a lot and it was just a nightmare. But you couldn't blame him for it. It was when he needed support more than ever and he wasn't really getting any.

"I just tried to pretend it wasn't happening, to block it out and think positively. But obviously you worry, especially with two young children. But I thought if anybody was going to come back from something like that it would be Julian, because he's so determined."

Mum Carol was aware of the impact of the injury on her son. "It hit him very hard – he did go very moody then. Because all he ever wanted to do was play football," she says. "People used to say to me, 'Oh, he'll never play again.' And I'd say, 'He will!' I always said he would play again and that he'd come back harder. I can remember saying it to a guy called Brian Biggs at work. His son was training to be a physiotherapist and he was saying, 'Oh no, my son's said this and that...' and I said, 'I'm telling you, Brian, he'll be back and he'll come back harder.' And Brian has never brought it up since."

Carol's most distinct memory of that time, however, is of the screw in her son's knee: "I can remember Kay playing with it. I said, 'What are you doing?' and Kay said, 'Tightening his screw!' Later on he had the screw taken out and he now keeps it in a plastic tube. I was looking at it once and went to take it out when I realised it still had skin on it and dropped it!"

Of course, there were occasions when Carol had to give her son some encouragement. "I think he was struggling mentally, deep down, but he wouldn't let people know," she says. "The more that people were writing him off, the more determined he became that he was going to do it. I remember when he went to the home games on his crutches. He'd get the biggest cheer of the day from the fans. They didn't care about the team, it was Julian they were more interested in seeing.

"The club treated him like s**t. They did him wrong... That's when you learn who your friends are" – CAROL DICKS

"But the club treated him like s**t. They did him wrong. And they didn't do anything to try and make it up to him either. That's when you learn who your friends are – some people just didn't want to know."

The people that did want to know, among others, were the Quinns. "I saw Jackie nearly every day," says Kay. "Her and Jimmy were brilliant, especially with the girls. There are not many people who would want to look after a couple of two-year-olds, but Jackie would always have them. I was really upset when they moved away." Other supportive friends included Keith and Wendy Berry, who lived in the next road in Billericay. "I'd probably have gone mad if it had not been for them," adds Kay.

Jimmy Quinn, who saw more of Julian than any other player at the time because of living so close by (and who also helped drive him in to London from time to time), had no doubts that he would successfully return. "As far as I'm concerned he was always very positive. Of course, we tried to encourage him as much as we could, telling him to keep doing his work and he'd be back sooner than he thought. But if Julian said he was coming back, it was as simple as that. A lot of other people would've folded and packed it in, but he knew right from the start that he was going to come back and for that he deserves a lot of credit."

During the latter part of the 1990-91 season, Julian wasn't the only Hammer to be sidelined through injury. Striker Trevor Morley was also forced out of action in March, although through rather unusual circumstances after being stabbed in the stomach in a 'domestic' incident. "Bish came in the day after it happened and said, 'Trevor's been stabbed,'" recalls Julian. "At first we thought he meant in a pub brawl or something. After the incident Trev went round to the next door neighbour's house and asked if they could call an ambulance. He told us afterwards that he could feel himself drifting away."

Typically, though, despite the seriousness of the wound to Morley, which ruled him out of nine games (including the FA Cup quarter-final tie against Everton – won 2-1 in his absence), his fellow colleagues still found time to have a joke at his expense. "John Green's got a skeleton in his physio room and Trevor walked in there one day and found all these knives stuck in it!" grins Julian. "He wasn't too happy about it at the time but he laughed about it later."

As for Julian's own rehab, his routine later started to include afternoon visits to the Collier Row Rollerbowl for use of their gym equipment, such as the leg machines, bikes, and stepping and rowing machines. As they worked together, John Green became aware of a significant moment in Julian's recovery. "In the end, Julian said to me, 'I crossed the road the other day and I just sort of broke into a jog without realising it – and I was surprised that I could actually jog.' At that point we started walking him on the treadmill, building up the speed and adjusting the incline. He trained for about another three weeks with his brace on – he was running and twisting and turning well but just to give that extra support we had a lighter brace done for him. It was easy to for him to move with that and he joined in training quite successfully with that. Then one day he turned round and said he didn't want the brace any more."

By that time it was the end of September and, back in the land of the living, West Ham had just embarked on their first campaign back in the First Division. With only one win in the first eight games (and a less than convincing new left-back in Mitchell Thomas, who'd been brought in during the summer for £500,000 from Spurs), Hammers fans (who'd spent the best part of the year writing letters of support to Julian) were eager to see their favourite return. While Green had initially targeted Christmas as the time for a comeback, the public had been warned not to expect Dicks back until February 1992. Not surprisingly, the *Sunday Sport* went one step further and declared in October that *'the brilliant full-back looks certain to miss all this season'*. The more informed papers were quickly confirming the progress Julian was making, stating that he was three months ahead of schedule. Green was eager to keep the reins on him, though. "There was a tendency for Julian to think, 'Right, I've trained a couple of times, now I want to go out and play.' I said, 'No, I think you should train for at least three weeks without playing.'"

Telemessage®

MPC8095 LMY2325 PBD0003 P13 1366 2740ROMF   22 NOV 1991/1633

Westham United Football Club
Green Street
Upton Park
London E13 9AZ

22 November 1991

TELEMESSAGE
JULIAN DICKS
WESTHAM UNITED TRAINING GROUND
SAVILLE ROAD
CHADWELL HEATH
ROMFORD

        BEST WISHES, NICE TO HAVE YOU BACK.
        FROM

        ALL THE STAFF AT
        WESTHAM UNITED F.C.

As the sight of a ball again began to focus in Julian's mind, his spirits picked up dramatically. "Once he started training again he was a lot better," confirms Kay. "I used to get really cross because around that time a few people who hadn't spoken to us for God knows how long were suddenly back on the scene again, phoning up for tickets. Julian would always be polite, but I wouldn't have anything to do with them. At least we knew where we stood."

Training during October and the early part of November, with a hole in his knee that looked like an eye socket without an eye in it (as another player stated at the time) as the evidence of what he'd been through, Julian pencilled in his first comeback game – a reserve outing against Ipswich Town at the Terence McMillan Stadium in Stratford, East London on November 27. "People were ringing up the club to ask where the game was," recalls Julian, "and somebody there had said it was at Upton Park. So a lot of people went over there instead!"

The Ipswich game was the acid test. As so many had said during Dicks' 13-and-a-half months out of the game, the only time he'd really know if he had what it took to play again would be when he was actually back out there, giving it one hundred per cent. "I think it was with him, because you wouldn't tackle any of the boys on the training ground as hard as you tackle in a game," says John Green. "When he made his first tackle at the Terence McMillan Stadium, there was a huge cheer from the ground as he clattered some bloke. The bloke stayed on the ground and Julian just got up and ran off. That was it then – he had no reaction afterwards."

Nobody was more apprehensive than Kay Dicks as Julian attempted his comeback. "I had the girls with me, my dad was down and I was dreading it," she admits. "I didn't want Julian to kick the ball – I just wanted him to run around for an hour-and-a-half. The thought is always at the back of your mind that he's never going to be the same player, or that he'd not have the same guts as before. He went in for a couple of tackles but it was as if he'd never been out. It was unbelievable – it was the same old Julian."

But Dicks had decided that he wasn't going to go into the game to merely pussy-foot around. "That was the test," he insists. "If I was going to test it properly, I had to get stuck in - and I did get stuck in. And I came through the game with no problems." Much to the delight of his family, in particular, although Ron Dicks admitted that he was "worried" about the game. But apart from Julian reporting "a couple of twinges", he was fine.

Billy Bonds was full of admiration for the way in which his player battled through and made a return. "Personally speaking, I think that injury would have finished a lot of players, certainly 75% of the players that I know. That was a very, very bad injury," says his former boss, who admits that he was never really aware of what was going on in Julian's head during that period. "He's got his own way of doing things and you didn't really know what he was going through. He wasn't that outgoing – maybe he spoke to one or two of the players a bit more about it – but you knew he was mentally tough as well as physically tough, so you always felt he'd probably be able to get over it."

That's not to say Bonds didn't occasionally fear for his player's future. "You always fear because, from a selfish point of view, he was one of our best players and we wanted him back," he admits. "And from a personal point of view you don't want to see a fellow's career end, especially when he's got young children. But he came through it and never missed a day's training after that."

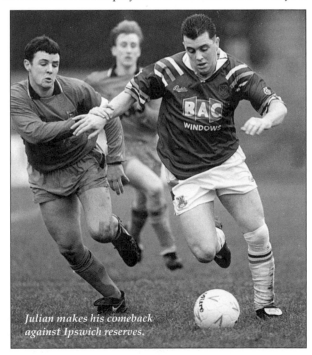

Julian makes his comeback against Ipswich reserves.

The fanzine's favourite returns to the action...

CHAPTER 14

FROM BILLY BONDS TO SILLY BONDS

TYPICALLY of Julian, his first-team comeback game against Sheffield United on December 21, 1991, saw him make an instant impact – unfortunately at both ends of the pitch. Despite showing no signs of having problems with his knee, it looked as if his big day was going to be spoiled by his 82nd-minute error, which allowed a through-ball to escape him and resulted in Brian Deane putting the Blades ahead. Just four minutes later, though, the Hammers were controversially awarded a penalty – and it was Julian who stepped up to crash it home.

"I remember just picking the ball up and putting it down and taking it," says Julian, who took advantage of the fact that £400,000 striker Mike Small (who'd been purchased at the beginning of the season and started taking the penalties in Dicks' absence) had been substituted. "It was a great feeling after being out for so long and the response from the fans sent shivers down my spine."

The supporters had given Dicksy a hero's welcome, acknowledging his courage and commitment to wear the claret and blue shirt again. Not only that, but they knew that if the Hammers were to stand half a chance of surviving in the top flight in that first season back, they were going to need him – instantly and at his best.

It didn't look good, though. With the likes of Kenny Brown, Tim Breacker and Mitchell Thomas coming into the backline during Julian's period out of the picture, the team had secured just four wins in 20 league games and the point against Sheffield United was the only one they picked up in seven games – the last of which saw Julian grab his second penalty since his return in the 3-1 home defeat by title-chasing Leeds United. "Mike Small wanted to take the kick," recalls Julian, "but so did I, so he said, 'Fair enough.' Their striker, Lee Chapman, tried to put me off by saying I'd put it over the bar, but I just kept my head down and stuck it away."

Dicks played hero *and* villain in the FA Cup third round meeting with non-league Farnborough Town – who conceded home advantage in the interests of crowd safety and their bank balance. Not that it made much difference, with the part-timers earning a creditable draw at Upton Park. Julian scored his first goal from open play since his return with a 66th-minute 15-yard drive that should have set up victory,

Julian's late penalty equaliser against Sheffield United in his First Team comeback match.

only for him to literally 'hand' Farnborough an equaliser after handling Dean Coney's shot in the penalty box.

The day was another landmark in Julian's career, with him reclaiming the captaincy from midfielder Ian Bishop, who'd worn the armband in his absence. Bish, although probably expecting the news, was none too happy about the situation. "Billy called Bish into the office and told him he was giving it back to me," says Julian. "Bish was quite bitter about it – he told me that's how he felt – even though he obviously didn't blame me."

Just weeks later, press stories started to emerge, claiming that Dicks was ready to quit the Hammers. *'Dicks: I'm Fed-Up'* was one national newspaper headline, above a story that claimed that Julian was disillusioned at Upton Park and was ready to quit following the silence from the club regarding his contract (which was due to expire at the end of the season). "I have played my heart out for West Ham since I joined them. I have worked my way back from injury two months ahead of schedule and I am bitterly disappointed that they have not even discussed a contract," he was quoted as saying in the story.

"I wasn't fed up," argues Julian. "I just wanted to get my contract sorted out and get on with my game. When you've only got so much left on it you wonder if they're going to offer you another one."

The comments in public certainly did the trick – within a week the club responded and the media spent the new few weeks speculating how much the new three-and-a-half year deal was worth. Despite the papers suggesting the deal would probably amount to somewhere between £400,000 and £750,000 in total, the true figure actually exceeded the estimates, being nearer £800,000 in reality.

While Dicks had pressed the issue, leaving the club with little choice but to put together a favourable deal for him (to have risked losing him would have been a

Julian celebrates his first goal from open play since his comeback - in the FA Cup meeting with non-league Farnborough.

Dicks: So lucky I didn't see red

By JACK STEGGLES

West Ham 1 Oldham 0

ANGRY Oldham players insisted Julian Dicks should have been sent off after a bust-up with Paul Bernard.

And Dicks, who responded to a Bernard challenge from the Latics midfielder, concedes they had a point.

"I suppose I was a bit lucky," admitted the skipper, who signed a new three-year contract immediately after the game.

Angry

"I got angry because Bernard caught me so high it has left me with stud marks all over my chest.

"That tackle I had gone in for was one of the worst I have ever seen and if I had gone their fella would have had to go with me.

"It looked bad for Dicks, who returned to first team action only six weeks ago after 14 months out with a serious knee injury.

For he had already been booked for a foul on Neil Adams when the flashpoint occurred.

But referee Keith Cooper settled for booking Bernard — and did not even speak to the Hammers full-back.

"It never crossed my mind to send Dicks off," said Cooper.

"I am certain he never threw a punch at Bernard. If he had done I would certainly have sent him off.

"And I settled for a booking for Bernard because his tackle was considered his tackle to be high, and dangerous, not malicious."

Dicks enjoyed the last laugh as Hammers clung on to a 34th minute Mitchell Thomas goal to boost their relegation fight.

■ Team mates try to restrain an angry Julian Dicks after he was the victim of a high challenge by the grounded Paul Bernard.

dreadful public relations move, especially in the light of the unrest between the fans and board following the attempted launch of the Bond Scheme, not to mention the poor team performances) his decision to sign – despite reported interest from former team-mate Liam Brady, then managing Celtic – was a display of loyalty on his part to West Ham. Many players, particularly in more recent times, would have been eager to jump ship in such a situation, especially with the club's relegation almost a formality.

Despite the grim picture, with the team rooted at the bottom of the table with a paltry 20 points from 23 games, Julian showed plenty of fighting spirit when talking about the position. "There will be people who might look at Hammers' position and say I should not have made such a commitment," he said. "But I think it shows my own belief that we won't go down at the end of the season. I missed out on all the promotion celebrations last summer and it's essential we avoid the drop."

It was tempting for some to doubt the sincerity of such words, particularly when survival was looking so unlikely, but Julian is adamant that such a positive stance was – as it is always – necessary. "I always genuinely believe that if we're not mathematically down there's always a chance," he insists.

Dicks displayed another sort of fight on the Upton Park pitch in the game against Oldham on February 1. And few could blame him, after the Latics' Paul Bernard flew in on Dicks with a wild lunge, missing his knee by the smallest of fractions. Retaliating instantly, the Hammers' left-back hurled himself at the grounded opponent, only to be dragged off by the mass of incoming bodies. "The ball was bouncing and as I went for it he came in with his foot up and just missed me. I didn't want another person putting me out – especially after what I'd been through – and it got to me," admits Julian. "Bernard was on the floor and I rushed over and got hold of him and said a few nice words."

> **"Bernard was on the floor and I rushed over and got hold of him and said a few nice words"**

With Dicks already having been booked earlier in the game, the press remarked on how he'd surprisingly managed to stay on the pitch after blatantly seeking retribution. "I suppose I was a bit lucky," said Julian after the game. "But it was one of the worst tackles I've ever seen and if I had gone their fella would have had to go with me."

Referee Keith Cooper denied taking a sympathetic approach to Dicks: "I am certain he never threw a punch at Bernard; if he had have done I would certainly have sent him off," he said. Yet it seemed obvious to most that the official had appreciated Julian's understandable anger and used his discretion, although the media felt he'd stretched that a little too far. *'The last 10 minutes was a grim Dicks show as he fended off retaliatory tackles and carried out a feud with any passing Oldham player. It was not a good example by the Hammers captain and it was a puzzle why the referee didn't take further action apart from a brief midfield lecture,'* wrote the *News Of The World* the next day.

"This was a big win, because we have some tough games coming up," said Billy Bonds after the 1-0 victory. He wasn't joking either – the Hammers proceeded to lose their next five league matches! Two of those – against Everton and Arsenal at home – will live in the memory of all those who attended, for all the wrong reasons.

When Dicks returned from injury, West Ham had just announced their intention to introduce 'The Hammers Bond' – a scheme which involved fans buying a bond (priced at £500, £750 and £975) in order to acquire the right to purchase a season ticket. The funds generated through the scheme would help pay for the redevelopment of Upton Park in the wake of the Taylor Report, which demanded all-seater stadia. Spending a reported £1-2million on the promotion of the scheme – with fans being sent detailed brochures explaining the concept, which threatened the sale of players (among other alternatives) if it was not successful – West Ham made an appalling error of judgement. It was an act of virtual blackmail that infuriated supporters (whipped up into a further frenzy by the campaigning of fanzine *Fortune's Always Hiding*), it showed scant regard for the faithful who'd stuck with the club through thick and thin, and it displayed little understanding of the nature of the

Julian retrieves the corner flag from a protesting fan during the game against Everton.

local support, while the timing (in a relegation season, following under-investment in the team) could not have been any worse.

The simmering bad feeling first overflowed after the 1-1 draw against Wimbledon at Upton Park on January 11, when an estimated 4,000 fans invaded the pitch after the game, demanding the scrapping of the Bond Scheme and the resignation of the West Ham board. It took up to two hours to empty Upton Park and the resulting publicity meant it was inevitable that more action would be follow. It did, during the match against Everton on February 29, when a demonstrator leapt over a wall, uprooted a corner flag and made his way to the centre-circle where he promptly plunged it into the ground and staged a sit-down protest.

> "I went to pick the flag up because everybody else just walked away. Actually, I pretended to stab him with it"

It was Julian who arrived at the scene first and the next day's papers were full of photographs depicting the left-back reclaiming West Ham's property. "I went to pick the flag up because everybody else just walked away," says Julian. "Actually, I pretended to stab him with it. I asked him what he was doing and he said he opposed the Bond Scheme. I said, 'We've got a football match going on – can't you make your protest afterwards, when the game's finished?' And a few more fans came on after that."

Another press photo showed Julian being confronted by an angry looking fan. "It's funny, because it looks like he's going to punch me," says Julian of the picture, "but the guy actually came up to me and said, 'I f***in' love you!' I just said, 'Oh, cheers.'"

"It looked like he was going to punch me, but the guy actually came up to me and said, 'I f***in' love you!' I just said, 'Oh, cheers.'"

The match – which Hammers lost 2-0 (although that seemed irrelevant) – was delayed for over eight minutes as police tried to clear the pitch. And the headlines next day were dominated by two players – one a present Hammer, the other a former one – who defended the supporters' view of the Bond Scheme.

'Julian Dicks and Tony Cottee amazingly supported the bitter Upton Park demo – even though they fear it will cost West Ham their First Division lives,' wrote one paper. 'The FA are bound to consider docking the club points...and that could seal relegation. Hundreds of fans streamed on a quarter of an hour from time. And bumbling West Ham have only themselves to blame. They have scored their biggest ever own-goal – the wretched and reviled Bond Scheme to raise money.'

"What has happened to the family club?" questioned Tony Cottee who'd faced the Hammers for Everton and witnessed the hostile scenes first-hand. "I could not believe what I was seeing. And what has happened to all the money they had from transfers, such as the £2 million they got for me? Of course I feel sympathy for the fans," he added, continuing to speak out against the scheme. " If you've got a family of four, how the hell are they meant to pay out for those bonds? From an outsider's point of view, it is quite unbelievable what is going on. It is very sad."

As a former West Ham player who still felt a great deal of empathy with the fans, Cottee was free to speak his mind on the disturbing events of that day. What wasn't seen to be so politically correct – at least by the West Ham hierarchy – was a current player backing the protests. But that's exactly what Dicks did in the aftermath of the game. "The fans are right. I agree with what they're doing," he was reported as saying. "It's not good for the club if it costs us points. But you can't ask ordinary people to pay out £975 to watch their football team before they've even bought a ticket. It's totally wrong."

Julian was indeed offended by the whole concept of the Bond Scheme. "Obviously I disagreed with it, because we were at the bottom and they were asking people to fork out £975 to watch a load of crap," he says. "It wouldn't have been so bad if we'd been at the top but we were struggling. And they spent nearly £2 million promoting the thing – you could have bought two good players for that!"

Dicksy's honesty when questioned by the media after the Everton game could not go unaddressed by the club and the subject was raised as soon as the players

"They were asking people to fork out £975 to watch a load of crap"

reported for training in the week. "On Monday morning Peter Storrie and Billy Bonds called us all in and said, 'You get on with the football and leave the rest to us.' They didn't single me out, they just

> "Julian wasn't the only one against it – I never backed the Bond Scheme either. I thought it was a diabolical liberty" – BILLY BONDS

said, 'Somebody has said things,' although they knew who it was. I said, 'You mean me, don't you?' and they said, 'Yes.' I told them that if I don't agree with something, then no matter what it's about, I'll say so. I didn't get fined but I got a bollocking for it."

As far as Peter Storrie and the rest of the board were concerned, though, the playing staff were in no position to air a point of view on the scheme. "All that was said to the players was that they shouldn't really air an opinion on something they didn't know the full facts about," says Storrie. "I think all players were just told to concentrate on football and put other things to one side. No-one was individually picked out – the squad was spoken to as a whole."

The Hammers Bond had put Billy Bonds in a difficult position. As manager of the club he was expected to act as an ambassador for the scheme and, when players backed the views of the fans whose protests were undermining the team's performances, he had to be seen to be taking action. The problem was that Bonds was totally against the fund raising venture as well.

"Julian wasn't the only one against it – I never backed the Bond Scheme either," Billy says. "I couldn't say anything because it was something the club was doing – I just had to sit on the fence and say nothing. To this day I've never said anything about it, but I was asked by the board to do certain things for the Bond Scheme which I refused point blankly to do. Nobody knows that. I was dead against it, so I would have shared Julian's views – I thought it was a diabolical liberty."

More than that, Bonds also blamed the Bond Scheme for destroying his team's hopes of First Division survival. "We were doing very well (19 points from 16 games) up to around November," he remembers. "We'd beaten Tottenham, won at Arsenal and drawn 0-0 at home to Liverpool, when we played superbly and Bruce Grobbelaar kept them in the game. Mike Small was going very well (having scored 13 goals). Then, all of a sudden, the Bond Scheme came out. I'm not saying it wouldn't have been a struggle, but I think we'd have survived that year otherwise.

"The Bond Scheme didn't help anybody because we were asking players to go out and play in an atmosphere that was very hostile. I remember the Everton game when somebody ran on and stuck the corner flag in the centre-circle. Some of the fans went over the top but generally you couldn't blame them for feeling the way they did. But it was very difficult for the players – nobody wanted to go out and play.

"The one thing about West Ham United Football Club was always its togetherness – the fans had supported the team through thick and thin and, even when the side was struggling, they knew when to get behind the players. But this was different. I was at West Ham 27 years and I've never known a year like it. It was just a nightmare season and the year deteriorated from the moment the Bond Scheme was announced."

The Everton debacle (which Tony Cottee remembered more for a clash with Julian – "There was one timely elbow I got towards the head region in that game and it was definitely from Dicksy. I don't think it was anything personal between him and me – he was just an aggressive type of player who would do things like that to put you off your game. And he got away with it, like a lot of hard men did in the late eighties and early nineties," says TC) was followed by a trip down to Southampton three days later and this time the fans' anger was vented at the team – for their dismal display in the 1-0 defeat. "What a load of rubbish!" was the cry and it was Dicks who backed the supporters again. "I heard the chants and sympathise with the fans," he said. "They paid £30 or £40 to come down and watch us lose and they're entitled to say what they like. When I was out injured it was those same people who kept me going. I'll never forget that and I'll always have time for them."

It was this kind of honesty that endeared the fans to Julian – as his mum Carol has always recognised. "He speaks up for them and gives it 110%," she says. "They'll never forget how he stuck up for them against the Bond Scheme. They still say that to me. They'll always back Julian, no matter what he does, because he backs them. He's never given up on the fans and they've never given up on him. He's honest. If he's asked something, he'll say what he thinks – right or wrong – because that's what he believes."

The Southampton game was followed by another 1-0 defeat – this time at Anfield (with Liverpool boss Graeme Souness declaring, "I'll be very disappointed if they go down – any team playing the way they do deserves to be in the First Division") – and then it was back to the intimidating atmosphere of Upton Park for the visit of Arsenal.

142

In a bid to avoid a repeat of the Everton game, the club drafted in an extra 100 police officers to take the total number on duty to 300. All was quiet, until Arsenal goalkeeper David Seaman realised he had two Hammers fans watching the game behind him – one laying and one sitting on his goal line! Not surprisingly, given West Ham's form at the time, the ball was up the other end with the Gunners on the attack, so it seemed like a good minute or so before the officials or anybody in authority realised the trespassers were there. Three more spectators then invaded the pitch and the game degenerated into yet another farce, with the result a formality (Arsenal won 2-0). "I think the fans had every right to protest," Julian states, "but not when the game was going on. They should have left it until after the games to protest. If people are running onto the pitch, everybody's concentration goes. It really didn't help."

> "Groves said to George Graham, 'I wanna come off!' But Graham just told him to get on with it as well!"

For all the rumpus over the Bond Scheme during the Gunners game, it was Dicks whose name dominated the headlines following his running battle with Perry Groves throughout the match. *'Perry Groves and Julian Dicks swapped tackles, elbows, abuse and bookings – then carried on their way after the game,'* wrote *The Sun's* Brian Woolnough in a story titled *'Dicks? He Kicks'*. "During the second half I said to Lee Dixon, 'If I get off this pitch in one piece I will be pleased,'" claimed Groves to the press afterwards. He continued: "I was lucky not to be injured and George Graham took me off for my own good in the end. I was booked but still got an elbow in the face. I asked the ref for protection against Dicks because he was kicking me, but all he did was say things to me that I have never heard on a football pitch. I am very upset about it." Man in the middle Brian Hill simply replied, "I say amazing things to everyone, even my wife!"

The encounter also made an impression on Julian but, as far as he was concerned, it was Groves who was guilty of play-acting. "Perry was playing either on the wing or wide right midfield and every time he got the ball I was there breathing on him," he remembers. "He was making the most of every tackle I made, rolling on the floor and complaining. He said to the referee, 'He's gonna kill me in a minute!' And the ref said, 'If you don't like it, get over to the other side of the pitch!' After a while Groves said to George Graham, 'I wanna come off!' But Graham just told him to get on with it as well! After that, he made the most of every tackle I made. But I enjoyed that day," adds Dicks who did get booked (for the fourth time in nine games) in the first half before things got more heated.

Bonds admitted that he considered taking his man off to avoid the threat of a red card, but insisted, "Twenty years ago it would have been passed as a good contest between two players." Not surprisingly, Perry Groves failed to show his face in the players' bar afterwards, which was just as well, as he'd have had Dicksy's mother to contend with. "I was standing by the door waiting for him," declares Carol. "Perry

*A slight difference of opinions
against Sheffield Wednesday in
February 1992 ends in smiles!*

Groves had done nothing but try and get Julian sent off. I waited for him in the bar but he never came in."

As has so often happened throughout Julian's career, his personal fortunes have improved as the team's have declined (or vice versa) and the remainder of the 1991-92 season was no exception. Sure, the goals for Julian dried up as West Ham slid to inevitable relegation (his last had been a header in the 2-2 FA Cup draw with Wrexham on January 25 – the Hammers were eventually knocked out by Sunderland in a fifth round replay), but his form was impressive enough for England manager Graham Taylor to call him up to the England B squad for the trip to Czechoslovakia (see England chapter). And more importantly, he played in every game after his return to the first-team, dismissing any fears about his fitness or form.

Draws against QPR and Leeds in March arrested the run of defeats, prompting Julian to declare "we can still stay up" while at the same time confessing that "draws are no good to us." What was most pleasing for Hammers fans to hear, however, was Dicks' determination to stick with the club, despite the

> **'I've signed a three-year contract and I'll see it through, even if we do go down'**

spectre of relegation. "I've signed a three-year contract and I'll see it through, even if we go down. I feel it's important to show loyalty. That's something that has gone out of a lot of clubs now. I'm happy at West Ham," he confirmed.

Consecutive defeats by Spurs and Chelsea (the latter seeing striker Clive Allen, signed from Chelsea for £250,000 on transfer deadline day, score on his debut) at the beginning of April did the Hammers' cause no good whatsoever, though, and despite a 4-0 thrashing of Norwich (in which Julian scored his last goal of the season and had a punch-up with Canaries defender Mark Bowen – who would join the Hammers himself in 1996), further defeats by Southampton, Manchester City and Crystal Palace all but nailed the lid down on the coffin.

There was still time for one moment of joy, though, with a home game against championship-chasing Manchester United. "I remember Kenny Brown scoring the winner," says Julian of the match which effectively cost Alex Ferguson's men the title. "The ball came in, it hit Kenny on the shin I think and went spinning into the bottom corner. When clubs like Manchester United come to Upton Park expecting to win, it makes the lads even more determined to get a result. Especially under the evening lights, which helps make for a great atmosphere – the crowd get behind you and it gives everybody a big buzz."

Reds manager Ferguson called the level of effort from West Ham's players "obscene" and Billy Bonds said afterwards that he wished he could bottle the passion shown against United – a point Dicks himself acknowledged. "I knew what he meant. I've never needed geeing up – I used to get fired up for under-nine matches on Saturday mornings – but all players are different," he said, no doubt puzzled by some of the motivation problems his team-mates seemed to suffer.

Yet again it left Hammers fans with the familiar feeling of wondering how their team could beat the big guys but fall to the little ones – and the defeat three days later at Coventry on May 25 only confirmed the matter, as West Ham went down 1-0 (with Julian vainly forcing the best save from 'keeper Ogrizovic) and dropped through the trap door.

"The only thing I can really remember was when everybody was walking off the pitch and I stayed out there to clap the West Ham fans," says Julian. "Even Coventry supporters who ran onto the pitch after the game said they admired me for staying out there and applauding the crowd. I think all players should do that, but they don't. When you've just got beaten it's not always the first thing you think of, but the fans pay good money and it doesn't cost anything to just give them a wave or a clap. But it was obviously a blow to be relegated."

Dicks spoke defiantly after the game. "Upton Park needs a good sorting out from top to bottom," he sneered. "Total change is called for. The stables need cleaning. I'm sick as a dog about facing the prospect of Second Division football, because it's a rubbish league. The thought of going to places like Barnsley or Bristol Rovers fills me with gloom. I still think we're better than half the teams staying up – and that includes Coventry."

As he picked up the Hammer-of-the-year award for the second time before the last home game against Nottingham Forest, though, he could at least look back on the season with some pleasure – which is more than could be said for the rest of the West Ham squad. "Somebody had to go down and unfortunately it was us," he says somewhat philosophically, "but it was nice for me to get back, playing 20-odd games and come through them without my knee playing up. And it was also pleasing for me to get the Hammer-of-the-year award. It surprised me because some players had played virtually all season." *(Julian maybe omitted to add that's why they didn't get voted for!)*

The 3-0 win over Forest was not just an amazing parting shot from the Hammers but also from striker Frank McAvennie – who scored a hat-trick after coming on as a second-half substitute in his farewell match. "It couldn't happen to a nicer bloke," smiles Julian, who established a friendly rapport with the roguish Scot during their times together at Upton Park. "I thought Frank was superb, a great bloke," he adds. "He was just himself and liked to enjoy himself. I got to know him quite quickly and we used to go out and have a good time. I don't think anything really affected him. All he seemed worried about was going out and drinking!"

> 'I'm sick as a dog about facing the prospect of Second Division football, because it's a rubbish league'

McAvennie had experienced a disappointing time in his second spell with West Ham, not helped much by his relationship with Billy Bonds. "It wasn't a good one," admits Julian. "Billy was a player when Frank was there the first time and knew

146

about his lifestyle – the clubbing and the Page Three birds on his arm. Billy was the total opposite – he'd go home and be with his family. And when he became manager he knew what Frank was like."

The uneasy mood between manager and player had little effect on the rest of the Hammers camp, but Julian was of the view that Frank was given a raw deal. "Just because there's a personality clash, it doesn't mean that somebody who's doing the business shouldn't be left in. It shouldn't matter whether you love him or hate him. At the end of the day it's all about man-management. But Frank was in and out all the time."

In some respects, Julian could relate to Frank's problems with Billy Bonds. After all, he hardly had the smoothest of relationships with the boss himself…

"I don't think anything really affected him. All he seemed worried about was going out and drinking!"
— ON FRANK McAVENNIE (LEFT)

"I was a right bastard with Billy Bonds, the whole time that he managed West Ham"

CHAPTER 15

RUN-INS OVER RUNNING

"I WAS a right bastard with Billy Bonds, the whole time that he managed West Ham. I used to argue with him a lot and walk off the training pitch. To be honest, I couldn't really give a toss about anything."

Needless to say, Julian and Billy Bonds didn't have the smoothest of relationships. It may certainly have been an improvement on the one he'd had with Lou Macari – there was none of the obvious enmity on Julian's part – but that didn't stop the two men having their run-ins throughout their time together.

Most of the problems occurred on the training ground, with Billy unhappy with what he considered a lack of commitment from Julian. The player, on the other hand, felt the finger was being pointed at him unfairly. "We'd have a five-a-side game and I'd work my bollocks off while other people would just be strolling around," says Julian. "Then it would come to the running but because I'd been chasing all over the pitch I'd be knackered and be at the back, along with Frank McAvennie, way behind everybody else. Then Billy would have a pop at me and that would really make me mad. So I'd say, 'Bollocks!' and just walk off. Quite a few times I'd just walk in, get my gear and go home."

Bonds wasn't the first Hammers manager to encounter Julian's well-known dislike of running. Former boss John Lyall had also experienced the player's reluctance to run during training sessions. "I spoke to him two or three times about it and pointed out that if he was doing an hour's work before the others had started, he'd be physically and mentally tired by the end of the main session. But he didn't seem concerned about it," says Lyall. "There are footballers who don't like the physical side, while there are others who will run forever. He likes to work with the ball because he likes football, but there is another side that's necessary. The likes of Billy Bonds would expect you to run."

The idea that Dicks was too worn out to run (as a result of his early morning work with the ball) did not wash with Bonds, though. "That's a lot of nonsense," insists Billy. "He knows that and I know that. His attitude stunk.

"I wasn't so much worried about Dicksy getting fit," he explains. "It's just not right when you've got young players at the training ground – such as the likes of

Danny Williamson at the time – and they see the club captain half-a-lap behind all the others, with the manager and his assistant yelling, 'Come on, get going!' You have to set an example to the young pros, especially when you're the skipper."

Julian's liking for smashing balls around in training and doing his own thing also caused problems on occasions, as Jimmy Quinn recalls: "I remember one day when Julian was out training with the kids and youth team coach Paul Hilton, and he was messing about, blasting balls all over the place. Paul said to him, 'Listen, I'm trying to train the kids here, if you don't want to do things properly can you just go in and leave it.' And Julian told him what he could do. Paul went in and told Billy Bonds, so later Billy said to Julian, 'Here, what's all this about you telling Hilts to eff off?' And Dicksy just said, 'And you can just eff off too!' and walked off."

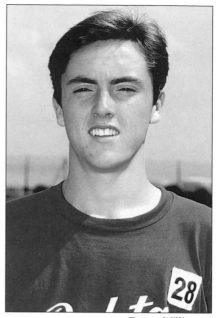

Danny Williamson

Danny Williamson has a similar memory: "The youths were doing shooting practice and if you didn't hit the target you had to do 10 push-ups. It was a bit ridiculous but all the lads were doing them, except for Dicksy when he missed on one occasion. I just remember him walking off and telling Hilts that he wasn't training with us any more."

Another training ground flare-up occurred during a five-a-side game. "Bish was literally on my back, on my shoulders, and his side went and scored," Julian recalls. "I said, 'That's a f***ing foul!' And Billy said, 'Bollocks!' So we're effing and blinding at each other for 30 seconds and I've gone, 'F*** off!' and walked in and gone home. I think it was Alvin who told me not to worry about it and to get on with it, but I said, 'Bollocks, I've had enough.'"

Bonds would invariably question Julian over such behaviour – particularly his attitude towards running and his habit of storming off in a huff. "He'd call me in, ask why I did it and I'd tell him," says Dicks. "Billy was the fittest man in the world, he could run and run and run, but everybody's not the same. Billy could work his balls off in the five-a-sides and when it came to the running he'd still be at the front, but I'm not like that. So they'd have a pop at me and I'd just blow up.

"I couldn't really talk to Billy. I'd go into his office and we'd try to talk but I'd just lose my rag and walk out. I'd be sweating and ranting and raving while he'd just relax back in his chair with a laid-back look on his face and it would just make me worse. I suppose it was a clash of personalities. I found it hard to chat to him – I don't think he had any sense of man-management."

Bonds' style of management resulted in a number of ups and downs with Julian. While many have drawn comparisons between the two people – based on their equally committed approach on the pitch – their personalities off it were very different and this proved a big factor in their relationship. It was something that Jimmy Quinn recognised during his 15 months under Bonds. "Billy's a lovely fellow but, now I'm a boss myself (at Reading), perhaps I can see that he wasn't really cut out to be a manager," he says. "You need to be a bit of a character and be able to have a laugh and a joke. I hope Billy doesn't mind me saying this, but he just seemed to be on the same level all the time. There are a lot more downs than ups in football and when you do get your good times you've got to be able to make the most of them and try and enjoy yourself. But whether we won or lost, or if something funny happened in training, Billy would remain the same.

"Because he was like that and Julian used to like having a laugh, one or two things would happen in training and Billy used to say, 'Bloody do it properly, Julian,' and Dicksy would say, 'F*** off!' – that sort of thing. Julian was very single-minded in his approach and if he didn't think something was right he'd tell you. If he didn't agree with you he'd tell you to eff off. To be fair, everybody had respect for Billy, because he was a legend, but sometimes he and Julian didn't see eye-to-eye on things."

Yet despite the moments of conflict, there was still a mutual regard between the two characters. "We used to have clashes," admits Julian, "but I know Billy's got respect for me and I've got respect for him. At the end of the day, if you argue you argue – that's the way of life. But I do look back and think, 'Oh, I used to tell the manager to f*** off!' But it was all split-second stuff."

Despite that respect, Julian's experiences during those times still left him doubting Billy's management, echoing Jimmy Quinn's sentiments. "I don't think Billy was cut out to be a manager, I really don't," he says. "Management is more than a nine-to-five job but Billy would be straight in the shower and off home after training to spend time with his family. Which is fair enough, people are different – he loved his family and that's all he wanted really."

> "There were times we could have come to blows. I would have loved to have chinned him a couple of times" – BILLY BONDS

Bonds, while always full of praise for Dicks as a footballer ("on the pitch he always gave me 110% – he was a terrific player for me," he says), has admitted that he and Julian are "different sorts of people" and that they had their conflicts. "We had our run-ins and he gave me a few problems," he says. "There were times we could have come to blows. I would have loved to have chinned him a couple of times and I'm sure he'd have loved to have chinned me!"

Leroy Rosenior

Not that Dicks was the only player to have crossed swords with Bonds. "He's had his moments," says Julian of his former boss. "Billy's offered people out. He offered Leroy Rosenior out once in training. Leroy went over the top on one of the young kids and Billy said, 'You do that again and I'll knock you out.' And Leroy went: 'Come on then! If you wanna go some, go some.' Anyway, it all got split up. Billy also had a go at Quinny, who offered him out."

The friction between Dicks and Bonds started to grow more significantly as Julian re-established himself in the West Ham side following his return from injury. Kay Dicks experienced the joy of witnessing her husband resurrect his career, only to see things ultimately begin to turn a sour as his attitude began to change. "It was a brilliant time for us, because he was back," she says. "But then he definitely changed – after being through a year of hell, he started getting cocky and developing a bad attitude. He ended up mixing with people I wouldn't give the time of day to and hangers-on we hadn't heard from for many months were suddenly back on the scene again. That used to cause a lot of arguments at home. I'd just say what I thought and obviously he didn't like it."

It wasn't just the 'hangers-on' who seemed to be fuelling Julian's ego – it was the supporters too. "I can remember going to the ground one day with the children," says Kay, "and this fella said to them, 'Your dad's God.' I just thought, 'Get yourself a life.'

"The trouble was that everybody was telling him how brilliant he was and, no matter what you do, whether you're a footballer or not, it's going to affect you," Kay acknowledges. "And Julian wasn't the same person I knew four years earlier. I just found it very difficult.

"It seemed to happen so quickly. Everybody noticed it – it wasn't just me. He had an ego bigger than a double-decker bus. We used to have terrible rows about the way he was but he couldn't see it, because he was like a god down at the club and everybody thought he was brilliant."

If the end of the 1991-92 season had ended disappointingly for Julian and Kay, the next 12 months only saw things deteriorate even more...

CHAPTER 16

OFF! OFF! OFF!

JULIAN was less than happy when he returned to Chadwell Heath for pre-season training in July 1992. Disillusioned that West Ham had not spent big in the summer (recruiting the likes of midfielders Peter Butler for £175,000, Matt Holmes for £40,000 and Mark Robson on a free transfer, after having sold Stuart Slater to Liam Brady's Celtic for £1.5m), he was concerned about the club's ambition to escape the First Division (as the old Second Division was re-named that year following the launch of the Premiership) at the first attempt and consequently sought talks with Billy Bonds about what was going on.

"Dicks was one of a number of players waiting to see Billy," revealed a 'club insider' in *The Sun*. "He didn't row with Bonds but you could say they had it out about the future of the club. No-one was holding back."

Explains Julian: "Teams were spending fortunes on players and we weren't spending any money. If money was spent, it was like two or three hundred grand. You can't really expect to keep up with the big boys if you're doing that."

Chelsea eye £2.2m Dicks

In the wake of the press speculating about Dicks' unrest, more stories started to appear linking him with a possible move to Chelsea. Despite the Hammers rebuffing Ian Porterfield's official approach – reportedly slapping a £2.2m valuation on their left-back – Julian was still the subject of an illegal approach. "I had someone inside Chelsea ring me up and ask what I thought about a move," he reveals. "I said that it didn't matter what I thought, it was whether the club wanted to sell me. And obviously if they wanted to sell me then it would be time for me to go. By all accounts Chelsea did make an official move but their bids weren't accepted.

"I'd have considered the move," he admits. "But, as I said to (managing director) Colin Hutchinson at Chelsea, if the club don't want to sell me then it's pointless me talking to him."

To further worry Hammers fans, concerned that the club might just cash in on their number one asset, there was a suggestion that Chelsea were offering misfit striker Tony Cascarino in a part-exchange deal. Fortunately, the price placed on Julian's head successfully intimidated all interested parties – including Crystal Palace and Wimbledon, both of whom would not have appealed to him.

While Julian had hoped the club might spend a good proportion of the Slater cash on quality players to help the Hammers' promotion bid, the most significant signing was that of assistant manager Harry Redknapp, who'd played for West Ham back in the sixties and early seventies, was a big friend of Billy Bonds and had proved his managerial credentials during a nine-year spell as boss of Bournemouth.

Harry was dismayed at the attitude of Dicks upon joining the club, however. "I arrived at the club off-season," says 'H' and on our first day back for pre-season training there was no Julian Dicks. He came in during the afternoon, having come back from holiday, and couldn't see any reason why he should have reported in on the morning with the rest of the players. He had a row with Bill and couldn't see why he was wrong to have done it – an attitude I'd never come across in all the years I'd been in football."

DICKS' CARR SMASH

The season could not have started in much worse fashion for Dicks. Just three games into the campaign, on August 29, he was sent off for blatantly throwing an elbow into the face of Newcastle winger Franz Carr (who'd made three appearances for West Ham during Julian's injury period) at St. James' Park. "I had the ball on the byeline and I just knew I was going to elbow him. And that was it – off. Not to this day do I know why I did it. I had it in my mind that I was going to elbow him and that was it – bang!"

> "I had it in my mind that I was going to elbow him and that was it – bang!"

What made it even more inexplicable was that there'd been no friction between the two players during the 74 minutes Dicks was on the pitch (in which the Hammers had gone two goals down), although he'd already been booked for a foul on Newcastle's Kevin Scott. *'He didn't even wait for referee William Burns' red card as the Newcastle fans in the 29,855 crowd pointed the way to the dressing room,'* wrote one reporter. After the game it was time to face the music, admitting to the press that he'd been stupid – "I deserved to get sent off. I can't say it was a day to forget because it's something I'll never forget" – and holding his hands up to the management.

"We'd played badly as a team," reflects Bonds, "and the sending off was the icing on the cake. We were losing 2-0 anyway, so I can't say Dicksy was the cause of us losing the game." Redknapp, on the other hand, was rather less philosophical about the incident. "He elbowed the fella straight in the face!" he recalls. "He'd had a roasting from Carr and threw an elbow and hit him in the gob."

The Franz Carr incident stands out as being one of Julian's darkest hours – because of the premeditation in the assault. Not only were there no excuses, there were no explanations as to why he'd deliberately lashed out. But even without the sending off at Newcastle – which meant Julian would miss games against Peterborough, Bristol City and Derby – Harry Redknapp had already become aware of how difficult Dicks was to control at that time.

"I felt he was nothing but aggravation. Every day there was a confrontation between him and Bill," says Harry. "I spoke to Julian and told him I felt he could play. There was no doubt he had a great left foot, was a good header of the ball and had lots of things going for him. It was just his attitude – if the ball went out for a throw-in during training he'd say it was his ball and want to have a row with everybody. If you told the players to report wearing shirt and ties for a game he'd say, 'Why can't I wear a f***ing tracksuit?' If you said they could wear tracksuits it'd be, 'Why can't I wear a shirt and tie?' That was what his attitude was like at the time. He'd become so powerful he was a law unto himself.

"I'd never come across anybody like him," continues Redknapp. "He started the season badly, was a bad influence on the team and when we played those three games without him, for the first time I could sense a different attitude in the dressing room."

West Ham won 3-1 at Peterborough, travelled to Bristol City and triumphed 5-1 and returned to Upton Park to draw 1-1 with Derby County, with Mitchell Thomas filling in at left-back.

Prior to the suspension, Julian had emerged as Hammers' hero by scoring both goals – a volley and header – in the 2-2 home draw against Bristol Rovers in the Anglo-Italian Cup, a competition that he admits was "a waste of time." Describing Dicks as *'a model of good behaviour'* by the *Evening Standard's* Ken Dyer the following day, the story confirmed West Ham's determination to hang on to their star – despite his problems and the continuing interest from Chelsea. "We have no plans to let Julian go to Chelsea or anyone else," declared MD Peter Storrie. "He doesn't want to leave and we don't want to lose him."

"It's always nice to be linked with other big clubs," confides Julian, "but it didn't make me think I was too good for West Ham or anything. I just got on with my game."

Another goal – a penalty – followed for Dicks as the Hammers won 3-0 at Southend at the end of September to qualify for the final stages of the Anglo-Italian Cup (on the toss of a coin after finishing level with Bristol Rovers on points and goal difference), but it all paled into insignificance after the following league game at Wolves on October 4.

Hammers fans at Molineux that Sunday will vividly recall the flare-up between Julian and Wolves' Steve Bull and Paul Birch which saw Billy Bonds needing to fly down the touchline – with jacket flapping in the wind – to save his defender from attacking one of the grounded players. "Bully had been getting away with murder during the game," remembers Julian. "I'd kick the ball and he'd come in and clatter me. So when I saw him coming in again I just followed through. Then Paul Birch came over and I had a pop at him as well. I can remember Billy running up and saying, 'No, no, no, leave it…' I suppose it was revenge because I'd had no protection myself. I can't remember what the ref said but I said, 'F*** off, you twat!' as he got the red card out. It seems quite funny when I look back."

With the match coming so close after Julian's sending off at Newcastle, there was no doubt that Steve Bull (for one) was looking to exploit the situation, going down at every opportunity and trying to wind Dicks up. *'Julian Dicks pointed an accusing finger at Steve Bull last night. Disgraced Dicks reckoned Bull's play-acting prompted referee David Allison to produce the red card,'* wrote one reporter. "That's the way Bull is," protested Julian after the 0-0 draw. "It's all right for people to go round kicking me but as soon as you kick people back it's blown out of all proportion."

'No, no, no, leave it!' Billy Bonds races to restrain Julian as he has a pop at Wolves' Paul Birch.

Such a feeling was shared by his former Birmingham team-mate Martin Kuhl, who could certainly relate to the situation. "Players like myself have had shin-pads broken but because we get straight back up nothing happens. Yet if we touch someone they squeal and we get booked. You should ask Dicksy how many times he's been scarred on his legs from people topping him. Because he's a hard man, though, he's supposed to take it."

Strangely, Billy Bonds does not remember running to Dicksy's aid at Molineux, but Harry Redknapp does recall feeling that his left-back had been a little hard done by on that occasion. "I thought it was a bit harsh that day, even though he did have a habit of throwing elbows into people's faces at the time," he admits.

Certainly, Julian realised that he was now a target – for referees, who expected him to get into trouble and felt pressured into clamping down, and opponents (like Bull) who went into games looking to exploit Dicks' explosive nature.

Weekly soccer mag *90 Minutes* asked the question: *'Is West Ham skipper Julian Dicks a victim of his own recklessness or are referees just picking on him?'* The story saw Julian complaining about the way the game was heading. "The game has gone soft. Sometimes I wish I had been playing the game when football was more competitive. The game was much harder in the old days. Players didn't exactly get away with murder but certainly there was more room for physical contact and genuine passion." Again, Martin Kuhl is in agreement: "If Julian was playing 15 years ago, nobody would say a word about him. The game has changed a lot – it's so quick now and you do miss tackles, but I've seen some of the things that he's done and taken no notice of what has been said about him."

Julian also reckoned his card was being marked at that time. "I've probably become a marked man where referees are concerned and it's hard to shake this reputation off."

Billy Bonds was aware that the problem needed to be addressed, however. "I don't know whether Julian's reputation goes before him but clearly we have to do something about these sendings off," he said as he announced that his player would be fined by the club, adding, "He knows the rules."

Three days after the Wolves game, Hammers were embarrassingly beaten 2-0 at Crewe (whose Gresty Road ground would soon be named as Julian's least favourite place!) in the Coca-Cola Cup – with Dicks picking up another yellow card. *'Dicks in trouble again as forwards flop,'* was one predictable headline afterwards. "I was booked against Crewe and the first thing the ref said to me was that I wasn't being victimised. What was the need to say that if it wasn't true?" he stormed.

> "I was booked against Crewe and the first thing the ref said to me was that I wasn't being victimised"

With the constant flurry of cards in Dicksy's face it was no wonder his position as captain was being questioned by some, but Billy Bonds insisted it would remain with his left-back – if only because he had few other options. "The only realistic alternative for the captaincy would be Alvin Martin," he said, "and he is not happy in the job."

Julian's last game as captain before commencing a five-match ban – as a result of the last sending off and going over the 21-point limit – was in the 4-0 walloping of Bristol Rovers on October 17 (scoring the second himself from the penalty spot). As he headed off to the sidelines for a month, he maintained: "I won't change the way I play, even if I get sent off again. Teams are always going to need players who battle and if there is a 60-40 ball in the other player's favour, I'm still going to go for it. I've been tackling that way since I was 10 years old, so I can't change now.

"The referee at Bristol even told me he would send me off if I tried to speak to him. But as the captain I have to speak to try and sort things out. And when I was fouled and nothing was given, Martin Allen was booked for telling the ref I wasn't the kind of player who just falls over."

Julian was indeed aware a problem existed but "didn't think about what I could do to cure it. I never asked myself that question. I've never sat down with Kay and said, 'What can I do?' I've never thought like that."

Despite the lengthy ban from domestic football, Dicks was allowed to compete in the Anglo-Italian Cup game at Cremonese. *'West Ham walked into an Italian dirty tricks war,'* wrote *The Sun's* Lee Clayton after the Hammers' 2-0 defeat. *'Billy Bonds' team were elbowed, punched, kicked and stamped... Bonzo's boys have been criticised this season for their increasing disciplinary problems, but they deserve praise here for somehow keeping their cool. Hammers full-back Julian Dicks was Cremonese's number one target. He was kneed in the face, punched and clattered by crude challenges. But to his credit, Dicks kept his cool and on the whole avoided confrontation.'*

> "Martin Allen was booked for telling the ref I wasn't the kind of player who just falls over"

Contrary to this report, however, Julian denies being singled out for special treatment by the Italians, claiming that it was striker Trevor Morley who took most of the punishment. "Trevor was battered in that game, he got really hammered," he says, before revealing for the first time what had taken place in the hotel the evening beforehand.

"Trevor, Kenny Brown and myself had a game of spoof in our room the night before the game. We got absolutely bollocksed! I was sharing with Kenny and Trevor's room was opposite. We finished the game about three o'clock in the morning and Trevor opened the door to leave and went smack, straight onto the floor! He was really out of it. We picked him up, took him into his room and he was really ill. And then he got really hammered in the game the next day!"

West Ham's hopes of promotion to the Premier League also took a hammering with Julian out of the side, the team only winning one of their matches – against Notts County – during his five-game absence (which felt like "five years" as far as he was concerned). Defeats against Swindon, Cambridge and Millwall meant that victory over Oxford – Julian's return game on November 21 – was imperative.

While he reclaimed the left-back birth, however, the captain's stripes would remain on the arm of Alvin Martin, who'd taken over again during Dicksy's absence. "Billy Bonds told me I have got problems and he doesn't want the captaincy to be one of them," explained Julian.

He put all his troubles aside, though, to score two 25-yard goals in the Hammers' 5-3 win. "He's got a left foot like a hammer," said Bonds afterwards, delighted to see Dicks respond in style after having had a 45-minute heart-to-heart with him 24 hours prior to the game. Unlike a lot of people offering Julian advice on how to clean up his act, Billy was at least able to draw on his own experiences of having got into hot water during his lengthy career. "I was very hot-headed and got into trouble myself," Bonds confesses. "It wasn't until I was maybe in my late twenties or early thirties that I started to calm down and think about things a little bit more. So from that point of view I did see similarities between us. We were both obviously very committed, physical players and I could see comparisons in that. I spoke to Dicksy a few times regarding that, because I could see why he was getting into trouble and I knew how he was feeling. As you get older you get wiser, which is why I tried to talk to him."

Julian's first manager, Ron Saunders, spent his last two years as a player at Charlton Athletic – during a time when Billy was starting his career. Certainly, the similarities between Bonds and Dicks did not escape the man who would go on to establish himself as a 'hard man' in the management world. "They had the one thing which attracted the crowds to them and made them support them as individuals," says Ron. "And that was heart, because they wore it on their cufflinks all the time. Both of them had this 'something' that their managers, team-mates and particularly the supporters love. And it's that they know what they're going to get out of them when they kick off – they're going to give you everything they've got."

Julian's two goals against Oxford – both from free-kick situations – gave everybody the opportunity to shift the focus back onto the positive side of his game. "That first goal was one of the best I've ever scored," he beamed, while his goalkeeping victim, Paul Reece, admitted: "When Dicks lines up for those free-kicks, it's like facing Stuart Pearce. His first goal was the best that's ever got past me."

Further goals in consecutive matches against Charlton and Luton, between Christmas and New Year, allowed the Hammers to draw both games as they pushed for promotion. The crunch game was at Derby's Baseball Ground on January 10, as the team took on the fellow promotion hopefuls knowing that victory would lift them to second place in the table. West Ham took a two-goal lead within 15 minutes and then...disaster! Dicks was ordered off by referee Alan Wilkie before half-time for his second bad foul on Derby winger Ted McMinn – his third dismissal in four and a half months and a record for any West Ham player in the history of the club.

Julian's third red card of the season came at Derby following a tackle on Ted McMinn (grounded). "Calm down, calm down," says Clive Allen.

"People thought, 'He's getting too big for the club.' And that's when they thought about selling me"

"I think that sending off annoyed me more than anything else," says Billy Bonds. "It was a massive game for us that day. Derby were just under us and if we could win that one it would put daylight between us and we'd be flying. Alvin Martin was struggling with an injury, we went two up and then Dicksy got sent off. Whether he meant it or not it was a wild tackle, right in front of the dug-out. Okay, he was going for the ball but it was a stupid, irresponsible thing to do and all of a sudden the whole game was in the balance – we might easily have ended up losing. Then I heard the fans chanting his name, which I just couldn't believe!"

Assistant boss Redknapp was no less furious about the incident, describing the second offence as "the most blatant foul ever seen!"

Not surprisingly, Julian's recollection of the second clash with McMinn is somewhat different to Harry's account: "I went in for the ball and never even touched Ted McMinn. And he went three or four feet up in the air!"

Photographs show Dicksy being shepherded away from McMinn, who lay curled up in apparent agony on the floor, by striker Clive Allen. "He was just saying, 'Calm down, calm down,'" recalls Julian of the man who "never swears" – suggesting that Clive just might have done on this occasion. "After I was sent off the fans were all singing my name, and then people thought, 'He's getting too big for the club.' And that's when they thought about selling me."

As Julian trudged into the Baseball Ground dressing room, his manager called

DICKS FACES RECORD BAN

him "an idiot". Whatever his explanations, there were obviously going to be further repercussions. "Both Billy Bonds and myself will talk to him," said Peter Storrie, with the FA's disciplinary chief, Eric Dinnie, also showing an interest. "Any player whose record is giving cause for concern could be called up for a chat to try to find out what's going wrong," he said.

Storrie didn't speak to Dicks – not as far as the latter is concerned, anyway – but Bonds did, the manager no doubt rather embarrassed about West Ham's worsening disciplinary record that season, having had seven men sent off (including Mike Small, George Parris, Trevor Morley and Matthew Rush). One soccer magazine asked, 'What's going on at the academy of football?' while one newspaper invited the public to air their views. 'Julian Dicks needs to calm down – as a West Ham fan I find his behaviour a disgrace,' was a view attributed to one Tracey Flack of Barking. 'For every red card a player receives, his team should be deducted a point. Then the likes of Julian Dicks might stop making those kamikaze tackles,' said Danny L of Manor Park, while others thought a change of club might be the ideal thing for him: 'If Julian Dicks doesn't change his ways, Billy Bonds should threaten him with a spell at Arsenal – that would cure his problems immediately!' reckoned Mrs L. Casson of Bow, while P. Lavous of Farnborough suggested, 'Sell Julian Dicks to Nottingham Forest. Remember Kenny Burns? He was a hoodlum until he joined Forest and Brian Clough turned him into Player of the Year – twice!'

Fact or fiction? We'll probably never know, but the question of what to do with Julian Dicks was undoubtedly the topical debate of the time. Former Birmingham hardman Mark Dennis – sent off a reported 12 times in his career – appeared in a *Daily Mirror* exclusive, offering his support. "I've known Julian since he was a kid at Birmingham City and he's no animal," he said. "His record looks bad, but that's only because he has a John McEnroe complex – he's a bad loser because he only wants to win. It's not all his own fault – he gets done for things other people would get away with, just as I did, just because his name is Julian Dicks. I saw the tackle at Derby and I've seen 2,000 far worse that didn't even earn a yellow card. Julian's trouble is that he's too enthusiastic. He wants to be seen as a macho man, but he's just not the kind of guy who goes out to maim people.

"The man who disappoints me more than Julian is Billy Bonds," continued Dennis. "Dicks will go out and die for West Ham, but Bonzo won't die for Dicks. He should be helping him channel his frustrations, not slaughtering him publicly. I'd rather Bonzo took Dicks into his office and gave him a right-hander than slag him off in the press. And stripping him of the captaincy was no way to help. Nobody knows the torture this lad is going through better than I do. That's why I've written to him, trying to help him sort his problems out."

Dennis did indeed write to Dicks. "Basically he said, 'Don't end up like me – you've got the ability, you're better than any other left-back, calm down and go and get the England shirt,'" says Julian, who responded with a phone call of thanks.

Dicks missed three games as a result of the Derby dismissal – the league wins against Bristol City and Leicester City and the dreadful 4-1 Cup collapse at Barnsley (with Kenny Brown taking the number three shirt) – and was back in the news again following West Ham's 2-1 victory at Watford on February 30. This time, though, it was for his *'new ice-cool temperament'* (according to one paper). *'Dicks kept his fists down after the challenging Charley's studs had dented the Hammers' star's chest. Instead, from the free-kick, Dicks powered upfield and provided a pin-point cross that was met by a Robson diving header for the first goal.'*

But Dicks was back in the dock a week later as second-from-top Hammers entertained leaders Newcastle at Upton Park. Yet while the media were talking about the *'horror tackle that put Robert Lee on the treatment table'* – *The Sun* (for which he was booked), Newcastle boss Kevin Keegan insisted: "Dicks has every right to go for a ball like that. It was one of those 50-50 situations so I have no complaints."

> "He was the only person who never slagged me off for my bookings and sending-offs" – ON BOBBY MOORE

"I did catch Robert Lee," admits Julian, "but it wasn't like some of the papers were saying, it wasn't malicious." There was also cause for Julian to show restraint after complaining to referee Keith Cooper that he'd been booked for his first foul while nobody in Newcastle's side had been penalised for "kicking lumps" out of Trevor Morley up front. "He said, 'If you speak to me like that I'll send you off.' So I just walked away and forgot all about it," he says.

By the time West Ham kicked another ball in competition, their former World Cup winning skipper, the legendary Bobby Moore, had passed away as a result of cancer. Three days after his death (February 27), the Hammers visited a maudlin Roker Park to play out a seemingly meaningless 0-0 draw, then returned to Upton Park – the gates and main forecourt of which had been camouflaged completely with banners, scarves, shirts, memorabilia and flowers from the tearful West Ham faithful – for the game against Wolves. "Everything was geared around Bobby Moore that day," recalls Julian. "The atmosphere was different to what it usually was. The public's reaction didn't surprise me at all because that's the way West Ham supporters are. Bobby Moore was a legend, he was unbelievable.

"I met him just once (while Bobby was on commentary duty at Upton Park) and he was the only person who never slagged me off for my bookings and sending-offs. On a one-to-one he never told me that I shouldn't do this or shouldn't do that. He just told me to go about my business the way I do and it would all work itself out."

As if he was seeking to make Wolves pay for what had occurred in the first game against them earlier in the season, Dicks seemed like a man possessed as he made a crucial tackle in the build-up for the first goal, made a significant pass to set up a penalty for the second – which he duly despatched home – had a piledriving shot tipped over and saw a header hacked off the line in his side's 3-1 victory. Not surprisingly, he was voted man-of-the-match and credited as being *'possessed with the battling spirit of Mooro.'* He was probably also amused by the booking of Wolves' Steve Bull!

If Dicks was hoping to keep his head down and stay low profile for the remainder of the season he was asking rather too much – especially as he started banging the goals in. He hit two – an unstoppable header and a poacher's effort – in the 2-1 win over Grimsby on March 9 and got another brace – this time both penalties – against Tranmere (in a 2-0 victory 11 days later) as his team snapped at the coat-tails of division leaders Newcastle. Typically, it wasn't all sunshine and light for Dicksy. He conceded a penalty in the Grimsby game (which was missed) and was so incensed at the decision that he pursued referee Alan Gunn across the pitch before being restrained by his team-mates. "He tested the referee's patience tonight but he was the difference between the two sides," said Billy Bonds. Between the Grimsby and Tranmere games the Hammers had lost their first match in 15 league outings – 1-0 at Notts County – and it was a day of double disaster, with Dicks picking up the booking that earned his fourth ban of the season. Far from being castigated by the press, however, he won sympathy for what *The Sun* described as *'a cruel caution. There was nothing malicious about his 52nd minute tackle on striker Kevin Wilson. But the theatrical reactions of Wilson and the County fans made it look like Dicks had committed a cold-blooded execution.'* "The ironic thing is I'm starting to get sympathy from opposing players!" commented Julian after the game.

Once again, it was time for more transfer speculation, with it being known that money was still required to fund the redevelopment of Upton Park following the inevitable collapse of the Bond Scheme. Hammers MD Peter Storrie denied that Julian was available, being quoted as saying, "Julian is not for sale...unless someone comes in with £4 million (a British record fee at the time)."

"If that was said, then they were just pricing me out of the market," states Julian. "With the season I was having they wouldn't have got that for me anyway. They'd have been lucky to have got £500,000 the way things were going!"

Yet somehow, a few days later, it was reported that Julian would be allowed to leave for £3 million, supposedly to fund team strengthening. The story had little obvious substance – although his dwindling popularity with the management behind the scenes may possibly have suggested some truth – but it was enough to disturb one fanzine, who ruffled the feathers of the fans somewhat by suggesting Dicks was Chelsea-bound. It was even alleged that extra security was brought in for the Tranmere game to avert the threat of a planned pitch invasion (that never occurred).

All the speculation as to what would have to be paid to tempt Dicks away from

Upton Park became irrelevant, though, when he seriously considered quitting the game after the events at Oxford's Manor Ground on March 23. It's the moment that Julian describes as "the lowest point of my career".

"Their centre-forward (thought to be Nick Cusack) stamped on my chest, right on the byeline, and when I got up the referee booked me. I felt like quitting then," he admits. "I was being victimised by referees and thought everybody was against me. I had six or seven stud marks on my chest and yet I was booked for it! I felt like quitting, I really did."

Dicks declared his threat to give up the game in the after-match press conference, yet the *Mirror* displayed little sympathy, claiming that Julian was *'lucky to escape his fourth red card of the season when he jumped up in retaliation and grabbed the throat of his opponent.'* And he also opened his heart to his father about his feelings at the time. "He told me he'd thought about giving it up," says Ron. "He was feeling rather low and said that if he could afford to he'd pack the game in, because of everything that had happened and being booked for things he didn't deserve. I've spoken to a lot of people who've seen the games and they've said he didn't deserve a lot of the cards. These are honest guys – they've not said that just because they're friends of mine.

"Of course, some of it is bound to be Julian's fault. You can't just keep blaming referees all the time. But I'd be gutted every time he got sent off," he adds, revealing that he invariably discovered the bad news via teletext. "I can't watch Julian on television. I'd go and see games live but I can't just sit there and watch it on the box – I'd probably end up kicking the telly in!"

Fortunately, Julian's depression lifted a couple of days after the 1-0 defeat at Oxford. "It only really lasted about two days at the most," he admits. "I came home, saw Kay and the kids, and I was able to put it all into perspective. I've got to work to provide for them."

Julian's fourth suspension of the season cost him games against Millwall (drawn 2-2, with recent loan signing David Speedie infuriating the Upton Park crowd as he failed to put away two one-on-one opportunities with the 'keeper) and Birmingham City (Bishop and Brown scoring unlikely goals in the last four minutes at St. Andrews to sneak a fortunate 2-1 win). With just seven league matches remaining, Portsmouth had put the squeeze on West Ham by going on a tremendous run and winning around 10 out of 11 games to overtake Hammers for the much sought after second promotion spot (with Newcastle clear at the top).

Yet Julian resisted any feeling of pressure – through his own problems or the threat of Pompey. "As soon as I step onto the pitch, it doesn't matter what other problems I may have. I just blank them out," he says. "It's also far better to be at the top than struggling at the bottom, so I wasn't feeling particularly tense."

The tension certainly got to a few others, though, especially after the 2-0 defeat at Luton on April 13 which saw Dicks get booked for deliberate handball to concede a penalty – leaving him just one card short of 41 points and his fifth suspension of the year. *'Wolverhampton official Gurnam Singh was thought by many to have let Dicks off when he deliberately prevented Kerry Dixon's goalbound shot from hitting the roof of the net in the 82nd minute,'* reported *The Sun's* Martin Samuel. "I feared the worst – I thought I was going," admits Julian.

With Bonds knowing he'd need all his best players at his disposal for the final four games, his patience was beginning to run out. As Singh ran over to Dicks at Kenilworth Road he was sure his player was about to be red carded (putting him out of at least the last two matches) and, with rumbustious midfielder Martin 'Mad Dog' Allen having exceeded the 41-point mark to incur a four-match ban (on top of the five he'd already missed through suspension), the West Ham manager was clearly worried that his team's promotion chances were being seriously undermined.

"We're sitting on the edge all the time because of their records and it has cost us dearly. Between the two of them they have missed about 20 games this season," complained Bonds publicly after the 4-0 win over Brentford (in which Allen was booked again). "That could cost us promotion."

Dicks was less than happy at being criticised by his manager in the press – and particularly the comments about endangering promotion. "If anything, Martin and I had done more to get the team promotion than cost us it," he argues. "It's wrong to

say things like that in the papers. Managers should call you into their office and discuss it there, not in the press."

Allen, too, was none too keen on what had been said by the boss. "Personally, I'm not too keen on managers slating players in public," he confirms. "It should all be done behind closed doors. But Billy would have regular chats with me and tell me to keep my mouth shut with referees, which was fair comment."

Despite his disciplinary problems (which saw him accumulate 57 points in total), Martin enjoyed the 1992-93 campaign. "It was a good season for both myself and Julian. We were both fully committed and it was a case of keeping the motivation, desire and effort to make sure we got promoted. It was probably my best season at West Ham. Billy put me in the middle and I had a good relationship with Peter Butler so we did a good job. But I used to get very involved in things, getting booked for tackles and dissent."

But Allen was not a character who allowed the negative aspects of the game to bother him. "He didn't really worry about things," says Julian of his former 'partner-in-crime'. "He'd always be bubbling. He was just one of those people – you couldn't get him down."

Glenn Hoddle wasn't bothered with Allen's disciplinary record, either, picking him for the Division One XI. "I couldn't have been doing too badly, despite what Billy went on record as saying," adds the Mad Dog.

As for what was said in the press at that time, by Bonds, or anyone else for that matter, the stories were not necessarily read by Julian himself. "My mum got all the papers and she'd tell me what was in them," he explains. Carol would also often talk to her son after games and question him on his bookings and sending-offs. "I'd have a go at him about it," she says. "He'd say, 'I was going for the ball.' I agree there were times when he only had to look at referees – I remember one occasion when he went to speak to a ref, who said, 'You talk to me and I'll send you off.' Julian said, 'I've got to speak to you, I'm the captain!' And the referee said, 'One word and you're off!' But there have been times when he's been a bit heavy-handed. I say to him, "You shouldn't have done that,' and he says, 'Why? I went for the ball.' It's his aggression – if the ball is there he'll go in to win it.

"There have been other times when he's got the ball but the player's gone up in the air. As long as he's made contact with the ball that's fine, as far as I'm concerned. The funny thing is, players don't seem to get booked when they clock Julian. I can remember when Mick Harford was playing for Luton and he put his elbow into Julian's face. I could see Julian's cheekbone rising on camera. What they wanted to do was put a hook into Julian's skull to bring his cheekbone back up. I said to Ju, 'He did that on purpose.' And he said, 'No, he never.' I said, 'Have you seen the video?' But he won't blame anybody. 'No,' he says, 'It's part and parcel of the game.' I said that they want to remember that when he does it!"

Ron Dicks occasionally spoke to his son about his disciplinary problems and offered his advice. "He always says to me that he's just going for the ball, so what can you say to him?" he asks. "Part of the problem is that most of these referees haven't played the game. I remember Paul Durkin, who refereed in the Western League when I played – he never played the game. I know Roger Milford quite well – he was an animal when he played but as a referee he's quite fair. If there were professional refs who'd had the experience of playing, you'd see a lot more understanding. But I think Julian's reputation went before him a lot of the time."

Throughout Julian's career, Ron has remained in contact with Ron Veal – the man who tracked his son's development as a kid – and the scout has continued to keep tabs on Dicks' fortunes. He's been disappointed with Julian's poor discipline but also recognised injustices. "I see other fouls being committed with nothing done about them, but if Julian had been responsible he'd have been sent off," says Veal. "The referees are not consistent – they're in for the kill with some people and not others."

The win over Brentford was a vital one for the Hammers – as was Martin Allen's last-second goal, which proved crucial at the end of the season. "Martin was a very whole-hearted player," says Julian. "He always gave 110%, although he did get a bit of stick from the fans at one point. But he worked hard and could score goals – and shoot from 50 yards!" he adds, referring to the Mad Dog's tendency to try one from unlikely distances.

Dicks himself got on the scoresheet with a penalty in the 2-1 win over Bristol Rovers at Upton Park on April 24, which nicely set up the final two games – away at Swindon Town and at home to Cambridge United. With second-placed Portsmouth losing at Sunderland on Saturday (May 1), the Hammers visited the County Ground 24 hours later knowing a win would take them level on points.

"I set up Clive Allen's goal our third one for Kenny Brown," remembers Julian, who had the shirt ripped off his back by a frenzied supporter on the pitch after the game. He also recalls receiving the man-of-the-match award from former Hammers star Jimmy Greaves.

West Ham's 3-1 win took them above Pompey through having scored one goal more (Allen's last-second strike against Brentford proving significant), so things could not been more delicately poised as they faced Cambridge at Upton Park on the final day of the season.

> "If I shot I'd get the glory but if I gave it to Clive it would be a certain goal. I thought, 'Give it to Clive!'"

"It was a crucial game – we had to win and hope it wasn't bettered by Portsmouth at home to Grimsby," Julian recalls. "We were 1-0 up (through David Speedie) for quite a time and then, in the last minute, their right-back received the ball in the box and was trying to play it out. I slid in, won the ball and saw Clive Allen in the middle. And I was thinking, 'Shall I shoot or give it to Clive?' If I shot I'd get the glory but if I gave it to Clive it would be a certain goal. I thought, 'Give it to Clive!' I slid it across to him and he slotted it home. Then all the fans ran on and it was bedlam!"

Fortunately the invading supporters – delirious with joy – were forced back so that the remaining few seconds could be played. The 2-0 win was enough to promote the Hammers (with Pompey winning 2-1) and relegate Cambridge. "I thought we performed a miracle that year," reflects Harry Redknapp, well aware that the team had done well in the face of a number of difficulties. "We got promoted but not because of Julian – I felt he caused a million problems at times and his form was patchy. Having said that, by the end of the season, we went and beat Swindon and he was absolutely magnificent. We came back to Upton Park for the last game against Cambridge, needing to win, and he was absolutely different class."

Harry's contribution to the Hammers cause was appreciated by Dicks also. "He's a good coach," Julian acknowledges. "Harry took most of the coaching and had more of a clue than Billy in that area because of his longer managerial experience. And being around better players helped him as well. It was nice, after years of struggling, to get back up."

Having missed most of the 1990-91 season through injury, Julian could at last enjoy his first promotion as a player, although he's still of the view that had the club invested more heavily nine months earlier they'd have given themselves a much easier ride. "If we'd have bought players we'd have won that division," he insists.

As far as Billy Bonds was concerned, it was the club's disciplinary record that season – Julian missed 13 games in all – that cost them not just a more comfortable route upwards but the First Division trophy. "I believe that if we hadn't had so many suspensions we would have won the title," he says. For all his problems with Julian during the campaign, though, he still had the highest admiration for his left-back as a player. "From a disciplinary point of view he'd been having a bad time – and that was of his own making,' says Billy. "But we kept trying to tell him that if he got that side of his game right, it would make him a much better player. I hated the troublesome side of him, some of the stupid things he was doing, but I loved the side of him as a player. He has a great left foot – it's like a cannon. I don't want to harp on about his disciplinary problems too much because he's a good player and that needs to be said as well. But his problems were holding him back. In that respect if was more his problem than mine. The team still had a bit of success – we got promoted and had some cup runs – so on reflection it didn't hold us back as such."

In the end, it was partly through the late efforts of David Speedie, brought in on loan from Blackburn in an inspired move by Bonds, that West Ham got promoted in 1993. "I got on fine with him," Julian says of the fiery Scot. "Harry told me that Kenny Dalglish had said not to put Speedie and me in opposite teams for five-a-sides! The fans got on his back a bit, especially during the Millwall game, but he did well for West Ham. He added a bit of bite and character."

Characteristics that hint at somebody already in the team, don't you think?

CHAPTER 17
O-KAY?

"NOW we'll have a jolly old knees-up!" was the rather unlikely quote attributed to Billy Bonds as the promotion party got under way. As the champagne flowed, Julian could reflect on the year 1992-93 with mixed emotions (once again). He'd contributed a lot to the promotion push, but his efforts had been undermined by the growing problems on the pitch with referees. On many occasions it seemed as if Dicks was tripping over the touchline at the beginning of each match and falling headlong into more trouble – culminating in his threat to quit the game after his booking at Oxford on March 23. But if life was difficult on the pitch, things were no more easy off it – particularly for Kay at home.

"Basically, he was a selfish pig," says Julian's wife of his behaviour at home during most of 1992 and the early part of '93. "He'd do what he wanted, when he wanted. He's always been very good with the kids, but they used to go to bed about eight o'clock and then he'd just do whatever he liked. And I'd just fit in around it. We didn't have much of a social life together."

> "Basically, he was a selfish pig" – KAY DICKS

Things had gradually deteriorated between Julian and Kay since their move from the Midlands in 1988. "After we moved down I wasn't in a position to go out to work and meet people because I was pregnant," says Kay. "I was stuck at home every day and hated it. I used to be back on the motorway to Birmingham every weekend, but as I got bigger that was difficult. So I didn't particularly like it at first, especially as it was very quiet where we lived. We were lucky that we met some nice people through the couple we bought the house from, Gary and Jane. And my sister came down quite often."

Kay had given birth to Kattie and Jessica in December of that year, but it was some time before she could take them to matches at Upton Park (and since then their appearances have been sporadic). "You can't drag two girls, one under each arm, to football. Then Julian was injured, so that wiped out another 14 months. They were about three or four before they started going to football – but they didn't understand and used to ask if they could go and play on the grass!"

The injury period incurred its own problems, of course, but the move down to West Ham had already had an effect on Julian's temperament. "He changed a lot when we moved down," confirms Kay. "I think it was because he was so popular at the club and so-called friends were telling him how great he was all the time. And I suppose it was bound to rub off on him. He could be a bit unbearable at times, to say the least."

After making his return from injury and emerging as Hammers' star man, Julian started to become even more self-absorbed. "He was absolutely full of himself by that time. I think he thought he was the best thing that had ever happened," declares Kay.

"I'd go out and get pissed out of my head – I'd just go straight to the pub"

Julian's tendency to land himself in trouble during games was also not helping matters. Kay often discovered if her husband had been sent off via teletext or through a phone call from a friend, and sometimes she'd hear from Julian during his journey back. "Sometimes he'd phone me on the way home on the coach. And I'd be straight down his throat," she admits. "What used to annoy me was that I knew that he could play without all that stuff – he's got the skill, he doesn't need to go ploughing into people.

"I'd be the first to have a go at him about it. But when I look back now at some of the things he's been sent off for, there's no way he should have gone. It wasn't always his fault. Sometimes I'd say, 'You stupid idiot!' but obviously I didn't know

Relaxing with 10 week-old Kattie.

"He's always been very good with the kids."

what I was on about so that used to cause problems. I'd probably be the last person he'd want to speak to about things. As soon as he walked through the door, I'd say, 'Have you been booked?' Not 'have you had a good game?' or 'did you enjoy the match?', but 'have you been booked?' I was probably driving him as mad as he was driving me."

But Julian was indeed guilty of bringing his work problems home with him. "I used to be terrible," he confesses. "If we'd lost (as the team were doing all too often in the early part of 1992) I'd go out and get pissed out of my head – I'd just go straight to the pub. We'd also have midweek games and I'd get lock-ins at pubs. I wouldn't say I was drinking heavily as such, just getting hammered after games. And what was going on during the 1992-93 season was causing problems as well."

Julian invariably took himself out to Brentwood with the people that Kay describes as "so-called mates" and hung out in wine bars. Players were barred from going out drinking on the two nights before any match, but, as Kay says, "The other nights, more often that not, he'd be out. I remember Christmas 1992 – it was the girls' birthday. I asked Julian if he'd come home and help me get their presents and stuff out and he came home totally pissed up. He was absolutely horrible and it just made me feel that he couldn't have cared less about any of us."

One theory about Julian's behaviour at that time is that he was trying to catch up on the sort of socialising he'd sacrificed as a result of getting married so early in life. "We were so young when we got together – remember, we were living together by the time we were 17 and married with two children by the time we were 19," reminds Kay. "Maybe he felt as if he'd missed out on things. I used to nag him to death, but I found it very hard to cope – with his job and his fame.

"He'd go out with people and they'd have women around them. And you'd have all these people coming back telling you things. I was absolutely paranoid – I didn't trust him as far as I could throw him. And he couldn't understand why not. It's very difficult when your husband's going out four nights a week and you're at home with the kids and people are phoning you up. It's very hard not to take any notice."

"I wanted to escape. I'd had enough" – KAY DICKS

The interest the press were showing in Julian and his family added even greater weight to the pressure the Dickses were feeling during this period. "They drove us up the wall," declares Kay. "We bought a repossessed flat in Billericay (in the autumn of 1992) and when the press found out about it they thought he was leaving me. Julian only bought it because he thought he was getting it cheap.

"The morning the deal had gone through the press were all outside the house. We had a car outside and they were waiting for him to chuck his stuff in it and go. But he went off to work and I went off to the local gym. I think one car followed him and one followed me. But they'd been there from about six o'clock in the morning."

As Julian's public profile – and notoriety – started to build, the Dickses' home came under even greater siege. "Someone put dog muck through the letter box and I had an endless amount of nasty phone calls. I had the police in at one point because it was getting so bad. It went from bad to worse and I just hated it because people wouldn't leave us alone. I don't know if they were jealous or what but there was always somebody wanting to have a go," says Kay, who confesses that the marriage came under great strain.

Kay lost her father, Peter, in April 1993 and, although other factors came into play, his death seemed to act as a catalyst for the couple recognising that things couldn't go on as they were. "I think we just realised we had to sort ourselves out or, at the end of the day, I was going back up to Birmingham to make a new life for myself. I didn't want to be stuck in seven nights a week with two children while he was off out. We just consciously tried to sort things out really."

The family had not planned to go abroad for any holidays during the summer of 1993 but after recent events a break in Tenerife was decided upon. "Things were getting better then," admits Kay, "but I still wanted to escape. I'd had enough."

But Kay wasn't talking about a holiday. She was looking for her and Julian to get away – for good.

CHAPTER 18

ON THE MOVE?

IF West Ham's promotion campaign had been fraught with controversy for Dicksy, the 1993-94 season hardly promised an easier ride – not on the evidence of the pre-season preparations.

Billy Bonds had spent just over £1.25m during the summer on two new recruits – winger Dale Gordon (from Rangers) and Charlton centre-half Simon Webster. But just four weeks after his move across London and a matter of days after the £525,000 transfer fee had been decided by a league tribunal, Webster was involved in a training ground clash which would – aside from ruling him out of the new season – effectively call an end to his footballing career.

"We were having one of our five-a-side games," recalls Julian, "and I went in for a 50-50 tackle with Simon. It was a block tackle and I went through and got the ball, crossed it and a goal was scored. I was up and down cheering and Simon was on the floor. We went over to him and he said, 'I've broken my leg.' I was gutted for him, especially as he'd just come to the club. I didn't really know him but I obviously felt for him."

There was certainly no suggestion from anybody who'd witnessed the incident that Julian was in any way guilty of a reckless or dangerous challenge, but he was disappointed at the newspaper coverage the following day. "Obviously, most of them had a field day," Dicks recalls. "The press reaction was annoying because they didn't know the facts. They just said that I'd broken his leg in training and that was it. People just assumed I'd gone over the top and smashed him to pieces, when it was just a block tackle. Fortunately, Simon then said in the papers that it was just an ordinary tackle and that was it."

Billy Bonds witnessed the clash and was satisfied that it was just one of those things that happens every now and again in football. "It was a straightforward challenge – the sort of thing you see on a training ground all the time," he says. "They both went in for the ball and Julian got up and Simon didn't."

A fortnight later Dicks' name was back in the news following a 'friendly' game at Leyton Orient, after being substituted for brawling with rival Warren Hackett. The

A half-time bust-up with Billy Bonds and Harry Redknapp at Coventry signalled the beginning of the end for Julian at West Ham.

Orient player had reacted strongly to a challenge from Julian, lashing out at him. "The player tried to punch me," recalls Dicks. "I caught him back, we had a grapple and the rest of the players got involved. But it was a natural reaction. When somebody throws a punch at you it's instinctive to hit back."

The team's dismal start to their return season in the top flight – a 2-0 home defeat by Wimbledon (the result somewhat overshadowed by the antics of Dons owner Sam Hammam, who daubed obscene graffiti on his own team's dressing room wall in order to stir his boys up!) and a 1-0 loss at Leeds United – had already forced speculation that Hammers might need to dispense with their biggest asset in order to fund the purchase of much-needed firepower up front. Billy Bonds had already attempted to lure 34-year-old striker Lee Chapman to the club but had lost out to Portsmouth in the close season. ("As we increased our offer he went back to them and they increased theirs – it was a crazy situation and we had to call a halt," said Peter Storrie at the time.) And with little money available as a result of the redevelopment taking place at Upton Park, Bonds and Redknapp knew they'd have to think very carefully about how to best use the resources available to them.

In retrospect, maybe the events of Saturday, August 21, helped make them arrive at the most crucial decision of their management partnership. With no points or goals in the opening two games, the Hammers headed to joint-leaders Coventry City. A Dale Gordon goal – his only for West Ham and the club's first ever in the Premiership – helped secure a vital 1-1 draw, but once again it was that man Dicks who was in the news following a yellow card that some thought should have been red.

> "I took off my shirt, threw it on the floor and said, 'Take me off then!'"

"I had the ball and was running out of our box with it and Sean Flynn had his arms all over me," explains Julian of the incident which took place just before half-time. "I just swung my elbow out and caught him. The referee booked *me* but gave *us* the free-kick, which I couldn't understand."

Dicks did his most to defend himself at the time, insisting that he'd merely shrugged Flynn off after being fouled and that his card had been a result of the Coventry man's play-acting. But the major fireworks took place in West Ham's dressing room. "I went in at half-time and Billy and Harry started having a pop at me, saying I could have lost us the game. Billy had a go at me and we just told each other to piss off. We had quite a flare-up really and Harry said, 'Well, take him off.' So I took off my shirt, threw it on the floor and said, 'Take me off then!' Billy calmed it down though and told me to get ready for the second half. If Harry had been manager then he'd have taken me off and chucked me out."

It's a game that the Hammers management remember particularly well and it's obvious that they were then, more than ever, of the view that their prize asset was also their number one liability. "He should have been sent off – how he was never sent off I will never know. He was completely out of order!" says Harry Redknapp.

'It was a match which left a question...would you buy Julian Dicks?'

"We'd gone one up and needed a win for our lives. We were playing ever so well when suddenly he smashed the fella in the face with his elbow and laid him out. We came in at half-time and we said to him, 'You could have cost us the game. It's irresponsible.' The next thing he wanted to do was have a fight with Bill! It's not the way to have success at a football club. I'd have taken him off."

But Billy didn't take Dicks off, despite fears of his left-back undermining the rest of the team's efforts. "It got a little bit out of hand," says Bonds of the half-time bust-up. "I wasn't necessarily just worried about Julian – it was the team as well. We could have lost him and then lost an important game. Those were the sort of things you'd try to get into his head but it took a fair bit of time for the penny to drop."

The Coventry incident was a typical example of Julian defending his beliefs. "I think if you stand up for what you believe in, then managers and players respect you for it," he says. "If the manager said you were crap and you thought you'd had a good game and just said, 'Yeah, alright,' then things are wrong. And if he said you were brilliant and you thought you were crap, and said so, then people would respect you for it. That's the way I've been brought up and I've always been the same."

The rumpus behind closed doors remained a private affair, but there was still much hullabaloo over the alleged elbowing on Flynn and subsequent booking. *'My immediate reaction was that he would be sent off, but I assume he received only the yellow card because the referee judged his action as retaliation,'* wrote Trevor Brooking in his Monday newspaper column, warning: *'If he continues in this vein he will repeat the misdemeanours of last season. Even the patience of Hammers supporters will wear thin if he continues to let them and himself down in this manner.'*

Reporter Ralph Ellis offered some support while making some astute observations. *'Dicks protested that it wasn't an elbow – that he simply tried to shake off an opponent who was climbing on his back. And from my viewpoint he just about deserved the benefit of the doubt. But the incident still exposed the flash of temper which is always bubbling under the surface and has made Dicks an easy target to wind up.'*

"To be fair, I've always had a temper when playing football. It always has been there and probably always will," Julian concedes.

The Ellis report had opened with the line *'It was a match which left a question...would you buy Julian Dicks?'* And the player himself, no doubt still fuming over the booking, the dressing room flare-up and seeing Coventry wipe out Hammers' lead (with a Roy Wegerle goal), told waiting press men after the game that "West Ham obviously want to get rid of me."

Any further misgivings the Hammers hierarchy may have had about selling Julian were blown away by the abysmal run of results over the next three weeks. A Clive Allen double in the midweek 2-0 home win over Sheffield Wednesday had

Julian flies in at Gordon Strachan during an early season game at Leeds in August 1993.

lifted people's hopes, but an appalling 4-0 Upton Park trouncing by Queens Park Rangers three days later, a 3-0 spanking by Manchester United at Old Trafford and a disturbing 0-0 home draw with bottom-of-the-table Swindon Town left everyone in no doubt – something had to be done, and quickly.

The presence of Liverpool manager Graeme Souness at Upton Park for the Swindon match indicated there'd already been movement behind the scenes. "I went up to a Liverpool game and said to Graeme, 'Look, we've got a fella here, he can really play, he's a bit of a nutter, but on his day when he puts his mind to it he's as good as anybody,'" reveals Harry Redknapp. "It was me who sold him to Liverpool. I thought a change of club would be good for him – he'd be less of a big fish in a small pond – and it might just sort him out. It would also be a good move for the future of West Ham."

When Souness ventured down to Upton Park for the Swindon game days later, few people were aware of him in the crowd, although reporter Harry Court wrote: *'It must have taken something special for Graeme Souness to travel all the way from Liverpool to Upton Park – especially with a home game against Blackburn today. But if there was anyone on display worthy of wearing a Liverpool shirt, then the Red machine must have serious problems under the bonnet. Maybe Souness was weighing up £2.5m Julian Dicks – but for a man with a heart condition, Souness is stretching it a bit to even contemplate linking Dicks and Neil Ruddock in the same defence.'*

Souness, who'd travelled down with right-hand man Tom Saunders (now a director at Anfield), has somewhat more positive recollections of what he saw that day, however: "We were sitting on the train to go back up to Liverpool and both of us said the same thing, that Dicks seems to have so much time and space when he gets the ball," says Graeme. "And we couldn't work out whether he was just clever when he got the ball or if people gave him extra respect – 'Go on, Julian, I don't really want to tackle you.'"

The 'Red machine' did indeed have problems 'under the bonnet' – at least at left-back, as far as Souness was concerned. "We had the problem of Irish players being considered as 'foreigners' and with David Burrows doing well we thought that maybe Steve Staunton was surplus to requirements and sold him to Aston Villa," he explains. "As time went on I became less happy with Burrows, though, and had seen Julian play many times and thought that he was my type of player. He catches the eye."

The first Dicksy knew of Souness' definite interest was before the training session the following Thursday, September 16. "I was just smashing a few balls around and Harry came out to me and said that if I wanted to go to Liverpool, he could sort it out for me," says Julian. "I was surprised that Liverpool had come in, given the reputation I had, but in a way I wasn't because the manager was Graeme Souness. And we know what he was like as a player! I said, 'Well, sort it out for me then.'

"After training I went into the office with Billy and Harry and they talked to me about it. They said that it had all been sorted and it was just a case of me going up to sort my personal terms out. Except that Graeme Souness at that point still had to talk to the players who would be transferred the other way. I knew two players were involved but not who they were."

The two Liverpool players concerned were left-back Burrows and midfielder Mike Marsh. It's suggested that the swap deal was finally agreed following an initial expression of interest from the Hammers in Marsh (who was allegedly over-priced at £1.5m by Souness) and a counter-proposal from the Anfield boss to exchange Burrows for Dicks. With the West Ham left-back being worth more than the Liverpool man, it was logical for Marsh to be included in the final package – indeed, many felt that it was a great bit of business by the Hammers. "Buggsy was a very good left-back in his own right and we'd seen Marshy play in a reserve game and he played ever so well," recalls Billy Bonds. "I don't think Marsh was too keen on coming down but in the end we persuaded him."

Dicks' recollection is that it was Burrows who was more unsure of the move, but makes the point that "once Graeme Souness wants you out, he wants you out". Julian travelled up to Merseyside that afternoon with agent Rachel Anderson and her husband, John. "We were speaking to Graeme on the phone on the way up there in the car, but he still hadn't got the players to go the other way yet. But he said that it wouldn't be a problem, he'd get them out.

"Graeme came to meet us in the Haydock Thistle Hotel, by the racecourse, and we sorted most of the deal out. He told me that I was his kind of player and that he didn't want me to change – he wanted me just the way I was. He then picked us up about eight o'clock on Friday morning to take us to the ground to meet the chairman and the secretary to complete the deal."

The agreed package included a weekly wage of £5,000 (negotiated up from the original £4,000 offered), £500 per appearance and a signing on fee of £300,000, but – money aside – Julian had already made his mind up after the Thursday meeting with Souness. "As soon as I met him I thought that he was the kind of guy I wanted to play under. He was straight. You looked at him and there was just something about him," says Julian, obviously impressed with the charisma of the Anfield boss.

Dicks had also discussed the move north with wife Kay. "She was pleased," he says. "We'd had a lot of stick down in London and she was happy to get away." During the previous months there had been slight rumblings of a move to Spurs but with the problems of the last 18 months still fresh in the memory, it was not a move that would have appealed to her. "I didn't want him to go to Tottenham," Kay insists. "I wanted to get away – anywhere. I'd have gone to Scotland. I just felt we'd got into a rut and we couldn't get out. We needed a fresh start, a total break away from everybody and just start all over again."

> "As soon as I met Graeme I thought that he was the kind of guy I wanted to play under"

Ironically, the Dickses had already set the wheels in motion to buy a new house in Little Burstead, having sold both their Billericay properties. Needless to say, they had to pull out as soon as the Liverpool move became known. "It's funny, I'd even got the cooker delivered and the bloke wouldn't let us have it back. He's still got it now!" laughs Kay. "I'd never been to Liverpool but I wanted to go. I didn't think they'd buy him, to be honest, and I was shocked. I didn't think he had it in him. But I couldn't wait to make the move."

Martin Allen considered Dicksy's move to Anfield as a reward for all his past efforts for the Hammers. "He deserved the chance to play for a big club," says Martin. "He'd worked so hard and played so well for West Ham that he had to go and play for a bigger club at that point in time."

By Friday, Marsh and Burrows had successfully been 'persuaded' that Upton Park would offer them much greater first-team opportunities and, with the deals secured, Julian then – in a chauffeur-driven limousine – went to join his new team-mates at their Melwood training camp. "I remember Bruce Grobbelaar throwing his kit at me while I was sitting down. They seemed like a good bunch of lads and made me feel welcome."

It was an exciting experience for Julian, as both he and the Hammers embarked on new adventures along different paths…

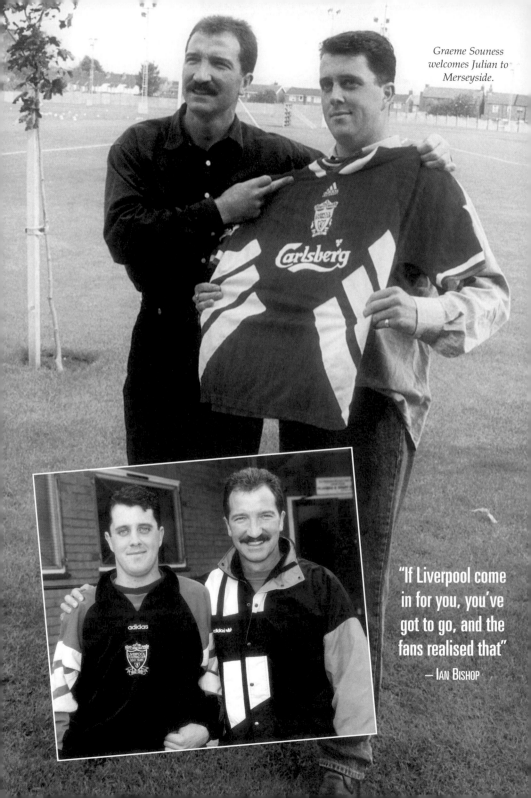

Graeme Souness welcomes Julian to Merseyside.

"If Liverpool come in for you, you've got to go, and the fans realised that"
— IAN BISHOP

CHAPTER 19

SOU FAR SOU GOOD?

DESPITE the speculation about Julian's possible move from West Ham, there was still something rather surreal about the photographs that appeared on the back pages of the national newspapers on Saturday, September 18. For there he was, in the red shirt of Liverpool, beaming proudly as he raised his arms and clenched his fists in a Mr. Universe-style pose.

As Hammers fans headed north for the game against Blackburn Rovers, there was obviously much debate about the sale of their favourite son. Although there was understandable disappointment at seeing Dicks in another club's colours, supporters had nonetheless recognised that change had indeed been necessary, while few could deny him the right to take such a golden opportunity to improve his chances of winning trophies and gaining international recognition.

Midfielder Ian Bishop, born in Liverpool himself, acknowledged along with the rest of the players that Julian had little option once the Anfield club had made their move for him. "If Liverpool come in for you, you've got to go – and the fans realised that," he says. "It didn't surprise me that a club like them came in for him because he was always our best player, standing head and shoulders above everyone else. It also didn't surprise me that he went, because you've got to have ambition and he probably felt he wasn't really going anywhere at the time."

There was also a degree of optimism among West Ham supporters, pleased at having seen two classy Liverpool players in Marsh and Burrows agree to join their club. The previous 24 hours had also seen the purchase of Lee Chapman (for £250,000), who'd decided that he'd been unable to adjust to the alien environment of the First Division and needed top-flight football. Contrary to some reports on the day, however, Chapman was not bought with cash acquired from the Dicks deal. "No money was involved at all," confirms Peter Storrie of the agreement that took Julian to Anfield in straight exchange for the two men from Anfield.

With three players making their debuts for West Ham, the team promptly notched up a memorable 2-0 victory at Ewood Park, with Chapman scoring the first goal of the afternoon. As crucial as the three points, however, was the team's convincing display which dispelled any fears the management may have had of experiencing a backlash from the travelling fans. "It wasn't a tough decision to sell Dicksy, because we needed to do something," says Bonds. "But it was a gamble because I knew if it didn't work I would get absolutely slaughtered. But the Blackburn game sorted everyone's fears out and after that we went from strength to strength."

> "I knew Bill wasn't happy with Dicksy being at the club and we just felt if was time for a change" – HARRY REDKNAPP

Julian may have been a little saddened at leaving the Hammers but the realisation that his sale had probably helped the situation at Upton Park offset those feelings somewhat. "I was gutted to leave but, as Harry and Billy had said at the time, they needed to sell players to keep the club up. I think Billy had been worried about letting me go because of the fans, but with them going to Blackburn and getting a result it would have eased the situation," says Julian.

"I think a lot of people were ready to have a moan during our first game without Dicksy," adds Redknapp. "He had a lot of support, but we won at Blackburn and it was all forgotten. I thought there might have been a backlash but I knew Bill wasn't happy with Dicksy being at the club and we just felt if was time for a change. No one player is bigger than West Ham United Football Club."

If the Hammers had faced a daunting trip for their first match without their former favourite, Julian's debut for Liverpool could not have proved a tougher baptism of fire – a Merseyside derby at Goodison Park. "I remember Graeme Souness saying to me, 'You've got something to prove.' And I told him that I had nothing to prove," recalls Julian of his first game, just 24 hours after making his move. "I said, 'If you didn't think I was a good player, you wouldn't have bought me. You know what I can do.' I think he thought, 'I've got a cocky bastard here!' But he'd have liked that, because he was the same. But I had a good game."

Dicksy indeed had a promising start to his Liverpool career, although it was a day of disaster for his new club. Not only did Everton (with Tony Cottee in the side) win 2-0, but it was the match that saw an on-field exchange of blows between colleagues Grobbelaar and McManaman. "The whole game was totally overshadowed by that incident," reflects Cottee. "Julian must have wondered what was going on because it was his first game and two of his team-mates were having a fight with each other!

"It was a very comfortable win for Everton on the day – Mark Ward (another ex-Hammer) got the first goal and I got the second five minutes from time – but I remember Dicksy having a very good game."

Julian was never going to have a problem remembering Cottee's effort that day – it came from *his* mistake! "The ball came down, I chested it, then TC came in and got it off me, nutmegged Mark Wright and beat Bruce in goal," he recounts. "But Graeme Souness didn't have a go at me. He just said I should have laid it off first time." Dicks had his own moments, though. *'Neville Southall had to be at his best to*

Taking a shot on his Liverpool debut at Everton.

keep out Dicks' 30-yard shot,' reported *The Telegraph* of his close effort to reduce the deficit.

As Julian impressed for his new club, mum Carol was completely unaware that her son had even left West Ham. "I didn't know anything about it!" she declares. "I was on holiday in Cyprus, we came back to our apartment from the beach and put the radio on for the football results. I had the kettle on for tea and the radio started talking about Liverpool. I sat there going, 'Oh Christ...' and it suddenly said that Julian Dicks was having a great debut for Liverpool. I screamed! Everybody rushed into the kitchen thinking I'd seen a giant spider or something. 'Our Ju's playing for Liverpool!' I said. We went out that night and bought six papers, and then rang him up to congratulate him."

Despite the intensity of the Merseyside derby, Graeme Souness had no doubts whatsoever of pitching Dicks into such an emotion-charged affair for his debut. "He's a big game player – he's got the temperament for things like that," he declares. The Liverpool boss had insisted at the Friday press conference that he had bought Julian for his tenacious approach and, although he hoped Dicksy had learnt from his previous misdemeanours, he had no desire for him to compromise his aggression. "I think we're alike in many way," reflects Graeme. "Maybe I was slightly better at controlling myself – in fact I must have been because I didn't get sent off as many times! But he's my type of player. He wants to win and he can play.

"The thing that people overlook is that he's a bloody good footballer. He's got a left foot that can open a can of beans and he's a good passer of the ball. When we got him to Liverpool people showed him a lot of respect. They would rather him pass the ball than confront him physically. For every player there is a settling in period but I was happy with him from day one."

Back at Upton Park, with Chapman grabbing another two goals in the 5-1 Coca-Cola Cup win over Third Division Chesterfield, and Burrows and Marsh fitting in snugly, many were suggesting that for all Julian's talents, the deal was already working out in West Ham's favour. Trevor Brooking, immediately after the Blackburn win, had expressed the view that the exchange deal was a *'decision which I believe will prove to be correct, and one which had to be made sooner rather than later. It would be silly to start drawing too many conclusions after one victory, but I feel far more optimistic and Bonzo now has a few extra options.'*

Trev also felt that the move to Anfield might bring out the best in Julian: *'This move could be the making or breaking of him. At West Ham his ability tended to allow him the luxury of coasting his way through matches, never quite having to fully extend himself. But at Liverpool he will be under the spotlight every week and it might just give him the impetus he now needs in his career.'*

> "You definitely get the benefit of the doubt from referees if you've got a Liverpool top on"

Conversely, it could also have been argued that with Julian being part of a better squad of players at Liverpool, the burden of pressure was shared among the team on the field, whereas at Upton Park the responsibility fell very heavily on his shoulders at times. "At West Ham a lot of things seemed to go through me and the fans expected a lot from me," he confirms. "But there were so many good players at Anfield it just made it so much easier. If you gave the ball to Jamie Redknapp or John Barnes or Ian Rush, you knew they'd do the business and you could go on the overlap and expect to get the ball back. So there was a lot less pressure on me."

The more comfortable playing situation also helped Julian address the disciplinary side of his game – at least as far as Souness was concerned. "There was so much expected of him at West Ham and maybe the pressure was off him," he reiterates to explain Dicksy's sudden improvement in that respect. That wasn't, however, Julian's theory as to why the yellow cards immediately dried up. "You definitely get the benefit of the doubt from referees if you've got a Liverpool top on – there's no two ways about it," he says. "I realised that on my debut. I got launched in, mistimed a few tackles and the ref (David Elleray) wouldn't book me. It was the same for Razor (Ruddock) as well. He was getting stuck in and getting the benefit of the doubt as well. If you mistimed a challenge at Upton Park you'd get booked more or less straight away. You might get the benefit of the doubt for one tackle, but not two or three. It stood out a mile – particularly at Anfield." Funnily enough, this wasn't something that team-mate at the time, Don Hutchison, was ever aware of. "I don't know what Julian's on about there," says Hutch, who remembers picking up more than his fair share of cards during his time at Liverpool.

184

Mike Marsh, Lee Chapman and David Burrows were beginning to look the part at West Ham. Marsh and Burrows were 'persuaded' to move south as part of Julian's move to Anfield.

Another difference Julian became aware of at Anfield was the occasional lack of atmosphere – which would no doubt surprise many given the legendary status of the Kop. "The Liverpool fans don't seem to sing," he declares. "They expect you to be winning and then they'll start singing – and that's when they're up there with the best. But if it's 0-0 or they're losing they don't want to know."

Liverpool fans had been used to winning, of course, but with Graeme Souness inheriting a side that was hardly blessed with youth, his job was to instigate change while trying to maintain the winning formula. Striker Nigel Clough had been signed from Nottingham Forest for £2.275m, while Dicks had been drafted in alongside another new face in defence, Neil Ruddock. The coupling of two of soccer's so-called hardmen prompted rumblings that, under Souness, Liverpool were abandoning their traditions and adopting a more physical approach to the game. *The Telegraph's* William Johnson had already made some cutting comments following Dicks' actual signing: '*The arrival of a new £1.6m signing in a chauffeur-driven limousine was symbolic of the way Liverpool have established themselves as giants in the modern game. Sadly, however, the occupant of the Bentley which pulled into the Melwood training headquarters was not in keeping with the style of a Rolls Royce club,*' he wrote bitterly. As far as Wimbledon's Vinny Jones was concerned, though, not enough fuss had been kicked up over the signings. '*Their disciplinary records are certainly on a par with mine, but because it was Liverpool doing the buying they got no more flak than if they'd signed Torvill and Dean! Can you imagine the fuss if our gaffer Joe Kinnear had brought that same tough-guy twosome to join me and the rest of Wimbledon's Crazy Gang? There would have been uproar!*' he complained in one interview.

The Liverpool players – Don Hutchison amongst them – still had their preconceptions of Julian as he signed to the club, though. "I was one of those people who thought he was a bit of nutcase. When somebody has been sent off that many times, that's all people see," says Hutch. "I didn't actually know that Julian was as good as he proved to be – I thought he was just a strong, hard tackling left-back. And then when you saw him play, you realised that there's more to his game than that. He's got a lot of skill."

Before the rest of the Premiership could get too worked up over having to face the 'tough-guy twosome', however, Dicks was sidelined after just six games by injury – to the same knee that had put him out of the game for 14 months at West Ham. "After the Oldham game (on October 16) my knee blew up and I went to see the club doctor," recalls Julian. "It was confirmed as just a small problem with the cartilage, though, and while it wouldn't heal as quickly as other people's because of what had taken place before, I wasn't worried about it."

Dicksy's injury was witnessed by his manager Graeme Souness. "I think it was Gunnar Halle who injured him with a late tackle. He wasn't happy with that challenge and the injury set him back a bit." Despite initial suggestions that he might need surgery, however, Julian declared himself fit for a Coca-Cola Cup tie against Ipswich, but then had to miss the team's 4-2 win over Southampton after Souness arranged for him to have his TEETH attended to. "As far as

> "Graeme made Julian go to the dentist and have all the work that needed doing on his teeth" – KAY DICKS

Graeme was concerned everything had to be right," says Kay Dicks. "He made Julian go to the dentist and have all the work that needed doing on his teeth. So he had to have about four teeth out.

Souness was the same with all the players – he was really on the ball with anything to do with health."

His teeth may have been in shape but tooth, er, *truth* be known, Julian's knee was proving a problem, with it eventually being decided that an operation would be required to trim the remaining cartilage in his left knee. Not only did this mean that he couldn't face his old West Ham team-mates when they arrived at Anfield for the game on November 6 (although he still met up with his ex-colleagues after they stayed in the same hotel as him) – which Liverpool won 2-0 – but he also missed the next couple of months.

Julian spent the early months in the north at the Haydock Thistle (scene of his original meeting with Souness), while Kay and the children – who stayed in an hotel in Essex following the sale of the Billericay property in order to keep the kids in school until the end of term – visited at weekends as he searched for a new family home. "I

> "I loved it because he was like a little fish again" – KAY DICKS

like looking for houses, but it's just the pain of moving all your gear once you've found one," he says. At the suggestion of Mark Wright and Rob Jones – two of the Liverpool players he'd established an instant rapport with – Julian started investigating around Chester. Ian Bishop's wife, Jane, had also confirmed to Kay the appeal of the area. "I went to see this house in a little village in Mollington and as soon as I saw it I liked it," says Julian. "So I called Kay, she came up and that was it. It was on sale at £290,000 and we offered £270,000, which was turned down. We liked it so much that we paid the asking price. Most of the place was damp because the couple selling only really used one room, but it was a lovely house."

Julian moved into the four-bedroomed house (situated in two acres of land) on December 10, with Kay, Jessica and Kattie following on Christmas Eve after taking a break in Lapland. ("I'd always wanted to take the children there," explains Kay of the unlikely holiday destination.) And they settled into their new home quickly. "It was lovely," declares Kay. "Within three months I'd have been quite happy to have stayed there for the rest of my life. I loved it. The school (Mollington Church of England) was lovely for the girls, it was easy to make friends and it was so easy going. We had lots of people visit and in no time it was as if we'd been there forever."

Kay was also happy with the change she saw in Julian – one that ultimately probably saved their marriage. "I loved it because he was like a little fish again," she says. "We used to go out and not get bothered because people didn't know who he was. It was a good job we moved when we did because I don't think I'd still be with Julian otherwise. You get to a point when you can only take so much."

Mark Wright was a nearby neighbour, while at the club Julian had also established an instant rapport with Don Hutchison and Harry Redknapp's son, Jamie. "I don't think he had any problems with getting to know people," reflects Graeme Souness. "Some of the players were maybe a bit wary of him at first,

"Julian's goal was a bit special," said Jamie Redknapp, pictured here congratulating his team-mate on his first Liverpool goal.

because of his reputation, but he was fine. He keeps himself to himself, he's got his own style and personality, but he was accepted and liked by the boys."

Julian made his comeback following surgery to his knee in the 0-0 draw at Sheffield United on Boxing Day, but a slight reaction ruled him out of the next two games, returning for the memorable 3-3 thriller against Manchester United at Anfield. The very next match saw Julian achieve something that few of his detractors would ever have considered likely – he celebrated his first goal for Liverpool before being booked! It came in the 3-0 romp at Oldham on January 15 (the club's ninth game unbeaten), in which Dicks crashed in a beauty from 25 yards. "Jamie Redknapp played me the ball, I controlled it and it flew into the top corner. And then everybody jumped on me!" he remembers.

"Julian's goal was a bit special," said Jamie afterwards. "He does it all the time in training and we've been waiting for him to do it in a game. So he's taken a bit of ribbing after finally doing it."

That particularly day was memorable for Graeme Souness for more than one reason, however, with Julian startling the players in the dressing room with a comment that indicated that certain things were not to be joked about. "Some of the senior players were messing around and talking about their wives," reveals Souness. "Somebody made a sort of locker-room type suggestion and Julian just turned round to the individual and said, 'Well, I would just kill you.' And he actually meant that. He had that look on his face. Everybody who was in the dressing room at that time thought, 'Christ, he means that.'"

Julian's habit of speaking his mind was something that Souness clearly appreciated, despite the fearsome image that the manager often projected. This was indicated in an early conversation between the two men after Graeme had been quoted on the left-back position. "He came out in the press and admitted he'd made a mistake in getting rid of Steve Staunton," Julian says. "If he hadn't have sold him he probably wouldn't have needed to buy me, but I remember saying to him, 'I'm a better player than Staunton anyway!' Graeme liked that – he liked people being upfront with him and a little bit arrogant, because he was the same himself."

> "If I was asked to pick the best 11 players I've ever worked with, he'd be one of them" – GRAEME SOUNESS

And there's no doubt that Souness enjoyed his relationship with Julian, to the extent that a genuine bond was established between the two. "I got on very well with him," confirms Graeme. "I had no problems with him at all. He'd give his opinion, I would welcome it, and he would listen to what I had to say. We never had a cross word the whole time I was there. Indeed, he's someone I would liked to have played with. It would have been a fair twosome in the team. I've signed a lot of players in my time and if I was asked to pick the best 11 players I've ever worked with, he'd be one of them.

"It's his attitude that appeals to me. He's wants to win and you've got to have people like that in your football team if you're going to be successful. Sometimes players can go a bit too far and overstep the mark, but unfortunately you can't just turn things on and off with a switch. But I felt I had a relationship with him and I could have helped him further. Unfortunately, I didn't get a chance to work with him for long enough."

Indeed, despite the brevity of their working relationship, something of a mutual appreciation society was formed. "I thought Graeme was superb," says Julian. "There was something about him. People weren't scared of him but you did what he said. His nickname was the Rottweiler – that's what they used to call him up there. To be fair, he was the governor – he ruled everything. Obviously the club wasn't his but he made it his. He was involved in everything and the chairman did what he said.

"But I don't think they gave him enough time. If you go in and change a side and buy players, it won't all gel together at once. You've got to give people time and I don't think they gave Graeme enough of it."

One of Souness' major problems at the time was keeping the established players happy while trying to integrate his own, younger purchases. And his approach to the task was not always appreciated by some. "Not by John Barnes, Ian Rush…the older players," reveals Julian. "If they weren't doing the business, he'd stick them in the reserves and they didn't like Souness for that. But that's the way he was – if you didn't do the business, he'd bin you. He dropped Rushy completely, not even using him as sub. John Barnes was another one. If you're not doing well, it doesn't matter who you are, you should be out of the side. At the end of the day, though, if you upset players, then they're not going to work for you," he says philosophically.

"Graeme said in the papers that he got rid of too many players too quickly, and if you do that then obviously you've got to bring other ones in. He was trying to get a younger side to prepare for the future but he didn't have enough time. They ousted him and that was it."

Come February 1994, and with an embarrassing home FA Cup defeat by First Division Bristol City tightening the noose around Souness' neck, his days were numbered. "The fans were calling for his head," admits Julian. "I remember losing one game and I drove Rob Jones home in my Porsche when I had the hump. I was doing 150mph down the motorway and Rob was holding on, saying, 'Slow down, slow down...'"

Eventually, with the team failing to consistently perform and the ranks divided in the dressing room, Souness' inevitable departure was announced. "It was the chairman who broke the news," remembers Julian. "He came to the training ground and said that Graeme had resigned and that Roy Evans was taking over for the time being. I think a few players were glad to see Graeme go, such as the players he'd dropped. No one likes to get dropped but he did it to quite a few so they were relieved to see him go."

Don Hutchison was not one of these people, however. "I adored Graeme, as Julian did," he says. "We thought he was honest and always told you exactly how he felt. Although it was Kenny Dalglish that signed me, it was Graeme who actually gave me the chance to play, so I owe him a lot really. I thought he was a good manager and I was very sorry to see him go."

Kay, who was more than happy with her new life, was also disappointed to see Souness leave Anfield. She had no reason to fear a change of boss, but she'd appreciated the efforts of the man who'd taken them up to the north. "Graeme was really nice and had made us feel very welcome, so it was a shame it didn't last very long," she says. "When he went nobody had a clue who was going to end up taking the job at first. Then it was announced that it would be Roy Evans. But I never really worried about it. I didn't know him well although I'd obviously seen him at the club. But I didn't realise how much Roy disliked Julian until he was actually in charge."

> "I didn't realise how much Roy disliked Julian until he was actually in charge" — KAY DICKS

CHAPTER 20

FROM EVANS TO HELL

A LTHOUGH most players are generally a little concerned if the manager who's bought them swiftly departs, Julian had no particular reason to fear the appointment of Roy Evans as Liverpool boss.

As assistant to Graeme Souness, he'd done nothing to oppose the purchase of Dicks ("I talked it over with Roy Evans and Ronnie Moran and they were all very keen on it," insists Souness) and the pair had a reasonable working relationship – to the extent that, although he was sorry to see the boss go, the player didn't feel unduly worried with the change.

"I hadn't seen too much of Julian before he came to Liverpool – I'd only really seen him on the television and I'd always thought he was a fantastic footballer. And I still believe that," says Roy. "I think we had a reasonable relationship when Graeme was manager. Julian is his own man and has his own character, but the majority of the time I found him a very decent lad. I think the only problem we had with him was a worry about his injury."

True, Julian's knee difficulties, following the Oldham clash on October 16, did indeed plague him during his Liverpool days. And throughout this period, West Ham physio John Green – who'd worked so hard to see Julian through to full rehabilitation three years earlier – continued to keep tabs on his former player's developments. "Julian had taken a bad blow to the knee – it was quite a nasty injury. They did some trimming of the cartilage but the main thing that Julian had was a bone bruise," John reveals, before explaining: " The cartilage is like a cushion between the two bones that meet at the knee and Brian Roper had taken one of the cartilages completely out, so there was no cushion there. One bone therefore smashed against the other and the bruise sat up on the surface. That's quite a nasty business and it takes a long time for that to heal.

"With that sort of thing we'd have said to Julian, 'You'd better have 12 weeks off.' You have to treat it with the utmost respect. But I think the people at Liverpool didn't really do that. Subsequently, Julian got a lot of swelling on the knee every time he trained."

Instead of being rested after the Oldham game, Julian had continued to try and

Being introduced to Stephanie Moore by John Wark at the Bobby Moore Memorial match at Upton Park.

turn out for the club. "You get players who can play with a bit of pain and others who can't – and Julian is obviously one of those that will," says Souness, while John Green was of the view that the player was pressured into playing. "Liverpool had made a big signing, they wanted him to play and they kept saying to him, 'Yeah, you can play but don't train.' So obviously he lost his fitness."

Given such handicaps, it was hardly surprising that Liverpool fans never saw Dicks at the peak of his powers. Ian Bishop, making regular visits to his home town, was aware of the disappointed reaction of the people on Merseyside. "The supporters were saying they weren't seeing the best of him," Ian admits. "I was telling people up there that he was going to be a marvel, a revelation. But they kept coming back to me saying he was injured a lot. When he did come back from injury, it was in a side that wasn't really the true Liverpool. They weren't going so well at the time and were having to rediscover the winning formula."

If Julian's season had proved difficult in respect of fitness and form, he was at least able to take consolation in the fact that he'd successfully convinced people of his rehabilitation ON the field, having not picked up a single booking in a Liverpool shirt by the time he came down to Upton Park on March 7 to take part in the Bobby Moore Memorial Match. To mark the opening of the new Bobby Moore Stand, the Hammers entertained an FA Premier League squad (managed by George Graham), including Glenn Hoddle, Liam Brady, Barry Venison, Brian McClair, Jason Wilcox, Dwight Yorke, Peter Ndlovu, Dean Holdsworth and ex-Hammers Tony Cottee and Dicks himself among the 22 players who enjoyed 45 minutes of football each. The gate of 20,311 raised an estimated £200,000 for the Bobby Moore Fund for Imperial Cancer as the

> **"I was delighted to be asked to turn out and I got a great response from the fans"**

Hammers won 2-1 (with Cottee opening the scoring for the Premiership) and although Julian may have forgotten who he was playing for when he accidentally pulled on a West Ham shirt again (when he was actually appearing against them), he certainly would not forget the emotion of the occasion. "I was delighted to be asked to turn out and I got a great response from the fans," he confirms.

The acclaim was nothing compared to what he received when he returned to the Boleyn Ground with Liverpool for a league game on April 23. During the six weeks following Julian's last Upton Park appearance he'd been booked for the first and only time in Liverpool's colours (against Everton on March 12) and scored his third goal for the club – a penalty that secured a 1-0 win over Ipswich Town at Anfield on April 9. Despite his spot-kick exploits with the Hammers, Dicks had only started taking penalties for his new club in the absence of Jan Molby and that was his second successful attempt (after putting one away in the 4-2 defeat at Southampton in mid-February).

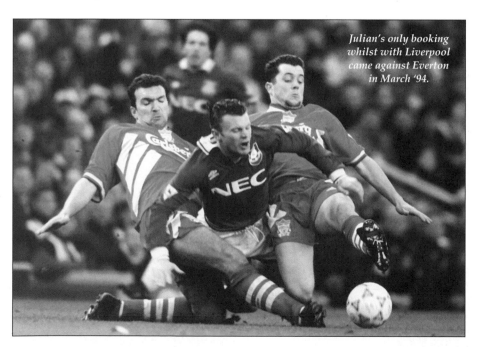

Julian's only booking whilst with Liverpool came against Everton in March '94.

Julian scores an historic goal from the spot against Ipswich.

"I may have only been there 12 months but I'm still down in their record books for scoring the last goal in front of the old Kop"

The significance of the goal against Ipswich was that it was the last one ever scored in front of the famous Kop End at Anfield (with the team failing to win their remaining two home games), Julian ensuring a little piece of Liverpool history for himself. "That's the highlight of my time at Anfield," he says. "I may have only been there for 12 months but I'm still down in their record books for scoring the last goal in front of the old Kop. They pulled it down shortly afterwards."

The game against the Hammers, however, was no less memorable for Dicks – thanks to the opposing fans alone. *'Julian Dicks was given a cheerily raucous homecoming,'* said one paper, while another acknowledged, *'Dicks was given a hero's welcome.'* "I knew I'd get a good reception because I've always had a good relationship with the fans, although it did surprise me how much of one I got – it was tremendous," Julian says.

So much so that he'd forgotten who he was playing for again! "I remember coming off the pitch at half-time and walking towards the *West Ham* dressing room. I walked past the away team door and I think it was Tony Carr (Hammers' youth team manager) who said, 'Where are *you* going?'" he laughs.

The game itself found Dicks up against West Ham right-winger Matthew Rush. "I know what Harry was thinking," says Julian. "Rushy is a quick lad and I think he told him to stop me getting forward. So every time I got the ball he was there. I remember West Ham's Tony Gale giving the second goal away when Ian Rush got onto the backpass and slotted it away. That's all I can recall really, apart from me and Razor (Ruddock) clattering Lee Chapman. Ludo kicked the ball out, it bounced and me and Razor both went in on Chapman and landed on him."

West Ham's fans may have missed Julian following his departure, but club physio John Green was keeping in much closer contact with him than he'd have anticipated. "Julian phoned me up to ask what to do about his knee and he came down a few times," reveals John. "Even at that stage we were talking about him possibly coming back and so I wanted to stay involved because I needed to know what was happening to the knee, just in case he did return."

Liverpool's 2-1 victory at Upton Park (their first away win under Roy Evans) kept the team in seventh place – a poor position given the club's tradition of winning trophies over the years. They eventually finished just eighth – behind Wimbledon and Sheffield Wednesday – and it was considered a big under-achievement. "They expect success every season and if they don't win anything then it's a bad year. So was finishing where we did – both the club and the fans expect a lot better," admits Julian.

Yet despite the unrewarding campaign, Julian was enjoying life at Liverpool. He'd played in the final 16 league games and Roy Evans had been quite happy with his form during the run-in. "I think Julian performed pretty well – his talent was never in question," affirms the Anfield boss. And after the traumas of the final couple of years down in Essex, Kay was settled into her new, hassle-free environment and very content. "I didn't go and see all the games but at home we had some brilliant times," she says. "We'd moved into the house and, thinking we were going to be there another three years, had everything done on it that was needed."

Julian's contentment was also apparent to his family, although Carol Dicks had become aware of the continuing division between the two camps of players at Anfield. "He was happy where he lived and the house he had," she confirms. "He got on with some of the players – the younger ones, such as Jamie Redknapp, Rob Jones and Robbie Fowler. But the older ones didn't want to know. The way I look at it, Julian had too much of a name to go to Liverpool and some of the other players didn't like it. The best one of the older ones was John Barnes, because he mixed with both sets. Whereas the likes of Ian Rush and Steve Nicol were 'yes men' to Roy Evans and just wanted to pick on the kids when they wanted their own way. But they couldn't get their own way with Julian. He used to tell them to sod off. On the coach you'd have the older guys down at the front with Roy Evans and the young ones at the back – Julian was always at the back.

"The Liverpool move could've been the making of Julian. I think the club would have been right for him if Souness had been there longer. But it seemed to me that Roy Evans just didn't want Souness' players in the side."

As far as Don Hutchison was concerned, however, any cliques among the players were purely down to how old they were. "I think it was just a thing of age groups rather than personalities," he says. "Obviously, if you're young and single you feel more comfortable with other lads your age, while others like Rushy would just do their own thing. But Julian was in the group that liked a laugh."

With the season over – a difficult one for both club and player – Dicksy looked forward to taking a break and starting afresh his first full season for Liverpool. No sooner had the print dried on the final league table, however, press stories started to suggest that Julian could be used as bait to bring David Burrows back to Anfield, following Evans' aborted bid to lure Steve Staunton (another former Liverpool left-back) to Merseyside again from Aston Villa – a move which in itself raised a question mark over Dicks' future. It was even suggested that West Ham had rejected a Liverpool attempt to set up some kind of swap deal. Evans denies the link with Burrows, while Kay remembers a chat with the Liverpool boss during the summer. "We were going to Cyprus and we saw him at Manchester Airport when he was going away with his family," she says. "There'd been paper talk and he came over to us and said, 'You take no notice of what you read in the papers, have a nice holiday.' I felt better after he said that, but when we got back it was just horrendous."

> "The likes of Ian Rush and Steve Nicol were 'yes men' to Roy Evans and just wanted to pick on the kids" – CAROL DICKS

It all started to go wrong for Julian following Liverpool's disastrous 4-1 humiliation by First Division Bolton Wanderers in a pre-season friendly on July 26. Roy Evans was so annoyed with the performance of the team – particularly the defence – that he made plain his views in the dressing room after the game.

"We got beaten 4-1 but I personally thought I'd had quite a good game," Julian declares. "We came in and Roy Evans had a go at Mark Wright, who had a go back. And that was it – he didn't say anything to me. The next thing I knew was that the manager was saying I was unfit and overweight in the papers the morning afterwards. I felt annoyed because I thought he could have called me in and told me, rather than going to the press. He was angry because we'd lost 4-1, but the only person he'd had a go at was Wrighty.

> "I didn't think that Julian, at that time, was as fit as I would have liked him to be"

"I went to see Roy and asked about the stories and he said, 'You're unfit and overweight.' I said, 'Well, why didn't you call me into the office instead of going to the papers?' To be fair, he did say, 'Yeah, I was wrong, that's what I should have done.' But obviously it was too late.

"He then repeated that I was unfit and I told him that pre-season was for *getting* fit. That was it really – he couldn't say anything else because he knew that was the truth."

Roy Evans was still annoyed at the Burden Park debacle, which he considered an embarrassment for Liverpool Football Club. "It's difficult to remember actual words that were said but obviously I wasn't a happy man on the night," says the Anfield boss. "I wasn't happy with the team's performance and I didn't think that Julian, at that time, was as fit as I would have liked him to be. Admittedly,

This pre-season friendly at Bolton turned out to be Julian's last outing in Liverpool's first-team and prompted Dicks' bust-up with Roy Evans.

there's the answer that it's pre-season and they're in the process of getting fit, but I just wasn't happy with the whole thing on the night. The next day, rightly or wrongly, I made a couple of decisions."

Those 'decisions' were to leave Julian Dicks and Mark Wright at home while Liverpool departed for their pre-season tour of Germany, where they were taking on Bayern Munich and Borussia Möenchengladbach, among others.

"I trained with the team after the Bolton game but then we had the trip to Germany," says Julian. "Rob Jones and I were talking to Ronnie Moran and I asked about bringing my passport in when he said, 'You're not going!' I said, 'What do you mean I'm not going?' He said it wasn't his decision and to go and see the manager. I went to see Evans and he said, 'You're not going, you're overweight and you're going to stay here to get fit.' I was annoyed at the situation but I didn't necessarily think that he was going to get rid of me or that I was on the way out. It didn't occur to me."

What did occur to Julian was to speak his mind to the press when they arrived at the training ground looking for a story following the team's departure without the two defenders. "I was bitter at being left behind so I thought I may as well just come out and tell the truth," he reveals. In the stories that appeared the next day, Julian not only disputed his manager's allegations that he was unfit and overweight but accused Evans of lacking "the bottle to tell me the truth that he does not want me in the team."

Dicks had no fears about opening up to the media, feeling he was purely responding in the same way as the Liverpool boss had done after the Bolton game. "I thought, at the end of the day, that's what he'd done to me," says Julian. "I'd told Roy in the office anyway that I thought he was a coward, as they left for Germany. I told him it was just an excuse. I said, 'If you want to get me out, then sell me.' And he said he didn't want to sell me. I said if he didn't want to sell me he should take me to Germany and he said, 'No, you're unfit and overweight.' And that's the way it was left.

"Maybe I was two or three pounds overweight," he admits, "but after six or seven weeks off you're going to put weight on. Sure, I used to have the odd day where I'd binge, just like any

> "I'd told Roy in the office that I thought he was a coward"

other footballer, but that's just part and parcel of the summer break. I had a punch-bag in my garage and used to spend time on that, and I'd go riding on my mountain bike, but nothing gets you ready for football unless you play games. You can run all day but as soon as you start playing it's a different kind of fitness."

Kay Dicks, however – who'd qualified as a fitness instructor – refuted claims that her husband had been 'pudding' weight on. "He was by no means overweight," she insists. "That was the first close season Julian had actually done work during the

DAILY STAR SPORTS NEWSPAPER OF THE YEAR

CHICKEN!

Evans hasn't got the bottle storms axed Anfield ace Dicks

■ BILL THORNTON

LIVERPOOL hard-man Julian Dicks last night made an astonishing attack on Anfield manager Roy Evans.

Dicks reckons he has played his last game for the club. And he accused Evans of not having the "bottle" to

Ossie's Samba party is put on hold

summer. Roy Evans just didn't like him – end of story. If he'd have been a stone lighter he'd have probably said he was too thin!"

Despite Dicks' newspaper attack on his manager, Evans refused to get further involved in a public dispute. "I didn't respond to the stories, otherwise you start a full-scale war in the press – and I wasn't prepared to do that," he says.

Not only did the Liverpool boss not respond but, according to Julian, he didn't even speak to him once the team returned from Germany. "He didn't talk to me for about 10 weeks," Dicks states, a suggested which is refuted by Evans. "I don't believe that we didn't speak for 10 weeks – I'd be surprised at that," he says. "I think we always said hello in the mornings. I'm not the sort of guy who holds any animosity towards anybody. I don't mind having an argument but I'm always prepared to talk to people."

Dicksy's situation at the club at this time was hardly helped by his poor relationship with coaches Ronnie Moran and Steve Heighway. The main cause of the problems with Moran was the difference in approach towards training between the two men. "I didn't get on with Ronnie," confirms Julian. "What they used to do on a Friday was have a five-a-side with rope or sometimes just have a piggy-in-the-middle, where one person is shoved in the middle and they have to get the ball. Then you used to do a few doggies (sprinting between cones). That would be it! They wouldn't let you have a football and you'd only be out for about 25 minutes and I'd not even be able to get a sweat on in that time. So I used to go and get a ball on my own and kick it against a wall and they didn't like that.

"I remember one row when Ronnie Moran told me to give him the ball. I said no and was effing and blinding at him and he said, 'You've only been in the game five minutes.' I said, 'Actually, I've been in the game for nine years!' But because he'd been in it for 40-odd years he thought I was stupid.

"I used to row with Ronnie every day. He grew up with Bill Shankly and he'd have his own way of training. I'd always been used to smashing a ball about for half-an-hour before training but when I tried to do that at Liverpool they didn't like it. They used to ask for the ball back and I'd tell them to piss off."

Such disputes had been witnessed by Graeme Souness during his spell as manager. "Julian wanted to be out with the ball but they liked him to warm up first," he explains. "But I know what he's talking about and who he is talking about, and he wouldn't have been the first person to have friction with that individual. But that person has been at the club a long time, has seen a lot of good players come and go, and he's done well for the club in his own way. It would have been nothing personal with Julian – he was like that with everybody who came to the club, especially those that came with a reputation."

There were other differences in training which Julian found hard to understand. "You also couldn't tackle in the five-a-sides," he says. "That's how it is up there. At West Ham you tackle, you kick people and you get a lot more out of the training than you do at Liverpool. And the more you train the more fluid you lose and the more weight you lose.

"Every day it would just be five-a-sides, a few doggies and then off home. At West Ham you'd do shadow play, corners and free-kicks, but at Liverpool it was the same every day. We might have a full game for about half-an-hour, but very rarely. Because that's the way that Shanks used to do things and it's just continued through the generations, the same routine. But then, if you're getting success from it, why change it?"

Why indeed? Certainly, the apparent reluctance on Julian's part to fall in line with Liverpool's own way of doing things appears to be one reason why the relationship was doomed. "It always takes two to tango and certainly, in some of the training sessions, Julian just wanted to play football – and didn't feel he had to do much running to do that," says Evans. "Our philosophy was slightly different to that – if you're talented *and* fit, that's a double bonus."

It wasn't just Julian's affection for working with the ball before training that staff at Liverpool tried to put a stop to – they also questioned the wisdom of him drinking coke before games, as he had habitually done so throughout his career. "I'd always drink two cans of coke before I went out at West Ham but they wouldn't allow it at Liverpool," he says. "They tried to stamp it out but I used to take them anyway because I was used to it. Roy Evans said to me, 'It's no good for you before a game.' I told him I'd been doing it for five or six years and was used to it. I just carried on and he let it go."

Surprisingly, it seems that one of Julian's main idiosyncrasies – that he never warmed up before playing or training – was more readily accepted, despite what Souness may have said about people not wanting Julian to go straight out with the ball. "They say that Alan Hansen never warmed up," Dicks explains. "He just sat there with his legs crossed and a cup of tea. He'd then put his top on and go out and play, so they were used to that."

Julian's problems with youth team manager Steve Heighway commenced the very day he'd signed for the club. "I never got on with Steve Heighway. On that first Friday, Graeme Souness introduced me to him and as I was shaking hands with him he was looking the other way. I thought, 'You arrogant twat!' and from that day I had no time for him. I was shaking his hand and he wouldn't even look me in the face!

"He just wouldn't speak to me. After a while he'd say good morning and I would totally blank him. They'd have their days when they wanted to speak to you and others when they didn't. There were many times I'd walk in and say good morning and then get blanked, so I just ignored them in the end.

> "As I was shaking hands with Steve Heighway he was looking the other way. I thought, 'You arrogant twat!'"

"It didn't bother me because Heighway was only the youth team manager. Obviously he had a great career and was there when Liverpool were booming, but I think there's a lot of jealousy over money. When he was playing they were getting nothing and we're playing now and getting paid thousands a week. It's jealousy."

The death knell on Julian's Liverpool career was sounded when he was exiled from first-team affairs and forced to train with the kids at Melwood. Quite simply, it was the final insult as far as Dicks was concerned, for there he was, a £2.5m-rated professional footballer, earning approximately £5,000 a week and training with school children!

"Ronnie Moran said, "Julian, go and train with that lot – the kids,'" he recalls. "Roy Evans didn't get on with Paul Stewart either, so it was Paul and myself lumped in with the kids. For the first two or three weeks I just got on with it, but when you're training with 15 or 16-year-olds there comes a point in time when you ask yourself, 'Is this worth it?' I mean no disrespect to the kids, because some were good players, but at the end of the day it was no good to me. I was just going through the motions and not even getting a sweat on in training."

Roy Evans, on the other hand, suggests that Dicks was only asked to train with the youths during the senior players' absence: "He only trained with the kids when the first team weren't there," he says. "If the first team are away, you've got to train with somebody."

Yet for all Julian's woes, he refused to initially allow his mood at home to be affected. "To be fair to him, he was really good," says Kay. "He knew he wasn't going to gain anything from being a pain in the behind, so he just went into work and got on with it, even though he was training with kids. But we had such a nice life where we were that it didn't get him down. Obviously he didn't want to spend the rest of his career like that. He was fine but I knew that he wouldn't be happy only turning out for the reserves."

Fortunately, during this period of isolation from the first team, Dicks did have one member of the coaching staff who took a more sympathetic view of his plight. "I always got on well with Sammy Lee, who was reserve team coach, and when I got bombed out he was more or less the only one who would speak to me. In fact, if it hadn't have been for Sammy, NOBODY would have spoken to me!"

Ultimately, though, Julian decided he'd had enough. "One day I thought, 'Bollocks to this!' I was only out there training for five minutes and I came in, had a shower and got changed and Sammy Lee came in after me. He said, 'What are you doing?' I said, 'I'm not being funny, Sammy, but I can't train with 12-17 year-old kids because it's doing nothing for me.' I said it was ridiculous. He said, 'C'mon, carry on training,' and I said, 'No, I've had enough. I can't handle it any more.'

"So I jumped in my car and went home. Roy Evans called me into his office the next day and said, 'What are you doing? Whoever I put you to train with, you train with,' and I said, 'I'm not training with the kids.' At the end of the day I'd rather train on my own, because at least I'd know I'm working myself hard. Training with kids is too easy for me. He didn't fine me but told me not to let it happen again. I said if he put me with the kids I'd do the same tomorrow and the day after that because it was getting ridiculous."

Reflecting his demoralised state of mind as the season began, Julian often consoled himself in his local boozer. "The pub was only over the road and, once I got bombed out of the first team, I was there more or less every night," he admits. "I wouldn't get rat-arsed, I'd just have a few drinks. But there were nights before reserve games when I'd go and get drunk. It was nothing against Sammy Lee – I thought he was great and respected him – but Hutch and I would go over for a few bottles. It was just the way I felt then – if I fancied a drink, that was it. I'd take things out on the beer."

> "The pub was only over the road and, once I got bombed out of the first team, I was there more or less every night"

Don Hutchison had also been edged out of the first-team picture by that time, following allegations that he'd exposed himself to women in a bar and newspaper pictures showing him with a Budweiser label stuck on his private parts! Although not bombed out of Anfield, the Gateshead-born midfielder was told by Roy Evans that he'd have to lay low for a while. "When the newspaper stories appeared he said to me that it would take a good few months before things would settle down and that I was going to have to spend a while in the reserves because the directors weren't too sure about what had happened," says Hutch, who was also excluded from the trip to Germany.

Watch those hands!... photocall fun with Neil Ruddock and Robbie Fowler.

Dispirited with the situation and feeling unwanted, the two players were very much in the same boat (heading nowhere it seemed). Not surprisingly, they started spending more time together, with Hutch even staying with Julian on some occasions. "When the lads went to Germany I stayed at Julian's house for a while and there was nothing else to do but enjoy yourself – go out and play golf and have a few beers," he says. "We'd go down the pub and have a few drinks – Julian, Mark Wright and myself – and be gutted that we weren't on that Germany trip. We were all in the same position. I was living alone and couldn't have sat around in my flat on my own, so it was good for me to get over to Julian's. Kay was fine. I got on with her and the kids, and it was like, 'Why don't you come over a bit more?'

"It must have been hard for Kay, having Julian around the house at that time, so I think it might have been a help for her that I was there as well and could go and play golf with him."

The experience of playing second-string football also did little to help the mood. "It's not easy trying to push yourself when you're playing Southport away on a really boggy pitch," says Hutch. "We were getting through the games so easily because of the difference in standard. So you don't even know if your fitness level is getting better or not."

Inevitably, motivation was at an all-time low. "Once I knew there was no future at Liverpool I did what I wanted," Julian admits. "There was one funny time when Hutch and I were playing in a friendly on the Saturday and we went over to the pub on Friday. We went over there about six o'clock and struggled out at three o'clock in the morning. Hutch was well out of his tree and we were playing stupid games. Near the pub there was a wall, only a couple of feet high, which he tried to walk along, but he fell off and landed in the main road. So I picked him up and took him home.

"I think we had to be at Anfield by mid-day, so I woke him up about 11.15am. I said, 'Come on, Hutch, we've got to go.' Of course, he'd only gone and puked up in my girl's bed! So we went to Anfield, got on the coach and he said, 'I'm gonna be sick!' I said that if he was going to be ill he should go to the toilet. He went to the lav and you could hear him! Sammy Lee was sitting right next to the door but never heard him, although I did. When he came out he was all white and his eyes were streaming.

"We both had pie and chips before the game but we won four or five-one and we both played well!"

"Then when we got to the game it was still quite early, so he said, 'I'm starving!' and went over to the chip shop. We both had pie and chips before the game – I think it was against Altrincham – and we won four or five-one and we both played well!"

While this was by no means typical behaviour from Julian – or Hutch, for that matter – he admits that players have been known to break the rules from time to time. "I've seen players have a drink on the Saturday before a match – go to the pub at 12 o'clock, have a couple of pints, then go to the game," he reveals.

Hutchison eventually found himself heading for the exit door at Anfield in an effort to get his career back on the rails. And it was West Ham, who'd been linked a number of the times with the talented Geordie, who offered the chance of Premiership football after having a club record £1.5m bid accepted. "When he knew that West Ham were in for him Hutch asked me what it was like there," says Julian, "and I said he'd have a great time down there. I told him the lads were brilliant and if he did well on the pitch the crowd would love him. He also knew Harry Redknapp through Jamie anyway."

Hutch didn't want to leave Liverpool but, like Julian eventually would, felt the only way to resurrect his career would be to start afresh elsewhere. "I had to just get away," he says. "It was just doing my head in and I couldn't go on any more." Unlike Julian, however, there was no personal feud with Roy Evans in Hutch's case. "There was no problem between me and Roy," he insists. "He's a hard person not to like because he's really friendly. At the end of the day he's got a job to do and that's to pick 11 players. But you don't see it like that when you're not playing. It's easy to say it now – 'he's got a job to do' – but if he doesn't pick you then you can't stand him for half an hour. That's what football is like. And when it goes on game after game you ask yourself, 'Does this fella not like me?'

"Roy actually asked me the day before I signed for West Ham, 'Are you sure this is what you want because I don't really want you to go.' It *wasn't* what I really wanted at all but at the end of the day I couldn't have carried on just playing for the reserves. It was something I *had* to do. You'd be a mug to say you wanted to leave Liverpool, unless things aren't right."

With his move to the East London club completed, Hutchison made his debut for the Hammers against his boyhood heroes, Newcastle United, on August 31, 1994. "We came down to watch him in his first game for West Ham," says Kay Dicks. "It was funny – it was quite nice to see everyone down at Upton Park again, although I was glad that it was just a visit. But within a few months we were back again."

Indeed they were. In fact, there was an air of inevitability about Julian's departure from Anfield. "I can remember him saying that he didn't think he'd play again for Liverpool," says Kay. "Mark Wright was having problems as well, which makes you wonder what could have been when you see that he's since done well for Liverpool and played for England again. But I think Julian knew deep down that he was never going to get another chance."

Ultimately it was Julian who forced the issue with Roy Evans. "I went into his office and said I wanted to get away. I said that I'd had enough," he says. "Clubs would come in offering loan deals but I didn't want to go on loan. I wanted to settle down, sign a contract and move my family wherever. Birmingham and Charlton both came in, but every time the gaffer mentioned anybody I just said, 'No, I don't want to go on loan.'"

Neither would Dicks put in an official transfer request, knowing that signing on fees would be lost, and although Evans had not actually admitted to Julian that he wanted to sell him, it was simply a case of waiting for a club to make an offer and seeing if it was acceptable to Liverpool. In the meantime, he continued to turn out for the reserve team, and found himself coming up against another former Hammer having a miserable time – Tony Cottee.

Cottee himself had repeatedly found himself out of favour at Everton and, after six years on Merseyside, was just a few days away from making a return to West Ham (now managed by Harry Redknapp following the controversial departure of Billy Bonds) when he was asked to put in one last performance in an Everton shirt – albeit for the reserves. "I'd spoken to West Ham and knew I would be leaving Everton, but they said they wanted me to play in the mini-derby game," says TC, referring to the Everton v Liverpool Pontins League clash. "The game was on the Saturday and I was due to speak again to West Ham on the Monday. Nobody ever really holds back in mini-derby games, so I reluctantly agreed to take part in the match – my last at Goodison Park – and picked up the team-sheet for Liverpool's reserves and there was Julian Dicks, playing at number five. I thought, 'Oh no, just when I want a nice easy game!' It was Liverpool's first season of playing with three centre-halves and they'd obviously taken it down to the reserves, so he was playing in the middle of defence.

"I quickly went up to Dicksy when the game started and we had a chat while there was a corner at the other end. He said, 'So you're going back to the Hammers then?' and I said, 'Yeah, and it looks like you'll be following me,' because there were rumours that he might be going back. He said, 'Yeah, maybe,' so I said, 'Well, make sure you don't kick me because we might be team-mates soon!' Needless to say, it was the tamest Dicksy performance I've ever come across!

"There was much made of his fitness at the time but he didn't look overweight to me. He comfortably got through the game. I think it was more of a personal fall-out between him and Roy Evans and the weight thing was an excuse."

"I didn't care whether Liverpool won or not"

Cottee indeed made his move back to East London and coincidentally made his debut for the Hammers in the 0-0 draw at Anfield on September 10, although the little striker survived less than an hour of action after being sent off for a retaliatory tackle on Rob Jones. Not that Julian would have seen the incident. "I didn't bother to watch the games I wasn't involved in," he explains. "At Liverpool you don't have to attend home games like you do at West Ham. Which was just as well, as I couldn't have given a toss. I didn't care whether they won or not."

By this time Dicks had already had word that there was a chance of heading back to Upton Park. "I remember Jamie coming into training, telling me off the record that his dad wanted me back at West Ham. I said, 'Well, here's my number, get your dad on the phone!' But obviously Harry had to do things properly. Stories were appearing in the paper and I'd go into Roy Evans and say, 'Is this true?'"

One such story linked Dicks with Tottenham, but although he'd have certainly considered any offer – "just to get back to playing first-team football again" – Roy Evans denies having had any direct approach from the North London club. The club had, however, heard from the Hammers. "I asked Roy if the West Ham stories were true," says Julian, "and he confirmed that they'd been in and offered silly money for me. I remember saying, 'Well, you want me to go and I want to leave, so sort a deal out.'

"I knew that was it – it was all over."

CHAPTER 21

HAMMERED AGAIN

WITH West Ham definitely looking to take Julian back to Upton Park, he could look forward to not only making a return to first-team action again but being embraced by the fans at what had become his spiritual home. The move couldn't come fast enough for him, yet not everybody was hoping that a deal would be concluded.

"When it looked like it was going to happen I just couldn't believe it," admits Kay Dicks. "I would rather have gone somewhere else. I didn't want to come back to London. I liked where I was living anyway – I was settled. I would have been quite happy for him to stay at Liverpool for four years and not played, but that's being totally selfish. I knew he wouldn't do that anyway and I would never expect him to.

"When Julian told me that Harry was interested in having him back, the first thing I said was that I wouldn't go. I didn't want to come back to West Ham – who acted as if they were doing us a big favour – for it to just be like it was before. But I wanted him to get back to playing football and for him to be happy, because there's nothing worse than when he's ready to play but not allowed to – it's horrible.

"I knew that a few clubs, such as Birmingham, wanted him on loan and I did say I thought that would be a good idea, but it wasn't what he wanted. I was trying to put off what I thought was probably going to happen anyway, just to prolong it a bit longer. But obviously it didn't work, although things took a while to sort out."

Indeed they did. Hammers wanted their man back, but having recently spent £850,000 on midfielder John Moncur, £1.5m on Don Hutchison and lost money on the Joey Beauchamp fiasco (with the £1m 'homesick' winger leaving for Swindon – in a deal that brought defender Adrian Whitbread to Upton Park – before playing a competitive game), they couldn't afford to immediately pay the £1m Liverpool were hoping to recoup on the player who'd been valued at around £2.5m when he headed north 13 months earlier.

Not only that, but there were also doubts about Julian's fitness. "There was a question mark over his knee – that was my reservation," admits Hammers MD Peter Storrie, well aware of Julian having needed an operation on the same knee during his time up on Merseyside. "Everyone was concerned about it," he says, revealing that a clause was inserted into the player's new contract relating to the injury. "If he'd had a problem with the knee then we could take another look at the situation."

But that wasn't the only reservation that people had about Julian returning to Upton Park. "*Everybody* opposed it," reveals Harry Redknapp. "I was on my own. I think everybody thought I was off my rocker. They all thought, 'What are we doing with him back here?' I'm talking about the directors and coaching staff – people who'd been at Upton Park during his time here before – who didn't see it as a very good idea." Following his gambling instincts, though, Harry decided to "take the chance".

> "Everybody opposed it. I think they thought I was off my rocker"
> — HARRY REDKNAPP ON TAKING JULIAN BACK TO WEST HAM

Harry Redknapp welcomes Julian back.

"Frank Lampard, my assistant, hadn't worked with Julian before but he went along with me. He said, 'If you fancy him, Harry, go for it.' I just thought that I could get him playing again and hoped that the penny had dropped with him and that, having been a failure at Liverpool, he'd come back a changed man."

Clearly, Harry was confident that he'd be able to avoid the difficult situations that had developed with Julian under Billy Bonds' management, although others were obviously concerned that they could have been welcoming trouble back through the door. "It was probably only Harry and I that wanted to bring him back," confirms Lampard. "When Harry says other people had doubts I think he's probably talking about other people higher up in the club, who had their reservations – the 'can you handle him?' sort of stuff. I'd heard some funny stories about Julian and they weren't all good, but I felt confident. I knew he'd not had a good time at Liverpool and that there was a worry over his fitness and his knee, but I'd obviously seen him play and I knew he had something about him that we needed."

Peter Storrie admits he had certain doubts about Julian's return – "I had reservations because when Julian left, a lot of people at the club felt he was prone to bookings and sendings off. It's obviously a problem if he's only playing a limited amount of games because of suspensions" – but refutes any suggestion that the board tried to influence the manager in his thinking. "I don't think Harry is referring to the board when he talks about people opposing the move – I think he's talking about his staff and the people around him. There's no interference from us – we employ a manager and he picks and chooses the players he wants. People had reservations but I wouldn't say everyone was against it."

The air of doubt spread to the players, with even midfielder Martin Allen admitting "we were all a little sceptical" and Tony Cottee agreeing that some people "were not so sure it was a good idea". The

> "I'd heard some funny stories about Julian and they weren't all good, but I felt confident" – FRANK LAMPARD

forward was pleased to see the deal being pieced together, however. "I was at Everton for most of his first period at West Ham so I couldn't comment on what had taken place before, but I was happy to welcome Julian back because in my opinion we were buying a very good left-back," he says. It was a view shared by Ian Bishop – "to bring someone like Dicksy back was a coup. It's great to have players of his calibre around" – while Don Hutchison was also eager to have his old Liverpool team-mate back alongside him again. "Julian told me about two weeks after I joined West Ham that Harry had come in for him," he says. "I couldn't wait for him to sign and was really hoping he would. But it seemed to take ages for the deal to be sorted out. For me, coming to a new club, there was nothing better than to have Julian helping me along because it was somebody I knew."

With West Ham off-loading midfielder Peter Butler to Notts County in a £350,000 deal, there continued to be media speculation about the club generating the funds to bring Julian home. "I knew Julian would see his time out at Liverpool if he had to," says Carol Dicks, "but as soon as they said he could be going back to West Ham I just knew he'd soon be home. I was overjoyed."

After much negotiation, a deal was eventually agreed between the two clubs. "Roy Evans called me in and said, 'West Ham have been in touch again, we've

RETURN OF THE DEVIL

By FRANK WIECHULA

JULIAN DICKS lost out on £500,000 to end his 13-month Merseyside misery.

And as Dicks revealed he took a pay cut to rejoin West Ham he fired a parting blast last night at Liverpool boss Roy Evans.

Dicks claimed Evans used his weight as an excuse to axe him, ignored him for three months and forced him to train with the kids.

Dicks, now shaven-headed and sporting a tattoo – Taz the Tasmanian Devil – on his right leg, was so keen to return he took an estimated £2,000-a-week pay cut.

Over three years, plus potential domestic and foreign win bonuses, that adds up to an estimated £500,000 total loss with Liverpool.

Excuse

Dicks, who plays against Southampton at home today, declared: "It's said I was overweight and unfit.

"But that was just an excuse – Roy Evans wanted me out of his side.

"He didn't talk to me for 10-12 weeks, so I couldn't really find out why that was.

"I was training with the kids, the apprentices. It was difficult there – he just bombed me out all together.

"Personally, I didn't think I had weight problems. But Roy Evans is the manager and he picks the side.

"I felt fit myself. I've never been the best trainer at running in pre-season.

"But at the end of the day I think it counts what you do on the pitch."

Slim-line Dicks, 26, said: "I haven't got any worries about my match fitness – I'm a professional footballer.

Weight

"I've lost just over half a stone. I was the same weight when I left here that I am now.

"If I was unfit then, I shouldn't really be in the game."

After 28 games at Anfield Dicks fell out with Evans after a 4-1 pre-season defeat against Bolton.

The defender was accused of being overweight and axed from a club tour of Germany and his Anfield career was over. But Dicks, who scored 40 goals for West Ham in 203 appearances, insisted: "I don't have anything to prove to Liverpool or anyone else.

"You don't become a bad player overnight. If one manager doesn't like you it doesn't mean the rest of them do as well.

"I'm full of confidence – my spirits never dropped in my time up there.

"I know what ability I've got and that's what really matters. Yes, I took a pay cut but it's great to be back.

"At the time when I went to Liverpool it was a great move for me and I don't regret any of it.

"I had a great contract there and could have stayed there for three years, just sat in the reserves and picked my money up at the end of the week.

"If Graeme Souness had remained boss I think I would still have been there.

Ambition

"I didn't want to go to a club that didn't have any ambition, aren't going to win anything – and West Ham want to win things and do well.

"The fans and players were good to me up there and I've got no regrets at all about going."

BALD OVER: Dicks is back with a new look and new tattoo (right)

Julian back with a £500,000 trim

Nice Tattoo see you

sorted a price out, you can talk to Harry,'" says Julian. Contrary to some newspaper reports at the time, which suggested that the Hammers had parted with half a million pounds, with more to follow in instalments, the actual initial payment to Liverpool was a mere £100,000. "It was a very small fee," confirms Peter Storrie, "with everything else based on the amount of games he plays and West Ham retaining Premiership status. It will total about a £1 million at the end of the day."

That 'day' is not expected to arrive until the year 2005, with it being understood that the agreement is for Hammers to pay £50,000 for every 25 games that Julian plays. "He's got to play an awful lot of games for Liverpool to get a million for him," laughs Redknapp. "He was so cheap it was silly. Liverpool just wanted him out and it was a massive loss for them."

The history of Julian's knee was clearly a major factor in Hammers getting him at such a knock-down price. "The negotiations were more down to my chief executive, but it was quite difficult in the fact that West Ham were aware of Julian's knee, so it was more about games played than a big transfer fee," confirms Roy Evans. The fact that Liverpool accepted such a loss, however, indicates how strongly they wished to get Dicks off the wage bill.

Having been given the green light, Julian contacted West Ham and agent Rachel Anderson, then travelled down on Wednesday, October 19 for a meeting with Harry Redknapp, Peter Storrie and club secretary Tom Finn at the Swallow Hotel in Essex to agree terms. The newspapers offered conflicting stories about his personal finances at the time, with one declaring that the move had cost Julian £500,000 as a result of accepting a reduced salary with the Hammers, while another boasted that the next three years would see him become 'a millionaire'. "That's a load of crap!" Dicks insists, admitting that he had to take "a very big drop" in wages to tie the deal up. Not that he immediately signed on the dotted line.

> "He was so cheap it was silly. Liverpool just wanted him out and it was a massive loss for them" — HARRY REDKNAPP

"They wanted me to sign there and then," Julian reflects. "Peter asked if I could sign straight away and I said, 'No, I've got to go and talk it through with the wife.' He wasn't too happy about that, but I said that I had to sort it out with her. Harry understood and I travelled back up to Chester that night. There was no doubt in my mind that I was going to sign. But I had to speak to Kay. I knew she wouldn't be happy, especially after all the flak we'd had during our first spell down at West Ham."

As far as Kay was concerned, though, Julian had indicated his decision even before heading south for talks. "He told me that he'd probably sign," she says. "He spoke to me and I just said, 'It's down to you, do what you like.' He'd have signed anyway, he just wanted to get back. He knew what people thought about him down at Upton Park."

And it was his relationship with the supporters that convinced Julian that sometimes you *can* go back. "People often say you should never go to the same club twice, but at the end of the day I think my situation was a bit of an exception because I really got on well with the supporters," he says, before elaborating on the conversation with Kay about the move. "She just said, 'I knew you were going to sign, so why didn't you just stay down there and sign?' I said I wanted to talk to her about it and she said, 'Whatever I say, you'll do what you want.' She was right really."

Dicks had also discussed Harry's reasons for wanting to bring him back to Upton Park and the ambitions of West Ham at that point in time. "Harry told me I was an exceptional player – he's always told me I'm the best left-back in the country and he wanted me back for my ability. He knew that I'd caused problems before but his son Jamie must have told him that I'd calmed down a bit and he took a gamble on me," he says. "I asked the club what their ambitions were and Peter Storrie said, 'We're going to spend money and get some good players in to lift the club to where it belongs – we're ambitious.' And I thought, 'It's the same old bollocks, they told me that before.'"

For all of Julian's cynicism, however, the deal was signed after speaking with Kay. And to prevent him from bad-mouthing the club he was leaving, Liverpool arranged for Dicksy's outstanding signing-on fees to be woven into the deal. "They owed me £130,000 and it was written into my contract, so that if I'd slagged Liverpool off it would be forfeited," he reveals.

Back in Bristol, there was a sense of disappointment from Julian's father that his son was walking out of Anfield and waving goodbye to what had been a once-in-a-lifetime opportunity. "I felt he should have hung on at Liverpool," says Ron. "He'd been having a good time up there and should have sat it out and bided his time. But I didn't say anything to him because I don't think he'd have taken any notice of me anyway. But he could have got back into the Liverpool side and played in cup finals since."

Julian had made his mind up though, but with the ink drying on the final contract the implications of the move started to hit home with Kay. "I was absolutely gutted," she confesses. "I didn't know what to do really. At the end of the day I was hoping that people wouldn't buy our house. Because then I'd have an excuse to stay there."

CHAPTER 22

WELCOME HOME

THE 'welcome home' banners were out in force at Upton Park on Saturday, October 22, as Julian made his return in a West Ham shirt for the league game against Southampton. "I had an exceptional reception," reflects Julian, while tears of joy were seen in the Bobby Moore Stand, courtesy of his mum.

It was a good day all round, with the Hammers winning 2-0 to shoot three places up to 12th in the Premiership. And even a booking for Dicks – after a two-footed lunge on former Hammer Paul Allen – couldn't spoil the homecoming party. "It's only a booking," Julian shrugged after the game, while Harry Redknapp laughingly suggested he'd tried to lay a bet that his new player would be booked in his first game back! "Ladbrokes wouldn't give me a price on it!" he joked afterwards.

Most of the talk was of Julian's hew hairstyle – or lack of one, with his head being shaved so that he was virtually bald! It made the 'Terminator' appear even more intimidating than ever, although his early games back at West Ham were never more than just tentative steps in the right direction again. His disrupted pre-season schedule and exile in the Liverpool reserves had clearly taken its toll on his fitness, which was evident in the Southampton game which saw Julian appear reluctant to go on those rampaging forward runs that had become a past trademark of his.

"Julian wasn't in the best of shape when he left West Ham and he wasn't in the best of shape when he came back," acknowledges Redknapp, who attributed it to the player's famous disinterest in running. Physio John Green, however, felt that the injury had been a major factor. "His condition was poor," he says, "because he hadn't trained. And he was overweight. It wasn't any fault of his own – it wasn't because he was out drinking or that he's a slob. He didn't really play particularly well for the rest of that first season back and I think it was all down to the fact that he wasn't fit and his knee was still a problem."

Julian's bulky frame when he returned prompted more debate as to whether Roy Evans had indeed been justified in having a go at the left-back during his last days at Anfield, but what the fans couldn't see was how the lack of first-team action had affected his condition. "It probably took me about half a dozen games to get back to fitness. I was very tired after the Southampton game," he admits. "Not playing had definitely had an effect. When you're shoved into the reserves, it's easy football and to jump back into the Premiership takes some getting used to."

The lack of fitness may go some way to explaining why, having only been booked once in the previous year, Julian was yellow carded no less than six times before the end of December – earning him 24 points and a two-match suspension. "It was probably partly due to adjusting again to the game. When you're not playing you lose your sharpness, so it was a case of getting back into the swing of things," he offers, although he was of the view that had he been wearing a Liverpool shirt he'd only have been booked two or three times. "I'm doing exactly the same things now as I was at Anfield," he complained at the time.

"He was a little bit rusty and a bit...humpy, for want of a better word," says Frank Lampard. "It had always been a problem with him – these bursts of madness. But we told him he had to channel his aggression in the right direction and, if you're going to be an aggressive player, you have to do it at the right times. There's no point doing things right in front of the referee. Now they're worse than ever, they pick up on every little thing, so you've got to be very careful about what you do and when you do it.

"You don't want to take that aggression away from Julian because it's a big part of his make-up. But he's toned it down in his own way – either through maturity or because the experience at Liverpool did him good in some ways. Whether it be through his family life and watching his kids grow up, I don't know, but he's definitely matured since his return."

Julian insisted upon his return to the Boleyn Ground that he'd changed during his year at Liverpool, but given his track record in the past it was no surprise that most of his words at that point were taken with large pinches of salt. But Harry Redknapp had definitely seen substantial signs of progress in his man – "there was a massive change in him as a person," he says – to the extent that the rash of early bookings in Julian's second period at West Ham did not really concern him. And there was definitely one significant development as a result of the Anfield experience – the realisation in Dicks' mind that he was expendable after all.

"If I was injured or suspended during my first time at West Ham I'd always get back into the side – no matter what I'd done," he admits. "Whereas at Liverpool, when Roy Evans binned me and didn't speak to me, perhaps it made me grow up a bit and think, 'Maybe I'm not indispensable.'"

The only time Redknapp did have slight misgivings about bringing Julian back was around the time of West Ham's home fixture with newly promoted strugglers Leicester City on November 5. "Hutch, Kenny Brown and I went out drinking on the Thursday before the Leicester game," Julian discloses. "We went out in Romford straight after training and got hammered – absolutely bladdered! If we'd just gone out and had a drink with some food it would have been okay, but it just went to extremes and carried on into the night. That was the first time I'd done that at West

Ham, but somebody rang up Harry and told him that the three of us were out on the town.

"Come Saturday, I scored a penalty to win the match, Hutch got sent off, while Kenny didn't play. Harry didn't say anything until the following Tuesday when he called Hutch into his office and had a go at him. He was fined two weeks wages for being sent off. Then he called me in and I said, 'Yeah, I made a mistake, I'm in the wrong.' And it was left at that."

Hutch was suspicious as to whether they'd been shopped by a mysterious phone-caller, however. "Harry's a bit shifty like that," he says. "He tried that with me once before, when he said he'd had a phone call from a mate telling him I was out on the piss. And I knew for a fact that I wasn't. But it's something Harry does. On that occasion he caught us out, but who knows whether anybody did make a call?

"I think Harry might have had a clue on Friday morning but when I got sent off he came alight a bit. If I'd have had a stormer of a game then probably nothing would have been said."

The incident was enough, however, to sow a seed of doubt in Harry's mind about having brought the two Liverpool outcasts down to Upton Park. "There was just that little spell when I thought I may have made a rick in bringing Don Hutchison and Julian back together," the manager admits.

The win over Leicester – who'd picked up just one point in their six away games at that time – was an important one, but it looked unlikely after Hutch's 37th-minute dismissal for two lunges at Lee Philpott. Hammers' 10 men battled away, though, and when John Moncur was brought down in the penalty box with 13 minutes remaining, it was left to Julian to smack home his first goal since returning to West Ham. He was also credited on his all-round performance: *'Franz Carr* (yes, he of the elbowing incident at Newcastle two years earlier) *showed glimpses of pace down the right flank before being effectively tamed by a series of fine tackles from Dicks,'* wrote *The Telegraph*. While Dicks was the hero of the day, there was no disputing who the villain was: "It's personal with me and Hutchison," stormed Harry to the media men after the match. "If he's going to let me down, he'll let anyone down," he added.

> "There was just that little spell when I thought I may have made a rick in bringing Don Hutchison and Julian back together" – HARRY REDKNAPP

"I wasn't seeing the kids and they'd start crying down the phone. It was hard"

The three points were needed though, with the team then hitting a rough patch and losing to the likes of Sheffield Wednesday, Coventry and QPR in the league and Bolton Wanderers (at home) in the Coca-Cola Cup. Since Julian had left there'd been a fair number of departures from Upton Park, including the likes of Colin Foster, Clive Allen and Mitchell Thomas (all sold for fees of less than £100,000 before the March '94 transfer deadline), Tony Gale (released on a free in the summer after 10 years service and exactly 300 league appearances), David Burrows (swapped for Tony Cottee) and, of course, manager Billy Bonds (on August 10, 1994). Yet, despite the purchase of Moncur, Hutchison, Cottee and Dicks (plus Dutch striker Jeroen Boere, acquired from Go Ahead Eagles for £165,000 shortly after Dicks went to Anfield), the team was struggling to find any rhythm, slipping to 18th place in the league after the Rangers defeat. "We were playing badly and giving stupid goals away," Julian admits.

It was also noticeable that Dicks still wasn't getting forward as often as he used to. "Roy Evans didn't like me to do that at Liverpool. He just wanted you to play in your position and stay there, and perhaps that crept over into my game at West Ham," he conjectures, although he does acknowledge that he started to take a more considered approach to attacking. "Before I was just bombing forward without worrying what was behind me, but now I realise you have to think about things. There's a time to go and a time to stay. And maybe, when I was struggling for fitness, I thought that if I got forward I wouldn't get back!"

In December Julian moved into rented accommodation in Chigwell. He'd initially been staying at The Swallow, but having spent a few months in an hotel when he first moved up to Merseyside a year earlier, he was anxious to have some privacy. "I said to Peter Storrie, 'I can't hack this, I wanted a rented house.'"

Kay, meanwhile, was still in Chester, trying to sell the property up there. "I wouldn't have left it empty – I've always sold what we've got before moving," she says. "If I'd have come down to Essex earlier I'd also have had to pull the girls out of school, so I stayed in Chester for a while. We actually thought we'd sold the place a few times but people were taking the mickey. We'd paid the original asking price on it, had spent a fortune on it and we wanted to get what it was worth. But people were messing us about – they knew we had to move and that I was on my own."

The couple would eventually get the £300,000 they were looking for, but only after some eight months – during which time Julian stayed in the terraced cottage in Chigwell with his dogs (buying a parrot for extra company!) and Kay remained in the north with the children. "It wasn't easy," she confides. "We used to go down to see him, mainly in Birmingham (at her sister's) but we spent too long apart. At the time it didn't bother me too much being on my own because I had the kids, but I think it was a bit selfish really. But for him it was like being a single bloke again, living on his own."

Despite meeting up "two or three times a month", it was still difficult for Julian. "I wasn't seeing the kids and they'd start crying down the phone," he says. "It was hard, but that kind of thing is part and parcel of being a footballer," he concedes.

What wasn't part and parcel, as far as Julian was concerned, were media inferences that Kay wasn't going to come down – at all! "They didn't actually come out and say it," he reveals, "but the implication was that she wasn't coming back. You'd try and tell people that she was moving down when the house was sold, but they didn't want to know."

What undoubtedly furthered the flames of rumour was the fact that Kay didn't join Julian even when the house was sold, with the problem then being that they didn't have a new house ready to move into yet. And again, there was also the children's

Crazy eyes!

schooling to consider. "I moved in with a friend, Caroline, on the Wirral for two and a half months until the house was found," says Kay.

The first seriously considered place was a 16th century farmhouse near Burnham, Essex, which was available for £225,000. "We had a surveyor look at it and he said it was riddled with woodlice, beetles and woodworm," Julian recalls. "He said it would cost £25,000 to put right so we told the bloke and offered to go halfway on the cost of the work but he said no. So we said goodbye." Eventually a house in Latchingdon, near Chelmsford, was located and the family were later reunited on June 10, 1995. Compared to their old home in Billericay the new property was relatively isolated, but still not enough for Julian's liking. "A house in the middle of nowhere would do me," he says.

Back on the pitch, the performances had started to improve – but the results didn't as the season moved past Christmas into 1995. Good home wins were secured against Nottingham Forest and Manchester City (the latter thanks to a Cottee hat-trick), but a home draw with relegation-threatened Ipswich and defeats by Wimbledon, Blackburn, Spurs and Sheffield Wednesday (the last two both missed by Julian as a result of the previously mentioned ban) saw Hammers sink to three off the bottom of the table (despite the introduction of Danish international defender

Swamped by team-mates after yet another crucial goal.

Marc Rieper and Northern Ireland winger Michael Hughes – both initially on loan deals). The team had played particularly well at Ewood Park and the 4-2 scoreline (bolstered by two Alan Shearer penalties) flattered the opposition immensely. "To get beaten 4-2 at Blackburn was a joke. That was probably our best display since I returned and we deserved something from the game," Julian insists, reflecting on the match which saw him score his first goal in open play after re-signing for West Ham.

The Sheffield Wednesday game (on January 23), however, was turned into a complete farce after referee Paul Danson – later re-named 'Dirty Danson' by the tabloid press – red-carded defender Alvin Martin (still proving his worth, despite his 36 years) for bringing down Owls striker Mark Bright on the halfway line. Most felt that Alvin had simply stumbled into the path of the forward, and with the incident taking place so far from goal the general view (almost without exception) was that it could hardly have been considered a sending-off offence. *'Worst Ever!'* stormed *The Sun* of Danson's dubious decision. But Julian had other views.

"I watched the game and thought that Alvin meant to bring Mark Bright down," he says in stark contrast to the rest of the planet. "I still think that now. We've had a joke about it but my personal opinion is that he meant to do it. He'd say he didn't mean to but I think he did."

Danson would later revoke the red card, substituting it for a yellow one, but apart from saving Martin from suspension it was too late to prevent another three vital points from going down the pan, with Wednesday having eased to a simple 2-0 victory on the night. It meant that the Hammers' next league game (following a drab 1-0 FA Cup defeat at QPR), at bottom-placed Leicester on February 4, was increasingly vital. But it was Dicks and Cottee who emerged the stars, with the former winning a tackle on Leicester's Mark Draper in the box, storming to the byeline and cutting the ball back for TC to score his 100th league goal for West Ham. Just before half-time, it was Cottee who set up a penalty kick for Julian when he was sandwiched by two Leicester defenders and the Hammers left-back made no mistake from the spot. City pulled one back, but West Ham could take plenty of confidence from their superior showing (in a match that saw young midfielder Danny Williamson make his first start of the season). "That was a big game," says Dicks. "Both teams needed to win but we won it quite comfortably in the end, despite the result being tight. We were much better than Leicester."

The success helped put a little daylight between the Hammers and the very bottom clubs but after picking up just four points out of the next 12 available (with a 2-2 home draw against Everton and a fine 1-0 victory at Arsenal thanks to a Hutchison goal) there was no escaping that dreaded sinking feeling as they languished in 19th place. And it was starting to affect both players and fans.

"It's bound to affect people in the team," admits Julian. "You don't want to go out thinking that we've *got* to win or we're down – you've just got to play your best – but when the crowd starts getting on to individual players it makes it harder for them. They start worrying about needing another win *and* taking the crowd on again. They did pick people out to have a dig at them," he continues. "They had a go at Bish, they had a go at Moncs… But it's just part and parcel of football."

Not that Dicks has ever had to worry about taking flak from the crowd, with the supporters acknowledging his commitment irrespective of how his own game is faring at the time. "Even if you're 6-0 down, the fans want to see you trying because they pay your wages," he says. "I always go out and give 110%. Even if I'm having a bad game I still want the ball. The fans aren't stupid, they can see when players are hiding."

For many, the turning point of West Ham's 1994-95 season came in the 82nd minute of the home game with Norwich City on March 11. The Canaries had been sliding down the table at an alarming rate but they'd looked like arresting their fall with a brace of goals in the Upton Park match – despite going down to 10 men in laughable fashion. It was an obvious case of mistaken identity, with referee Martin Sims (who'd just replaced the injured Alan Wilkie) dismissing Andy Johnson for the professional foul clearly committed by Spencer Prior. "I hadn't realised the wrong bloke was sent off until somebody told me during the game," Julian admits. With eight minutes remaining, Cottee pulled one goal back and he rescued a vital point (and perhaps more importantly denied Norwich another two) with a late equaliser.

From that time onwards the Hammers would lose just one more match, going on an 11-game run that amassed 18 points as they headed for Premiership safety (while Norwich eventually fell through the trap door). A significant moment came with a stunning Dicks goal at Nottingham Forest, when he fired in a curling 25-yard free-kick to put the team ahead. "I remember that free-kick well," says Julian. "Hutch was on the bench and he said to the rest of the lads, 'If we all stand up he'll score.' So they all stood up, apart from Keith Rowland, I hit it well and it flew into the top right-hand corner."

The Hammers were pegged back on that occasion, but Dicks was on target again in the next game, grabbing a penalty in the 3-0 home demolition of Wimbledon as the team leaped out of the bottom four.

Julian reached a regrettable milestone at Ipswich Town four days later, however, when he was booked for the 50th time in West Ham's colours after bringing down Claus Thomsen from behind. The incident ended in an unsightly fracas as Hutchison's crude intervention to try and pick up the grounded player appeared to see him catching the Ipswich man on the head with his boot!

After an impressive 2-0 home win over Champions-elect Blackburn Rovers (which saw Simon Webster finally make his first-team debut following his clash with Dicks back in the summer of 1993, although he would eventually quit the game in the autumn of '95) and a draw with QPR, Julian's last full game of the campaign was in the 1-0 defeat at relegation rivals Crystal Palace. "We still needed one more win to be safe so people were saying we had to get something at Palace, especially with the two games remaining. We had to keep on fighting."

*That 25-yard curling free-kick against Forest... the bench were on their feet **before** he took it!*

The good news was that the two games were both at home. The bad news? That was that they were against Liverpool and Championship-chasing Manchester United. The match against his former club saw Julian meet manager Roy Evans for the first time since his departure. "He asked me how I was doing," he says, "but I've got nothing to prove to Roy Evans or Liverpool. You just get on and do your best." With the Anfield club already having qualified for Europe (via their Coca-Cola Cup win) and Don Hutchison in inspired mood against his old team, the Hammers promptly romped to a thrilling 3-0, status-preserving win that lifted them to 13th position. Julian, however, survived just 11 minutes of the match against his former team-mates. "I'd gone on the overlap and went to cross the ball," he recalls of the incident that ended his season. "John Scales came in and as I kicked I went through across the bottom of his boot. I didn't feel anything crack but I couldn't walk on it because I was in so much pain. I tried to play for another two or three minutes, but I couldn't run it off. I went for an X-ray the next day and I was told that I'd chipped my ankle bone.

"We had the end-of-season trip to Australia the following week and the surgeon said, 'You're not going,' because the ankle would swell up on the plane. So I rang up Harry and told him that I'd broken my ankle but still wanted to go to Australia and he said, 'Fair enough, it's up to you.'"

The day before the team headed Down Under, they had the small matter of taking on Manchester United, who could still clinch the title if they won at Upton Park and saw Blackburn held at Liverpool. Yet again, though, and for the second time in four seasons, West Ham denied Alex Ferguson's team the Championship. Winger Michael Hughes put the Hammers ahead and, despite a frenzied assault on their goal for the majority of the game, they held out for a memorable 1-1 draw.

"United knew they had to win and with just 20 minutes to go they were just bombing the ball up front. Andy Cole had three or four great chances but it just wasn't to be, mainly thanks to Ludo who played a blinder that day. Even though we were safe, we're all professionals and we went out and did the job. All the lads performed brilliantly and, of course, it stopped Manchester United from winning the championship," says Julian, not the least bit disappointed to see his boyhood heroes fall yet again on East London turf. "Not one Man Utd player came into the lounge after the game – they were so gutted I think they just got on their bus and shot home."

Just over 24 hours later, and against the initial advice of the surgeon, Dicks stepped onto a plane at Heathrow Airport. But while the rest of the Hammers squad had arrived at the terminal by coach, Julian, Hutch, Kenny Brown and Matthew Rush had other ideas, turning up in a stretch limousine and making a grand entrance in front of the rest of the lads!

On the plane, however, Julian's ankle started to give him

> "It was so painful I said to the doctor, 'You've got to get this thing off, it's throbbing!'"

some major grief. "He was basically dancing around on his leg and it started to swell up badly inside the plaster," recalls John Green.

"It was so painful I said to the doctor, Ges Steinberg, 'You've got to get this thing off, it's throbbing!'" Julian remembers. "So he went to get a kitchen knife and then started to saw the plaster off. It must have taken him about 40 minutes. He pulled if off and there were all these black blisters on the bottom of my foot."

> "We went to the Sydney Opera House and Martin Allen loved it, but Hutch, Moncs and me were like, 'Yeah, so what?'"

"Ges has still got blisters himself to prove the story," adds Green. "But Julian's foot was okay, as long as he just walked on it and didn't play any football. It was a shame for him because he could have done with finishing the season by playing over there in Australia."

Not that Julian was particularly bothered about missing a few "mickey mouse friendlies". The club played games against Western Australia (drawn 2-2), Victoria (drawn 1-1) and Australia U-23 (won 1-0 and lost 4-0), but were criticised in the local media for not putting out stronger sides and accused of not taking their visit seriously. Such complaints hardly acknowledged the long and difficult season the Hammers had just endured back home or their tight schedule Down Under.

"The lads had no break," complains Julian. "We were playing, getting pissed up in the night, then flying off in the next morning, staying in that evening, playing again the next day, going out in the evening, then flying off again. It was ridiculous. We had four games in eight days and it was just stupid, especially after the season we'd just played. People expected us to put our first-team out but that wasn't realistic – not with injuries piling up."

The trip to Oz was Dicksy's first and, once the novelty had worn off, he started to find it all rather boring – especially with not playing. He was also less than impressed with some of the cities visited, especially Sydney. "It was a shit-hole," he says. "We stayed in Kings Cross and it was full of prostitutes and was filthy. I didn't like the place whatsoever, although Surfers Paradise was nice when we got there.

"Martin Allen was buzzing out there, though. He's a real sightseer. We went to the Sydney Opera House and he loved it, but Hutch, Moncs and me were like, 'Yeah, so what?'"

But despite being underwhelmed at playing the happy tourist, Julian in fact played a vital role in offering support to Martin, who was worried about his father's poor health back home. "Julian was good to me when my dad was ill," says the Mad Dog. "Being on the other side of the world when my dad had a very short time to live wasn't easy. I was hanging around with three people – Don Hutchison, John Moncur and Julian – which might surprise people really. Although they're rogues they were quality blokes. I'll always remember how Julian treated me at that time – he was very kind."

CHAPTER 23

SAINT JULIAN

B ACK from Australia, Julian spent the rest of the summer break settling his family into the new Latchingdon home and taking things easy to allow his ankle to heal. The injury naturally prevented him from doing too much training during the close season, so he inevitably missed the Hammers' trip to Germany in July for the game against TSV Munich 1860, which marked the 30th anniversary of the European Cup Winners' Cup final between the two teams. Julian was clearly missed, though, with some laughable defending resulting in a 4-3 defeat.

And Dicks also had to duck out of the remaining friendlies too. "Basically he wasn't fit enough," explains physio John Green. "When we went down to Devon for the pre-season tour, Julian and I had about five consecutive days of hard running – he trained a hell of a lot harder than anyone else who went down there – and that's when he started to come through again."

Harry Redknapp was also anxious that Julian would not aggravate the ankle and potentially jeopardise his chances of starting the season, particularly with the tough start that faced the Hammers. "Harry told me to do my running but not to bother playing on it," says Julian. "I could have played in some of those games but he wanted me to leave it as long as possible to get it 100 per cent right."

As usual, the bookies were tipping West Ham for relegation. There was nothing new about that, of course, but for the team to be made *favourites* for the drop (at 150-1 for the title) – with the clubs that eventually did go down: Manchester City (50-1), QPR (66-1) and Bolton (100-1) all given shorter odds – was somewhat unjustified. "Most of the pundits had us relegated before a ball had even been kicked," Julian complains, "but I thought we'd do well. We'd finished the previous season well and I could see us being comfortable in mid-table. But we didn't get a good start."

Indeed they didn't. And neither did Julian, as he looked to kick off the season with the home match against Leeds United on August 19. "I was late for the game. I was going down the A127 and I rang Harry to say that I was going to be late because the traffic was horrendous," he recalls. "I got to Ilford and he passed me onto Frank who directed me round the back doubles. You're supposed to be at Upton Park by

1.15pm and I turned up at ten past two! It was boiling hot as well. I had a shocker that game."

The game had started well enough, with Danny Williamson putting West Ham into a fifth-minute lead, but two quality strikes from on-fire Ghanaian striker Tony Yeboah secured the points for Leeds. And points were indeed hard to come by for the team in the opening weeks. A visit to Old Trafford saw a 2-1 defeat and the dismissal of recently-signed Dutch striker Marco Boogers for a crazy challenge on United's Gary Neville (with Julian holding David Beckham and Steve Bruce at bay as they sought to remonstrate with the offender), and although draws were gained at Nottingham Forest and at home to an under-performing Tottenham side, things worsened considerably with the derby defeats at home to Chelsea and away to Arsenal, with the results being virtually overlooked amidst the controversy of Julian's tangle with John Spencer at Upton Park and his red card at Highbury (detailed elsewhere).

But Dicks wasn't the only Hammer making headlines for the wrong reasons. £800,000 import Marco Boogers was at the centre of a farcical situation, with the tabloids announcing *'Barmy Boogers goes off in caravan!'* as the forward failed to return from a trip to Holland to be with his pregnant wife, complaining of a stress disorder after failing to get picked for West Ham's starting XI in the early games.

Many were of the view that the Boogers affair undermined the team's efforts at this stage, but it's not an opinion shared by Julian. "We just had a good laugh about it," he says. "With all the funny headlines it became a big piss-take in the end. The problem for Marco, coming from Holland, was that he wasn't used to people tackling in training. We'd go straight through him and he'd want to have a row with people."

Following the explosion of adverse publicity after the Arsenal game, the pressure on Dicks as West Ham travelled to Second Division Bristol Rovers for a Coca-Cola Cup game on September 20 was predictably immense. "I was well aware that all eyes were on me," he says. "I was speaking to somebody afterwards and he told me that the press box was jam-packed. They were watching me, just waiting for me to slip up again. One or two of the papers had said that I was a skilful player, but all the rest just said I was an animal and was dirty. But I just had to shove it out of my mind. As soon as I cross the white line, all I think about is football and trying to win."

Those hoping for Julian to fall in the Rovers game were sorely disappointed, with him being as good as gold throughout Hammers' 1-0 victory. And headlines of the right variety were won the following weekend at Upton Park when he coolly despatched two penalty kicks past the despairing left hand of Everton's Neville Southall to secure West Ham's first league win of the season. "Again the press box was full, waiting for one slip, ready to hammer me again," he says. "But I scored the goals, we won the game and things calmed down a bit. Harry stuck up for me in the papers and that helped." Redknapp indeed praised his player for the way he came through the game. "I thought he was excellent today," said the boss afterwards. "He's got himself into problems and he's got to get himself out of them, but he coped very well today and when he gets on and plays football he's a very good left-back."

Harry quite rightly gave short shrift to press men wanting to focus too much attention on the next booking that Dicks picked up, in the televised 1-0 win at Wimbledon on October 16. "There were five other bookings out there as well tonight, why aren't you talking about them?" snapped Redknapp after one reporter had brought up Julian's yellow card for a foul.

It was hardly surprising then when Julian declared his reluctance to accommodate the media after matches: "The press wanted to speak to me after the Everton game but I just blanked them. I don't even bother speaking to them any more."

Dicks had by then already banged in another penalty, to set Hammers on the way to a 3-0 home victory in the second leg of their cup tie with Bristol Rovers. And another followed at Upton Park on November 4, although it came in rather different circumstances, with the team collapsing 4-1 to Aston Villa. "That's got to be the worst game I've ever played in," he says. "We just didn't get going and everything we did seemed to go wrong. You can cope with one or two people playing badly but when everybody plays badly you've no chance."

It was indeed an off-day for the Hammers. Prior to that disaster, they'd gone five games unbeaten in the league, bolstered by the return of striker Iain Dowie (back in September in a cheap part-exchange deal that took Dutch striker Jeroen Boere to Crystal Palace) who'd struck the winner at Sheffield Wednesday and what should have been the clincher in the home game against Blackburn (ultimately cancelled out by Alan Shearer's last-minute equaliser).

The improved form couldn't prevent West Ham from being tipped out of the Coca-Cola Cup by Southampton, though, and once Julian's three-game ban was announced after being found guilty of bringing the game into disrepute for the Spencer incident, the Hammers would have to face Bolton, Liverpool and QPR without their influential left-back.

> "That's got to be the worst game I've ever played in"
> — AFTER THE 4-1 HOME DEFEAT BY ASTON VILLA

With Keith Rowland filling in, though, the team did well, spanking bottom-of-the-table Wanderers 3-0 on their own turf, working hard to secure a 0-0 home draw with Roy Evans' men and picking up all three points when a late Tony Cottee goal edged out 10-man Rangers at Upton Park. Incredibly, after such a difficult start to the campaign, Hammers had now lifted themselves to a place in the top 10 of the Premiership and cries of 'we're gonna win the league' could be heard emanating from the bars of The Boleyn pub after the win over QPR.

Dicks returned for the away trip to Blackburn on December 2, but despite scoring his fifth penalty of the season there was little joy to be had in the 4-2 defeat (which could've been a lot worse had Hammers not found some resolve after going four goals down in 64 minutes) which saw Alan Shearer net a hat-trick (one a penalty after being clumsily challenged by Julian).

And things did not get any better in the Sky televised game at Goodison Park on Monday, December 11, with goalkeeper Ludo Miklosko getting sent off for challenging Daniel Amokachi as the Everton player headed towards goal. Many thought it was a harsh decision – "it was a penalty but I didn't think Ludo should have gone," complained Redknapp – but with the Czech traipsing off, the question was who would have the courage to don the 'keeper's shirt. Cue our man Julian…

> "I got a bit of stick from behind the goal – 'you fat bastard' and things like that"

"Nobody else wanted Ludo's shirt, so in the end I thought somebody's got to do it. So I took Ludo's shovels off him and went in goal. I treated it all as a big joke because there was only going to be one result. We were already 1-0 down and the first thing I had to do was face a penalty. TC told me to go to my right but being left-footed I would have gone to my left. I went to the right and the ball went the other way!

"It was enjoyable, though. I got a bit of stick from behind the goal – 'you fat bastard' and things like that – but in the second half I was in front of the Hammers fans who sang 'England's No 1'. I had a good time."

That was despite conceding another goal when he could only parry Amokachi's shot with his hands for Ebbrell to slide in and score. "Hutch told me that if I'd tried to kick the ball I'd have got there, but thinking like a goalkeeper I went down with my hands," he explains. Julian's heroics did, however, land him the man-of-the-match award, courtesy of Sky's viewing punters. "I

In goal at Everton, December '95.

got a bottle of bubbly for my troubles, which I've still got unopened – it's not the best champagne in the world," smiles the budding connoisseur.

A late comeback thanks to two goals within 120 seconds 10 minutes from the end of the home game against Southampton brought some relief, with West Ham winning 2-1, but there was more misery up at Middlesbrough two days before Christmas with the Hammers overwhelmed 4-2 by Bryan Robson's Juninho-inspired side. Boro's fourth goal was credited to Hendrie, but video evidence suggests that as Dicks and the striker slid in to meet Pollock's cross, it was possibly the man in light blue (rather than red) who got the significant touch to put the ball past Miklosko. "Pollocks!" was the word that Dicks seemed to utter as the goal was awarded (or something like that!). A long range shot from Julian a couple of minutes from time brought a hint of respectability to the scoreline, but – although nobody could possibly realise at the time – Dicks picked up what would ultimately prove to be his last booking of the season. Needless to say, had anybody laid money at their local bookies on this being the case, they'd have got very, very good odds indeed!

"Juninho had the ball and I steamed in, but with his quick feet he knocked the ball on as I took him out," recalls Dicks of his yellow card clash. "The referee booked me and I had a go at Juninho for rolling about all over the floor. Then he got booked for a foul on me. I was defending in the corner and as I got the ball I could see him coming. As I went to clear the ball he came in and clipped me and we both landed on the floor. I got up and saw the ref going for his card and I told the official there was no need to book him. Juninho and I had been having a go at each other but when I tried to save him he was grateful. He thanked me, even though the ref still still booked him."

What was more amusing for Hammers fans watching the highlights on Match Of The Day that evening was the commentator's suggestion that the concept of Juninho fouling Dicks was beyond the realms of possibility – as if brilliant Brazilians don't commit offences, least of all against 'hard men' like Julian.

Genuine farce was witnessed at Maine Road on New Year's Day, however, when the Hammers were forced to field rookie Neil Finn (three days past his 17th birthday) in goal as a replacement for the suspended Miklosko, after reserve 'keeper Les Sealey injured a calf muscle. Despite his gallant efforts, Manchester City sneaked their way to a 2-1 victory that set the relegation alarm bells ringing at West Ham, with the team having lost four of their last five Premiership matches.

An FA Cup win over First Division Southend United at least avoided a potentially embarrassing situation, but in the league the woes continued, with Hammers losing to 10-man Leeds United (after former West Ham striker Lee Chapman, on loan at Elland Road, was sent off by referee Paul Danson for elbowing Marc Rieper) and then being unlucky to concede the points to Manchester United in a lively match at Upton Park on January 22.

Eric Cantona scored the only goal of the game for the Reds, but that was incidental as all the post-match scrutiny centred on not the winning strike or even Nicky Butt's sending off for up-ending Julian, but a challenge made by Dicks (okayed at the time by the ref) on striker Andy Cole a few seconds before the dismissal of the United midfielder. "Had Cole not taken his leg out of the way, he would have carried it off the pitch himself," blasted Sky TV's Andy Gray, once again turning the spotlight of media attention very much on Dicksy's involvement. "I got fouled by Nicky Butt yet I got the blame for it all – it was obviously just my reputation going before me," says Julian.

And he was supported by his manager also. "The TV people *would* highlight that tackle, wouldn't they?" stormed Redknapp. "It's out of order what they said about it and it's not the first time they have dug Julian out. He went in to win the ball and he did not break anybody's leg. The referee gave nothing for it and it didn't make it right for Butt to go in late on Dicks."

Eric Cantona attempts to calm things down as Roy Keane and Julian clash over Nicky Butt's sending off.

The referee, Stephen Lodge, defended his position after the game and highlighted the fact that he didn't have the benefit of replays to assist his decision-making process. "Judgements have to be made in a split-second with two angles of vision. From my view I didn't see the Julian Dicks tackle as a foul. I did see what I considered to be a second cautionable offence by Nicky Butt."

With Sky replaying the incident over and over again and Andy Gray re-iterating his point of what *could* have happened to Cole if contact had been made, the press predictably followed their lead the next day. "I got the rollicking in the papers and Nicky Butt got off scot-free!" Julian protests. "This kind of thing has happened so many times. It's not as if I've gone out to break somebody's leg – I just don't do that. But that's what some people have tried to portray me as, somebody who just goes out and tries to snap opponents in two.

"The people who saw the Manchester United game will have seen it wasn't my fault – it was a genuine attempt to win the ball – but people who don't go to games will have just assumed, 'Oh, he's at it again.' People like to jump to the same old conclusions because that's the way the brain works – they put two and two together and get five.

"Andy Gray seems to be making a career out of having a go at me. The fact that I am Julian Dicks, a player with a certain reputation, seems to make me an easy target. I don't think he's got it in for me as such, but other incidents occur and they've only replayed them a couple of times. But when it's me it gets shown hundreds of times!"

Team-mate Danny Williamson, who was closest to the United incident, certainly had some sympathy with Julian. "The TV people made a lot of it," he says. "During the game the tackle didn't really look like much – Julian just went in as he always does. But Andy Gray picked it out and said he'd gone over the top and that's what started it all. If he hadn't have commented I think it would've been forgotten. It was a great game as well, but all the papers were concerned about was Julian's tackle."

Predictably, Andy Gray subsequently defended his comments. "I call it as I see it and I would call it the same whether it were Julian Dicks, Ray Wilkins or Mother Theresa," he said.

If Dicks was getting weary of the media scrutiny, then so were the FA. "Do we have to react to every tackle in every Premier League game just because it's shown on Sky and involved Julian Dicks? I can't see any action being taken on this one," said a spokesman in the aftermath of the game.

> "Do we have to react to every tackle in every Premier League game just because it's shown on Sky and involved Julian Dicks?" — AN FA SPOKESMAN

And indeed there was none. But the controversy raged for a few days, with one photo of the game exposing a skirmish taking place between Dicks and United's Roy Keane after the sending off. "He had a pop at me, saying I should have defended Butt and told the referee not to have sent him off," reveals Julian. "I said, 'What, like you would have done for me!' I wouldn't mind but it was as if I'd rolled over and played dead. But I just got up and walked away. People take all sorts of liberties with me but when I'm clattered I don't roll around as if I'm dying."

The United game was to mark a watershed in West Ham's season. Not only would Julian avoid controversy for the rest of the campaign but he would prove influential in a side that would respond to the growing fear of relegation (having now lost six out of seven league games) in emphatic style – commencing with five consecutive Premiership victories.

The run started with a 3-2 home win over Coventry City on January 31 – a game which could have left both teams on the same number of points on the fringe of the relegation zone had the Sky Blues triumphed on the night – and continued with another Upton Park victory three days later, this time over Nottingham Forest. That game had seen 19-year-old Portuguese star Dani (on loan from Sporting Lisbon) make his debut as a late substitute, and the striker swiftly won many friends when he scored after just five minutes of the televised game at Tottenham on February 12. His instinctive header followed a Williamson corner and a volleyed shot from Dicks that goalkeeper Ian Walker could only parry into the path of the Hammers new boy. "He did well against Spurs," recalls Julian of Dani's sensational start. "It's always nice to beat Tottenham – I think they thought it was going to be an easy ride. The pitch was diabolical, really bad, but we played well and could have had four or five quite easily."

"I was over the moon to score at Chelsea. I ran behind the goal and gave it the big one"

As it was, Hammers had to make do with a 1-0 win but it had the pundits pouring praise upon the East Londoners for their flowing football in dreadful conditions that Spurs used as an excuse for them having resorted to long-ball tactics. *'West Ham staged a TV presentation of Beauty & The Beast at White Hart Lane as heart-throb Dani and he-man Julian Dicks combined to defeat a stunned and disbelieving Tottenham,'* wrote the *Daily Express*, while *The Sun's* Martin Samuel scribbled, *'Upton Park's very own United Nations pulled together to produce their greatest performance in years.'*

With Croatian international defender Slaven Bilic (a then record signing at £1.65m) making his debut, and Dani making an instant impact, the cosmopolitan nature of Harry Redknapp's revamped side escaped nobody's attention. And it seemed to be working wonders, with the Hammers on a great winning run. With nine points from three games in the bag, the team headed to Chelsea, with Julian well aware that he was likely to face abuse from the home crowd following the much-publicised Spencer incident at the beginning of the season.

"I could hear some of the barracking and knew it would happen," he says. "But they're entitled to do that. They pay to get in, they can boo whoever they want. But if people have a pop you just have to get on with your game and try to prove them wrong."

But Dicks did more than that, sticking two fingers up at the Stamford Bridge faithful with a perfectly taken header to bring the Hammers back into the game after dropping behind to an early Gavin Peacock goal (as they struggled to adapt to a new three centre-half defensive formation). "I was over the moon to score. I ran behind

Julian heads Hammers' equaliser at Chelsea. A sweet moment after being booed all game!

the goal and gave it the big one. I knew there were Chelsea fans there because West Ham were on the side of the tunnel," says Julian, while Hammers' end-of-season video commentator stated, "That's one in the eye for David Mellor!" Actually, it was also one in the eye for Dicksy himself, after a clash with Blues defender Frank Sinclair left him with a lovely shiner.

With Danny Williamson plundering the winner, West Ham left West London with a famous victory and another three points under their belts. Next up: Premiership leaders Newcastle!

"We were on a high after the Chelsea game and with the confidence flowing we went into the Newcastle game with nobody thinking we would get beaten," Julian says. "Once you get that feeling you can go on and beat anybody and we proved a lot of people wrong that night. We outplayed them and beat them quite easily. It was Faustino Asprilla's first start for Newcastle and he got lumps kicked out of him by Slaven, Rieps and me. Every time he got the ball we were there and after a while he didn't fancy it. He was moaning at everybody."

Kevin Keegan's men slipped to a 2-0 Upton Park defeat (the second goal coming from Tony Cottee after a Dicks header), and from that moment on the Toon Army's Premiership lead was to be gradually further eroded.

Buried in the Hammers' winning streak (and probably from most fans' memories now) was a little trip to Grimsby in the FA Cup. The original fourth round tie at

Upton Park was drawn 1-1 and so the team found themselves visiting Blundell Park for a replay just 48 hours after their energy-sapping endeavours against Spurs. The First Division side cruised to a surprising 3-0 victory, but while some were questioning the fairness of the Hammers having to play such an important game so soon after fighting an epic battle at Tottenham – a match that had been put back two days due to the demands of Sky TV – Julian refutes any claims that tiredness could be used as a valid explanation for such a lame performance: "When people say that I think it's just an excuse," he offers. "We train a few hours a day, usually have a day off in the week and play 90 minutes on a Saturday. If you get tired after that there's got to be something wrong with you. Personally, I could play three sets of 90 minutes in three days. I wasn't tired, although maybe other people were, but generally that's just an excuse.

"They just played better than us and wanted to win more. Every time we got the ball they hassled us and when they got the ball we only had four or five who chased them. You can carry one or two players but five or six is pointless. I was gutted after that result. The thing is, they were a crap side, they really were. The mood on the coach home wasn't the best."

Fortunately, the Hammers had bounced back in style against Chelsea and Newcastle, but all good things have to come to an end at some time and the run of league wins came to an upsetting halt when Arsenal visited Upton Park on February 24. A mistake from on-loan American John Harkes allowed the Gunners to take a second-minute lead through John Hartson and eventually land all three points, despite incessant pressure from West Ham. It looked as if Hammers' dominance (*'It's not often you get a one-horse race and that one horse fails to win it,'* said *The People*) would pay off when they were awarded a a second-half penalty, but – unknown to all those present – Dicks was suffering from the effects of an earlier clash. "I can't remember the challenge but what I've been told is that the ball was bouncing, I went in for it and Ray Parlour came in with his arm up and just caught me on the side of the head."

It was therefore a rather concussed Julian that put the ball on the spot and attempted to beat England 'keeper David Seaman, who's been known to stop the odd penalty in his time. And there was certainly something rather 'odd' with Dicksy's spot-kick, with it tamely heading towards the middle of the goal and Seaman saving with his feet. "All I can remember is him running up and not hitting it as well as he usually does," recalls the grateful Seaman. "I managed to save it with my legs or feet. He came up to me afterwards and asked about the penalty."

Indeed Julian needed to, for he could remember nothing of the game at all, not realising how lucky he was. "I realised straight after the game that I couldn't remember any of it," he (just about) recalls. "I can remember asking the ref if I'd missed a penalty because there was something in the back of my mind telling me I might have missed one. He said, 'Yes,' and I asked what the score was and he said it was 1-0. I've watched it since on telly and it was a disgraceful penalty."

The Daily Telegraph made the valid point that, with Julian suffering from double vision, the sight of being faced with two David Seamans was probably rather daunting for him!

"I came off after the game, saw the club doctor and he told me that I was quite badly concussed and that I'd put myself on autopilot. It was just instinctive for me to carry on playing and put the ball on the spot when we were awarded the penalty. I had to get a mate to take me home," he reveals.

Carol Dicks remembers the afternoon well (even if her son doesn't), despite not being able to make the game: "Julian still doesn't remember that Saturday. He told us that Bernie brought him home, although he didn't know the route and so Julian told him how to get back. Yet he doesn't remember it. Apparently the referee asked him who he thought the best player on the park was and our Ju said, 'You are!'"

The Arsenal game may go down as a 'forgettable' occasion for Julian, but it was a rare day of disappointment amid a period in which his stature grew immeasurably – on two levels. Not only was his form becoming ever more impressive – debatably as a result of him more recently moving into a left centre-back position (alongside Rieper and Bilic) – but he'd gone a dozen games without a booking (hands up if you can name the previous time that happened!). It was clearly some achievement, particularly given the rigidity of the new laws that were being rigorously enforced by the officials.

> "I saw the club doctor and he told me that I was quite badly concussed and that I'd put myself on autopilot"

Julian's explanation of what many deemed a transformation around this time was that he was simply enjoying his game a lot more. "Maybe the new faces (such as Bilic, Dani and the recently recruited Ilie Dumitrescu from Spurs) at the club helped make a difference," he speculates. "The training was a lot more enjoyable – we played a lot of five-a-sides, the English versus the foreigners – and with us winning games, everybody was on a high and coming in happy. A few years earlier, when we were struggling, you'd come in and just not feel into it. Nobody likes losing."

Things were also a lot happier in Julian's home environment. Kay may have returned to Essex the previous summer with a certain amount of trepidation but, despite the traumas experienced in the earlier part of the season, she'd coped reasonably well – mainly as a result of her new resolve and a change in her own character. "I'm totally different now. I don't take any notice of what people say, which helps," she says. "I'm a lot stronger now. I don't know if it's for the better or worst but I'm not the same person I was a few years ago. You just can't let things get to you.

"You always worry when you come back that it's going to be the same again, but it's been much better. I've got all the friends in Billericay that we already had and we've met some nice people around here in Latchingdon. We're really lucky."

More significant than Kay's personal development, however, was the maturity shown by Julian following his return from Anfield. And nobody was aware of that more than his wife. "I think he changed as a person during the time we spent at Liverpool. He'd grown up a lot," she declares. "If we'd have moved back down and things had ended up like they were before, then I'd have just gone. At the end of the day, I don't have to stay."

The change in Dicks was acknowledged everywhere, however. "He's a totally different character to what he was first time round," states Peter Storrie. "The difference is like chalk and cheese. You wouldn't recognise him from the person who left us in 1993. Perhaps going to a big club and being left out of the side hurt his pride a bit.

"We've all spent time with Julian – Harry, Frank and myself – and I think he's got respect for us," he continues. "I would like to think that he's listened to some of the things we've said. But he's concentrated on football – that's been the main thing. He's focused himself on the games and he's getting older – he's definitely more mature."

That maturity was acknowledged by Julian's father Ron, who witnessed in games he saw against Forest and Wimbledon that his lad was showing a significant development. "He didn't go in for any tackles he wasn't going to win," he says. "In the past, he was tackling when it was 60-40 in the opponent's favour and at that level they're either going to do you or you're going to take the player out. But he wasn't doing that. He was taking his time and just going in for tackles that he knew he was going to win."

> "You wouldn't recognise him from the person who left us in 1993" – Peter Storrie

The view that Julian was mentally in tune with his game was shared by striker Tony Cottee. "With the clampdown and change in the rules I thought, like everyone else, that it would make it harder for people like Dicksy and those who like to compete and tackle," he admits. "But his record was very good and I think it was down to the fact that he concentrated on his football. He wasn't getting involved with people, winding other players up or doing the niggly stuff. Instead of going into tackles and maybe looking to pull or push people, he was winning the ball and distributing it well. His football did the talking and in my opinion he should have got an England call-up."

There was indeed a clamour for Julian to be selected by Terry Venables (detailed in a later chapter), as the 'new-improved' Julian Dicks continued to impress with his performances and conduct. His agent Rachel Anderson was of the view that he was at last accepting responsibility for his own actions. "He has people telling him what to do and what not to do every day of his life, but it's about helping somebody to understand that they're in charge of their own destiny," she says. "There's a limit to what you can do when it's a team game, but he realises that if he loses his cool with the referee, for example, then it's nobody's fault but his own."

There was no greater example of Julian's improved temperament than in the drawn game at Villa Park towards the end of the season, when Aston Villa striker Savo Milosevic attempted to antagonise Dicks by bearing his head down on him in a touchline incident. "We were 1-0 down and the ball went out for a throw-in," Julian recalls. "I knew it was ours because the linesman was flagging our way and Milosevic was fannying about with the ball to waste time. I pushed him out of the way to get the ball and he came over, forced his head down onto mine and pushed me. I just laughed at him – if you laugh at people it usually makes them worse. The referee booked him and I just got on with it."

Ron Dicks, acknowledging how he has mellowed himself over the years, was of the opinion that Julian had perhaps followed in his footsteps in that respect. "He's older now and as you get older you mellow. I was probably as bad as him in terms of discipline but as I aged I started to improve," he reveals, before making a valid point about the Hammers' form. "Another big difference for Julian could be that West Ham had been playing quite well. When you're struggling for your life it's a bit different. It was the same when he was at Liverpool – they were in the top half of the table and he only got booked once. I think he definitely grew up when he was there."

Dicks was similarly restrained when, in the home game against Manchester City on March 23, he was up-ended by Steve Lomas who received a red card for his indiscretion. Said *The People*: '*West Ham's reformed wild man, who refused to get involved when Lomas was sent off, was given a glowing reference by City manager Alan Ball. He said: "The penny seems to have dropped with Dicks at last. He's much more mature now."*'

Manager Redknapp also recognised that, investing faith in Dicks by handing him the captain's armband for the City game. It was the first time Julian had led the side out since losing the captaincy in October 1992 as a result of his five-match ban (with Steve Potts – axed for the game against Alan Ball's men – having carried the responsibility since that time). And he would continue to do so for the rest of the season.

The Hammers promptly won the City match 4-2, memorable as a result of two sensational goals by Dani and Dicks. And with Iain Dowie scoring two typical headers, every West Ham goal was a trademark effort from each player. While Dani eluded the defence with a silky run, as if the ball was attached to his foot, before drawing the goalkeeper a fraction and sliding it under his body from an acute angle, Dicksy collected a ball across the edge of the penalty area from Michael Hughes and blasted into the top left-hand corner from nearly 25 yards in sensational style. It featured in March's *Match Of The Day* 'Goal-of-the-month' competition and had Hammers fans drooling. In fact, if the TV clip had shown the complete build-up, involving Bishop and Hughes on the right wing, then it could well have won the award. As it was, it was voted West Ham's goal of the season by supporters in a *Hammers News Magazine* end-of-season poll.

"I got the ball and just lashed at it," shrugs Julian. "I always like to shoot when I get a chance. I don't think (goalkeeper) Eike Immel expected me to shoot. I watched it fly in and when it hit the back of the net I was gone!"

Such a goal proved that, despite the centre-half role that Julian had adapted to in the second half of the season, his instincts to get forward had not been compromised. The theory for some was that this new position also helped him avoid making rash challenges, with him having a full-back or wing-back to assist in the bottom left corner of the pitch which hence left him less exposed than perhaps he'd been in the past. Frank Lampard is sympathetic towards such a view ("with Keith there you virtually had two left-backs so it probably did help him"), while Harry Redknapp states that he simply made the change to "suit the team".

"I wanted to get Keith Rowland in on the left-hand side and it suited Julian to move to centre-half so it worked okay for us. But the left wing-back position is where I'm looking to play Julian in the future. You've got to be super-fit to do that job and I think he's in better shape than ever."

Another significant change in Julian during the 1995-96 season appeared to be his physique. The debate about his weight which had taken place after his return from Liverpool became a distant memory as a slim-line Dicks continued to terrorise both attackers and defenders with the season nearing its climax. The City goal marked his ninth of the campaign and praise was earned from all quarters, on top of the *Evening Standard* 'Player-of-the-month' award he'd already received for February.

"Julian is in better nick than he's ever been in his life," said Harry Redknapp, adding: "I've looked at him stripped off and he's a different boy to what he was."

Even though most parties claim that Dicks had not lost that much weight as such, all were in agreement that he was in better 'shape'. "People have made a big deal about his weight, but he's only around four pounds lighter than when he was at Liverpool," says Rachel Anderson. "But he has changed shape. Maybe it's in the type of training – I don't think he does as much weightlifting as they used to at Liverpool. And he also realises now, just like anybody else, that an athlete has to look after their body. Unfortunately, sometimes they have to be the wrong side of 25 before they really take it seriously. He's not a fanatic about it, though. He eats well – good food and bad food – and still has the odd drink."

Kay was especially pleased to see the improvement in her husband's condition. "He's done really well with his weight," she says. "He's lighter now than he's been for years. I think he lost a little bit and felt better for it and so now wants to keep it that way. He eats a lot better now. He still has a beer now and again, but he's more aware of what he should and shouldn't be consuming."

Perhaps the most significant factor was that McDonald's was no longer just down the road, as it had been at previous places. It's something that Julian jokes about but it just might have a touch of relevance. "I definitely feel fitter. I haven't cut my food down and I eat what I like, although I probably don't eat as many burgers," he concedes.

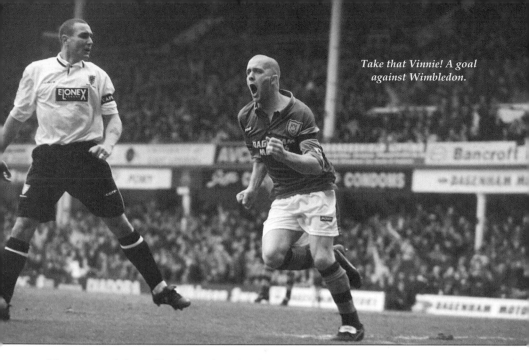

Take that Vinnie! A goal against Wimbledon.

The responsibility of looking after the dogs at home may also have contributed to Dicksy's improved physique. With Julian having to get up at 7am to feed and clean them and let them out, plus needing to feed and handle them during the day, it's all more demanding on the body and Kay feels that it's really since the demands of the dogs have grown that he has lost more weight.

Despite a great run of games without bookings, Julian was still threatened with suspension should just one more yellow card be waved in his direction before the end of March. He was on his best behaviour, though, and successfully crossed the calendar threshold which allowed more bookings before any ban would be incurred. It was all academic, however, as Dicks made it through to the end of the season with a completely clean bill of health.

In fact the only occasions when refs had to make note of the number three in their books was when they were registering his goals, with Julian following up his March goals against Middlesbrough (a penalty) and Man City with further strikes – both headers – against Wimbledon (whose Vinnie Jones also scored, somewhat fortuitously) and, on the final day of the season, Sheffield Wednesday.

Dicks had revealed his feelings about not wanting to be considered for England's Euro '96 campaign a few days before the last Hammers game, while, in typically honest fashion, also insisting he'd have no second thoughts about condemning Wednesday to relegation (with the Hillsborough club still mathematically vulnerable). "I'd said I didn't care if we sent them down so after that I had to do something against them," he says. "I popped up and scored in the second half and it was nice to end the season with a bang."

Even though it seemed as if the day was likely to end in anti-climactic fashion, with Sheffield's Jon Newsome grabbing a last-minute equaliser, the one point gained on the day still proved enough to secure Hammers tenth place in the Premiership – eclipsing rivals Chelsea and finishing in their highest position since the club's best-ever performance of third exactly 10 years earlier. "We didn't realise what the situation was until we got back into the dressing room, but it was a nice end to a good season and it's the highest I've ever finished with West Ham."

There'd been the odd disappointment in the run-in, though. The Hammers had been completely outplayed at Newcastle, being lucky to escape with just a 3-0 defeat ("they were superb that night," says Julian), although Steve Potts had harshly been sent off. During the 2-0 loss at Liverpool, in April, Dicks was subjected to boos from the Anfield crowd. "I think it was because I'd spoken out about them not singing and said things about Roy Evans. But I spoke to him and a few of their players and things were fine." And the last defeat of the season came, rather embarrassingly, at QPR in the final away game, which saw Rangers relegated despite their 3-0 victory romp.

The irony was that while Harry Redknapp was ranting and raving at the

deficiencies of the defence on the day, former West Ham boss Billy Bonds – then youth team manager at Loftus Road – was sitting in the opposite dug-out drooling over Julian's talent. "I was sitting with Ray Wilkins," recalls Bonzo, "and Dicksy hit a great pass from one side of the field to the other. Ray said to me, 'Cor, he's got a left foot,' and I said, 'Yeah, it's as sweet as a nut.' He's got a left foot he can do anything with.

Celebrations after Julian's goal against Sheffield Wednesday in the last game of the season.

"As a footballer, I had the utmost respect for his ability," Bonds continues. "That's never been in doubt. He's a smashing player and the best compliment that I can pay him is that he could have played with some of the best players I played with at West Ham. He'd be well at home with some of the best.

"From a football point of view he never let me down. He was terrific. And I think he's started to settle down a little bit now and, as he gets older, he'll only become a better player. He had a good season for the club that year and it was evidence that he's calming down and losing a side of his character that a lot of people didn't like when I was in charge there. But he's a quality footballer and the fans at Upton Park will always love somebody who's got the talent and wants to put their foot in and have a go."

Not surprisingly after such a woeful display at Queens Park Rangers, it was Harry Redknapp who wanted to 'have a go' – at his players. And so he did in the dressing room after the game, much to the

> "The best compliment that I can pay Julian is that he could have played with some of the best players I played with at West Ham" – BILLY BONDS

annoyance of Dicks who felt that it was the team as a whole – not just the back five – that had failed to defend. But his own reaction reflected how much he'd changed in recent times. "What I used to do if I was barracked by the manager after a game would be to automatically say, 'F*** off, you're wrong!' and have a big ruck. But if Harry has a go at me now I just say, 'Fair enough,' and then go and see him Monday morning – as I wanted to after the QPR game. It's much better to talk one-on-one and I've done it a couple of times with him."

Having said that, Julian has always demanded outright honesty from his managers. "I always believe that if the team has played badly but two individuals have played well, the manage should say to those players, 'You played well and you played well, but the rest of you were crap.' If a couple of players have played badly, the manager should point them out in front of everybody. The only people that have really done that are Ron Saunders and Graeme Souness.

"But I get on well with Harry. He showed faith in me when bringing me back, because most people wouldn't have touched me with a bargepole. And I think I've done okay for him."

The fans thought Julian had done 'okay' also, voting him 'Hammer-of-the-Year' by a country mile – an award he publicly received at the Sheffield Wednesday game on May 5, following an initial presentation at the Supporters' Club a few days earlier. And just two days after wrapping up the Premiership season in goalscoring fashion, Dicks hit the back of the net again, this time with a brilliant 30-yard shot in an Upton Park friendly against Dani's Sporting Lisbon to commemorate Hammers' centenary season (with the young Portugal star playing his last game for West Ham before returning home, and veteran Alvin Martin also bidding a final farewell).

Despite his typically valiant efforts in the 4-1 defeat, however, Julian confesses that motivation for such a game was not easy. "Sporting Lisbon may be a great side but once you've finished the season, the last thing you need is a friendly in front of a couple of thousand people (with just 4,361 in attendance). I was told I'd only be playing for half the game but ended up staying on for the whole 90 minutes. It was nice to be shaken by the hand by the Lisbon players after scoring my goal, though."

With the 1996 'Hammer of the Year' trophy and runner-up Iain Dowie.

Julian could at least look back on the season with a deep sense of satisfaction, not only in his own excellent form but the performance of the team as they embarrassed the 'experts' prophesising relegation with a top-half finish. "I think we had a great season," he reflects. "We started off quite badly, so it could have been even better. It was certainly nice to know we weren't going to be relegated with a good part of the season still to play. And, hopefully, if we buy some more players, we can push on and go for Europe in future."

Nobody was probably more pleased with Dicks than Harry Redknapp, however. He'd taken a gamble, stuck his neck out and followed his instincts – and Julian had repaid that confidence to the extent that the manager had formed a completely new opinion of him – not just as a player, because he more or less knew what he was getting there – but as a person.

"Whatever his problem was before, he's sorted it out and he's a completely different lad. He's a pleasure to work with now," beams Harry. "He may not have won the crowd over immediately when he first returned, but I think he's done that now and that second year he was absolutely superb.

"His attitude is 100 per cent better than it's ever been. He never misses a day's training, he's the first one out on the training ground and he'll go through a brick wall for you. He was my Player-of-the-year by a mile. Iain Dowie was a good second, in my opinion, but Dicksy well deserved his Hammer-of-the-year award.

"I've said what I thought of him when I first came here but I *like* him now. He's a good lad basically. I've made him captain again and he's responded brilliantly. And he's got magnificent talent, a great left foot, he's a great header of the ball, has a terrific right foot and was on the verge of getting back into the England team. So full credit to Dicksy – it's all down to him."

CHAPTER 24

JULIAN FOR ENGLAND?

I F Julian had a pound for every time his name has been mentioned in connection with the England team, he'd be a multi-millionaire. He's been touted as a future full international since the days when he was invited into the England youth squads for training in 1986 ("the main thing I remember is going out for a beer one night" is Julian's chief recollection!), yet since that point in time – when his Birmingham manager John Bond refused to allow him to participate in more sessions because he disagreed with the coaching philosophies – the links with England have been controversial, to say the least.

Bond bitterly opposed the ideas that were being preached to England youngsters by regional coaches under Dave Sexton. "I've heard disturbing reports that some people at the FA (a reference to coaching boss Charles Hughes) are trying to convince Bobby Robson to play the long-ball game. If the England youth coaches are going to continue to ask Julian to do that, it's best that he doesn't go," argued the Birmingham boss (a decision that Dicks was content to go along with at the time).

It didn't stop Bond tipping his bright young prospect for future England honours, though, as he continued to impress for the Blues. "In three or four years he'll be playing for England and be worth his weight in gold," he said in January 1987.

Less than 18 months later, following his transfer to West Ham, Julian got his first big international break when he was called up for the England U-21 Toulon Tournament in France. Disaster struck, however, when he was sent off in the game against Mexico after making a challenge on an opponent. "Even to this day I know I played the ball and the player just rolled over and over," Julian insists. "I thought the referee was going to book him for play-acting. But he got his card out and sent me off. I hadn't even been booked!"

Manager Dave Sexton was reasonably understanding after the incident – "he just told me not to worry about it and that it was one of those things" – and, after missing the semi-final of the competition, Dicks was picked in the team (that he recalls including David Rocastle, Nigel Clough, Michael Thomas and Nigel Martyn) for the following game. "I played in the final when we lost 4-2 to France. That was when I had a big row with Dave Sexton."

The dispute stemmed from a show of frustration from Julian as he trudged into the dressing room after the disappointing defeat. "Two of their goals were offside," he complains. "So I kicked a ball which then hit a bucket of water and it went everywhere. Dave Sexton said to me: 'Do that again and I'll knock you out.' So I said, 'Well, come on then!'

"Things were heated for about 10 or 15 seconds and I think it was David Rocastle who told us to leave it. Sexton was usually mellow and laid back, but we'd just been beaten in the final so perhaps he had the hump about that. Maybe he was still annoyed about my sending off in the quarter-final, I don't know, but he hasn't spoken to me from that day. We got to the airport and he thanked every lad, but he refused to speak to me."

As far as Dicks was concerned, his performances had otherwise been fine. "I must have done okay – at least in the earlier games – for me to get my place back for the final," he argues.

Back at Upton Park, the hope was that the sending off would not ruin his chances of further recalls. "I really hope the the FA don't hold that against him," said Alvin Martin, the last Hammer to achieve major England recognition (having made the last of his 17 appearances against Paraguay in the 1986 World Cup). "It would be a waste. He's too good to be frozen out."

Frozen out he was, though, never getting another call-up for the Under-21s. "As far as I was concerned it was because of the sending off and the argument with Dave Sexton," reckons Julian.

The next season saw relegation for West Ham, with Dicks picking up 11 bookings, and the following campaign got off to a similarly inauspicious start, prompting new Hammers boss Lou Macari to declare: "Change your image or forget an England place." The story, in November 1989, saw Lou admit: "I know Dave Sexton was very disappointed when Dicks was sent off for the England Under-21s against Mexico. Julian just doesn't realise the harm he is doing to himself. He is one of the most talented young defenders in the country but unless things change he could do himself out of an England career."

"Dave Sexton said to me: 'Do that again and I'll knock you out.'"

It was a point that Julian readily acknowledged. "I accept my reputation could have damaged my England chances. That's something I may have to live with," he said.

After bagging the goal to take West Ham through to the fifth round of the Littlewoods Cup, even the press were rueing his lost opportunities at full international level. *'Julian Dicks, West Ham's Littlewoods Cup goal hero, will look jealously at those players taking part in the England matches against Italy next week,'* wrote *Today's* Rob Shepherd on November 11, 1989. *'Dicks is certain his tarnished reputation has cost him international recognition, although he is now being touted as a challenger for Stuart Pearce's vulnerable left-back slot. But next week Tony Dorigo will play for the*

Julian was sent-off in his England Under-21 debut.

England B team, while Nigel Winterburn has been drafted into the full squad as cover.'

"I've no doubt that if it was judged on ability alone, I would have a good claim to be in the frame. But I know there is a black mark against me as far as England is concerned," explained Dicks of his omission.

With terrible timing (a habit of Julian's throughout his career), he was then sent off the following week in the explosive cup game against Wimbledon, sparking all sorts of headlines about Upton Park's 'night of shame'. Not surprisingly, he admitted a couple of months later: "I think my international chances are pretty slim at the moment. I'm playing in the Second Division and I have a pretty bad disciplinary record. But I'm learning to control my aggression and in a year or so I hope to be pushing for a place in the England squad – especially if we regain First Division status."

The Hammers were to fail in their bid to return at the first attempt, of course, and the events of the autumn of 1990 were to push any thoughts of England well out of Julian's mind, as he set about coming to terms with his ligament injury and the very real threat that his career might well be over.

Ironically, that fateful Bristol City game on October 13 saw him attract headlines not about the damaged knee but the booking he received: *'Dicks is one of the most talented left-backs in the country but he'll never receive full international recognition unless he rids himself of his bad boy image,'* said the ever-so-wise *Sun*.

Just five months after fighting his way back to the West Ham first-team a good year later, Dicks received the ultimate reward (well, almost) for his efforts and courage when he was called up by Graham Taylor for the 'England B' game in Czechoslovakia on March 24, 1992. *'Dicks to Czech in for Taylor,'* announced one headline as Julian was drafted in among a number of replacements following 10 withdrawals from the original squad (Liverpool's David Burrows being the left-back who'd had to pull out). "When a door closes on one player it opens for another," explained Taylor.

'Julian Dicks will complete a fairytale return to the international scene with England B

Le Tissier, Smith, Sinton, Dicks, Jobson and Shearer line-up before the 'B' international in Budejovice.

today,' wrote Jack Steggles. *'Dicks thought he'd blown his England chances after getting sent off for the England Under-21 four years ago.'*

"Although I didn't deserve it, to be sent off was a real blow. It's definitely gone against me and put my career back. So I'm finding it hard to believe what's happening to me at the moment. It was the biggest shock of my life when I got the call up on Saturday," Julian declared as he tried to absorb the good news. For the record, the team that took to the field that day in Budejovice was as follows: Martyn (Palace), Barrett (Villa), Palmer (Sheff W), Jobson (Oldham), Dicks (West Ham), Sinton (QPR), Batty (Leeds), Thomas (Liverpool), Le Tissier and Shearer (both Southampton) and Smith (Arsenal), with subs Woods, Dorigo, Hurst and Dixon.

Julian played the full 90 minutes in the 1-0 friendly victory and was bubbling when he was next interviewed by *Hammers News.* "The new England management said that they were not concerned about what had happened in the past – just to go out and play my usual game," he said. "I enjoyed the experience but the football was a different style to what I've been used. The Czechs passed the ball well and slowed the game down. The winger I was marking 'cheated' a bit because whenever I went on the overlap he didn't bother to chase back with me. So if our attack broke down, I had to be careful not to get caught out of position.

"It was frustrating at times. They tend to make a meal of any 50-50 tackles and roll all over the place. I felt like getting stuck in but you can't do that at international level. The bloke I was marking was taken off in the second half which enabled me to get forward more. I got in a few good crosses and had a shot – right-footed too – that went just wide."

With front-runners Stuart Pearce and Tony Dorigo both sidelined for the next trip – to Moscow on April 29 to take on the CIS – Julian would have fancied his chances of gaining a first full cap, especially with him and Graeme Le Saux being the only two left-backs in the party of 34 for the two games. But it was Le Saux who got the nod for the full England team, with Dicks having to console himself with a second 'B' appearance. "I've been told that I'm in the country's top 40 and it's encouraging to be involved again.

> "I think McMenemy just wanted to assert some authority. They treat you like children"

The whole experience of being away with England gives you a boost," he said philosophically afterwards.

What wasn't revealed at the time, however, was what took place at the airport on the return journey home. "Carlton Palmer, Chris Woods and myself went to the upstairs lounge to have a couple of beers," says Julian. "Lawrie McMenemy (Taylor's assistant) came up after a while and asked what we were doing. We said we were having a couple of drinks and he said, 'Leave your beers and get through.' We thought we were boarding the plane but we got through and everybody was just sitting there in the departure lounge. There was no plane, nothing, and we just sat there for about an hour. I think McMenemy just wanted to assert some authority. They treat you like children. They don't realise you're in your mid-20s – they treat you like kids."

It's not known what effect the incident has had on Dicks' chances of further international recognition, but it clearly did him no favours – "the story must have got back to the FA, and I don't think Woods or Palmer have figured since," he says.

The two East European trips with Graham Taylor and Lawrie McMenemy did at least open Julian's eyes to what was going on in the England camp at the time. The most disturbing thing for him was the lack of pre-match discussion about the games they were going into. "All we'd do is kick balls about in training and that was it. It wasn't like they laid the team out and said, 'This is what *you* do, this is what *you* do...'" he says.

Not that the training techniques for the full England team impressed him too much either. "I was watching them train one day, doing some shadow play, and Graham Taylor told Paul Stewart to kick the ball as far as he could," begins Dicks. "Paul Stewart said, 'You what?' Taylor said, 'I want you to kick the ball as far up there out of play as you can and then we'll put pressure on them.' I thought, 'That's the England manager speaking. We can't play like that!' But that's the way he wanted to do it and that's the way they did it.

"It was sad. He was the England manager and he was asking people to just wellie the ball 70 yards out of play. It was ridiculous."

Despite the emergence of Graeme Le Saux, there was still every hope that Julian could push for a place for the USA '94 World Cup finals, assuming, that was, that England would qualify. Just when Dicks needed to put a consistent run of games together for West Ham, though, he undermined everything with three dismissals in that four-month period in the first half of the 1992-93 season.

"In our opinion, he could be the next England full-back. He's got the ability and he's young enough to do it – but he won't with his disciplinary record. That's what's keeping him out of international honours in the game," said exasperated Hammers MD Peter Storrie after the third sending off at Derby.

"The fact is that potentially he is a good enough player to wear an England shirt – but only if he sorts himself out," reiterated Billy Bonds.

Julian had clearly put himself out of favour with Graham Taylor, with the manager electing to play centre-back Martin Keown out of position at left-back (following the loss of Pearce, Dorigo and Winterburn through injury) in the 2-2 draw in the World Cup qualifier against Holland at Wembley on April 28, 1993.

Hammers News editor Tony McDonald campaigned on Julian's behalf: *'He is still no angel, but then neither are one or two England stars, like Gascoigne and Paul Ince, who have had their fare share of problems with officials too. England is not so well blessed with talent that it can afford to dismiss Dicks so lightly. I believe he is the most skilful left-back in the country at the moment. I think England should give him another chance. Or does good technique, skill and sheer determination count for nothing these days?'*

As Julian looked to the 1993-94 campaign, attempting to put his troubles behind him, he was adamant an England place was still available to him – if he sorted his act out. "This is a make or break season for me England-wise. I would love to go to the United States if we qualify but I have got to prove myself and not get booked every game."

In October 1993, Julian made the move that many thought would see him finally make that elusive step up to full international status – he joined Liverpool. "As soon as he went there, I said, 'That's it, he's going to play for England now,'" admits Ian Bishop.

"The next step is England now," said brother Grantley at the time. "If he can get his discipline in order – I'm sure that will happen at Liverpool – he can go on and play for his country. Stuart Pearce is 30 and will have to retire one day."

> **"As soon as he went to Liverpool, I said, 'That's it, he's going to play for England now.'"** — IAN BISHOP

And with international honours usually a formality once a Liverpool shirt is pulled on, Julian declared: "I am wiping the slate clean. Seventy per cent of my game is aggression but I have spoken to a lot of people about my disciplinary record. I know it cost me the chance of an England call-up last summer. Hopefully

Liverpool will get into Europe next season and playing for them will help my international prospects."

We'll never know what might have been had Dicks not been hit with injury so early in his Liverpool career, but his much improved disciplinary record was at least acknowledged in the latter part of the season. *'Dicks has only been booked once this season. If the intent is there, it will be a change that many people, including England manager Graham Taylor, will welcome because there are few better left-backs and his record of 29 goals in 152 league games for West Ham is an extraordinary ratio for a defender,'* applauded Peter Ball of *The Times*.

During his year at Anfield, a magazine article (in the wake of England's ultimate failure to make USA '94) speculated about an ideal winning team for the 1998 World Cup. Whether writer Ian Ridley was a closet Hammers or Liverpool fan has not been revealed, but Dicks was his definite choice for the left-back berth. *'Blackburn's Alan Wright and Graeme Le Saux and Spurs' Sol Campbell fall into the attacking category, but the team is going to need a tougher presence. Liverpool's Julian Dicks, despite the furore regarding his disciplinary record, has the attributes – enthusiasm and energy – to fill the position and, at 29 in 1998, will have the experience too,'* he wrote.

Sadly, next England supremo Terry Venables was not so convinced. Julian's expulsion from the Anfield ranks may have seen him lose his best opportunity for a call-up in some people's eyes (if not Julian's – "it shouldn't matter what club you're at, if you're good enough you should be picked," he argues), while his form in his return season at Upton Park, although improving throughout the campaign, failed to see him seriously threaten Le Saux, who'd emerged as the manager's first choice.

A serious ankle break for the Blackburn player coincided with Julian's best form for many years in the 1995-96 campaign and, with a complete transformation in terms of discipline (avoiding a yellow card for 25 games in total) the clamour for Julian's elevation to full international status had never been greater.

'Julian Dicks gave an exhibition of all-round full-back play in West Ham's 2-0 win over Southend that could make him a surprise contender for England's European Championship squad,' wrote the *Daily Mail* in January.

'Dicks has matured and is playing better than ever,' expressed the *Daily Telegraph* after he helped Hammers to a win at Chelsea in February.

'The West Ham defender is in sensational form and an obvious candidate for the left-back spot made vacant by Graeme Le Saux's horror injury,' said *The Sun*.

'In purely footballing terms, he is an England class defender,' claimed the *Evening Standard*.

"In my eyes, Julian is the best left-sided player in the country. If Terry Venables can pick a better left-back than Julian, I haven't seen him," said Hammers team-mate and Danish international defender Marc Rieper in support of the press campaign that was building to get Dicks called-up for the remaining friendlies prior to Euro '96.

"I believe I'm good enough to play for England," insisted Julian in the April 1996 issue of *Hammers News Magazine*. "People might say that's being big-headed but I know I've had the ability since I've been playing football. It's just my disciplinary record that's probably kept me out. Of course, it would be nice if I did get a call-up but I won't lose any sleep over it. It would be great to play for England – all I need is for people to give me a chance," he added.

Julian's mood soon changed, however. It's doubtful that he'd have taken any notice of the positive press, but there was a growing feeling that a call-up to the squad was more likely than not, with Venables having no obvious cover for Stuart Pearce. *'Terry Venables is ready to hand Julian Dicks a shock England call-up against Bulgaria. Coach Venables has sent chief scout Ted Buxton to watch the defender three times. And Buxton has given Venners a glowing report,'* wrote *The Sun* on March 19, while the *Daily Mirror* declared on the same day: *'Julian Dicks will make a late bid for England's European Championship squad with a debut call-up tomorrow. The Hammers tough guy is set to be rewarded for the best form of his career by winning a place in Terry Venables' squad for the friendly against Bulgaria at Wembley.'*

The call never came for the Bulgaria match, though. But hopes were raised when it was announced that Terry Venables was making a personal appearance at Upton Park on April 13 to watch the game against Bolton Wanderers.

There was a unique sense of collective hope within the crowd that Julian would reproduce his impressive form of the previous six months against Wanderers, to the point that there was a united cheer when something he attempted came off and an audible sigh of disappointment if a tackle was lost. Starting the game in a traditional left-back position, however (for the first time in months), it seemed a nervy performance from Dicks and he lacked the commanding authority that had pushed him to the brink of a call-up.

"Julian didn't have a particularly good game," admits Frank Lampard. "I think he'll be the first to admit that and it didn't help his cause. But Ted Buxton had been raving about his other performances."

Buxton had indeed cast an eye over Dicks on a number of occasions, including the Middlesbrough game back on March 9, when he'd shaken Julian's hand and spoken to Hammers coach Frank Burrows. "I got Ted Buxton to come to Upton Park and watch him quite often," says Peter Storrie. "I spend a lot of time with Terry Venables and I pushed Julian for a long while."

With the England boss having previously denied Dicksy the call-up, however, there was a degree of cynicism in some quarters about his visit to the Hammers. "The only reason that Venables was there that day was to keep the press quiet," insists Carol Dicks. "He had no intention of picking Julian – it was just to say he'd watched him. Julian didn't have one of his best games but he played in two positions and he had a better second half when he was moved into the middle.

"Julian came into the players' bar and people were asking him if Venables had spoken to him, and he said, 'No, he hasn't spoken to me. He's not gonna speak to me.' I heard that Slaven Bilic had chatted to Ted Buxton and the subject of Julian was brought up. Buxton supposedly said to Slaven, 'Tell Julian to grow his hair.' What's his hair got to do with playing for England?"

> "If they're picking people on their hairstyles then it's a bit pointless playing for England at all"

Despite what Carol says, Bilic apparently offered words of encouragement to Julian following his conversation with the England scout. "Slaven came and told me that I was probably going to figure in the squad for the Croatia friendly on April 24, but I never really thought in my own mind that I would get in," says Dicks, although he admits: "There were rumours going around that it's because my hair is too short and all that kind of crap. If they're picking people on their hairstyles then it's a bit pointless playing for England at all really."

The debatable topic about Julian's visual image is addressed elsewhere in this book (chapter 26), but it's worth making the point here that a lack of hair hardly thwarted Paul Gascoigne, Mark Wright, Steve Stone and Alan Wright's bids for international recognition prior to Euro '96.

Needless to say, Julian did not get the much anticipated call-up for the Croatia game. And to add salt to his gaping wounds, both Philip Neville and the aforementioned Wright were called up as cover for Stuart Pearce. It was the ultimate insult as far as Dicks was concerned, to the point that he told the author of this book that he would reject any last-minute call to the international set-up, should it

KICK OFF, Saturday, May 4, 1996   1

SunSport's Saturday

soccer pullout No38

KICK OFF

STUFF YOU, TEL

'd sooner build a dog kennel than play for ngland, blasts Dicks

ANDERTON . . . fit again

Anderton targets Euro slot

By JANINE SELF
DARREN ANDERTON
has told England coach
Terry Venables: "I

suddenly arrive. The plan was for Julian to reveal his intention to snub any late request for his services in the following month's issue of *Hammers News Magazine*, but when a tabloid reporter fired the relevant question to him as he was leaving a training session near the end of the season, he was unable to hold back. And there it appeared on the cover of *The Sun's* Saturday Kick-Off supplement: *'Stuff You, Tel!'*

Dicks repeated the sentiment again in *Hammers News Magazine* the following week: "The truth is that I don't want to go and play for England – not under Terry Venables," he said. "If he called me tomorrow, I'd just say, 'No, thank you.' Because if I did get picked now I'd only be an after-thought. To be honest, I'd rather spend the summer building dog kennels."

The stories attracted a mixed reaction, with some questioning the wisdom of verbally sticking two fingers up at the England set-up, while others supported Julian's honesty. "I don't know if it was the right way to do it," says Ian Bishop, "but, fair play to him, he spoke his mind, which I suppose is something a lot more people should do. Julian speaks his mind but he knows he can back it up with his football. I think he knows he's the best left-back in the country and his attitude is that if other people don't think that, that's down to them. I certainly think he played well enough in the second half of that season to have been included for the European Championships."

Fellow team-mate John Moncur also supported Julian in his actions. "As a friend of his, I'd stick by anything he says. If that's what he wants to do, it's his decision and I wouldn't question it. Julian says what he means and means what he says and that's one of the things I like about him," says Moncs, whose opinion is that Julian was definitely disappointed to have missed out. "He wouldn't be human if he didn't want to play for England. I think he was disappointed because over the years he's proved himself to be one of the best left-backs in the country. Maybe there was a little bit of anger there on his part because he knows how good he is."

Dicks did indeed say when he meant, to the extent that he came clean about his views on the national side. "I don't care whether England win or not," he admitted. "It doesn't bother me. I haven't watched an England game since the World Cup in 1990 because I find the games boring. But that shouldn't matter. I didn't go and watch Liverpool but that didn't stop Graeme Souness from buying me."

"Venables must have something against me"

Dicksy's parents had mixed views on the story. Indeed, Carol had already discussed the issue with him. "Julian told me that if Venables wanted him in the summer, he'd tell him he could stuff it," she confides. "I said, 'You can't say that!' and he said, 'Oh yes I can!' He told me that if he can't get picked after the games he played that season, he's never going to. I said that it might come and he just said, 'No, ma, I don't want to know.'"

Ron Dicks, on the other hand, had no doubts about his son's act of defiance. "I'd have done it weeks earlier," he says. "Why have him watched six or seven times when he played really well and been 'man of the match' in most of those games and then not pick him? All it does is build his hopes up, because he does want to play for England, without a doubt."

Kay Dicks, meanwhile, had no idea that Julian was going to speak out so openly, even though she was well aware of what her husband was thinking. "I was surprised when I heard about the story," she admits. "I was at a dog show and I thought people were taking the mickey when they started talking about building dog kennels. I know that anything he says usually gets taken out of context and distorted, so I rang Julian up and asked him if he'd seen the paper."

Ultimately, though, she understood Julian's frustration with the situation. "I think he'd had enough of people phoning up asking about England. He doesn't pick the side. The press build up all the speculation and when nothing comes of it they love it because it's another story. At the end of the day, though, he should be playing for his country."

People's immediate reactions obviously placed a small seed of doubt about his move in Julian's mind, however, with him seeking the advice of Frank Lampard. "One morning he just said to me, 'What do you think, have I done the right thing?' I just said, 'Well, it's your decision, you make your own mind up.' I wouldn't want to say that he was wrong. Technically I suppose he was wrong, but he's the sort of lad who says something and means it. At least you know where you stand with him."

Ultimately, though, Dicks' outburst was more an act of instinct than considered thought. "It was building up and up and in the end I just let rip," Julian explains. "The thing is, you've got people being called up for the England squad who shouldn't even be in the club sides. I'm better than Stuart Pearce, Graeme Le Saux, Philip Neville and Alan Wright. Some people may think I'm a big-headed bastard but that's just the way I feel. I scored 11 goals last season and we had no full-backs who were anywhere near that. You pick the players who are in form and I don't think Terry Venables did that. So he must have something against me – even though he once tried to buy me for Tottenham.

"But no-one's had a go about what I said. My friends told me I did well to speak out because I've just been honest. Harry's not said a word, although all he's got to worry about is me playing well for West Ham."

Harry concedes the outburst won't have helped Dicksy's cause "especially if he does want to play in the future" but hopes that it won't stand in his way. Peter Storrie also expresses the view that "Julian didn't do himself any favours – it was ill-timed" but felt that such stories in the press are often taken with a pinch of salt. "If Terry had wanted to bring him into the squad I don't think it would have bothered him," he says. "Terry's the sort of man who would have rung him up and said, 'What's all this nonsense?'

"He was close to getting a call," adds Storrie. "I think one of the main reasons why he didn't get there – and this is just a personal opinion – was that Terry already had two players, in Gascoigne and Ince, who are notoriously a bit volatile and liable to go at any time. And whilst Julian had obviously done a fantastic job before the European Championships, his reputation was still there before him. I think they may have felt that having three possible sparks in the team was too much to run with in a competition where the referees might be very hard and firm with tackles. But only Terry will know the reasons why he didn't pick him."

That hasn't stopped people speculating as to why the big call-up never came – least of all Julian himself. "I think I'm blacklisted," he says. "It's because of my reputation, the bookings and dismissals. I think I was first blacklisted for the U-21s after being sent off in the Toulon Tournament, because there was no reason why they shouldn't have put me in the next squad. I also think the airport incident with the B team counted against me. Somebody must have told the FA about that.

"I think the top people at the FA make the decisions. The manager says what his squad is and they probably say, 'You're not having *him* in the team.' That's my opinion."

Over Land and Sea

£2

OLAS 110   Issue Date 23/3/96   Manchester City

A public message to Terry Venables:

Forget the dicks you've picked - get the real one in the side - Julian Dicks

60 pages Incorporating Home Alone

It's also the opinion of father Ron:
"Terry Venables may have picked the national side then but I think he'd had a directive about Julian from Bert Millichip or Graham Kelly because of his disciplinary record. I think the manager only went to see him against Bolton to keep the media quiet. I was sure he was going to get called-up until that game, but he didn't select him for the following squad and now I don't think he'll ever be picked for England. But it does annoy me. If he's not been the best left-back in this country over the last year I don't know who has."

It's also feasible that Dave Sexton has influenced people above him following the dressing room dispute in France. "Dave Sexton said to him, 'You do that again and I'll smash you,'" says Carol Dicks. "Julian said, 'You and whose army?' and Sexton looked at him as if to say, 'You'll never play for England again.' It's the FA who approve the squad."

It seems hard to believe that a spilt bucket of water could have upset Sexton so much, but there's no doubt that Julian's frustration was construed as an unacceptable display of petulance. "He kicked the bucket over because he doesn't like losing," says former scout Ron Veal, showing an interest in Julian's progress. "I know the kid. He likes to win every game and he's passionate. I think Dave Sexton put a block on him after that.

"I'm very disappointed because he should easily have represented England at senior level. You need people who know they've got the shirt on. I saw Gazza sticking his tongue out at the camera while on England duty but you wouldn't see Julian do that. He may go in hard for the ball but that's different – it's a man's game. When I look at some of the people called up before Euro '96 it seems as if Venables was giving away caps like confetti."

> "I saw Gazza sticking his tongue out at the camera while on England duty but you wouldn't see Julian do that" – RON VEAL

Former Hammers team-mate Jimmy Quinn, however, feels that Julian may have stood more chance of being pulled into the England squad after the Toulon incidents if Venables had been managing then. "I think there were one or two people in the camp at that time who thought that if you did the slightest thing wrong you couldn't be involved any more," he states. "If Terry Venables had been in charge he would have played again.

"Julian is without doubt one of the most talented people I've ever played with. I've been involved in international football for the last 11 years and played with and against a lot of good footballers, but I've never seen anyone with better feet than Julian. If he'd have concentrated a little bit more on his fitness earlier he could have been the best left-back this country's ever seen. It's a shame that someone of his talent hasn't played on the full international stage yet. I just can't understand why he wasn't picked for the European Championships."

Frank Lampard is probably close to hitting the nail on the head when he says that it's likely to be the combination of Julian's temperament and the mentality of the continentals that was putting most doubt into the England manager's mind. "You've got to keep your tongue in your cheek when you're playing for England," he stresses. "You know what some of these foreigners are like – you've only got to blow on them and they go over. Maybe that was in Terry's mind."

Unfortunately, Mr Venables did not respond to requests for him to contribute towards this book.

Whatever the reasons for Julian's continuous omission, though, there's no doubt that double standards came into play. While doubts remained about his temperament, nobody seemed to question that of Paul Gascoigne, who had been booked on something like 16 occasions in his first season for Rangers. In fact, how many of England's European Championship squad could lay claim to going 25 games without a yellow card?

"The FA obviously don't believe in rehabilitation," says Carol Dicks sarcastically, making an obvious reference to the likes of Tony Adams and Dennis Wise who were still selected after being found guilty of far greater crimes (off the pitch) than kicking a bucket of water over or being sent off.

The question following the Euro '96 finals, of course, was whether new England manager Glenn Hoddle would hold any past comments or misdemeanours against Dicks – assuming he's interested in him in the first place, that is.

"I spoke to Julian about England after Euro '96," reveals Tony Cottee, "and asked him if he felt things would change under Glenn Hoddle. He just said, 'I'm not overly worried about the situation – if it happens it happens and if it doesn't it doesn't.' In a way, that's a good way of dealing with life because you can't make things happen. He did everything he could last season and still he never got the call-up he deserved, so he couldn't have done any more."

As Dicks commenced the 1996-97 season with West Ham, it remained to be seen whether the call would finally come. "A new manager has taken over and if he was to pick me I'd play for him," he states. "But I don't really expect the situation to change. And if it's true that Glenn Hoddle stopped John Spencer speaking in my defence after the stamping allegations then I don't think I've got much chance of getting picked anyway."

The early signs under Hoddle's management did not look good, especially with Stuart Pearce being coaxed out of 'retirement' for the World Cup qualifying games against Moldova in September 1996 and Poland in October, following the Forest man's initial announcement to terminate his international career after Euro '96.

And to make matters worse for Julian, Everton left-back Andy Hinchcliffe was then called up for the two squads, making it even more unlikely that Hoddle had been convinced by Julian's improvement over the previous year. And *The Sun's* comment, following West Ham's league visit to Goodison Park in October 1996, further proved the injustice: *'Andy Hinchcliffe has jumped ahead of Dicks in the England reckoning – but there was no comparison here.'*

And there's no shortage of support from some of those who have worked with Julian over the years. "He should be an ever-present in the England team," says Lou Macari. "I definitely think that had he been fortunate enough to play at West Ham in the era of Billy Bonds and Trevor Brooking, he wouldn't have been so misguided. Had he played with the real professionals I think he'd have been a great, great England player. And he still could be if he could force his way into the team. But people only see his reputation.

'Andy Hinchcliffe has jumped ahead of Dicks in the England reckoning – but there was no comparison here'
– The Sun, October 1996

"If you were the England manager, you'd look at him and pick up vibrations from certain media reports and games he's played in and think: 'Let's steer clear of him.' But the right place to have Julian is ON your side. Going to Liverpool was a golden opportunity for him and they probably didn't weigh him up properly. I'm quite sure Roy Evans never got hold of him, put his arm around him and said, 'You're an England player – now go out and prove it.'"

Evans doesn't deny that Julian still has the potential to achieve international honours, however. "I think he's got enough talent to play for England, that's for sure," he says. "He's a great talent, football-wise. The regret is that it just didn't work out for him at Liverpool. With the (three centre-back) system that we play now, he'd have probably been excellent."

Former Birmingham team-mate Martin Kuhl makes the valid point that Julian would probably have stood more chance of international honours if he was born in another country! "If he was Italian, he'd be in their team," he insists. "But in England you've got the bigwigs at the top asking themselves: 'Can we have him in the team?' It's just the fact that he's got a disciplinary record – it's something that's cost a lot of players opportunities. I remember Frank Worthington always saying that Mark Dennis should have played for England. It's the same with Dicksy, it's the fear factor – will he blow up? But the foreign teams do it, they've got their hard men who get booked and, if you want to win things, sometimes you've got to pick these sort of people."

> "He goes down as one of the best left-backs who've never played for England" – GRAEME SOUNESS

Graeme Souness, another hardman of old, still believes that Julian has the potential to represent his country. "Most certainly," he agrees. "I would think he's quietly disappointed that he's not already played. It's certainly not been through lack of ability. As far as I'm concerned, he goes down as one of the best left-backs who've never played for England."

The key, ultimately, is whether Julian can allay any lingering fears that the England supremos may have of him 'sparking' or 'blowing-up'. The potential is still there, as Billy Bonds proved in his own time. "I got called up late in my career, when I was in my thirties, and maybe if my disciplinary record had been a little bit better and I'd have thought about things a bit more, I'd have got involved earlier. I saw Julian quoted as saying he'd have loved to have broken into the squad and maybe he realised that if he carried on the way he was he would never have had a chance."

"The hope is that he has learned," adds John Lyall, "because he's such a good footballer. Last season I saw that the England people were looking at him and that was a level that we always felt he would definitely play at and gain full caps. He's a Stuart Pearce type – he's got the same power, quality and determination – and even now it's not beyond him to get an England cap. He wouldn't let anybody down."

SOCCER STAR'S TWINS ATTACKED

ATTACK: Julian Dicks

Dad's stamping sparks off school revenge on girls, 6

Julian a hard man? No he's just a big girl's blouse

DICKS FACING FAN BACKLASH

By FRANC

JULIAN DIC
£500,000 to
Merseyside

And as Dicks reveal

ts premium offer **KS** SUPER SPORT -

Jules sale

Stop the agg
Dicksy –
you'll be

CHAPTER 25

THE PRESS(URE) GAME

THE role of the media in helping to shape the public's view of Julian cannot be under-estimated. Ever since the Bristol papers revealed his school's concern over him leaving home to join Birmingham City at the age of 14, Dicks has become a figure the press have loved to write about, whenever the opportunity arises.

This, of course, has been largely down to Julian himself. His footballing talents initially built his popularity with the fans, but his cult status at Upton Park – developed through his full bloodied approach to the game and his honest relationship with the supporters – has helped make him a character that sells newspapers. And *character* is a key word, with Julian's habit of speaking his mind often providing the media with something to work with.

He's also given them every opportunity to cultivate his 'bad boy' image, with his many dismissals and regular involvement in controversy. And, as we all know, the press love nothing more than a piece of controversy. Once an identity has been established with the public it can be cynically developed and exploited, and Julian's reputation as one of soccer's 'hard men' is a tag that, once pinned on, has been hard to shake off.

A familiar feature of the press is their habit of building somebody up in order to then shoot them down. It happens in all areas of the entertainment industry, with celebrities occasionally regretting their fame as the media look to cash in on their status and public profiles. It's a ploy that Julian has become painfully aware of during his days in football.

"They like to put you on a pedestal so that they can chop it from under you," he says. "I don't know why they do it. Maybe they like to stop people from getting too big for their boots. It's probably just what's been bred into a lot of journalists – and it does sell papers."

Dicks first experienced such treatment in his early years at West Ham. "The papers were building me up, after I got into the England U-21 side, saying I should be playing for the full team. Then I would get booked or sent off and they were saying that I didn't deserve to play for England."

Julian looks over the 'Hammers News Magazine' with his agent Rachel Anderson. Most press enquiries are dealt with by her these days.

Of course, it's the media's job to make the most of any story, but what's happening in modern times is that the press – particularly the tabloids – are producing exaggerated responses to situations in order to make for more thrilling copy. When somebody plays well it's like the second coming of the Messiah, while being sent off is the equivalent of committing mass murder (particularly for a player saddled with a bad image). It all makes for super-large headlines, screaming at you from the page, with the aim of enticing you into the story. "I've learnt the hard way about how they work and I'm very cynical about the press now," Julian admits. "I haven't got a very good relationship with them."

> "I've learnt the hard way about how they work and I'm very cynical about the press now"

Things weren't always so bad, though. Back in the days at Brum, following Dicks' explosion onto the scene as a tigerish teenager, the early coverage was all positive although there were other, more established players in demand by the press. "I didn't get too much attention – nothing like there is now – because I didn't have the profile," says Julian. "They didn't have too much to write about so the press left me alone really.

"They started taking more of an interest when I joined West Ham. It mostly stemmed from the bookings and sendings off. Then the bandwagon got rolling and they were all jumping on and taking pops at me."

Julian started to establish relationships with press personnel during this period, as he emerged as a figure of interest. As well as developing some feeling of confidence and trust in the staff of the club's monthly publication, *Hammers News*, Julian also got to know reporter Lee Clayton (a West Ham fan), then of *The Sun* and latterly chief soccer writer on *The Star*. "I knew Lee more as an acquaintance than a friend, in that I'd rather talk to him than the rest of the press crew. I got on well with him but then he stitched me up. I opened the paper one day and saw that he'd called me an idiot or thug – or something like that – in a match report. I don't blank him or anything but I just wouldn't really give him too much of my time now."

Not surprisingly, given his three red cards, the 1992-93 season hardly saw Julian's name out of the headlines. That was when the media scrutiny intensified for the first time and the press were forever on his doorstep, creating all sorts of pressure on the Dicks family. "The press didn't do us any favours at all," says Kay of that time. "Once they've got it in for you, that's it really."

And it must have seemed as if history was horribly repeating itself in 1995, when Dicks was accused of stamping on Chelsea's John Spencer, was sent off five days later at Arsenal and then made the front pages of the tabloids for the very first time with the story about his daughters being picked on at school. Yet, despite all the aggravation, Julian ironically admits: "All publicity is good publicity football-wise, even if it's for getting booked or sent off. My way of looking at it is that if you weren't any good they wouldn't write about you. If you were just a run-of-the-mill player they wouldn't give you the time of day."

> **"I got on well with him but then he stitched me up"** – ON THE STAR'S LEE CLAYTON

Being good enough to attract press interest is one thing, being singled out for special attention is something else, as Julian discovered to his woe with the explosive *News Of The World* front page allegations of his sexual infidelity while on holiday in Tenerife in May 1996 (see chapter 33). Now he wasn't just a name worthy of column inches, he was (like Paul Gascoigne) a specific TARGET – not just for the soccer writers but the main news hounds. It's a fact not lost on some of Julian's West Ham team-mates.

"He's a target because he's a name," says John Moncur. "The people who put out the Tenerife story only did that because of the person that Julian is. They've done it because they think they can earn money out of it. I think it's disgraceful that newspapers write stories like that."

Moncur has seen it all before with his good friend Gazza, of course. "In a lot of ways I think they're similar in character," he declares. "They've definitely both got that will to win. I also think they've both got a lot of bottle – on and off the field – with the way they deal with certain things. They've taken so much flak off the press and had to develop a thick skin because of the amount of people looking to put them down."

Gascoigne has indeed experienced the downside of fame, with his every move being scrutinised, while Julian has also been the victim of his own success. "It's because of how well he was playing and all the publicity he got about the England thing towards the end of the season," says Ian Bishop. "That's why they've targeted him. It could have been anybody in that Tenerife story but he was getting publicity so that's why they picked him out."

Dicksy's image also had something to do with it, as far as Tony Cottee was concerned. "He's a big name and a cult figure at West Ham and people like to try their luck with characters like that," he says. "He's got to be thick-skinned because he's created his image and he's got to deal with that. If he goes out with 10 lads and there's a punch-up you can bet your life Dicksy would get the blame for it. That's just how it is but he seems to deal with it very well."

Indeed, there's a general acceptance now in football (as there is in most other areas of entertainment) that if you put your head above the parapet, then it will quickly be shot at. "It's just the way it is for all top players at the moment," adds Danny Williamson. "You only have to look at what happened to the England players before Euro '96. The papers are always looking for a story. With the Tenerife thing, I was told that the *News Of The World* sent a reporter out there because they knew the team were there. So you've got to watch your back."

In terms of purely his football, however, 1995-96 had seen Dicks gain lots of positive press, with many writers linking him to an England place. Not that Julian took any of the plaudits too seriously. "It could soon hit rock bottom again," he warns. "They were pushing me for England but if I do get sent off again it'll be splashed all over the back of the papers and I'll get called a thug again."

Nowadays Julian tends to ignore most of what's written, generally only looking at match reports if a paper is laying around at the training ground. "I don't think half the reporters go to the game," he says. "You read their reports and it's as if they were watching a totally different game. It's funny really – they've never played the game yet they try to give marks on how a player has performed. If a centre-forward has a crap game for 89 minutes but then pops up and scores, they give him a seven or eight out of 10. Yet if someone's done well for 80 minutes and gets booked or sent off, he gets two or three."

Dicksy's view of journalists has also dimmed as a result of noticing a change in emphasis in match reports. "The Manchester United game (in January 1996) was a classic example," he says. "They didn't want to write about the game, just the incident with Andy Cole. That's all they wrote about and then they stuck the marks out of 10 at the bottom. Obviously they can highlight the tackle, but they should write about the game. It's all wrong."

Adds Kay Dicks: "Julian doesn't tend to do too much with the football press now unless it's sorted out with his agent first. It's just not worth it because everything he says gets twisted around."

CHAPTER 26

MEN BEHAVING BALDLY

I F Julian wasn't a man behaving badly in the majority of the 1995-96 season, he was at least a man behaving BALDLY! His shaved head – which he first unveiled following his move back to Upton Park from Liverpool in October 1994 – has been a constant topic of debate since his return.

Many have argued that by having a strict cut that's so much more intimidating, he's reinforcing the stereotyped view that most people have of him (lumping him in with the likes of Vinnie Jones etc). It's also been suggested that the skinhead style has done little to help his image with referees and opposing supporters and that it's been a serious handicap as he tries to convince people he's not the thug he's sometimes made out to be.

Despite the opinion of others, Julian has always been adamant that he'll wear his hair exactly as he likes. "People say I should let my hair grow but there are loads of players with short hair and nothing is said about *them*," he argues. "It doesn't matter what I look like or what image I've got, people should judge me on how I play. People just jump on the bandwagon. Even when I used to have my socks rolled down they used to call me a thug. The papers used to say I didn't look like a player because my shirt was hanging out!"

The question, of course, is why Dicks decided to shave his head in the first place. While some may suggest that it was to consolidate his tough guy image, Julian insists it's purely a matter of practicality. "When my hair grows it goes all wavy and it really annoys me. It's here, there and everywhere and you've got to put gel on it. And I got bored with it. Now I just get up and go out, without even thinking about my hair. To be honest, I'd like to let it grow like Bish's, I really would. I have tried to let it grow but it gets so unmanageable I just think, 'Sod it, I'll have it all off.'"

It's wife Kay who is called upon to keep Julian's hair short, but it's not a popular move with mum Carol. "I don't like him with his head shaved," she says. "I've told him: 'Let your hair grow.' But all he says is that it's nothing to do with me. I just make him worse. There was a time a while back when he'd let his hair grow and we were over at his place. We were saying how young he looked and he said, 'Kay, I'll have my hair cut later.' And he had it all off!"

Julian wasn't always bothered about the waviness of his hair, though. "It was very wavy when I was a kid. It wasn't long but it was down on my neck," he says. "When you're that young you're not really bothered but as you get older it starts to get on your nerves."

The first serious change of hairstyle for Julian came in his Birmingham days, when he had his locks highlighted. "That was Kay's idea," he explains. "We were good friends with a hairdresser in Birmingham and she did them for me. They lasted about six months, until they grew out, but I liked them at the time."

The next radical move, in 1989, was to have his head shaved at the sides so that his hair was angled in the shape of a 'V'. "It was just something I wanted to do for a change. I actually fancied a 'Mohican' but don't think it would have gone down too well at the club. The lads gave me enough stick as it was," he reveals.

> **'If you want your hair shaven at the back and sides, and short and spikey on top, you ask for a 'Joolian Special'** – THE SUN

It was even claimed in one Hammers match report that Julian's V-style had been adopted by local hairdressers. *'East End barbers have even named a hairstyle after the cult hero,'* wrote Lee Clayton. *'If you want your hair shaven at the back and sides, and short and spiky on top, you ask for a 'Joolian Special'.'* "It makes me look streamlined, but it doesn't make me run any faster – although I wish it did!" he joked.

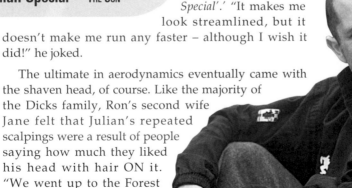

The ultimate in aerodynamics eventually came with the shaven head, of course. Like the majority of the Dicks family, Ron's second wife Jane felt that Julian's repeated scalpings were a result of people saying how much they liked his head with hair ON it. "We went up to the Forest game," she recalls, "and he'd grown his hair a bit. We said he looked

'Shoot' likened Dicksy to Sidney, one of the Bash Street Kids in 'The Beano'.

really good and that was the worst thing in the world to say. If we'd have said, 'You look bloody awful!' he'd have kept growing it. But because we said how good he looked, he got Kay to shave it off again. It's almost as if he thinks, 'If people like me this way I'm going to change it.'"

"I asked him why he'd shaved his head again," says Ron, "and he said he couldn't be bothered to mess about with it. All he had to do was get up and polish his head and he was ready!"

Julian's 'wavy' hair was also missed by his agent Rachel. "He's got this thick, curly hair and I think it's lovely. But he doesn't like it. He just prefers his head bald," she says.

While the debate over Julian's head continued, particularly around the time of the Spencer/Arsenal incidents in September '95, his improved performances and discipline overall allowed him the freedom to do what he wanted with his hair. "He's an individual," explains Rachel, "and has always wanted to shave his head. He just feels confident now that his behaviour on the pitch is good enough so that he can now do that."

> **"The haircuts stand out and make him recognisable. I think he likes to have an audience"** – FRANK LAMPARD

Frank Lampard is of the view that the trademark skinhead was another way of Julian establishing his own individuality. "The haircuts stand out and make him recognisable. I think he likes to have an audience," he says. Nobody at West Ham, however, has suggested to Dicks that he change the style. "Julian is his own man and does his own thing," says Tony Cottee. "That's one thing you can't change about him. You can't pull him into the office and tell him not to have his hair cut or wear a goatee beard. He's the type of lad to whom you've just got to say, 'Dicksy, go out and play.' And all credit to Harry Redknapp, he's done that and let him get on with it. He's pulled him in a couple of times when he's needed to, but in the main he's let him get on with it and he's reaped the rewards. If you tried to change him you wouldn't get the same Dicksy."

West Ham's management team of Redknapp and Lampard have indeed been aware of this point and it's reflected in their handling of the player. "You have to talk to Dicksy, but you only go so far because he's the sort of lad who's got his own way of doing things and own ideas," confirms Lampard. "And I think you have to deal with people like Julian – and others at the club – by sowing little seeds in their mind. You don't bang the drum too much at them because if you do they start banging the drum back. Everyone is different and with Dicksy I always think you get a better response by being level-headed and decent about things rather than getting into a slanging match."

While Frank and Harry were happy to let Julian continue being billiard ball-headed, the irony is that it was Kay – who was doing the shearing – who felt it could invite problems. "He didn't do himself any favours with his hairstyles," she says. "I know that shouldn't come into it – if you want your hair green, purple or whatever, it should have nothing to do with the job you do – but unfortunately it does."

It hasn't just been Julian's hairstyle which – rightly or wrongly – has inevitably influenced people's perceptions of him. There's also the Terminator nickname and his four tattoos. It's generally accepted that he was tagged Terminator by the West Ham fanzines after his "I'll be back!" declarations following his knee injury in 1990 and it was something Dicks indeed appreciated. "I like things like that, they give me

The 'Peter' tattoo... and just look at all that hair!

a buzz, even though I've never actually thought of myself as The Terminator," he says, while acknowledging that perhaps it perpetuates the negative view that some have of him. "It probably does, but so does my hair, my dogs and various other things about me, so a name is not going to make much difference." He's also enjoyed the many caricatures that have appeared of him over the years. "I think some of those things are really funny. There's been quite a few in all but it's just a bit of fun. Some people might take offence but I always just laugh at them," he says.

Julian's four tattoos include a cross featuring the name Peter (in honour of his deceased father-in-law) on his left arm, an image of the devil on the other arm, a cartoon character known as Taz on his left calf and a reproduction of the cover of 'Slash's Snakepit' (the first solo CD from the Guns N' Roses guitarist) on the inside of his right thigh. "I had that one done in Australia. It cost £75 for that and took about four hours. That hurt, that one!" he says. "But I do like tattoos. I'd have loads of them if I could. I had the cross on my arm done first and liked it so much I had a few more."

For some, it all makes for an intimidating character. Add in the aggressive style of Dicksy's play on the pitch and it's inevitable that many people have a misconception of what he is really like as a character. It's a fact confirmed by Martin Allen, who's been running soccer schools since 1990 and been delighted to involve Julian with the coaching of young kids. "Of all the professional players who help out, the most outstanding is Julian Dicks," says Martin. "People see him on the TV with his skinhead, tattoos, aggressive attitude and perhaps boisterous behaviour on the field and when I tell them that Julian Dicks works at my soccer schools it's like, 'Crikey, you have *him* there working with *children*?' As if you couldn't trust him or expect him to turn up. But if the truth be known, he is the first to arrive each day, at 9.15am, he's straight out onto the pitch and he plays with the children right through until 3.30pm in the afternoon. The last person to come off the field is Julian Dicks covered in sweat."

So keen was Julian to be involved, that he even continued coaching during his year out with injury. "Part of his rehab that year was to come and work at the soccer school in Basildon," reveals Allen. "He was out there all day every day, even with his brace on, playing with everybody. The staff and the parents of the children couldn't believe how dedicated he was.

"Julian loves kids. He turns up and he has them piling up on top of him. He tells the children to eff off and calls them little s-h-i-t-s and all that sort of stuff, but the parents watch from the sides and they love it. I always tell him to watch his language, but he's unique and you've just got to let him get on with it and do it his own way."

During their five-year relationship at West Ham (which ended when Martin joined Portsmouth in the autumn of 1995), Allen was able to gain an understanding of Dicksy's psyche, being able to relate to feeling misunderstood and having his own concerns about the way he was perceived by others once he was labelled Mad Dog. "It used to worry me that people used to think of

> **"When I tell people that Julian Dicks works at my soccer schools it's like, 'Crikey, you have him there working with children?'"** – MARTIN ALLEN

me as Mad Dog, when I was running my own company, doing lots of charity work, running my schools and had two well brought up children. I used to have a bit of a hang-up about that," admits Martin. "I thought people might see me as just a thug with no brain who used to go round shouting at referees and arguing at people, rather than a deep thinking and sensitive person, who can be aggressive and shout at people. There's something else there. It's my hope that one day I'll go into management and I don't want people thinking: 'How can he manage a football club when he's some kind of lunatic?'

"At times I did play along with it and enjoyed it. There was often the chance for me to have a laugh with the supporters, especially over by the Chicken Run, and we used to have some good times. But the name stuck."

But as for Julian being misunderstood, Carol Dicks has the opinion that his looks are a definite factor. "I've told him that his hairstyle doesn't help his image but he says it's nothing to do with anybody else. 'I'll do my hair the way I want,' is what he always says," she admits. "I do get annoyed. He is misunderstood and it's all to do with his 90 minutes football on the pitch. We took our friend Steve's wife, Carol, to Upton Park for her first football match not long ago and we introduced her to Julian in the players' bar. She couldn't believe it was the same bloke who was on the pitch. She said she could understand why people thought he was a nutcase, because of the hard way he plays and his determination to win, but off the pitch she thought he was entirely different."

Don Hutchison, who was sold to First Division Sheffield United for approximately £1.2m in January 1995 but has kept in touch with Julian on a regular basis by phone, has also surprised curious acquaintances with his explanation of his mate's character. "The kit man at Sheffield asked me recently what Dicksy was like and I shocked him when I said he's the quietest man you'll ever meet in your life," he says. "You see him at home with his family and dogs and he's so quiet. But get him on the football pitch and he's a totally different character. People don't see the talent he's got – that's the thing. It's a shame he wasn't picked by England for the European Championships."

But given Julian's playing image, people will probably always have the wrong impression of him as a person, something appreciated by his team-mates. "He's misunderstood by a lot of the public because of the way he plays," confirms John Moncur. "But those who know him closely know exactly where they stand with him

and what he's like. The press will try and say certain things that go along with his style of play to keep the bad boy image going. But he's as good as gold really."

Julian was caricatured as a member of pop band East 17 by '90 Minutes' magazine in their 1995 calendar.

CHAPTER 27

WILL THE REAL JULIAN DICKS STAND UP?

S O, who is the REAL Julian Dicks? Is he as loud and brash as his on-field persona suggests? Or is he, as Don Hutchison proposes, a quiet man who only comes to life when putting his boots on? Or is it a question with no simple answer?

Certainly, for anybody who's met Julian's parents, the temptation is to say that, for starters, his character would seem to draw heavily from that of his father. "I think he takes after me more than his mum Carol," verifies Ron. "He's got the same temperament as me. Julian was always very quiet and so am I. He is also very shy. When he's out with people he doesn't know he doesn't say too much. He's got to really get to know people first. Of course, when he's with his mates he's one of the lads."

There are those, however, who view Julian's reserved nature as being less of a shyness and more of a wariness. "I'd say he was wary of people he doesn't know and it takes him a while to get to know people and decide whether he can trust them," says Ron's wife Jane. "Ron's the same and so is Grantley – there are a lot of people who dislike Grantley, but that's because they don't know him. Sometimes he can come across as being rude, because he's not open and gushing with people."

Julian himself is undecided as to which of his parents he might take after most. "It's hard to say because my dad was all for football, the same as me. He always taught me to look after myself on the pitch," he says. "But my mum was much more of a softy with us – as I am with my kids – and I spent more time with her when I was younger and was closer to her. So I probably take after both my parents in different ways. But people looking in from the outside would be able to see more in that respect than I probably can."

As well as the influence of his parents, it could also be reasoned that Julian's experience of leaving home at the age of 14 and growing up in an older environment – at Birmingham City Football Club – has significantly helped shape his character. "I think apprentice professionals and young boys in that situation grow up very quickly but in lots of ways they miss out," says former boss Ron Saunders. "Julian coped very well. He was always a little bit shy, but then a lot of the boys were. A lot of these lads develop certain parts of their mind so that they become quite strong characters, although most of them also become slightly introverted."

Ron may be speaking generally there but some would say he's come up with a stunningly accurate description of the kind of character that Julian has become, without necessarily intending to do so. While Dicksy's aggressiveness on the pitch has led to misunderstandings about him as a player and a person, his introverted nature has also (as Jane says) given others the wrong impression. And as already suggested, it indicates that Julian is not the easiest of people to establish a rapport with.

"He's not an easy person to get to know," confirms ex-team-mate Martin Allen. "He's not a very confident person in his speech but once you get underneath and round the back of him, he's very confident and cocksure. He finds it very difficult to stand and have a conversation with outsiders, but put him in front of 30,000 on a football pitch and he thrives."

> "You know if you're his friend — and you probably know if you're not!" – JOHN MONCUR

John Moncur shares Allen's view but states: "You know if you're his friend – and you probably know if you're not! I see myself as a good friend of his. Certain things he does make me laugh and certain things I do make him laugh. We can give each other stick and we know full well that nothing is meant – on or off the field. It's that sort of relationship. But having known him for over two years now he's the sort of person I would definitely trust. When you can trust someone, that's when you know that you can call them your friend.

"He can be a little bit brash at times. But deep down I don't think he's a nasty person at all. He's always been good with his family and he thinks a lot of them. He's obviously got a lot of spirit but that's what makes his character. And he's a good character."

As far as Tony Cottee is concerned, it's the fact that Dicksy is so "different" that makes him so intriguing. "We're very dissimilar characters but that doesn't have to stop you getting on well with people. I can honestly say that I've got on great with Dicksy since he came back to the club. We've never had a problem and we can talk to each other. He's completely different to any other player I've ever met. I've come across a few eccentric characters – like Neville Southall, for instance – in my time but Dicksy's a little bit different to all of them. I get the impression that he's the way he is at football – noisy and doing his own thing – but when he goes home he's a different man, a family man. But when he's with the lads and playing football, he's got another side of his personality that comes out."

If any player should understand Julian it's Ian Bishop, who's been his room-partner on Hammers trips in latter times and who still refers to him as 'Norm' – a nickname suggested by Phil Parkes and Tony Gale, who thought that Dicksy resembled the character from TV comedy *Cheers* while sitting in a hotel bar during a pre-season trip to Scandinavia some years ago. "I suppose we're both good natured people," says the Bish. "People won't believe that of Norm – those who don't know him that well and just see the aggressive side of him on the football pitch – but he's one of the nicest people you could ever get to know. He'll do anything for you."

Bish got to know Julian upon joining the Hammers in December 1989, the pair becoming friends after a night out. "There was myself, Julian, David Kelly and Allen McKnight, and I think we went to Hollywoods in Romford, which was one of Dicksy's haunts at the time. We hit it off straight away and that's when we first became mates.

"I think he's matured – as a player and a person. He's got two lovely little girls, his wife Kay is a lovely girl as well, and when he's away from football you wouldn't really recognise him. I'd even go as far as saying he's quite soft. He looks after the people he cares for – his family and his friends. On the football side he looks after his team-mates as well when he's out there on the pitch. He's even curbed his temper on the field too. And Harry's made him captain again which shows he's more responsible and that people have got respect for him."

Even closer than Bish to our character under scrutiny is agent Rachel Anderson, who's been looking after his affairs since 1992. Rachel – previously involved in marketing and merchandising, as well as being an aide for former FIFA president Sir Stanley Rous – first became involved with Julian during a period in which he was experiencing "a few problems" and, knowing Kay through an aerobics course they were both on, she offered to help. "Perhaps the person advising him at the time didn't necessarily have his best interests at heart and I suggested a couple of ways of dealing with things that seemed to work. That's when he said that perhaps I might do a better job of looking after him than the so-called experts."

Many might think it's not an easy life looking after 'The Terminator' but Rachel insists it's "a piece of cake – he's a pussycat really", before elaborating on the kind of person Julian really is. "He's quite stubborn but very kind, which can lead to problems," she admits. "Sometimes he says yes to everybody and everything because he doesn't want to upset anyone and unfortunately he can be put upon. He's also quite shy, but once he gets to know somebody he's a friend for life. I could guarantee that a friend of his could phone at three in the morning and he would be there to help. By the same token, if somebody did him wrong, they'd no longer exist. It's as simple as that."

Like all people, though, Julian's character has evolved and he admits now that he's changed substantially as a person since his early years in the game. "I think, as you get older, you look at things in different ways," he concedes. "When I was 19 or 20 I was like a bull in a china shop. I'd just go out and have a row with anybody. But now I have a laugh at things. As long as I do well for West Ham and I'm getting paid well, that's all that matters really. I've got my family, which is the most important thing. As long as I've got money to look after them I'm happy."

DADDY DICKS

THE responsibilities of marriage and being a father of twin daughters has undoubtedly brought about a change in Julian's character – as it would in most people, to be fair. His parents could see a more "responsible" side of their son emerge, while nowadays they see a very definite maturity. "I think he's more content now," says his mum. "He's happier now than he has been for a long time. Maybe it's because, after he leaves football on a Saturday, he's got his family and his dogs to take his mind off things."

As a father, Julian describes himself as "soft-centred", admitting that he's easily manipulated by his girls. "Kattie and Jessica wrap me around their little fingers. Kay says that and I deny it, but they do," he confesses. "They'll go to see Kay and say, 'Can we go down to the shops for some sweets?' and she'll say no. Then they'll come and find me and I'll take them down to the shops. I'm like that with anybody's kids. My sister-in-law's son wanted some golf shoes. He was only seven and she wouldn't buy him any because he was growing so quickly. So I took him down the golf shop and bought him a pair. That's what kids are there for really – to spoil!"

Julian's affection for children has not gone unnoticed by those around him. "Nobody would believe what he does for kids," says Carol Dicks. "People don't know how he takes presents to hospitals at Christmas. He was at Great Ormond Street hospital recently to see a little boy. And we were at his house once when his doorbell went and it was kids asking for autographs. He came back in, got a photo off his wall and said, 'Who do you want it signed to?' I've never seen him refuse a kid an autograph and he'll get very annoyed if anybody else does."

(Whether it's kids who have been stealing the family's rubbish out of the bins in his drive remains to be seen, but there have been several occasions where mysterious 'beings' have pinched the refuse. One can only speculate as to what they've been hoping to find, but with Julian keeping so many dogs, you can work out what they've mostly been shoving their hands into!)

According to those close to the couple, they've changed in the respect that while Julian was always more cavalier in his approach to spending money, with Kay being rather more cautious with the purse strings (keeping one eye on tomorrow), it's now the latter who is more relaxed about splashing out on the kids and the home. While one member of his family puts forward the idea that "Julian has matured in the respect that he now thinks about the future more", he insists: "I'm just the same – I live for today. But Kay's turned around. Years ago, if we decided we needed a new carpet for the living room, I would say, 'Let's go out and get it,' and she'd say, 'Let's save up and leave it for another year.' If I wanted a new set of golf clubs I'd just go out and buy them, but she wasn't like that. But now, if she wants something, she just goes out and gets it. She's just ordered a

The Dicks family... Kay, Julian, Jessica and Kattie.

new car, but she wouldn't have done that a few years ago. I don't know what's brought about the change. Maybe it's living with me!"

The key, possibly, would seem to be in the Dickses' improved financial position. Whereas money was tight when they first met (with Julian earning just £20 a week), they can at last now enjoy the comforts of an affluent lifestyle. "If you've got the money then you may as well spoil yourself," says Julian. "You might get hit by a bus tomorrow and you can't take the cash with you. But if you have kids you have to have money to look after them. Touch wood, I've always had money and been able to say, 'You can have this, you can have that...' But at the end of the day, if anything happens to me then the family are cared for anyway – that's the main thing."

> "Kattie and Jessica wrap me around their little fingers"

BEHIND CLOSED DOORS

AS Tony Cottee has already indicated, a different side of Dicksy emerges when he's in football mode or among the lads. In the dressing room, the signs are that Julian has no fears about making himself heard. "He is loud, there's no doubt about that," says Cottee. "He makes people laugh, has a good swear up when he wants to and is a character – and you need characters around you in the dressing room. He's very good for team-spirit in my opinion."

> **"He's always got something to say, although sometimes I think he shouts for the sake of it"** – FRANK LAMPARD

Danny Williamson agrees with TC's verdict. "He's loud!" he echoes. "Julian's the first to jump on somebody if there's a bit of stick going round. He'll join in and rib somebody but it's all good natured."

Dicksy's more vocal nature is confirmed by the Hammers' assistant manager. "He's always got something to say," says Frank Lampard, "although sometimes I think he shouts for the sake of it. People say he's aggressive but he's not really off the pitch. He just likes to hear his own voice now and again."

While Julian can supply plenty of volume in the dressing room when he wants to, he rarely tends to open up too much on the effects of victory or defeat after a game. "He's loud and shouts and swears, but he keeps his thoughts to himself," says John Moncur. "He doesn't show his feelings as much as other players do, particularly after defeat," confirms Danny Williamson. "He's either got a way of dealing with it or hiding it. Maybe he just accepts it and knows there's another game around the corner. I can't say I've seen him taking defeat too badly."

This is a far cry from the character who stormed into the England U-21 dressing room and smashed a ball against a bucket of water in anger back in 1988. Like Tony Cottee, on the face of it, it would seem that, with the help of time, Julian has come to terms with accepting defeat philosophically – as any professional player ultimately needs to. "He can be the same in defeat as in winning, very down the middle, and that's the best way to be," says TC. "I've learnt that myself over the years. I don't think you get anything through being totally high through winning or totally low through losing, and I think Dicksy is the same. He just gets on with it."

And wife Kay confirms that, with the exception of the 1992-93 season, she's rarely had to suffer too many sulks after a Hammers defeat. "He's very good actually in that respect," she says. "He might get annoyed and frustrated but he wouldn't come home in a mood now because they've been beaten. He'd often say that there was no way the team should have lost and he does get frustrated if he thinks everybody hasn't given everything. I think that gets to him more than if they lose."

This is not to suggest, however, that Julian has suddenly become a good loser – just that he tends to keep his feelings to himself and doesn't take defeat out on other people. "He hates to lose," says Kay, "and even though he's fine, he's certainly got a different smile on his face when they win, especially if he's picked up the man-of-the-match award. He loves to win and that's all he wants to do, whatever he's doing."

Indeed, never suggest to Julian that he is a 'good loser'. "If people lose and accept it I think there's something wrong with them," he states defiantly. "I can't understand people who say that they're good losers – what's the point in playing then?"

TIME TO LAUGH

DESPITE Julian's intensity at times, he's always there if a laugh is to be had – particularly on the team coach. Invariably, the choice of music being played (if not his own) would inspire him into action. "Martin Allen used to bring stupid tapes onto the coach so I'd snap them up and throw them out of the window. We ripped two or three of his tapes up and he didn't bring any more so I think he got the message. He'd buy some stuff like 'Dance Mix' or something, which used to drive me mental. But it was all done for a laugh," he says.

Indeed, it would seem that 'Mad Dog' was often the target for pranks while travelling to away games. "Martin was reading his book one day and he was on the last four or five pages so, when he wasn't looking, I ripped the last two pages out. He took his book and got off, but he never did say anything!

"I remember an occasion when John Moncur was sharing a room with Martin Allen," continues Dicksy. "Moncs went down to the petrol station to get some chocolate and there was nothing in there apart from dog food. So he bought it and, while Martin was eating downstairs, Moncs poured all this dog food in his bed! If you pour water on dog food it kind of expands so I chucked a bottle of water over it and this stuff went all over the place. Martin got the hump about that!"

I'LL DO IT MY WAY

F Julian has a trademark as he prepares himself to play football, it's doing things unconventionally. It all comes down – intentionally or otherwise – to Julian being his own man and doing things his own way. "The best example I can give you of Dicksy being different is his lack of stretching before training or playing," says Tony Cottee, as bemused as anybody else by it. "Every player has to stretch their muscles and do a warm-up, but Dicksy goes out, sits on the ground or stands around talking, does no exercises and yet he can still smash a ball further than anybody else after they've done their warm-up."

The sight of Dicksy bounding straight into action, without the obligatory stretches, has always left other players scratching their heads – Martin Allen included. "Many times we'd be running round Chadwell Heath when we'd stop in one of the corners and the coach would suggest some stretches to do," the Mad Dog recalls. "Julian would just lay on the floor with his hands behind his head and look at the sky with not a care in the world. But he'd be striking balls without a problem and join straight in without pulling a muscle or getting injured. I used to ask John Green how he could do it and he just said that he was remarkably strong and unbelievably supple."

The physio offers the following explanation of how Julian can defy the accepted laws of physical preparation: "It's difficult to explain but some people, bio-mechanically, must be almost perfect human beings for what they do. Every now and again, sport throws someone up like that. Athlete David Bedford also apparently never warmed up. Billy Bonds never did a warm-up and look how many games he played. And if you look at the leg contours of Julian and Bill, they're very similar – they've both got bandy legs!

"There seems to be an argument that some people have developed in a way where their bone and muscle length is just about right for what they do. So they're not as vulnerable to injury as they might have been if they were different. If someone like Tim Breacker tried to play for three days without stretching, he'd be a physical wreck. He's one of the fittest players we've got, but he needs to stretch every single day, before and after training. Yet Julian doesn't.

"Julian has acclimatised to the way he is and has a consistency to his training which he hardly ever breaks. If Harry says he can have two days off, you can guarantee that on the second day he will train regardless."

However, Green acknowledges how Julian has started to show a more educated approach to his training in recent times, particularly since his injury. "Julian is getting a little bit more sensible now," he says. "When the weather was bad last season we had a bit of a problem because we played a game and trained for three consecutive days on the hard astroturf of the indoor pitch which caused his knee to start swelling up. I told him I thought he should have a day's rest and he turned round and said, 'Yeah, I think I should as well.' I've never heard him say that before.

But he's obviously more aware of what's going on with his knee now. He knows when to take a day off and he knows when to train a bit harder."

Julian's attitude towards training has often been maligned as a result of his legendary dislike of running and the number of arguments encountered with various bosses, but, as Martin Allen confirms, he's actually a good trainer. "People sometimes think he's lazy and can't be bothered but, to the contrary, he's one of the best trainers I've ever come across," he says. "Despite the running, when it came to five-a-sides, crossing and shooting, and his rehabilitation with John Green after his injury, he was spot on."

In the tradition of Bobby Moore and Frank Lampard, among others, Julian has always worn plenty of heavy clothing while training in order to increase the level of sweat. But it's the goalkeepers facing him in training who've often had to do the sweating – Les Sealey among them. "People don't even see Julian in training," remarks Ian Bishop. "He just goes out and starts banging balls into the top corner. Les Sealey was here for a year and a half and I think Dicksy shattered his confidence. He'd be firing shots past him from outside the penalty box while the rest of us were having a cup of tea and putting our feet up in the changing rooms, waiting until the last minute before going out. Les would be shouting his mouth off all annoyed and we'd realise Dicksy had been planting balls past him all over the place. He's got the best left foot I've ever seen."

But if Julian's preparation for training has been unique, so has his pre-match routine which involved drinking two cans of coke. As already detailed, it was a habit questioned by a number of perturbed managers, including Lou Macari and Roy Evans. Yet, according to John Green, there was nothing necessarily bad about the practice. "If Julian's digestive system can cope with that amount of fizzy drink then that's not a bad thing," he says, "because coke contains quite a bit of sugar and he's going to get energy from that. For most people it would be diabolical because they wouldn't be able to run around, but Julian is obviously used to it. He never has a problem with his fitness level towards the end of the game."

It's a routine that's worked for Julian and is also indicative of his approach to playing football – ie. if something doesn't interfere with a player producing the goods, then people shouldn't dictate about lifestyle. And that includes drinking during the nights before games. "I know players shouldn't do it but if they perform on a Saturday I can't see anything wrong with it," Dicks says. "If people are in a routine and want to do something they should be allowed to do it, as long as it doesn't affect their game. It's like George Best said – he used to go out on a Friday evening, get home at four in the morning, get up at mid-day and go out and play a blinder. If somebody gets hammered the night before and then plays a crap game, then they should get fined. But if they want to do that and they play well, then that should be fair enough."

ONE FOR THE LADIES?

THERE have been numerous references to Rachel Anderson throughout this book – including earlier in this chapter – and Julian's involvement with her immediately sets him apart from all other players (apart from, more recently, Don Hutchison and Keith Rowland) because she is the world's only licensed female agent.

"I get a bit of stick about it," admits Dicks. "People say, 'What does she know about football?' But as far as I'm concerned she doesn't need to know anything about the game – it's about contracts and business. And she's done very well for me in terms of negotiating deals and handling the press on my behalf."

"I get a bit of stick about it" – ON HAVING A FEMALE AGENT

Which leads us to the debate about women in football. Julian may be happy with a female agent, but he's less than impressed with the idea of women becoming more involved in the playing aspects of the game. "I've watched women's football on telly and you get them coming up to you after games saying they should be paid the same as men or that they should be playing against the men – and I think that's totally ridiculous. They're talking about mixed sides and that's ludicrous.

"I think football is a man's sport. Well, it's supposed to be, but I'm not so sure with the way the refs and the FA are going!"

Mention of referees takes us onto the issue of female officials – as has already started, in isolation, at the lower levels of the game. "I think it's ridiculous," says Julian. "Referees get a load of abuse from players and fans and if you get a woman who's not, say, very broadminded, then you're going to have a few problems. Refs are bad enough as it is, let alone with women coming into the business. The officials don't know enough about the game as it is – so having said that, maybe they can't get any worse!

"I can't really see it happening – but hopefully I'll not be around if it does!"

CHAPTER 28

BROTHERS IN ARMS

EVERY now and then, generally when various cup competitions are in full flow, the media turn the spotlight onto the other member of the Dicks family who also plays competitive football – Julian's brother Grantley.

On more than one occasion the press have sought out the elder of the two Dicks boys for an interview in order to present the players' contrasting achievements, such as in January 1994 when Julian returned to his home town to take on Bristol City with Liverpool in the third round of the FA Cup, while Grantley was travelling with Vauxhall Conference club Bath City to Stoke in the same competition for a rare meeting with league opposition.

Following an interview with *The Sun's* Steven Howard, when the reporter visited Grantley's home in the Bristol district of Ashton, a double-page feature emerged with the heading of *'Bruise Brother II'*, highlighting the player's 24 bookings in 66 matches and opened with heavy references to the brothers' liking of bull terriers as pets.

Ultimately, Grantley considered he'd been stitched up. But it's not something he should have been surprised about, given his profile as Julian's brother. "I get plenty of stick because of who I am around the non-league scene," says Grantley. "Wherever I go I get abuse from the crowd, especially when we play a London club. They say things like, 'Grantley Dicks is a homosexual.' They call me a w***er and say, 'You're as bad as your brother', '...as crap as your brother', '...as fat as your brother'. I get it all the time, certainly for the last four years or so, but it doesn't make any difference to me. It didn't happen so much when I was playing in the Western League, because that just involved local teams. But now we travel all over the place and, with a couple of thousand watching, people know who you are."

The footballing fortunes of the two left-backs may appear to have differed – and it's been the obvious angle for the media to exploit – but scout Ron Veal (the man who watched both boys at school level) refutes any suggestion that Grantley was the one who failed to 'make it' in the game. "Grantley *has* made it as far as he's concerned – at non-league level. He's happy and that's the main thing," he says, before offering some explanation, at least in part, as to why the brothers' careers have travelled individual paths. "Julian wanted to be the best and trained and practised and knocked the ball around from morning until night when he was a boy. Grantley wouldn't do that, he'd be out doing other things. But he wasn't a bad player."

Even though Grantley describes his young self as "a fat lump" and "not the fastest player in the world", he must have shown some potential as a kid, for Ron Dicks had high hopes for his first son. "Grantley was the one I thought was going to make the grade early on and be a pro," says Ron. "I thought he would be the more capable of the two boys. I think it was Julian's size that I doubted, because he was very small. Even when he was 14 he was only about 4ft 11 and seven-and-a-half stone.

"But he's a good player, our Grantley. I'd say the only thing between them when they were younger was their passing ability, which Julian had the edge on. But people develop at different ages – Julian developed very early on while Grantley probably developed a bit later. I was the same. I developed when I was

Grantley Dicks

around 27, because I was still playing park football up until then."

Unfortunately, despite Ron's initial hopes, Grantley's development came rather too late (being turned down for the Bristol Boys team) for him to attract interest in the way that Julian did. "I think that if you're not involved when you're 18, unless you're lucky you're not going to make the grade," he acknowledges.

After leaving school Grantley attended college on a graphic design and printing course, remaining at home with his parents until they separated and later marrying girlfriend Lianne. His career would see him work at a firm of printers as a bookbinder before going into partnership ("until I was stitched up"), while more recently he's been employed as a warehouseman. On the pitch, meanwhile, he progressed through the Bristol leagues, playing for Redwood Lodge, Clandown, Odd Down, Paulton Rovers and then – making a step up – Bath, who he joined in 1991.

But while their lives have differed, there's no denying the similarity in personalities between the two brothers. Just as Julian takes time to come out of his shell with people yet to win his trust, so does Grantley. And the more familiar the two are with people, the more comfortable they are. "I get louder when I'm with people I like and trust," says Grantley, also pointing to the pair's calm nature off the pitch. "Since I was 18 or 19 I've never lost my temper big-time outside of football. And I don't think I've seen Julian really lose his temper, not when I've been out with him. I think we're both the same like that."

Mum Carol is obviously best-placed to point to the two boys' similarities. Perhaps surprisingly, she describes both of them as "loners", although Grantley would seem to be a little more accessible. "They've both got their friends but I think you'll find that Grantley mixes more than Julian does. Having said that, Grantley seems very moody at times – and that reminds me of his father!" she says.

Other members of the family also recognise the brothers' identical characteristics. Grantley's wife Lianne has only ventured to London on a limited number of occasions but it's been enough to convince her how the two men have emerged from the same mould. "I would say that Grantley and Julian are very much alike in their ways," she says. And as far as Ron's wife Jane is concerned, you can add their father into the equation. "When you see all three of them go out onto the pitch it's like looking at the same person. They all run the same!" she states.

But there's more to it than running the same, of course. With Julian inheriting his father's aggression and competitiveness, it's inevitable that Grantley has as well. "He goes in hard," admits Carol, "but he doesn't seem quite as hard as Julian. Grantley always wants to win, but he doesn't seem to take it to heart so much as his brother. He never did as a kid. But they're still like two peas in a pod – they'll both go in to win that ball."

When time permitted, Julian would occasionally watch his brother in action. "I still watch Grantley play and I can see myself in him and some of him in me," he confirms."

The most obvious comparison made, especially by the media, has been the two players' disturbing disciplinary records, with Grantley reckoned to have amassed approximately 90 yellow cards since the age of 16. In the early days Grantley's biggest problem used to be "backchat" – as his mum puts it – but dissent has hardly figured on his crimesheet over the last five or six years, which have seen him sent off four times in all with Bath.

> "They're still like two peas in a pod – they'll both go in to win that ball" – CAROL DICKS

The 1992-93 season had him collecting 13 bookings (resulting in a four-match ban and £25 fine from the officials at Lancaster Gate), while the following campaign saw him sent off twice and incur a five-game ban – all before January! Less than 12 months later, Grantley was red-carded in Bath's FA Cup first round tie with local rivals Bristol Rovers. "It was my first game back from suspension," he admits, feeling aggrieved at having his big day ruined, especially with the family watching. "He said it wasn't a bad tackle but I was there at the game and I thought it was," says father Ron.

Inevitably, it's felt that Grantley's poor disciplinary record damaged his potential to play at a higher level, despite establishing himself with Bath (whom he describes as "the Wimbledon of the Conference" in terms of financial clout, with him picking up around £120 per week). "His career did suffer," confirms Ron. "I think a league club would have taken a chance on him if it hadn't have been for his disciplinary record – I honestly believe that. I'm not talking about a Premiership club (although he did have a trial with Forest in 1992), but perhaps a Second Division club would have given him an opportunity."

Like Julian, however, Grantley feels that his reputation results in him rarely getting the benefit of the doubt in situations. On many an occasion he's felt that his card has been marked before he's even stepped onto the pitch. "Referees know my name before they even book me," he says. "When I got sent off against Rovers the ref never even had to ask my name, so obviously he knew who I was before we'd even started. I know for a fact that referees talk about me, because I used to know a couple who did it."

Not surprisingly, Grantley doesn't have the highest opinion of the men in the middle. "The referee I had last Saturday was terrible," he declares. "I asked him if he'd ever played football and he didn't answer me. The problem now is that they're all robots, because they've got the man in the stand giving them marks. They're all thinking, 'I've got to do it right by the book.'"

Away from the game, the two brothers have maintained regular contact, speaking on the phone at least once a week and keeping an eye on each other's soccer fortunes. Ironically, they saw more of each other socially after Julian's move to Liverpool. "With Bath we used to sometimes play around Liverpool and we stayed up there a few times," says Grantley. "At the end of the 1993-94 season we went to Spain on tour and instead of going to South Africa with Liverpool Julian came away with us to Magaluf and got to know all the lads. He was quiet for the first few days, until he got to know everybody, and then he was just like one of us. All the Bath lads reckoned he was brilliant. And he must have had hundreds of kids coming up and asking for autographs and photos during that week, but he was happy to sign for everybody."

But there's no envy on Grantley's part in respect of Julian's fame and fortune. "I'm not a jealous person," he insists. "I may have perhaps been a *little* envious when he went to Birmingham at 14, because I was just a young lad, but fair play to Julian – I'm proud of him. I'd like to be up there, obviously, but I don't talk nastily about him behind his back or anything. It would have been nice to have been a pro, but to get the real benefits you've got to be at the top. There are a lot of pros in the lower divisions of the Football League who have to work as well as play."

"Basically, Grantley has got the best of both worlds," concludes Carol Dicks. "He's got his job and he's got his football which he gets paid for. And he's happy."

CHAPTER 29

BARKING UP NEW TREES

I F Julian has three loves in his life, with his family and football at the head of them, then his dogs must come next. So much so that, when he decides he's had enough of professional football, the animals will provide his next livelihood. "As soon as I finish playing I'll concentrate on boarding and the breeding of my dogs," he declares.

Julian presently has eight dogs – six bull terriers, one bulldog and a rottweiler (the guard dog). One of the bull terriers, Jack, and the bulldog – strangely named Lilly! – are housedogs, while the remaining five animals are housed on the two acres of land that make up the Dickses' back garden. And with planning permission being granted in August 1996 for Julian to have 24 kennels built on his land for boarding purposes, there's nothing to stop him proceeding with his business plans in the future.

Julian has always loved animals, of course, but his attraction towards bulldogs didn't begin until living in Billericay during his first spell with West Ham. "I'd see people walking with these big white things but didn't know what they were. But I thought, 'Now those are what I call dogs!' And I'd love to have one," he recalls.

Wife Kay was less than enamoured with the idea of Julian's new idea for family pets, however. "I didn't like bull terriers – I used to think they were ugly," she admits. "But we got our first one in 1990 and that was it – I got more interested. They're just so lovely, they're proper little characters."

The Dickses picked up their first dog by contacting their local kennel club and being put in touch with a woman in Welwyn Garden City. "She had two puppies and one wasn't very well – it was lucky to have survived," Julian remembers. "Kay felt sorry for it so that was the one we decided to have. We called her Lizzy and used to take her out and look after her, but she died at one and a half years of age."

By then Jack had been bought, with Julian and Kay becoming good friends with breeders John and Mandy Young in Wickford, from whom they've since acquired the rest of their dogs. "Since getting our first dog I've always wanted more and more," says Julian. "But I couldn't because we didn't have a big enough back garden."

"The only way Richard Littlejohn can get an audience is to be sarcastic and talk crap" – KAY DICKS

That problem was solved when the family moved to Chester. "I bought all the bricks and wood to build kennels in my back garden but things didn't last long enough up there for me to get started," Julian says. It was during their time up north, however, that the couple started regularly attending shows and warming to the idea of displaying their own dogs. "Once you've got one and learn more about the breed, I suppose you just want the perfect dog," explains Kay.

With Julian back at West Ham, and with much more land to accommodate kennels at the property in Latchingdon, the Dickses' involvement with the dog scene increased substantially. Because of Julian's footballing commitments on Saturdays, it's Kay who's attended most shows around the country (more recently with a video camera) in order to look at the competition as they plan to show their first dogs. "The point is to try and make champions of them," Kay explains. "To do that you have to win three championship shows (or tickets) and there are 37 tickets a year available to win. Once you get into it, it's addictive and you want the best."

Although Julian has a certain profile on the dog scene, it's Kay who has most appreciated the social aspect of it all. "Our social life revolves around the people we know through the dogs. People might chat to Julian about football but they're more interested in what's winning in the ring. I've met probably some of the nicest people through the bull terriers," she says. Thankfully, these friends were reasonably understanding, following TV and radio presenter Richard Littlejohn's scathing attack on Dicks and his dogs in his *Mail on Sunday* column in the spring of 1995. "We found out through some friends that he'd written about me, saying that I'm vicious and aggressive like a bull terrier," says Julian. "Littlejohn doesn't even know anything about the breed and yet he's slagging the dogs off!

"Jack's as soft as anything. I wouldn't entertain a dog if he was vicious and have never had one that's been aggressive. But you get people like that writing in the papers. And people got the hump about it and wrote in to complain."

Littlejohn's unnecessary comments also enraged Kay. "There was a caricature of Julian with a snarling bull terrier under his arm and it was suggesting they're both dangerous animals," she says. "He was just being ignorant. I think people shouldn't write things when they don't know what they're on about. It's like me having a column in *The Sun's* sports pages – I'd write a load of rubbish and that's what Mr Littlejohn did. It's like his programme – the only way he can get an audience is to be sarcastic and talk crap."

Despite nobody on the dog circuit necessarily blaming Julian, the reaction was still one of anger, as Kay quickly recognised. "I went to puppy training shortly afterwards and people weren't happy because the dogs are their living. A lot of them were also annoyed because they know Julian and are aware he's not like that.

Out for a stroll by the River Dee whilst with Liverpool.

"I don't know why it is, but people think he's different to everybody else just because he kicks a ball around. And we're not, we're just normal people who have normal interests and people don't seem to be able to leave us alone.   Princess Margaret has got bull terriers but I haven't seen a caricature of her with a snarling dog under her armpit. It just annoys me."

Julian, meanwhile, seemed more irritated about the breed being misrepresented than himself. "A dog can't defend itself," he says. "It can't stand up and say, 'You're wrong!' But people who breed them can and that's what they did.

"Some people might hold *me* responsible for it all but I couldn't really give a toss about them," he adds. "I just get on with the people that *I* know through the dogs – *they* know what I'm like and that's what matters."

It can safely be presumed that the odious Littlejohn received plenty of angry letters – enough to get up his nose anyway – because he was back to unleash another assault on Dicks at the end of May, this time in the *Daily Mail* (a paper presumably scrapping their sense of quality control in order to compete with the livelier tabloids). Quick to pounce on the *News Of The World* story (see chapter 33), alleging Julian's involvement with a 17-year-old girl while on holiday in Tenerife, and desperate to believe every word of it, Littlejohn seized the opportunity to slur the player's character even more: *'Dicks announced that he would not be available to represent his country this summer because he was planning to spend more time with his dogs. We all, mistakenly as it turned out, assumed he was referring to his bull terriers. Apparently not,'* he wrote, before reiterating the claims of the Sunday paper. *'They were later spotted at a nightclub called Busby's, which they left when Dicks went outside to be sick. You couldn't make it up, you really couldn't,' he added,* before making one final dig: *'Most of the people who go on holiday to Tenerife couldn't point to it on a map.'*

The irony of the piece was that it strongly suggested that Littlejohn believes everything he reads – and surely he, more than anyone, should know better. But what else would you expect from a Spurs supporter?

The end of May also saw Julian breeding his first dogs. "They call it rape, that's what it's called in dog terms," he explains. "The stud dog does 'the business' with the bitch and it's then 63 days until the puppies are born, give a day or so. And that's when the hard work starts."

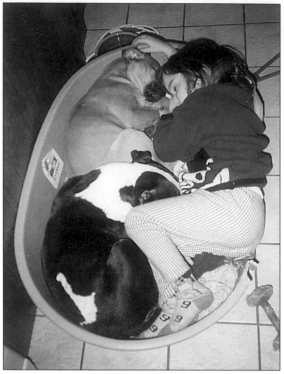

Jessica grabs 40 winks with Red and Jack.

The Dickses spent the latter part of the summer of '96 looking after the litter of four puppies, three of which went to new homes after eight weeks. Looking after all their dogs, as Julian suggests, is indeed a tiring business – "I didn't realise what hard work it was," verifies Kay, who reveals that Julian gets up at 7am to feed and clean them – but the hope is that a puppy will be good enough to show and ultimately prove itself a champion. "You just keep your fingers crossed that it's going to be good enough to go into the show ring," she adds.

Julian and Kay's first dogs to be shown in early 1997 are a stud named Loco and a bitch named Holly. "It would be nice to go to a show and see your dog come first," says Julian. "You can win best of breed, best opposite sex, best colour or whatever. Once your dog becomes a champion the stud fees come in and people want your puppies. It's all about money. You're looking at £450 for a puppy and £150-200 to mate your dog with my stud dog.

"Just think: £200 for a quick bonk!"

CHAPTER 30

ONCE A ROCKER...

PASS through the front door of Julian and Kay's home and there's a fairly good chance that you'll hear the unmistakeable hard rock sounds of Guns N' Roses, Iron Maiden or Metallica blaring out at a fairly painful volume. "I think it's absolutely awful – he drives me mad," complains Kay, whose preferred music is that of the rather more restrained Mariah Carey and other chart acts. "Julian comes in from work and my music goes off and his goes on – twice as loud!

"He'll stick the golf on the telly, have his music blaring out from the house and then he'll go up to the kennels. And if you turn it off he goes mad. We'll have a barbecue with lots of people round and he'll have his music blasting across the garden. Nobody likes it. It's all just noise and swearing, although I don't mind Guns N' Roses so much – I suppose I've got used to them over the years!"

Julian's love of hard rock music is just one thing that sets him apart from the majority of footballers. "He's an 'eavy bastard!" quips Frank Lampard, who, along with the rest of the Hammers camp, has had to endure Dicksy's taste in music on numerous coach trips around the country. "I think he likes to think that he's a bit different by liking it – it makes him stand out."

And it's something the other players have come to accept – if not enjoy. "I hate his music!" blasts John Moncur. "But it's all part of his image – Satan, no fear, all that. It's all part of Julian being his own man."

Julian's response is that it's only fair that he gets a chance to listen to his favourite music on the coach, with the rest of the squad enjoying their Luther Vandross and the like. "Most of the players are into soft soul or love music," he complains. "I'll listen to one of their CDs but when I shove one of mine on all hell breaks loose. They want me to turn it off but because they've had one on I'll have one on. Slaven Bilic likes my music and so did Dani, but apart from that no-one else does."

Dicksy's interest in music, particularly the hard rocking kind, had always been minimal as a kid, but the sudden emergence of LA rockers Guns N' Roses in 1987 made a big impression on him and captured his imagination for good. "My brother was the one with the record player when I was younger and I was never that interested," admits the man whose tackles are heavier than a stack of Megadeth albums. "But as soon as I discovered Guns N' Roses that was it really. I'll listen to all heavy music, including stuff like Metallica, but Guns N' Roses are my favourites. If I stay in on my own I'll shove four or five of their CDs in and listen to them all night. I went to Germany to see them in concert with my agent's husband, John, about three years ago. And I also saw them at the Milton Keynes Bowl a while back."

Julian displays the gold disc which marked 100,000 sales of Iron Maiden's 'Seventh Son of a Seventh Son' album.

Despite admitting that he gets a little self-conscious when being recognised at such events – "I like to let myself go but it's difficult when you get people watching you. They're probably thinking, 'Look at that idiot!'" – Julian would love to experience the thrills of being in the (cowboy) boots of the likes of singer W. Axl Rose or guitarist Slash from G N'R. "I'd love to lead the lifestyle of Guns N' Roses," he says. "It must be great to perform in front of 80,000 people. Obviously there are things you can't do, like go shopping or whatever because you'd get mobbed all the time, but there's a downside to everything."

Unlike a lot of footballing celebrities, Julian is not the type to insist on backstage passes or VIP treatment. "I won't do that unless they're offered to me. I'm not the kind of bloke to say, 'I'm Julian Dicks, can I have some tickets please?' But for the likes of Def Leppard and Iron Maiden, we get offered passes anyway because I know people in the bands."

London metal giants Iron Maiden's unstinting allegiance to the Hammers has been well documented over the years, although founding member and bassist Steve Harris is now the only real fan remaining in their ranks (with relatively new guitarist Janick Gers, for example, supporting his native Hartlepool!). Early Maiden albums would have 'Up The Irons!' messages on their sleeves, while a claret and blue scarf would never be far away from the PA on stage. "I like their music and they first came down to the training ground one day during my first spell at Upton Park," reveals Julian. "They knew I was interested so they brought down some CDs and T-shirts, and they've sent me some stuff as well."

Such is their relationship that Julian was invited to Maiden's special 'Raising Hell' performance at Pinewood Studios in 1993 – the last to feature long-time vocalist Bruce Dickinson. "The gig was for their fan club and friends and only 1,000 people were allowed in. A colleague of Steve Harris had a video camera and I did an interview for them. We also had a drink afterwards and it was a good day."

Since that occasion Harris has met Julian a number of times, mostly after games at Upton Park (which he attends as often as Maiden's touring, recording and promotional schedules allow). "He seems a really nice guy – very quiet and unassuming – which surprised me a bit because of the image he projects on the pitch," says Steve. "But, then again, I get that as well. Because I'm aggressive on stage people think I'm going to be the same when they meet me. So I can relate to Julian in that respect.

"When I first met him I was feeling a little bit unworthy. And it was the same when Bish (who Steve got to first know through playing tennis) introduced me to Slaven Bilic. (Indeed the feeling was mutual, with Bilic trekking as a young kid into Italy from the former Yugoslavia just to buy Maiden albums!)

But it's Julian's commitment to the Hammers cause that has always endeared the bassist to him. "The thing is, he's always shown that he really loves to play for West Ham," says Steve, who attended trials at Chadwell Heath himself at the age of 14. "Julian gives 100 per cent for the club and is an excellent player. Not only is he tough but he's a good passer of the ball. I was gutted when he left for Liverpool, so I was really pleased to see him return.

"As far as I'm concerned he should be in the England team. Maybe his visual image hasn't helped him to be selected, but you can't really spend time worrying about that – it's his performance that matters. That's what he should be judged on."

> "I hate his music. But it's all part of his image – Satan, no fear, all that" – JOHN MONCUR

Despite Steve's support of Julian, he's not seen fit to try and clone the player's shorn hairstyle, preferring to retain the same straggly locks that have warmed his shoulders for over 20 years (the band released their 'Best Of The Beast' compilation to mark their double-decade mark in autumn 1996). And as for the likelihood of Dicksy trying to grow his hair Harris-style, don't put any money on it!

FIDDLING ABOUT

WHAT Julian has done, however, is pick up an electric guitar for himself. He bought it during his first period at West Ham, although he won't pretend he's mastered it at all. "I can play a few notes, although I've had no lessons or anything. I just turn it up as loud as possible, fiddle about and do my best to annoy people.

"I also get on the piano every now and again. I'm still trying to learn 'November Rain' by Guns N' Roses but I can't get anybody to teach me just that one song. They want me to learn about reading music and I'm not into that."

ON YOUR BIKE

L ISTEN to Carol Dicks talk about her passion for motorbikes and it's tempting to assume that this is where Julian's interest has come from. "I love motorbikes," says his mum. "Going back years when I was single, I was always out on motorbikes – Triumphs, BMWs, BSAs..." Indeed it was a BSA 250 that Julian and Grantley first enjoyed riding about on when they were still living at home in Bristol, as Carol recounts: "At the back of our house in Kenmare Road there was a field which they used to go over to with their dad. It wasn't ideal because it was up and down and full of brambles, but it was well away from the road so there were no police or anything. They used to ride that bike around there, although Julian would only have been about 12. Of course, I got on the thing, took it down the field a little bit and then fell off into a blackberry bush. Did they laugh? They picked the bike up and left me in the brambles!"

The first bike Julian actually owned was a KMX 125 scrambler, when he was about 20 after joining West Ham, and he followed up with the likes of a Varago and a Honda. But the bike of his dreams, however, was a Harley Davidson. "My mate bought a Harley and I thought it was lovely," he remembers. "'I'll get one of them,' I thought to myself. I'd bought my Honda on the Saturday and my mate got his Harley on the Monday. The following Saturday I went down to the Harley shop in Leigh-On-Sea and bought myself one for £9,600."

Julian's choice was a 1300cc Harley Davidson Fatboy. "It was a beautiful bike, it really was," he insists. "But I couldn't get it insured because of my legs. Companies were quoting me like £15,000, which was more than the bike was worth! So I thought, 'Sod it, I'll ride it anyway.' And if I got caught I'd take the consequences.

"I used to ride it to work on a nice day, and wear all the leathers, but I had no insurance or anything. I must have had it for four or five months and done about 500 miles on it. The lads loved it. I gave Bish a lift up the road on it one day. I remember riding it to work once and getting on it and zooming off after training. Billy Bonds came out and asked Charlie, the security man, 'Who's that?' Charlie said, 'It's Julian,' and Billy said, 'What the f***in' 'ell's he doing on one of *them?!*'

"The club didn't even know I had the bike. I told all the lads and made a big noise every time I rode off, but the management never asked about it so I never told them. They only got to know about it when pictures of me on it started to appear in a few magazines, but I'd already sold it by that time."

With Julian having no insurance the sale of the bike was inevitable, not necessarily through fear of getting caught riding it illegally but the threat of having the Harley stolen. "We'd been out one day and when we got home the garage door was up and the alarm on the bike was going off," he says. "Luckily there was a car in front of the garage so nobody could get the bike out. But I realised I had to sell it because there was the risk of losing nearly ten grand's worth of bike. I sold it in the end for about £7,500. It's a shame because I really miss it."

A BIT OF A CLUBBER

IF Julian ever had to hang up his boots to pursue any other sporting activity, you could bet your life that his choice would be golf. He watches it on the TV, reads the magazines and plays around twice a week. As already detailed, Julian first got bitten by the bug while out injured in 1991, with it eventually becoming part of his rehabilitation course. "My brother-in-law in Birmingham first asked me to go and play golf with him and I said, 'Nah, it's a poof's game!' He told me to come and have a try, so after two or three weeks I went over to see what it was like.

> "I've smashed up loads of clubs"

"I used his clubs and I was hitting the balls around and after playing one round I thought, 'Yeah, I love this game.' So I went straight to a golf shop and bought myself a set of clubs. The next day I went and had another game and it's just gone on from there really. You get the bug and just want to do better and better."

Unfortunately, and most irritatingly for Julian, after reaching a certain standard he realised he wasn't improving at all. "When I first started playing I just used to put the ball down and smack it!" he laughs. "And I used to play well. But once you start thinking about things, such as what to do with your feet, hands and arms, that's when it all goes to pot!

"So I've had a couple of lessons, because I was playing and just getting worse and worse. I went down and saw one of the local pros, Graham Packer, and he sorted me out with my grip and style. He's so technical it's unbelievable. You've got to have the grip, the stance, the body alignment – everything. I now play about once or twice a week, off a handicap of seven. Moncs is off four, so he's a very good player."

Having played with him regularly, Moncur can attest to one thing: Julian plays to win! "It is hard because you can go out one day and play very well, then the next day you can have the biggest stinker ever known," says Julian. "I've smashed up loads of clubs. I remember we played down in Plymouth, at St Mellion, and I bought a brand new seven wood which cost me about £220. I hit one ball and missed, so I went 'smack!' on the floor. It was made of graphite and just smashed. I just slung the club into a bunker. It gets you so mad, but when you have a good game it's like the best thing on earth."

Many people play golf for relaxation purposes, but such is Julian's level of commitment and competitiveness, he rarely leaves a course feeling 'relaxed' as such. "Even if you're playing on your own, you want to do well. Even if you're playing for nothing, I still want to beat you. I can't see the point in playing anything if it's okay to lose," he states.

> "I enjoyed it and it took a lot of aggression out of me"
> — ON CLAY PIGEON SHOOTING

Such a philosophy is an integral part of Julian's character that's been well recognised by Kay. "He's just very competitive," she says. "Whatever it is – even a game of scrabble – he plays to win."

SHOOTING PRACTISE

AS if Julian doesn't do enough 'shooting' on the pitch, he's now doing even more in his leisure time – of a different variety. For he now owns three shotguns and two 2.2 Magnum rifles. His interest in the pastime started following his move to Liverpool. "Mark Wright got me into clay pigeon shooting," he reveals. "You could hear the noise of it in the distance from where I lived and I'd never done it before so we went and had lessons, down at North Wales Shooting School. Kay thought she was better than me, although I wasn't so sure! But Mark Wright and I went quite a few times. I enjoyed it and it took a lot of aggression out of me."

Nowadays Julian can regularly be found rough shooting on a friend's farm, pursuing rabbits, hares, pheasants and pigeons (singled out because of their 'pest-value' – "I only shoot vermin," he emphasises). "I have the same competitive approach to shooting – you can't let a rabbit get away, you've got to shoot it. I wouldn't say I was the best shot but I can hit a fair few. I've taken rabbits into work and the lads will take them down to the butchers and get them gutted. I won't shoot things, though, if people are not going to eat them. I won't shoot anything just to leave it or throw it away."

Of course, the availability of guns has become a major topic of debate in recent times, with the government discussing the possibility of banning certain weapons such as handguns (following the tragic Dunblane shootings). Although Julian owns no handguns, he once expressed an interest in obtaining one for target shooting but licences were only available to people who'd been members of an appropriate shooting club for six months. But he is unconvinced that such rules or any law changes would make much difference in terms of such weapons being abused. "These laws are not going to stop anybody from committing crimes," he says.

"I think I'd vote against banning handguns. It's a sport for a lot of people and they do enjoy it. And I enjoy what I do. The point is, if people want to get hold of guns, they can go and get them on the street corner anyway. If you want to part with two or three hundred quid, you can get a gun - no problem. So I don't actully think banning guns would make much of a difference. But I can understand the Dunblane families taking a different view, of course. And I can sympathise with those people."

Indeed, it's even been suggested that certain knives are banned also. Julian uses knives "for rabbitting and fishing" but asks the question: "Where do you draw the line? If you ban knives, you've got to ban lots of things. But I can understand the call to ban the carrying of knives in the street. Even a pen-knife can kill people."

HELLO, JULIAN, GOT A NEW MOTOR?

JULIAN is the first to admit that he's "got a fascination for cars", which he attributes to his dad Ron. So much so that he's had probably more vehicles than he can accurately remember, estimating around 40 to have passed through his hands over the last 10 years. "He's had cars we haven't even seen if it's been a fortnight between visits – they've been and gone," says his mother.

Carol can also remember early evidence of her son's affection for cars. "He was learning to drive and he'd say, 'I'm gonna take the car to bed.' What he'd do was get in the car, take her for a drive round the block and come back onto the drive. He'd say, 'I had to warm her up before she went to bed.'"

His first car was a green BMW 1602 – "pea green" if you believe Julian or "lime green" if you prefer the word of Carol. "Then he had a Maestro, I think, which used to talk to you about putting your seat belt on. He'd just leave the engine on so the thing was talking all the time!"

Despite his interest in cars, the large turnover has more to do with Julian getting bored of them easily. "I'd say I'm like that with most things," he admits. "I drive each vehicle around for five or six months, sell them and get another one."

When Porsche comes to shove.

Since that first BMW, Dicks has driven Sierras, Granadas, Mercs and Porsches, among others. "I've had three Porsches – the first one was a red, H-reg Carrera 4, which was a lovely car. I sold that and bought a brand new Porsche Carrera convertible, which cost £62,000. I only sold that because it was too small and I couldn't get the kids in the back. Then I picked up two Mercs, then sold one of those and bought a BMW convertible. The third Porsche was made in 1979 but it had a new body, new wheels and was immaculate, despite doing over 104,000 miles. I got rid of that to get a Daihatsu jeep for my shooting trips."

And, like most top footballers, there's the sponsored motor – a Mondeo (a far cry from his first sponsored vehicle – an FSP Polynesian, which Julian describes as "a Lada-type car"). He also drives another BMW and the aforementioned jeep, while Kay has a Mercedes estate in which she can transport the dogs. But knowing Julian, he'll probably have sold the lot by the time you read this!

I'LL BE BACK!

THEY call Dicksy 'The Terminator' – and it's entirely appropriate, for Julian loves to watch Arnie movies. "I do like to watch films when I can," he says. "I like stuff like the *Terminator* movies, the *Rocky* films, *Pulp Fiction*, *Natural Born Killers*... But I also like *Legend Of The Fall*, with Brad Pitt, which is superb. If it's a good film it doesn't matter even if it's soppy – I'd watch it."

BOOKED!

JULIAN had never shown a great interest in reading, but that was until his mum bought him some books on American Indians such as Geronimo and Sitting Bull. "We got a telling off from Kay because she doesn't see him for hours on end as he's off reading his books," she says. One of Julian's favourites is *Bury My Heart At Wounded Knee*, which tells the history of the American West from the Indian point of view. "He's never been one for reading but he's got quite a few books in his study now."

CHOP JUEY

UNKNOWN to many, Julian developed an interest in martial arts – more specifically ishinryu karate – a few years ago and could even be seen in full regalia on some promotional cards for tutor Simon Kidd.

"I posed for a few cards to help him out," explains Julian. "I just had a couple of lessons and learnt a few moves – more for protection really. But it's not something I've really pursued."

However, Kidd – a fifth-dan black belt – was quoted recently on Dicksy's interest: "He's very keen on the sport and is improving all the time. He's already moved up a couple of grades and has the ability to make a name for himself."

WHO'S A PRETTY BOY THEN?

THE remaining member of the Dicks family to get a mention here (after Kay, daughters Kattie and Jessica, the eight dogs and recent addition of puppies) is Pepsi, the macaw. Julian acquired the bird while living on his own in Chigwell after returning to West Ham, costing him the princely sum of £850.

Introducing Pepsi

"Parrots and macaws fascinate me," says Julian. "They're pretty to look at and they can speak. Pepsi can swear with the best of them! But mostly it's just 'hello', apart from when Kay is around – he doesn't like her! I think whoever had him before must have been a woman and hurt or mistreated him. He likes the kids, though."

Julian's agent Rachel recalls meeting the bird for the first time: "He looked very bald and unhappy (the bird, not Julian) when he bought it, but now he lords it in the living room. Animals react very well with Julian."

Remembering her son's affection for the adopted seagull he brought home as a kid, Carol Dicks thinks there'd have been every chance that Julian would have found himself a career working with animals had his footballing efforts not paid off. And Rachel has witnessed the player's tenderness towards living creatures. "We were going to a presentation in Cheshire, which he was going to earn quite a bit of money for," she recalls. "As we were driving along, he saw an injured bird in the road. We screeched to a halt, got out and saw it was a blackbird. So we had to do a U-turn, go back to the house and get the address of the local vet. But when we realised it was going to die we gave the bird some brandy so that it could at least die happy. But that's the sort of thing that Julian will do."

And then there's Nicholas – the horse that Julian bought during his first period at West Ham. "It was 15 and a half hands – a big old thing," he says. "It cost me three grand but I couldn't get any insurance so I had to let it go. I probably lost about a thousand pounds when I sold it, but that was nothing compared to the enjoyment I got out of it.

"I used to go up to the stables in Billericay at six o'clock every morning before going to work. It may sound silly galloping round fields but it's quite thrilling when you ride it very fast."

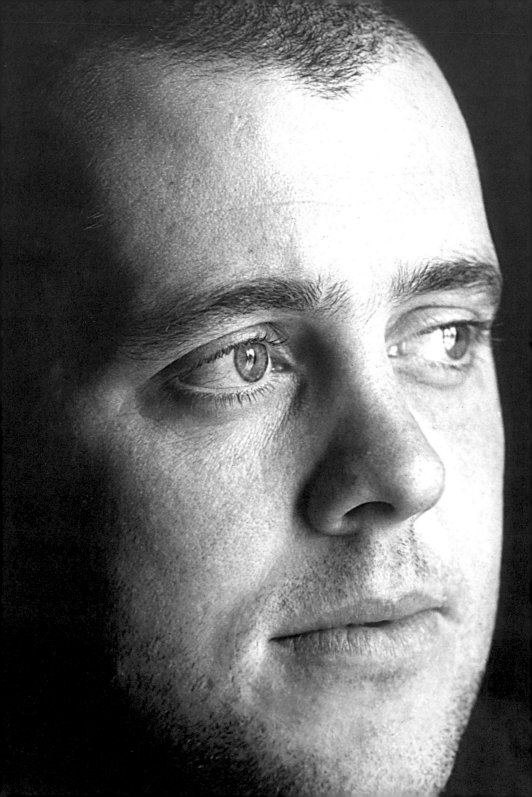

CHAPTER 31

MUM'S THE WORD

THOSE supporters who sit in the upper tier of the West Stand at Upton Park may well be familiar with a female voice that can frequently be heard airing an opinion on what's taking place on the pitch – especially if it involves Julian. For that voice belongs to Carol Dicks, arguably her son's biggest supporter – and critic.

"Everybody up there knows who I am and they all know I'll slag anybody off – and that includes Julian," says Carol, who attends every home match and many of the away ones with boyfriend Martin – a lifelong Hammers fan. And it's fair to say that, given her vocal profile, she's something of a cult figure in the West Stand. "I enjoy watching Julian but I get more nervous than he does. People ask what's wrong if I'm quiet. And I've had my fair share of arguments as well," she admits. "It was the same when I was watching Julian over at the parks when he was younger. I remember effing and blinding with one man, but it was only during the game. At the end he said, 'Sorry about the language, love, do you fancy a drink?' and it was all forgotten. And that's the way Julian is – it's all during the 90 minutes and then it's forgotten.

A visit to Carol and Martin's home is all that's required to see how much pride they they have in Julian's footballing achievements. West Ham and Dicksy paraphernalia is everywhere – videos, books, magazines, photographs, ticket stubs…you name it, they've got it on shelves, on walls, in cabinets, in cupboards or in drawers. "I don't think there's anything out that I haven't got – including all the unofficial T-shirts!" Carol beams.

"People say to me that I must be so proud of him and I *am* proud of him. I was in our works canteen once and I wrote our Ju a letter. And as I was writing it I was crying and the ink was getting smudged. I just wanted to tell him how proud I was. I do tell him to his face, but he just thinks it's mum talking for the sake of it. So I wanted to put it down on paper."

They won't have been the first tears that Carol has shed over Julian or the Hammers. "I think Upton Park has seen more crying than anything from me," she says. "When we lost the Division Two championship in 1991, when Notts County beat us and Oldham scored an extra-time penalty in their game to overtake us, I was on the terraces crying. And, of course, both times he's gone down with West Ham I've ended up in tears!"

Carol and Martin have continued to follow Julian's fortunes, wherever they have lived, even making the 500-mile round-trip from Manchester when the couple lived and worked there in the late eighties. The pair then returned south in 1989, setting up home in New Malden, Surrey, with both securing positions at the Post Office. "We were training in the first week and it was already around the office that Julian Dicks' mum was going there to work," explains Carol. "They thought I was a big black mama because his name was Julian and he'd been transferred from Birmingham! I had to say, 'Sorry to disappoint you, lads!' Some of the people at work have met Julian and they say how quiet he is, that he's nothing like me."

> "They thought I was a big black mama because his name was Julian and he'd been transferred from Birmingham!"

There's no doubt that Carol is indeed more obviously extrovert than her two sons. And, not surprisingly, given that there is also no great facial resemblance, most people are surprised when they establish her identity as Julian's mum. "They don't believe me," she reveals. "I don't know what they expect really, but they're surprised to see you working for a living. I don't think people expect me to be so friendly and they also don't expect me to be in The Boleyn pub next door to the ground either."

Carol and Martin can often be found in the popular watering hole on the corner of Green Street and Barking Road in London's E13, after having joined Julian in the players' bar after matches. "We go into The Boleyn after every home game, with our friends Keith and Jerry, and even the landlady knows who I am now," Carol says. "We were chatting to some people once and Martin said, 'This is Julian's mum.' They said, 'No, you're not.' I said that I was. And they said, 'No, you wouldn't be in here if you were Julian's mum.'

"We were in there one night and there was a little kid, who looked a bit backward. He had a photo album of the West Ham players and nobody was taking any notice of him. So I asked him who he had in there and he was showing me all the players when he said his favourite one was Julian Dicks. Suddenly, Jerry came along and said, 'Alright, Dicksy?' – that's what he calls me – and the kid looked at me and said, 'Did he call you Dicksy?' I said, 'Yes, I'm Julian's mum,' and they went mad!

"Another one of his friends came up and said, 'Can I ask you something – can I buy you a drink? Only, I want to say that I bought a drink for the person who brought God into the world.' They told me how he was their idol, how he stood for everything they wanted at West Ham and how he could never do anything wrong. They even took a picture of me. Sometimes it seems I'm more famous than he is!"

Carol and Martin's visits to the players' bar are generally the only occasions when Julian seems particularly willing to discuss the events of the game. "You get more out of him up there than you do at anytime throughout the week, because he's still got football in mind. But once he leaves Upton Park that's it," says Carol. Martin, on the other hand, will occasionally talk to Julian about his performances if they visit for the weekend or go for a drink. "Generally it's something he's cocked up on," says Martin. "A few years ago I said to him, 'I expect you to play well, so I'll just remind you of the bits when you don't.' But if anybody else turns up we just change the subject.

"He's like most people – even though you don't necessarily enjoy talking about your work, you discuss the good and bad things that have happened. You don't want to go to a pub and talk football with everybody. But people think: 'He's a footballer, he must want to talk about it.' Sometimes I'll ask about the tactics, such as why they've switched from four to five at the back and things like that."

Generally, however, Julian is reluctant to talk about 'work' too much when 'out of the office'. Off the field he invariably puts his mind towards other things, particularly with the responsibility of looking after his dogs at home and getting his kennels built. And if he is thinking about football, then his thoughts are mostly kept to himself. Except, of course, when he's asked his views on something while still in a football environment, in which case Julian can be as outspoken as anybody. It's something we've already seen, particularly when he felt strongly about the Bond Scheme at West Ham in 1992 and came down very heavily on the side of the fans, in spite of the on-pitch protests seen. "It may not have been wise but it was definitely honest of him," says Martin. "It certainly didn't endear him to the management, obviously. I haven't discussed it with Julian, but when you think about the way the club treated him when he was out injured, it was certainly a nice way of keeping the fans on his side and dropping the board in it at the same time. Looking back, it was a nice way of getting back at them and that was just by sticking up for what he believed in."

> "I said, 'If you've got something to say about my family, then come out and say it.'"

Inevitably, Carol has found herself debating issues with people at work as a result of the controversies involving Julian, not least following the stamping allegations after Chelsea's John Spencer was injured in the game at Upton Park in September 1995. One male work colleague, with a rather warped sense of humour, thought it would be funny to stand behind Carol and stamp on the floor four times, before saying, 'Oops, it's an accident!'

"I said, 'If you've got something to say about my family, then come out and say it.' I just looked at him with contempt and walked off," says Carol. "I didn't speak to him for ages and he came up to me and said, 'Have I upset you, Carol?' I said, 'Am I speaking to you?' And he said, 'No.' And I said, 'Well, you've upset me then, haven't you?' He said he hadn't meant to and I said, 'You shouldn't have done it then!'

"My language at times has been atrocious but when anything like that is concerned I get annoyed, because there's no need for any of it. Martin nearly punched somebody at work because of it and if he had have done he'd have lost his job."

Another flare-up took place when the couple went to see the Wasps rugby team in action and a Chelsea supporter (a friend of a friend) said that Julian had deliberately stamped on Spencer's head. "I said, 'He f***ing never!' They say I went white! I nearly had him. Martin said, 'I'm stepping in here. If I was you, I'd re-phrase that.' I went potty! I said, 'Before you say that, what did the FA do? They weren't convinced he did it either, so before you start on me or my son, get your facts straight!' I would have hit him."

Carol was understandably deeply upset when the guilty verdict was arrived at after the FA enquiry over the Spencer matter. "I got a call at work from Kay saying that they'd found him guilty. I said, 'You've got to be joking!' I was gutted and was in tears. I thought it was disgusting. Shortly afterwards, Asprilla got a one-match ban for an elbow and nothing for being found guilty of a head-butt!"

Needless to say, there are a few people around who won't be receiving any Christmas cards from Carol in future, including Sky soccer analyst Andy Gray ("I could kill him") and politician and radio/TV presenter David Mellor, who blasted Dicks after being sent off at Arsenal a few days after the Chelsea game.

"We were with Julian the following week and I was sitting there, plugged into the radio, and I was listening to every word that David Mellor said. And he did nothing but praise him! I said to Martin, 'This can't be David Mellor!' But he told me that he was a typical two-faced politician. I was waiting for Mellor to say one bad word and I'd have rung him up."

The next explosion of controversy took place when the

"I'll bet you a tenner you end the season with more points than Everton" – On The Terraces.

tabloids splashed stories of Julian's kids getting 'attacked' at school on their front pages. It was a time when everybody was trying to keep a low profile – even Carol. "Julian told me as we were going to the next game that I should be careful because the press would be out. And he warned me that they may be trying to get in touch with me. His agent Rachel gave me her number in case the press started hassling me. But nobody got in touch and I kept my mouth shut at football. It was a one-off but I did it!"

> "Whenever anybody mentions West Ham now, it's Hurst, Moore, Peters...and Dicks!"

Thankfully, following those times, Julian went on to have an outstanding season for the Hammers, keeping his nose clean and producing probably his best ever form. Martin has a theory about Julian's improving disciplinary record: "When he was getting sent off all the time, most of his bookings came when he'd lost possession and was trying to recover. It would be his determination to get the ball back that would get him into trouble. But he's getting cover now, especially when playing five at the back. If he does lose the ball now it's not just down to him to win it back, you've got Bilic or Rieper or Rowland or whoever. Most of the bookings in his career have come as a result of trying to retrieve a lost situation."

Julian's impressive form in the 1995-96 season had many campaigning for an England call-up, not least Carol and Martin. "We're all convinced he's the best left-back in the country and a lot of people think he should have been playing for England for years," says Martin. "Yet before Euro '96, he was third in line, behind a couple of cripples. They say that Julian's got to grow his hair, but they then picked Villa's Alan Wright – a five-foot dwarf with no hair either! I know it's a strange concept in our politically correct times, when the FA have to be seen to be doing the right thing, but wouldn't it be nice if you saw an England line up and you could say, 'Oh, they're going to go out and try to win tonight.' The bottom line is: do they want to win or don't they?"

Julian's rejection at international level in the build-up to the European Championships ultimately led to him declaring his unavailability should Terry Venables have wanted to draft him in as a last-minute replacement. The announcement provoked a range of opinion, with many people questioning the wisdom of it, but Martin could understand Julian's frustration. "It probably went on for so long that he thought, 'Yeah, I'd love to play for England, but I've probably played the best I've ever played – it'll be difficult to improve on this – and I'm seeing people getting into the international set-up who shouldn't even be playing Premiership football.' He probably thought it best to tell them to shove it and for him not to worry about it anymore.

"Julian will probably be the most famous player that never played for England. You think of the greatest moment in English football – winning the 1966 World Cup – and it's Hurst, Moore and Peters. Whenever anybody mentions West Ham now, it's Hurst, Moore, Peters...and Dicks!"

CHAPTER 32

HE'S GOT NO HAIR EITHER!

THERE have been a lot of changes at West Ham United in the years following Julian's arrival in March 1988 and just one established first-teamer survived at Upton Park until the close of the 1995-96 season – Alvin Martin (although Steve Potts was to become a regular in 1988-89, at right-back, and still remained at the club as the 1996-97 campaign got underway).

Since John Lyall brought Dicksy to the Hammers, Alvin has witnessed the ups and downs of his team-mate's career from the closest proximity and been well-placed to acknowledge the change in his character during those eight years (which ended when Martin moved to Leyton Orient in the summer of 1996). And as far as Dicksy's evolution as a player goes, the period at Liverpool would appear to have been significant.

"Looking back across Julian's two periods at West Ham, I noticed that he was more mature after he returned from Anfield," says the centre-half. "He was on a road that was going nowhere in his time at Liverpool and when he came back to West Ham I think he knew where he was going. And that has resulted in him playing the best football of his career since. Julian had to grow up – if he hadn't have done then maybe he'd have gone down the same road as Mark Dennis.

"He returned and realised it was do-or-die the second time. If it hadn't have gone well at West Ham in the second period he'd have probably ended up going lower and lower – I don't know where he'd have gone from there. But he's responded to the opportunity that West Ham gave him. It was right for him to go to Liverpool at the time and it was right for the club. But by leaving it really taught him a lesson on what a great club West Ham is. I think he's the first one to put his hand up now and acknowledge that."

It's generally thought that many players would have been happy earning good money on Merseyside, whether they were in the first team or not, but Alvin insists that that view is not necessarily compatible with the mentality of footballers: "Their lives are always geared into how things are going on the pitch," he says. "If somebody's performing well, then that joy spills over into his social and family life.

But things didn't go well for Julian and if it's not happening on the pitch, it doesn't matter how well you're getting on with your team-mates or how lovely your house is. The only thing that matters is going in every day, looking forward to training and the next game because you're playing well – that's when everything else falls into place.

"And that's the way it is now for him – he's enjoying his football. When he came back he'd grown up as a person and he wasn't doing anything rash. Julian obviously recognised a weakness in himself that people could wind him up and that he was playing into their hands. He's worked on that and he's a better player for it."

They don't come much more experienced than Alvin – aged 38 when he left West Ham, having enjoyed his second testimonial at the club – and he knows that, in football as in life, you can never say never. And that goes for Julian making misjudgements. "We're all liable to do something rash," he states. "Even now at my age, when you're involved in a football game that you want to win, you're always liable to do something you thought you were past doing. You never get it out of your system – some people call it winning, some call it not wanting to lose, some call it professionalism or having that extra five per cent of aggression – whatever you want to call it, Julian's got it and I like to think that I had it.

"I even did something in the heat of the moment that I shouldn't have done during pre-season with Orient. So Julian might, at some stage, do something that you can't legislate for because it will be in the heat of the battle. But now he's starting to think things through a little bit more. He's got to grips with that side of his game and character and he's able to control it."

That 'side of his game and character' – as Alvin puts it – was never more apparent than during the 1992-93 season, of course. But for all Julian's problems at that time, he never sought the advice of his more experienced fellow defender. "He won't discuss football and, as far as I knew, he never spoke with any team-mates about his problems," says Martin. "I wouldn't have expected him to come up and talk to me about his problems. Now and again he'd probably have known what I'd have said anyway!

"I've offered loads of advice on the pitch and we've had our little fall-outs. We've had our arguments on the pitch when not a lot of common sense has been spoken. But there's a common respect between us. We both knew that, say in training, we didn't wallop each other because then it might get out of hand. I think we have a mutual respect and I'd like to think there's as much on his side as there is on mine. If you told me I had to pick a team for a game we've got to win to save our lives, he'd be in my side. That's the greatest compliment I can pay him."

Throughout the course of their relationship at West Ham, Alvin has been able to witness the development of Julian as a person, but concedes, "I think he's changed slightly but openly I still believe he is a shy person. I'm not a psychologist but I'd say there is a shy part of his personality that maybe the football and the image of being an aggressive player tends to mask."

Martin has also become aware of the contrasting aspects of Julian's personality that make up his overall character. He's seen Dicksy's outspoken nature, for example – "I don't think he'll ever go into the diplomatic corps! He's a lad who wears his heart on his sleeve and if somebody asks him a question and he feels at liberty to answer, he'll tell the truth. He won't say something that he doesn't believe, which is an admirable quality, although I don't think it's one you could take into management!" – yet he knows as well as anybody how introverted the player could be in the dressing room when it came to discussion about the game. "When we had team meetings, people

"If you told me I had to pick a team for a game we've got to win to save our lives, he'd be in my side"

would give their opinions on things but Julian would be very subdued – even in more recent times," he says. "He's the kind who'll say, 'Give me the ball, get me on the pitch and I'll play.' He's not one of those people who analyses his game – he's a natural player and he plays to his strengths."

One of those 'strengths' was his resolute character during his year out injured – an experience that Alvin himself has had to overcome in his career. "I've been there myself with serious injuries and then you find out about people. But I don't think I ever doubted that Julian would come back," he says. "One of the main differences between people like Julian and those I met when I joined Orient is that they haven't got the strong will that he has. If Julian or I go out and don't play well it will upset him and it will upset me. He's got personal pride in his performance. He's got application and attitude. When he got injured, he realised what it entailed and he worked as hard as anybody can. Whether it be long running or pumping weights, he knew what depended on it and he got there. But I always expected him to because he's got a very strong will and that's one of the attributes that makes him a winner."

The two topics of debate during the 1995-96 season – apart from Julian's much improved disciplinary record – were the merits of a prospective England call-up and his newer role as a left-sided centre-half for West Ham. With Martin having played in the middle of defence and gained 17 caps for England, his opinion is one to respected. "As far as I'm concerned, he's got the best left foot in the country," he offers. "He's a good defender but I wouldn't say he was the perfect defender – the same as I wasn't or even Bobby Moore for that matter. But what you've got to do when you play at that level is make the most of what you've got.

"Julian is a better player than Stuart Pearce going forward and is probably better one on one. The one thing that Pearce has got over him at the moment is control and concentration. Playing at centre-half would improve his concentration. And if he is playing there for West Ham, who's to say he can't play for England in that position? I think Glenn Hoddle wants people who can play on the ball but he doesn't want people who are going to get sent off."

The latter part of the 1995-96 campaign saw the calls for Julian to wear an England shirt grow substantially, but it wasn't something he spoke at great length about with any of the other players. "I don't think he was ever confident that it was going to happen, to be honest," says Alvin. "I think he felt that his reputation was not going to let it happen. That's the only indication I ever heard him express. But I don't think he's overly bothered by it. Bonzo was always like that – if he gets picked he gets picked.

"I still think he could get the call," continues Martin. "I've got a lot of respect for Glenn Hoddle and he's a manager who will pick teams who can play. He likes people who can pass the ball and be attack-minded – and Julian comes into that category. And if he's good enough, I think Glenn will play him. There's no reason why he shouldn't get linked with playing for England, even at centre-back."

CHAPTER 33

SUMMER SCANDAL

J ULIAN and Kay Dicks have been through enough to know that periods of peace can never be taken too much for granted but, if they were in danger of assuming that their lives would remain forever untroubled following the successful 1995-96 campaign, the events of the weekend commencing Saturday, May 25, 1996 would rock their worlds enough to remind them that there's no room for such complacency.

Kay first became suspicious of something taking place that day when, while Julian was out playing golf, the family phone rang a number of times only to have people hang up upon hearing her voice. After a while she assumed the calls were being made by members of the press hoping to catch Julian picking up the phone. "That's not necessarily unusual – we've had loads of calls like that," says Julian. "But when I got home the phone rang again and so I answered it to hear a woman saying she was from the *News Of The World*. She said they had a story linking me with a girl in Tenerife and asked if I had anything to say. I told her I had nothing to say but if they printed anything I'd sue them because it was all lies."

Indeed, Rachel Anderson, Julian's agent, made immediate contact with the *News Of The World* upon hearing of the calls on Saturday and stressed that the story was untrue, would create untold distress among Julian's family and that the paper would be leaving themselves open to the threat of legal action should they publish such allegations.

Tenerife had been the hotspot that Julian and a number of other West Ham players (including Keith Rowland, Ian Bishop, John Moncur, Robbie Slater and Iain Dowie) had visited earlier that month as a post-season club holiday (with Julian having been nominated as the man in charge of the party). Ten days or so had passed since the players' return and, apart from one or two of them needing a few days to recover, it appeared that the trip had come and gone without incident – until that early evening phone call, which saw Julian warn his wife that the press were up to something. "Julian said, 'Look, I've done nothing, whatever they write is a load of rubbish,'" says Kay.

Dicks had arranged to spend the evening out with a mate (leaving Kay at home with his mother Carol), visiting Dukes nightclub in Chelmsford, but his time there was short-lived. "We got into the club just after 11 o'clock," he recalls, "and the manager came up to me and said, 'Your mum's on the phone.' I felt like I was just 15 again! But she said, 'Kay's leaving.' I asked her what she meant and she told me the press had been on the phone again and that Kay was going. So I asked the manager to order me a taxi and I came home. I got through the front door and, to be honest, I lost my rag with Kay a bit because she should know what the papers are like by now. All they want to do is stir shit up."

Having experienced hassle from the press before, Kay had decided the best way of escaping the media attention was to retreat to her family in Birmingham. "I just didn't want to be at the house the next morning," she explains. "It wasn't that I wanted to get away from Julian, I just didn't want the aggravation. I was really upset because we'd had it all before. Things had been okay for a while but it just made me think, 'Here we go again.' I believed Julian from the moment he told me what was happening, but it's the hassle from everybody else I was dreading. Although at that time we didn't realise then it was going to be all over the front of the paper."

With things calming down, Kay decided to remain at home for the evening. "Julian said, 'Even if you're not here on Sunday morning, they're still not going to leave you alone, are they?' So I stayed, got up the next morning and his mum went down and got the paper."

When Carol returned with the *News Of The World*, nobody could quite believe their eyes. Carrying a front page headline of *'Sex romp shame of married soccer star'*, the tabloid alleged over the course of its first three pages that Julian had enjoyed *'nights of passion with a besotted 17-year-old fan'*. The story, credited to Helen Carter, went on to claim that the West Ham star had been *'cavorting'* with teenager Leeann Cronin in the hotel room she shared with 22-year-old Jo Mitchell, who was attributed with a number of quotes.

"When Kay saw the headlines she went ballistic," recalls Julian. "But when she read the story and looked at the pictures she realised there was nothing in it, although she was still very upset about the whole thing."

Kay, like most intelligent people, recognised the lack of substance – "it was a story about nothing" – but she still found it hard to comprehend. "I just couldn't believe it," she says. "It was all over the front of the paper. I was so upset."

Six photographs accompanied the report – a head shot of Julian taken on his first day back at West Ham, a family picture with a caption stating how *'Dicks likes to play the family man'*, one of Lineker's Bar (which Julian visited), a solo snap of Leeann, one of Julian holding a bottle of beer (used as the main colour image on the inside spread to imply his guilt, claiming that he was *'getting well-oiled'*) and, finally, a blurred shot that supposedly showed the pair of holidaymakers walking along together. Significantly, Julian was positioned to the far left of the picture (not revealing who else he may have been walking with) while the indistinguishable female about five

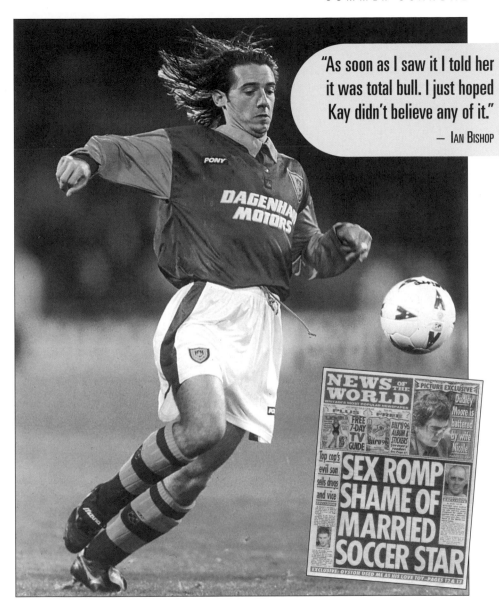

"As soon as I saw it I told her it was total bull. I just hoped Kay didn't believe any of it."

— IAN BISHOP

feet behind him was on the far right (it not being clear whether she's on her own or part of a group of people). With this last snap claiming to depict Julian and Leeann as they *'head for her bedroom'*, the natural query from most readers would have been why, if a photographer was tracking them, there wasn't a more conclusive picture (such as the two of them entering a building together, for example).

Not that Kay necessarily needed to see the printed story to confirm her belief in Julian's explanations the previous evening. "When you get a phone call like that, he'd have had to tell me if he'd done anything," she says. "He had no idea he was being followed around out there, so if he had have been guilty of something they could well have had evidence. So he had to be honest with me.

"Julian was so angry when he saw the paper," she adds. "He was absolutely fuming. He actually told me that they could have had pictures that looked a lot worse, because obviously the players got girls coming up to them and asking for photos."

Indeed, with the resort of Playa de las Americas being packed with British folk on their hols, the West Ham players (and no doubt the other English football teams out there at the same time – including, it's thought, Wimbledon) were of course recognised as celebrities and approached for conversations, autographs and photographs.

"I spoke to loads of West Ham supporters out there," says Julian. "It was cup final weekend but there were loads of Liverpool supporters out there, so they obviously knew who I was as well. Keith Rowland and I watched the final between Liverpool and Manchester United and then went on a Mexican night with the reps, up in the mountains. We came back, went down to Lineker's and talked to so many people – you lose count in the end. Obviously we were doing what normal people do on holiday – enjoying a few drinks and having some photos taken."

Julian does indeed recall Leeann – "when I saw her in the paper I could remember speaking to her" – *and* the newspaper reporter. "She was a pain in the arse," he insists. "She wouldn't leave me and Keithy Rowland alone so I told her to eff off. So she obviously got the hump."

To say that Dicksy got 'the hump' when the paper alleged his infidelity is something of an understatement. "It really annoyed me because having bad press over getting sent off is one thing, but when they write stuff like that it affects not just me but my whole family. It's a real liberty."

Julian and Kay's daughters were indeed affected, even though they were on holiday in Spain with Kay's sister at the time. "The papers were obviously available out there and people were knocking on the children's doors. So I had to bring them home," says Kay. "Everybody was upset. The kids are not stupid – they'd seen their picture in the paper and wanted to know why."

Many were surprised that the paper had gone so big on the story, running it in all their editions across the country, but Julian was philosophical about it. "I'm not really surprised because I know what the media are like," he says. "They'd built me up through the season, saying I should be playing for England and all the rest of it, and it was another way of knocking me down. That's what they do."

Dicksy's room-mate on the trip, Ian Bishop, was certainly shocked when he saw the allegations. "It was my wife Jane who saw the story first and called me downstairs," he recalls. "As soon as I saw it I told her it was total bull. The photos didn't show anything, the story didn't really say anything and I said I just hoped Kay didn't believe any of it."

Kay didn't, of course, but her concern was that other people might! "The thing that upsets me more than anything is that people do believe what they read in the papers," she admits. "Some people even said that if they'd have been me, they'd have taken Julian for every penny he's got. So *they* obviously believed it."

Julian and Kay's real friends may not have credited the story with too much truth but, thinking that the Dicks household was probably under siege on that Sunday, they all allowed the couple some peace (Bish included – "I thought I'd let the dust settle before ringing," he admits.)

> "Some people even said that if they'd have been me, they'd have taken Julian for every penny he's got" – KAY DICKS

"It's really weird – we have got some pretty good friends but nobody phoned," confirms Kay. "Everybody thought the same – if I needed anything I'd make the call. They all thought our phone would not stop ringing so didn't like to bother us – it was really strange! But my friend Caroline came down from Liverpool that day and we all went out on the Sunday night and got drunk!"

Kay's instinctive reaction at the time may have been one of anger – "I felt like going round to those girls' places and giving them a good hiding but, as it happens, they've been talking to their lawyers as well (for the matter is also, at the time of writing, in the hands of Julian's legal people) – but that subsided a little, even though things took a while to return to normal. "It wasn't until I'd seen everybody again," she says. "Like the first time I went to a dog show afterwards, people didn't know what to say to me. True friends have been as good as gold, but I could tell a lot of people were very uneasy with me. That's hard to deal with. And I had no idea what was running through their heads either."

As to why Julian was considered appropriate for such coverage is a matter of debate. Clearly, it's thought in some quarters that such stories sell papers and there's no doubt that, like pop stars, highly paid footballers in the present age are afforded a much greater 'celebrity' status than players of old. And as such, they're going to be targeted for big stories whenever possible. Other scenarios that appeared in the summer and autumn of 1996 support this view, with the likes of Ryan Giggs and Robbie Fowler, for example, gaining big publicity as victims of the 'kiss 'n' tell' stories. It seems that single young men, if they're in the public eye, can't do what other single young men do – at least not without somebody trying to cash in and exploit a star name.

As far as Kay Dicks was concerned, though, the media's motives in Julian's case were even more sinister. "They just don't like him and why that is I don't know," she says. "I know Julian's had his problems on the pitch but it's not as if he goes out drink-driving and doing things to genuinely deserve front page headlines. All his problems have been through his football, not his home life. I'm sure the press would really like to find something to land him in it. Somebody's got it in for him. But what else can they do?"

The News Of The World also alleged that Julian propositioned their *'blonde undercover reporter'*, begging the question as to why they had such an employee in that position and following footballers around bars in holiday resorts. (The story also featured a panel which asked: *'Did you meet a star on holiday? Maybe you even had your picture taken.'*)

"It's disgusting that they send people abroad to follow you round – you've got no privacy," complains Kay. "Maybe you can't expect any in Tenerife, a popular holiday resort, but you should be allowed to go away at the end of a long season and have a break."

With the popular press continually encroaching on people's privacy – with *The Sun*, for example, publishing pictures in October 1996 that alleged to show Princess Diana stripping at a window (only for the paper to have to apologise in humiliated fashion after the photos were proved to be fake) – the calls for restrictions to be placed on the media seem to grow all the time. "I think something has got to be done about it," says Julian. "If something happens on a football pitch then it's fair enough – the press are entitled to write about those things because that's what they're there to cover – but when they go into people's private lives, that's when it's got to stop. Something will happen about it one day."

It's a point of view shared by Kay, particularly after her husband's summer headlines. "It's the nastiest thing they've ever done," she states. "It's not something they should be allowed to do – it's disgusting. That kind of story would split some families apart. For people who can't take the aggravation it could ruin their marriages, it could ruin their lives. But I think I've got through the worst of it and I'd never let it get to me."

Julian, too, is adamant that he's not going to allow such tabloid treatment to influence his future behaviour. "If you let certain people from the press like that rule your life then you wouldn't have a life," he argues. Unfortunately, he also feels he'll always be a potential target for a big story. "As long as I'm playing football, they'll always be on my case," he insists. "If something happens and I'm around, then they'll link me because they want to sell papers and get a few quid in."

Thankfully, however, none of the headlines – football-based or not – have made him rue his level of achievement and public profile. "I generally like being well known," he says. "It's nice when people come up and say hello to you and ask for an autograph. The only thing I don't like is when you're out for a meal with friends or family and people keep coming up to you. But it's all part and parcel of the job," he acknowledges before confirming defiantly, "I don't regret my profile at all."

CHAPTER 34

WHAT NEXT?

AS the "hap, hap, hap...py Hammers" – as the Boleyn Ground's public announcer would say – commenced the 1996-97 season, hopes were high down Upton Park way.

Not only had manager Harry Redknapp recruited no less than SIX players – comprising Romanian international striker Florin Raducioiu (a record £2.4m buy), Portuguese forward Paulo Futre (one of the world's most expensive players, with all his fees combined, although he arrived from AC Milan on a free transfer), £1.9m centre-half Richard Hall from Southampton, versatile defender Mark Bowen (on a free from Norwich), striker Steve Jones (back with the Hammers for a second time following a couple of years at Second Division Bournemouth) and Northern Irish winger/midfielder Michael Hughes (signed on a free, like Futre, under the Bosman ruling from Strasbourg after one and a half seasons at West Ham on loan) – but the fixtures computer (for once) generated an opening list of matches which, on paper, seemed rather kind.

With home encounters against the likes of Coventry, Southampton and Wimbledon, plus a trip to newly-promoted Sunderland among the first six games, fans were looking for a good start to support the club's bid to improve on the previous season's tenth place – which would take some doing considering the progress made by most Premiership clubs in a summer that had seen a wealth of foreign talent arrive in England after the European Championships.

The Hammers team that stepped out onto the perfectly clipped Highbury turf on August 17, however, bore little resemblance to the one Redknapp would have wanted to name against Arsenal, with arguably just five of the outfield XI likely to have been first choices (injuries taking their toll). A 2-0 defeat was a natural outcome and with the situation hardly improving for the home game against Coventry a few days later (Hammers gaining a 1-1 draw after going behind), three points were essential against Southampton (managed by Julian's former Liverpool boss Graeme Souness) the following Saturday. A win didn't look likely, though, after a Dicks error allowed the Saints to take a horror lead.

"Slav headed the ball down to me and when I tried to control it on my thigh it skimmed off me and Neil Heaney got in and whacked it into the back of the net," he says, holding his hands up. "I was gutted! I really did feel awful. I thought, 'Here we go – another shitty result.'" A Michael Hughes goal brought the team level, though, and a few minutes later Dicks was being asked to put the ball on the penalty spot. "That was my opportunity to make amends for my mistake," he says. "There was no way I was going to miss that. I kept my head down and smashed it into the bottom corner."

The first three games had allowed Julian to extend his run of games without a yellow card to the unlikely-sounding total of 25 – an incredible feat given the stringency of referees in recent times – but, ironically, it all came to an end on September 4 at the ground at which he'd last been booked (nine months earlier) – Middlesbrough's Riverside Stadium. Julian had already complained in frustration to the officials about a number of things – "I thought they were an absolute disgrace!" he storms – but his yellow card, after closing in on £7m Italian international striker Fabrizio Ravanelli, took the biscuit. "I didn't touch him but he just fell to the ground. Ravanelli screamed when he went down and I thought he was dead!

Go on, give us a kiss! Julian enjoys some banter with Slaven Bilic.

"It doesn't bother me getting booked, but if you are going to get booked you want it to be for something you've done – and I never touched him. That annoys me. And as for what I said to the linesman, who was just a few yards away, it's not something you'll be able to print!"

The game – in which the Hammers were overwhelmed four goals to one (the 'one' being a very good one, though, by Hughes) – also saw Dicks subjected to some intense abuse from the partisan crowd. "Every time I touched the ball I got booed, but it didn't bother me," he insists. "I enjoy things like that – it doesn't affect me at all."

Performance-wise, however, it wasn't one of Julian's greatest games, but – for all his obvious frustration on the night – he did at least keep himself on the pitch. "Three or four years earlier, those were the type of situations where I used to lose my head and get sent off. But I'm 28 and if I haven't learnt by now I never will."

A dour 0-0 at Sunderland followed and a dreadful 2-0 home loss to Wimbledon followed that, but the Hammers performed brilliantly to win 2-0 at Nottingham Forest, on September 21, despite being reduced to 10 men after Marc Rieper was red-carded early in the second half. Incredibly – and unforgettably for all West Ham fans present – the team extended their lead within 60 seconds of Forest's resulting free-kick!

> "From the knee downwards, to the bottom of my foot, I couldn't feel a thing. It was like my leg had been chopped off"

An unfortunate 2-1 home defeat by Liverpool came next (with Dicks hitting the bar with a spectacular shot from distance), while Hammers' luck was out even more when they trekked to Everton on October 12. Not only was Portuguese international Hugo Porfirio (another astute loan acquisition by Redknapp) denied a clear-cut penalty but the Toffees gained a 1-0 lead when Julian was off the pitch receiving treatment. "I was quite frightened," he admits. "I went past Michael Branch and his knee hit the side of my right one. From the knee downwards, to the bottom of my foot, I couldn't feel a thing. It was like my leg had been chopped off. But physio John Green told me that I'd hit a nerve and it would come back after five or 10 minutes. And while I was off they scored!

"I went back on for the kick-off and after a couple of touches Bish gave the ball to me. I still couldn't feel my right foot and as I went to kick it with my left my right leg buckled and I nearly fell over. The bench asked if I was all right and I told them that I couldn't feel my foot. It was quite scary."

The feeling gradually reappeared over a period of 20 minutes or so with Julian finally getting a late consolation spot-kick but, as West Ham moved into the rest of the autumn/winter campaign, the hope was very much that the life would quickly return to the team and results would improve. Many blamed the number of injuries the team had encountered in the early months, but Julian had little sympathy with such a view. "That's more of an excuse," he claims. "The people brought in are all professional footballers and if they can't do the job then they shouldn't be in the side."

And things did pick up, with the Hammers securing three consecutive home wins (against Leicester, Nottingham Forest and Blackburn) at the end of October. The Leicester game had seen Julian collect his third yellow card of the campaign (following another in the match v Wimbledon) and Julian was once again publicly critical of the man in black's handling of the match. "The referee was disgraceful," he blasted in the following day's papers. "I didn't shake his hand and I don't blame the Leicester players for not doing so either."

Referee Mike Riley had enraged the Foxes by sending off captain Steve Walsh - a decision which Julian also disagreed with. Having said that, the sympathetic way in which the press covered Walsh's 12th red card of his career did not escape Dicks. "That's a lot worse than me, " he insists. "I'm not being disrespectful to Walshie but his profile is totally different to mine. His red card hardly made the news, yet when I get sent off it's all over the papers!"

With the autumn debate about the worth of foreigners to the English game raging hard in the media, and West Ham, still in the bottom half of the table, there were suggestions that the club's policy of importing European talent was not working out, with it proving difficult for the English players to strike up a rapport with the newcomers. But such an idea is kicked into touch by Dicks.

"I think we've got a good bunch of lads and we all get on okay with each other," he says. "Raducioiu and Futre have had their injuries but the lads have made them feel at home and I think they like it here. Obviously, you get better banter with English players, but we enjoy good banter with Slaven and Rieps and have a good laugh with them."

Talking of laughs, plenty were had in the autumn of '96 as 'Forever Blowing Bubbles' – a CD compilation of Hammers hits – was released onto the market, most notably for the track entitled 'Julian Dicks – The Terminator' by Flat Back Four. It's a novelty song of classic proportions and Julian's daughters, Kattie and Jessica, haven't stopped playing it (much to the annoyance of mum Kay!).

Back on the pitch, Julian had started the season playing in a left-sided centre-half position, with Richard Hall sidelined as a result of a bad foot injury. The likelihood, however, as Harry Redknapp has already suggested, is that Dicks would then move into a left-sided wing-back position – despite the player's own slight doubts. "I'm not really one of those people who can get up and down quickly – I'm not built that way," he claims, while conceding, "Obviously, if it comes to it, then I will play there. But if Harry asks me where I want to play, I'd probably say as a left-sided centre-half or at left back."

If Harry was looking to relocate Jules out on the left, then he must feel that Julian has the capabilities. September press claims that Dicks had signed a new four-year,

Still vocal after all these years!

£10,000 deal at West Ham, however, were unfounded – despite what had been reported. With his contract set to expire at the end of the 1996-97 season, negotiations were expected to take place some time during the winter period – a deal that would, presumably, keep Dicksy at the club he loves most for the rest of his career.

So, how do you close a book such as this on one of soccer's most intriguing and controversial characters – somebody held in the highest esteem by Hammers supporters but still regarded as something of a villain by many opposing fans?

Maybe the best way of bowing out here is to simply allow a few of the people involved in Dicksy's career to voice some parting words...

"We used to say that there aren't too many 28-year-old teddy boys – and players are the same. They grow up." – Former Hammers manager **John Lyall**

"Dicksy's not misunderstood. If you're honest, he hasn't been sent off when he shouldn't have been. But people always identify with quality footballers and over at Upton Park they've always loved somebody who puts their foot in and wants to have a go." – Ex-West Ham manager **Billy Bonds**

"When Julian concentrates on playing football, he's as good as anybody." – Liverpool boss **Roy Evans**

"If I was still at Liverpool, then so would he be. I hope that when he finishes his career, people look back and remember him for being the fantastic footballer he is." – Former Liverpool and current Southampton manager **Graeme Souness**

"If you're going into war, you want somebody like Julian Dicks alongside you." – Ex-Hammers team-mate and current Reading co-manager **Jimmy Quinn**

"He loves it at West Ham. He's part of the fixtures and fittings at Upton Park. When he arrives there it's like: 'Dicksy's coming home...'" – Former Hammers team-mate and current Pompey midfielder **Martin Allen**

"The fact is that he hasn't got what he deserves through his football – and that's international recognition." – Hammers team-mate **Ian Bishop**

"I don't think he'll ever reach his true potential – playing for England – but I'm proud of him." – Father **Ron Dicks**

"The fans think the world of him." – West Ham MD **Peter Storrie**

"You only become a cult figure one way – by playing well. When I was running pubs it was always 'Dicksy this, Dicksy that...' from the punters." – West Ham assistant boss **Frank Lampard**

"He's a very changed person. I'd love to see him end his career at West Ham and be his manager for the next four or five years." – Hammers manager **Harry Redknapp**

NOT THE END

DICKSY'S CAREER RECORD

GAMES AND GOALS

Season	Club	League		FA Cup		Lge Cup		Others		Total	
		Apps	Gls	Apps	Gls	Apps	Gls	Apps	Gls	Apps	Gls
1985-86	Birmingham City	23	0	1	0	2	0	0	0	26	0
1986-87	Birmingham City	34	0	1	0	2	0	2	0	39	0
1987-88	Birmingham City	32	1	3	0	2	0	0	0	37	1
1987-88	West Ham United	8	0	0	0	0	0	0	0	8	0
1988-89	West Ham United	34	2	6	0	7	0	2	0	49	2
1989-90	West Ham United	40	9	1	0	9	4	2	1	52	14
1990-91	West Ham United	13	4	0	0	2	1	0	0	15	5
1991-92	West Ham United	23	3	6	2	0	0	1	0	30	5
1992-93	West Ham United	34	11	1	0	1	0	6	3	42	14
1993-94	West Ham United	7	0	0	0	0	0	0	0	7	0
1993-94	Liverpool	24	3	2[†]	0	3	0	0	0	29	3
1994-95	West Ham United	29	5	2	0	2	0	0	0	33	5
1995-96	West Ham United	34	10	3	0	3	1	0	0	40	11
1996-97	West Ham United*	17	3	0	0	4	1	0	0	21	4
TOTALS		**352**	**51**	**26**	**2**	**37**	**7**	**13**	**4**	**428**	**64**

[†] Includes one abandoned game

* As at 10/12/96

DISCIPLINARY RECORD 1984-1996

Contrary to the popular belief that Julian has been sent off on nine occasions during his career to date, the FA's disciplinary records only confirm SIX domestic dismissals from 1984-1996. Add in red cards in games for Birmingham youths v West Brom in 1984 and England U-21s v Mexico in 1988 and the total dismissals on record amount to eight. As for the number of yellow cards, er, we lost count…

1984-85 Birmingham City

20/10/84	v Port Vale	(H)	Reserves	▪ Cautioned for persistent infringement
27/10/84	v Southampton	(A)	Reserves	▪ Cautioned for foul tackle
1/12/84	v West Brom	(H)	Reserves	■ Sent off for foul & abusive language
11/4/85	v Brighton HA	(H)	Reserves	▪ Cautioned for foul tackle
1/5/85	v West Ham Utd	(A)	Reserves	▪ Cautioned for foul tackle

1985-86 Birmingham City

2/9/85	v Aston Villa	(A)	Reserves	▪ Cautioned for persistent infringement
12/10/85	v Millwall	(H)	Reserves	▪ Cautioned for foul tackle
22/10/85	v Coventry C	(H)	Reserves	▪ Cautioned for dissent to referee
30/10/85	v Norwich City	(A)	Reserves	▪ Cautioned for persistent infringement
5/2/86	v Oxford Utd	(A)	Reserves	▪ Cautioned for foul tackle
16/4/86	v Tottenham H	(A)	FL Div 1	▪ Cautioned for foul tackle

1986-87 Birmingham City

7/8/86	v Bideford	(A)	Friendly	▪ Cautioned for persistent infringement
23/8/86	v Stoke City	(A)	FL Div 2	▪ Cautioned for dissent to referee
30/8/86	v Derby County	(H)	FL Div 2	▪ Cautioned for tripping an opponent
3/9/86	v Brighton HA	(A)	FL Div 2	▪ Cautioned for foul tackle
13/9/86	v Huddersfield	(H)	FL Div 2	▪ Cautioned for foul tackle
23/9/86	v Middlesbro	(A)	Lge Cup	▪ Cautioned for tripping an opponent
4/10/86	v Barnsley	(H)	FL Div 2	▪ Cautioned for foul tackle
15/11/86	v Millwall	(A)	FL Div 2	▪ Cautioned for persistent infringement
13/12/86	v Shrewsbury	(A)	FL Div 2	▪ Cautioned for foul tackle
27/1/87	v Swindon T	(H)	Reserves	▪ Cautioned for foul tackle
28/3/87	v Barnsley	(A)	FL Div 2	▪ Cautioned for foul tackle
20/4/87	v Reading	(H)	FL Div 2	▪ Cautioned for foul tackle
5/5/87	v Blackburn R	(A)	FL Div 2	▪ Cautioned for dangerous play

1987-88 Birmingham City

22/8/87	v Aston Villa	(A)	FL Div 2	▪ Cautioned for foul tackle
29/8/87	v Bournemouth	(H)	FL Div 2	▪ Cautioned for adopting an aggressive attitude
15/9/87	v Blackburn R	(H)	FL Div 2	▪ Cautioned for foul tackle
10/10/87	v Reading	(A)	FL Div 2	▪ Cautioned for foul tackle
7/11/87	v Hull City	(A)	FL Div 2	▪ Cautioned for dissent to referee
14/11/87	v Leicester C	(H)	FL Div 2	▪ Cautioned for persistent infringement
28/12/87	v Shrewsbury	(A)	FL Div 2	▪ Cautioned for foul tackle
2/1/88	v Swindon Twn	(H)	FL Div 2	▪ Cautioned for foul tackle
5/3/88	v Bradford C	(H)	FL Div 2	▪ Cautioned for foul tackle
8/3/88	v West Brom Al	(H)	FL Div 2	▪ Cautioned for foul tackle

1988-89 West Ham United

10/9/88	v Wimbledon	(A)	FL Div 1	▪ Cautioned for persistent infringement
3/9/88	v Charlton Ath	(H)	FL Div 1	▪ Cautioned for foul tackle
24/9/88	v Manchester U	(A)	FL Div 1	▪ Cautioned for foul tackle
22/10/88	v Newcastle Utd	(H)	FL Div 1	▪ Cautioned for dangerous play
1/11/88	v Derby County	(H)	Lge Cup	▪ Cautioned for obstruction
26/11/88	v Everton	(H)	FL Div 1	▪ Cautioned for foul tackle
11/1/89	v Arsenal	(A)	FA Cup	▪ Cautioned for foul tackle
22/3/89	v Norwich City	(A)	FA Cup	▪ Cautioned for foul tackle
1/4/89	v Tottenham H	(A)	FL Div 1	▪ Cautioned for dissent to referee
13/5/89	v Everton	(A)	FL Div 1	▪ Cautioned for foul tackle
23/5/89	v Liverpool	(A)	FL Div 1	▪ Cautioned for foul tackle

1989-90 West Ham United

8/9/89	v Swindon T	(A)	Reserves	▪ Cautioned for obstruction
9/9/89	v Swindon T	(H)	FL Div 2	▪ Cautioned for a foul tackle
16/9/89	v Brighton HA	(A)	FL Div 2	▪ Cautioned for persistent infringement
30/9/89	v West Brom	(H)	FL Div 2	▪ Cautioned for a foul tackle
7/10/89	v Leeds Utd	(H)	FL Div 2	▪ Cautioned for shirt pulling
22/11/89	v Wimbledon	(H)	Lge Cup	■ Sent off for persistent misconduct
6/1/90	v Torquay Utd	(A)	FA Cup	▪ Cautioned for persistent infringement
18/2/90	v Swindon T	(A)	FL Div 2	▪ Cautioned for persistent infringement
24/2/90	v Blackburn R	(H)	FL Div 2	▪ Cautioned for persistent infringement
3/3/90	v Middlesbro	(A)	FL Div 2	▪ Cautioned for a foul tackle
21/4/90	v Oldham Ath	(A)	FL Div 2	▪ Cautioned for foul play

1990-91 West Ham United

25/8/90	v Middlesbro	(A)	FL Div 2	▪ Cautioned for obstruction
8/9/90	v Leicester C	(A)	FL Div 2	▪ Cautioned for a foul tackle
29/9/90	v Sheffield W	(A)	FL Div 2	▪ Cautioned for tripping an opponent
13/10/90	v Bristol City	(A)	FL Div 2	▪ Cautioned for adopting an aggressive attitude

1991-92 West Ham United

1/2/92	v Oldham Ath	(H)	FL Div 1	▪ Cautioned for dissent
22/2/92	v Sheffield W	(A)	FL Div 1	▪ Cautioned for dissent
3/3/92	v Southampton	(A)	FL Div 1	▪ Cautioned for persistent infringement
14/3/92	v Arsenal	(H)	FL Div 1	▪ Cautioned for foul tackle
1/4/92	v Tottenham H	(A)	FL Div 1	▪ Cautioned for foul tackle
14/4/92	v Southampton	(H)	FL Div 1	▪ Cautioned for ungentlemanly conduct
18/4/92	v Manchester C	(A)	FL Div 1	▪ Cautioned for tripping an opponent
22/4/92	v Manchester U	(H)	FL Div 1	▪ Cautioned for foul tackle
25/4/92	v Coventry C	(A)	FL Div 1	▪ Cautioned for foul tackle
2/5/92	v Nottingham F	(H)	FL Div 1	▪ Cautioned for foul tackle

1992-93 West Ham United

23/7/92	v in Scotland	(A)	Friendly	▪ Cautioned for foul play
25/7/92	v in Scotland	(A)	Friendly	▪ Cautioned for adopting an aggressive attitude
29/8/92	v Newcastle Utd	(A)	FL Div 1	▪ Cautioned for a foul tackle

319

29/8/92	v Newcastle Utd	(A)	FL Div 1	■ Sent off for violent conduct
8/9/92	v Arsenal	(H)	Reserves	Cautioned for persistent infringement
27/9/92	v Portsmouth	(A)	FL Div 1	Cautioned for shirt pulling
4/10/92	v Wol'hampton	(A)	FL Div 1	■ Sent off for second cautionable offence
7/10/92	v Crewe Alex	(A)	C.C. Cup	Cautioned for foul tackle
26/12/92	v Charlton Ath	(A)	FL Div 1	Cautioned for foul tackle
10/1/93	v Derby County	(A)	FL Div 1	■ Sent off for second cautionable offence
21/2/93	v Newcastle Utd	(H)	FL Div 1	Cautioned for foul tackle
13/3/93	v Notts County	(A)	FL Div 1	Cautioned for foul tackle
23/3/93	v Oxford Utd	(A)	FL Div 1	Cautioned for foul tackle
13/4/93	v Luton Town	(A)	FL Div 1	Cautioned for hand ball

1993-94 West Ham United
| 20/8/93 | v Coventry C | (A) | FA Prem | Cautioned for adopting an aggressive attitude |

1993-94 Liverpool
| 13/3/94 | v Everton | (H) | FA Prem | Cautioned for foul tackle |

1994-95 West Ham United
22/10/94	v Southampton	(H)	FA Prem	Cautioned for foul tackle
26/11/94	v Coventry C	(H)	FA Prem	Cautioned for foul tackle
30/11/94	v Bolton W	(H)	C.C. Cup	Cautioned for foul tackle
17/12/94	v Manchester C	(H)	FA Prem	Cautioned for foul tackle
26/12/94	v Ipswich Twn	(H)	FA Prem	Cautioned for showng dissent
31/12/94	v Nottingham F	(H)	FA Prem	Cautioned for foul tackle
11/3/95	v Norwich C	(H)	FA Prem	Cautioned for adopting an aggressive attitude
17/4/95	v Ipswich Twn	(A)	FA Prem	Cautioned for foul tackle
30/4/95	v Blackburn R	(H)	FA Prem	Cautioned for foul tackle

1995-96 West Ham United
15/8/95	v Woking	(A)	Friendly	Cautioned for foul tackle
11/9/95	v Chelsea	(H)	FA Prem	Cautioned for shirt pulling
16/9/95	v Arsenal	(A)	FA Prem	■ Sent off for second cautionable offence
16/10/95	v Wimbledon	(A)	FA Prem	Cautioned for foul tackle
28/10/95	v Sheff Wed	(A)	FA Prem	Cautioned for foul tackle
23/12/95	v Middlesbrough	(A)	FA Prem	Cautioned for foul tackle

1996-97 West Ham United
4/9/96	v Middlesbrough	(A)	FA Prem	Cautioned for foul tackle
14/9/96	v Wimbledon	(H)	FA Prem	Cautioned for foul tackle
18/10/96	v Leicester City	(H)	FA Prem	Cautioned for foul tackle
16/11/96	v Newcastle Utd	(A)	FA Prem	Cautioned for foul tackle

As at 10/12/96